Eugenics in Austra [barcode] D1760393
Striving for Nationa. Fitness

Diana Wyndham

Series Editor
Robert A Peel

PUBLISHED BY THE GALTON INSTITUTE

British Library Cataloguing in Publication Data

Wyndham, Diana
  Eugenics in Australia: Striving for National Fitness
  1.Eugenics – Australia - History
  I.Title
  363.9'2'0994

  ISBN 0950406678

First published 2003 by The Galton Institute, 19 Northfields Prospect, Northfields, London SW18 1PE

Printed and bound in Great Britain by The Chameleon Press, 5-25 Burr Road, Wandsworth, London, SW18 4SG

Contents

About the Author

After completing a PhD in history from the University of Sydney, Diana Wyndham was awarded a Norman Haire Fellowship from the university's faculty of medicine in 1998. Previously, she was co-author (with Stephania Sidelecky) of Population and Perish: Australian Women's Fight for Birth Control (Allen & Unwin, 1990), written with the support of an Australian Bicentennial Grant.

Acknowledgement

I wish to thank board members of the Galton Institute for their decision to publish, and extend my sincere thanks to Robert Peel who has been a splendid editor. The seeds of this book were planted while I was librarian at the Family Planning Association of NSW in the 1970s and a board member of this organisation in the 1980s and 90s. The germination began with Australian Bicentennial Authority-funded research in 1987 which resulted in a book published by Allen and Unwin in 1990 – Populate and Perish: Australian Women's Fight for Birth Control, which I wrote with Dr Stefania Siedlecky.

This grew into a PhD thesis at the University of Sydney and I thank my supervisors, Professor Roy MacLeod and Dr Judith Keene. I also acknowledge help from Professor Mark Adams, Linda Brooks (Galton Institute), Dr Lyndsay Farrall, Dr Lesley Hall (Wellcome Institute), Martha Harrison (American Philosophical Society), Professor Daniel Kevles, Dr John Laurent, Humphrey MacQueen, Rosa Needham (FPA NSW), Dr Stefania Siedlecky, Dorothy Simons, Professor Richard Soloway, Dr Richard Travers, Alison Turtle, Dr Ann Williams and my greatest supporter, John Wyndham.

I found valuable archival material in the Eugenics Society Archives at the Wellcome Institute for the History of Medicine, the Marie Stopes Papers at the British Library, the Galton Papers at the University College London, the Margaret Sanger Papers at the US Library of Congress, and the American Eugenics Society Archives at the American Philosophical Society. I am indebted to the librarians who produced the four volume Bibliography of Australian Medicine and Health Services to 1950 and the NSW Parliamentary Library's extensive Newspaper Index 1910-1975: these sources listed relevant books, speeches, conference papers and newspaper items and, as well as revealing the presence of 'gems', showed where they were – predominantly in Sydney's Mitchell Library or in the Fisher Library at the University of Sydney.

List of Tables

List of Figures

'Introductory wall panel, "The Relation of Eugenics to Other Sciences', based on a paper by Dr Harry H Laughlin, Plate 1, in *A Decade of Progress in Eugenics* [1034], Scientific Papers of the Third International Congress of Eugenics, 21-23 August 1932 (New York: Garland, 1984).

The *Women's Suffrage Banner: Trust the Women...* (1908) painted by the Australian artist Dora Dora Meeson (1869-1955). Reproduced by permission of Lt Col. Simon Hearder on behalf of the heirs in copyright. Courtesy of Parliament House Art Collection, Joint House Department, Canberra, ACT. The banner was carried in London by an Australian contingent of women at the Women's Suffrage March on 13 June 1908. Australian women won the vote in 1902 but British women, who began their suffrage campaigns in 1866, remained without the vote until 1919.

A fund-raising appeal in the *Charities' Gazette and General Intelligences*, Official organ of the Benevolent Society of New South Wales, 25 September 1919, p. 11. This and the illustrations in Figures 21, 22 and 24 were provided by Petrina Slaytor. All are reproduced with the permission of the Benevolent Society of NSW.

Poster by Norman Lindsay (1879-1969) whose work spans the fields of painter, illustrator, cartonist and author. The poster appeared on the cover of the 1 December 1908 issue of *Lone Hand* and was used in publicity for the boxing heavyweight title of the world, held on Boxing Day 1908, at Sydney's newly-built Stadium. Sixteen thousand men watched as black American boxer Jack Johnson made history by defeating his white opponent, the Canadian Tommy Burns. Reproduced with permission of the Norman Lindsay Estate and the Image Library, State Library of New South Wales

Abbreviations

AA	Australian Archives
AAASR	*Australasian Association for the Advancement of Science. Report*
ACER	Australian Council for Educational Research (Melbourne, Victoria)
ACT	Australian Capital Territory
ADB	*Australian Dictionary of Biography*
AGPS	Australian Government Publishing Service (Canberra, ACT)
ALP	Australian Labor Party
AMCT	*Australasian Medical Congress. Transactions*
AMG	*Australasian Medical Gazette* (Sydney) 1895-1914
AMJ	*Australian Medical Journal* (Melbourne) 1856-1914
ANZAAS	Australian and New Zealand Association for the Advancement of Science
ARHC	*Australian Racial Hygiene Congress.* Report (Sydney, 1929)
EES	Eugenics Education Society (London), 1907-1926
EESNSW	Eugenics Education Society of NSW (Sydney) 1912-1922
ER	*Eugenics Review* (London) 1909-1968
ESL	Eugenics Society (London) 1926-1989, then the Galton Institute
ESV	Eugenics Society of Victoria, 1936-1961
FPA	Family Planning Association
Govt. Pr.	Government Printer
ICMJA	*Intercolonial Medical Journal of Australasia*
IFR	Institute of Family Relations (Sydney), Director Marion Piddington
Johns	*Johns's Notable Australians*, 1906; title varies *Johns's Notable Australians and Who is Who in Australasia*, 1908; *Fred Johns's Annual*, 1912, 1913, 1914.
LD	*Labor Daily* (Sydney) 1922-1940
MJA	*Medical Journal of Australia* (Sydney) 1914 +
ML	Mitchell Library, Sydney

NHMRC	National Health and Medical Research Council, 1936 +
MUP	Melbourne University Press (Parkville, Vic)
NLA	National Library of Australia (Canberra, ACT)
NSW	New South Wales
Qld	Queensland
RCDBR	*Royal Commission on the Decline of the Birth-Rate and on the Mortality of Infants in New South Wales* (Sydney: Govt. Pr., 1904), 2 vols
RHA	Racial Hygiene Association of NSW
SA	South Australia
SANSW(IG)	State Archives of NSW. Inspector General of the Insane. From 1876-1917 it was IG for the Insane, changing to IG of Mental Hospitals from 1918-57
SUP	Sydney University Press (Sydney, NSW)
UNSWP	University of New South Wales Press (Kensington, NSW)
UQP	University of Queensland Press (St Lucia, Qld)
Vic	Victoria
WA	Western Australia
WEA	Workers' Educational Association
WWW	*Who Was Who*, + cumulated index 1887-1990 (London: Black, 1991)
Who's Who	*Who's Who in Australia* (Melbourne), *Herald and Weekly Times*, 1922 +

Series Editor's Preface

Robert Peel

The word "eugenics" was invented by Francis Galton in 1883. Twenty years later it was in widespread use, its connotations were clearly understood and, above all, its perceived relevance to contemporary social issues ensured its universal approbation. For, although eugenics was a serious, but ultimately unsuccessful, contender in 1904 to provide the theoretical underpinnings for the then emergent academic discipline of sociology in Britain it was those who saw it as an instrument of social amelioration who came together in 1907 to establish the Eugenics Education Society, the first of its kind in the world.

Differential fertility, alcoholism, "feeble mindedness," pauperism and above all declining physical and mental fitness – these were some of the issues which, it was hoped, eugenics would help resolve. Sybil Gotto, the "virtual founder" of the Society and its General Secretary until 1920, had been a venereal disease campaigner. Leading members of the Committee of the Moral Education League resigned office in order to offer themselves for election to the new Society's Council which also attracted important figures from the Malthusian League which for forty years had urged its own panacea for the world's problems.

Members of the original Council of the Eugenics Education Society were thus already skilled in the arts of advocacy, protest and fund raising. Significantly, one of its first acts in 1908 was to petition the Home Office against the threatened closure by the LCC of its homes for inebriate women. Its success ensured that the Society henceforth would enjoy consultancy status with government. The Council's administrative expertise also enabled it quickly to build up a sizeable and distinguished membership whose listings in the early Annual Reports have been likened to a roll-call of Edwardian worthies.

From its start the Eugenics Education Society envisaged the formation of branches to which end it drew up regulations and published a model constitution. In Great Britain branches were formed in Glasgow, Edinburgh, Belfast, Liverpool, Oxford, Birmingham and Cambridge. In New Zealand a meeting called to inaugurate the Dunedin Moral Education League ended by declaring itself a branch of the Eugenics Education Society.

Elsewhere, in more than twenty countries of the world, autonomous eugenics societies were formed by groups of enthusiasts either independently of or in only loose association with the London-based Society. As well as embracing the basic tenets of the older Society each had special interests based on their own circumstances. In the United States and Canada the problem was immigration; in Hong Kong quarantine regulations; in Sweden the problem of welfare finance and in South Africa miscegenation. The organisations set up in the several states of Australia also had both generally shared and unique characteristics which emerge clearly from this excellent study. The former included birth control, national fitness and alcoholism. Special concerns included the falling birth rate and the threat of uncontrolled immigration (the "yellow peril"). As in Britain, the policy of sterilisation was neither embraced nor advocated at any time by any Australian eugenics organisation, although this will not prevent critics and reviewers from indulging in what John Turner has called the "zealous laying of posthumous blame".

The Australian eugenics movement, like its counterparts elsewhere, had its blemishes as well as its triumphs and both are objectively recorded in this volume. And once again they are both common to all such organisations and specific to the continent.

The Galton Institute is glad to have the opportunity of publishing this important book. Its own existence was, coincidentally, ensured by the generosity of Henry Twitchen, who made his fortune in Australia and for many years contributed a substantial annual sum to the then Eugenics Society and on his death in 1930 bequeathed to it the whole of his estate valued at £57,000. It is good to learn from Dr Wyndham's study more of the life of this benefactor.

It was an Australian, Lyndsay A Farrall, who catalysed the new revisionist historiography of eugenics in a bibliographical review published in the *Annals of Science* in 1979. Although a small number of academics in various disciplines and on both sides of the Atlantic had published scholarly work in the 1960s and 1970s it was Farrall's achievement to bring these together and to suggest primary and secondary sources of further research. Most importantly he placed eugenics firmly within the mainstream of post-Darwinian social theory. More than 2000 articles and over 100 books on eugenics have appeared in the ensuing thirty years as a result of Farrall's article. The publishers hope that he will be gratified by this most recent addition to that corpus.

Introduction

People often laugh about eugenics or loath it and much recent historical writing has been similarly cursory, inaccurate and dismissive. It has been widely misinterpreted and misunderstood, leaving questions unanswered and answers unquestioned. However, eugenics is not a bizarre scheme created by harmless eccentrics, neither is it an evil, obsolete aberration which ended in Hitler's death camps: this year the governments of Canada and Sweden revealed that between 1935 and 1975 thousands of their 'unfit' citizens were forced to undergo eugenic sterilisations. So far, $34,000 compensation per person has been provided to 200 Swedish victims but this will not finalise one of the most devastating scandals to shake modern Sweden. It has also been revealed that many people who were mentally ill, retarded, socially undesirable or homosexual were forcibly used for experiments, lobotomized or even killed, in efforts to perfect Sweden's genetic stock.

Since the 1980s interest in eugenics has been stimulated by the expanding possibilities of genetic engineering and reproductive technology and by the resurfacing of theories about race and intelligence. This book attempts to provide a historical context in which to judge whether these developments should be joyfully welcomed or fearfully resisted. Between 1905 and 1930, eugenics movements developed in more than 20 countries but for many years the vast literature on eugenics focused almost exclusively on its history in Britain and America. While some aspects of eugenics in Australia are now being documented, the history of this movement needed to be written. From 1911 to 1932, a loosely-defined collection of eugenics-related goals for increasing the nation's fitness were accepted as the norm. However, while eugenics flourished in this period – and its aims were considered scientific, worthwhile and achievable – the idea of producing biologically better people had become suspect by the 1930s. Eugenics' positive aura was replaced by a shadowy and sinister memory as the subject entered fifty years of historical hibernation, emerging after it had undergone extensive documentary cleansing.

1

While I have consulted some secondary sources, I have wherever possible relied on medical and other archival sources in an attempt to understand the social, political and economic background of the period, to place the study in context, and to analyse eugenic thinking. The list of successful doctors, lawyers, academics and politicians who espoused eugenics reads like a *Who's Who of Australia* for the first half of the 20th century. However, when their obituaries were written, in almost all cases their interest in eugenics was not mentioned. Although eugenics is no longer publicly advocated, its history has relevance for the generations living in the era of the Genome Project and beyond.

The *Macquarie Dictionary* defines eugenics as the science of improving offspring (or the whole of the human race), especially by the careful selection of parents. The word 'eugenics', from the Greek *eugenes* meaning wellborn, was first used in 1883 by the versatile British scientist Sir Francis Galton (1822-1911). Drawing on ancient ideas and stimulated by the writings of his half first-cousin Charles Darwin, thirteen years his senior, Galton expressed eugenic beliefs as early as 1865 but astutely waited until 1901 to launch his scheme[1]. The timing was well judged: people were excited by Mendel's rediscovered laws of heredity, and the Boer War was causing panic about Britain's national efficiency, it's racial health and the Empire's future. Gratified by his audience's response, the octogenarian Galton promoted eugenics for the rest of his life, invoking both the authority of religion and the sacred aura of science.

In Britain, from the 1780s, dreams of progress had fuelled the industrial revolution. By the 20th century those who had benefited from machine-made improvements began to dream of producing better people. Their fantasies were encouraged by Charles Darwin's famous upwards-and-onwards conclusion to *Origin of Species*. He said there was 'grandeur in this view of life' and that people could confidently expect 'a secure future of great length' with 'progress towards perfection'. Eugenics was eagerly accepted in the early 20th century, partly because it was in keeping with the wish to build a better Australia that would outstrip the achievements but avoid the poverty and unrest of the industrialized northern hemisphere. Initially it was endorsed as a scientific means for achieving the utopian goals of human betterment and by the 1930s eugenics was being promoted in more than 20 countries. However, after World War II, few people were prepared to advocate it openly and, around the world, most eugenic-oriented organisations continued but changed their names. For example, in the 1930s the American journal *Eugenics,* with its subtitle 'A Journal of Race Betterment' became *People*; in the 1950s the *Eugenics Quarterly* became *Social Biology*, in the 1960s Australia's Racial Hygiene Association became the Family Planning Association and in a recent metamorphosis, Britain's Eugenics Society has become the Galton Institute. Most eugenists had a chameleon-like ability to adopt a new identity as a geneticist, sociologist or social demographer.

In the 1930s eugenics claimed nests in many disciplines (**Figure 1**) but often these links were tenuous, transient or illusory. Margaret Spencer captured the complexity of such relationships in her 1992 response to my questions about her father, Dr Howard Cumpston, who became Australia's first Director-General of Health in 1921, when she said he mused about people calling him a eugenist but agreed 'perhaps he was in a public health sense, meaning that community and individual good health, freedom from disease, give progeny the best start in life'.

Eugenics could be an all-encompassing philosophy for the committed such as Sir John Macpherson (1858-1942), the founding professor of psychiatry at the University of Sydney who, in the 7 June 1924 issue of the *Medical Journal of Australia,* considered that eugenics embraced 'all those legislative and municipal measures which aim at good housing and drainage, better conditions of labour, pure food regulations, general hygiene, the abolition of dangerous drug habits, and increased facilities for early and efficient medical and surgical treatment to those in need of them'. The causes which other eugenists endorsed ranged from censorship, sex education, temperance and prevention of venereal disease, to pure food regulations and the health and happiness of babies. Many people calling themselves eugenists were muddled or mischievous. Some used eugenic arguments to validate special pleading, for instance suggesting that cars served a eugenic purpose by enabling country people to widen their marriage choices.

Figure 1: The Relationship of Eugenics to Other Sciences[2]

In Australia, Catholic clergy were implacably opposed, politicians were tentative, workers were distrustful and the press often treated eugenics as a joke. Some people confused the goals of pronatalism (to increase all births) with those of eugenics (to increase eugenically desirable births), or thought that eugenics and eurythmics were the same. During the initial fervour, the *Telegraph* speculated on 29 April 1912 that eugenists in London were as numerous as angels in heaven, and it was reported to be 'warmly welcomed' in America. It also attracted cranks and cynics: the *Sydney Morning Herald* (11 March 1914) warned that only 'the serious-minded' were invited to join Sydney's new Eugenics Education Society and George McKay joked in *The Soldier* on 27 June 1919, 'if eugenics had been the rule, some of us wouldn't have been here to study it'. There was competition between eugenists, and eugenic organisations in Sydney and Melbourne were such fierce rivals that they reached a consensus only once, in 1929 at the Australian Racial Hygiene Congress. While the Sydney-based Racial Hygiene Association (RHA) had visions of going national, a separate Eugenics Society of Victoria (ESV) was formed in 1936, an action which the RHA's Lillie Goodisson described as being in 'shockingly bad taste'. Neither organisation attracted a large membership. In 1950 Edith How-Martyn, a pioneering British birth control campaigner, was disappointed about the lack of interest in eugenics in Sydney. By then the RHA showed little interest, perhaps believing as John Maynard Smith does, 'eugenics can wait; birth control cannot'. The RHA, which in 1933 began to provide contraception, survives as the Family Planning Association, while the ESV, which remained eugenics-oriented, did not survive. Both groups helped to legitimise discussions about sexual matters and contraception; an ESV member said when the Society closed in 1962, 'we were the pioneers in this country and the subject which we presented to the public stimulated discussion and aroused controversy'. Eugenists, because of their interest in heredity, helped to foster research in human genetics.

Comments are coloured by memories of Hitler and fears about human clones or designer babies. So naturally, because of its bigoted definitions of unfitness in terms of race, class, ethnic and religious preferences, eugenics provokes heated and simplistic responses. Germain Greer provides a good example of such emotion-loaded, data-free reactions in *Sex and Destiny* when she said that eugenics was 'more barbarous than cannibalism and far more destructive'. It deserves more careful consideration; although old eugenics is dead, born-again eugenics may emerge in the era of the Genome Project. While Australians resisted attempts to build better babies for the good of the state a more subtle, harder to resist form may come, allowing consumers to shop for scientists willing to shape a genetically enhanced future for their children.

The history of eugenics provides the foundations on which to make intelligent appraisals of the difficulties which genetic advances pose for human rights, decency and ethics. Two seminal works on the history of eugenics are by an Australian, Lyndsay A Farrall and an American, Daniel J Kevles. Farrall's pioneering PhD thesis, *The Origins and Growth of the English Eugenics Movement, 1865-1925* was written in 1969 and in 1985, popular and academic interest was galvanized in 1985 by Kevles' best seller, *In The Name of Eugenics: Genetics and the Uses of Human Heredity*. This has been followed by a number of national and comparative studies of eugenics, particularly in Germany, Canada, and Latin America, some of them revealing long-hidden secrets. This archives-based study of Australian attempts to produce human thoroughbreds contributes a new chapter to the diverse histories of the movement.

---

[1]Many scholars mistakenly claim that Galton was Darwin's nephew or first cousin. Milo Keynes gave precise details of the complex relationship between Darwin and Galton whose grandfather was the physician, poet and philosopher, Erasmus Darwin. See *Sir Francis Galton, FRS: The Legacy of His Ideas*. Proceedings of the 28th Annual Symposium of the Galton Institute, London, 1991, Milo Keynes (ed.) (London: Macmillan in assocn with the Galton Institute, 1993), 4.

[2]Introductory wall panel, "The Relation of Eugenics to Other Sciences", by Dr Harry H Laughlin, Plate 1, in *A Decade of Progress in Eugenics* [1934], Scientific Papers of the Third International Congress of Eugenics, 21-23 August 1932 (New York: Garland, 1984). Stephen J Gould noted in *Hidden Histories of Science*, Robert B Silvers (ed.) (London: Granta Books, 1997), 64-65, that 'Ernest Haeckel produced the first historically important tree of life in 1866'.

1. Preserving Australia's National Stock

The role of eugenics in Australian history might have been forgotten, like most special interest groups which briefly flourished early last century. However, several things set it apart from the ephemeral groups which left no trace: the eugenics movement left written records, it made an impact and, most important of all, there are now fears that it may rise again. Eugenics was initially endorsed because it offered respectable solutions to problems troubling the new nation such as the need to revitalise an apparently degenerating population and to avoid invasion. Eugenics built on the earlier 'survival of the fittest' theories, providing hope that science would transform Australia into a new-world utopia. Eugenists argued that instead of relying on cruel and haphazard laws of nature they would use humane, systematic and scientific methods to eliminate the unfit.

Early last century anthropologists reported that a new Australian type was emerging. To optimists this marked a shift towards utopia. To pessimists these changes showed that Australia's white population was declining in quantity and quality – twin perils which they called 'racial suicide' and 'racial decay'. Optimists and pessimists both responded by combining notions about efficiency and progress with eugenic ideas in their attempts to boost the white population, fill the continent's 'empty spaces', improve national fitness and avoid Asian immigration or invasion. As a result, the imported ideas of social Darwinism and eugenics were eagerly accepted in Australia before the first world war and the notion of eugenics was promoted by many eminent Australians. The views were derived from Britain and America but some uniquely Australian influences were also at work. Many doctors who laid the foundations of Australia's public health service were eugenists and the two main eugenics organizations – the Racial Hygiene Association (RHA) and the Eugenics Society of Victoria (ESV) – were family planning pioneers.

Vitality or Decay? The Calibre of Colonists and Aboriginals

The writing of two men, Herbert Spencer (1820-1903) and Charles Darwin (1809-1882), prompted the concerns now known as social Darwinism. In 1852 Spencer coined the terms 'survival of the fittest' and the 'struggle for existence'. These were adopted by Darwin, who accepted these phrases as 'more accurate' than his term 'natural selection'.[1] Debate continues about social Darwinism[2] and whether eugenics should be seen as the most enduring aspect of it. While social Darwinism has been disparaged as the great nineteenth century fetish, in America, Britain and Australia it was eagerly invoked to justify struggle and competition. It supplied the philosophical basis for the theory that war was inherent in nature and ennobling with the result, in Barbara Tuchman's opinion, that 'Darwinism became the White Man's Burden. Imperialism acquired a moral imperative'.

In Australia, fears about the calibre of colonials were calmed from the 1870s by news of sporting successes, particularly cricket victories, against England which proved that British blood had not been thinned by antipodean summers. However, some sceptics wanted proof of mental *and* physical national fitness. The University of Sydney's motto *Sidere Mens Eadem Mutato*, usually translated as 'the same mind under different skies', hints that there were also fears about our mental fitness. When transportation ceased, fears about the stain of convictism were replaced by fears about the physique of the 'Australian race'. For example, in 1872 a Melbourne paper considered that people were shrinking and feared that 'Anglo-Australians' were becoming 'as stunted in their growth as the former possessors of the soil'.[3] Five years later, freethinker Henry Keylock Rusden (1826-1910) said in the *Melbourne Review*:

> "The survival of the fittest means that might – wisely used – is right. And thus we invoke and remorselessly fulfil the inexorable law of natural selection (or of demand and supply), when exterminating the inferior Australian and Maori races, and we appropriate their patrimony ... though in diametrical opposition to all our favourite theories of right and justice – thus proved to be unnatural and false. The world is better for it."[4]

Rusden presented this as an onerous chore but the 'the replacement of the Aborigines throughout America and Australia by white races'[5] was presented by the temperamental British scientist Karl Pearson (1857-1936) as an uplifting cause for satisfaction. There was no sense of shame, either, in a 11 January 1888 report published in Melbourne's *Age* newspaper which justified Aboriginal deaths, from 'the readily contracted vices of the Europeans', as being 'beneficial to mankind at large by providing for the survival of the fittest'. The likely author was George Barton (1836-1901), NSW's 'first purely literary man' and a 'potent preacher of social Darwinism', who made the much-quoted suggestion that whites should 'smooth the dying pillow' of the Aboriginal race. He also influenced his brother Sir Edmund Barton who as Prime Minister became the 'principal architect of the White Australia Policy'.

Barry Butcher convincingly argued that in the nineteenth century Australia was used as the world's anthropological quarry, with studies of Australian Aboriginals providing the 'evidence' for Charles Darwin's evolutionary theories. Once accepted, they gave scientific legitimacy to the belief that Aboriginals were inferior and destined for extinction, a view which Australian pastoralists and politicians had long held.[6] The 'most fruitful' anthropological data to be mined by Darwin (and others), came from Professor (later Sir) Walter Baldwin Spencer (1860-1929) whose work, as a zoologist, anthropologist, collector and art patron, enhanced the status of Melbourne University and earned him a world-wide reputation. In 1901 Australia had reluctantly funded a year-long study of the Aborigines of northern Central Australia by Baldwin Spencer and anthropologist Francis James Gillen (1855-1912). The grant was made only after 77 eminent Englishmen (led by Sir James Frazer author of *The Golden Bough*) had petitioned the Victorian and South Australian Governments on the grounds that it was 'to Australia, more perhaps than to any other quarter of the globe, that anthropologists are now looking for the solution of certain problems of great moment in the early history of science and religion'.[7] Baldwin Spencer was a Fellow of the Royal Society and from 1887, Professor of Biology at the University of Melbourne where he was the first to employ female lecturers and associate professors.

This liberalism contrasted with his 1913 Report to Parliament, signed as Special Commissioner and Chief Protector of Aborigines in the Northern Territory. Spencer's Report included plans for farming along the remote Daly River, although he knew it would drive the Aboriginals off their land because they would not have access to water holes and farms would destroy their food supplies.[8] John Mulvaney described Spencer's Report as a 'comprehensive but costly blueprint for Aboriginal welfare' which was 'tabled' and forgotten. While Spencer's notions were paternalistic, authoritarian and social Darwinian, they were also innovative and advocated the creation of extensive reserves. These positives which Mulvaney identified (and Spencer's role as the first academic anthropologist to receive government appointment as a policy-maker[9]) were ignored in the 1982 criticism that, if this were the policy of the Chief Protector of Aborigines, 'God save them from such friends!'.[10]

There were no positives in the policies promoted from 1915 to 1940 by the British-born Protector of Aborigines in Western Australia, A O (Auber Octavius) Neville (1875-1954), whose influence started in 1905. As a result of his urging, the Western Australia's Aborigines Act sanctioned the removal of part-Aboriginal children from their parents. After the adoption of NSW's Aboriginal protection policy in 1909 it was illegal for part-Aboriginals to live on reserves and the powers of the Aboriginal Protection Board were increased in 1915 and 1918. The aim of 'breeding out the colour' (by segregating the 'best' Aboriginals on reserves and assimilating the others) may have been influenced by news of America's 'greatest problem' in the 1930s, the racial strife fermented by a mixture of the 'worst' (poorest) blacks and whites.[11] Aboriginal assimilation became official Commonwealth policy in 1937 but it had flourished in a *de facto* fashion for years, prompting the anthropologist A P (Adolphus Peter) Elkin (1891-1979) to warn that it contributed to the detribalisation or extinction of the Aboriginal people.[12] These policies have been denounced as the ultimate eugenic solution but sixty years ago most people were either unaware of them or unconcerned about the consequences.

However, in one of the many paradoxes of Australian eugenics, in the 1930s a group formed to promote eugenics was fiercely *opposed* to the official doctrine and was severely castigated for its defence of Aboriginal rights. The group, the Racial Hygiene Association (RHA), was influenced by the feminist and human rights activist Mary Montgomery Bennett (1881-1961), pioneering overland motorist Francis Birtles (1882-1941), and anthropologist Ralph Piddington (1906-1974), son of Albert and Marion Piddington. British-born Bennett warned the policy would cause 'the disappearance of the native race'. For years she had seen the hardships which Aboriginals in Western Australia experienced, taught them and crusaded on their behalf. Predicably, Bennett was attacked by officials, who tried to divert the public from her accusations by claiming that she 'suffered from ill health, sometimes severely' and had an 'obsession' about Aboriginals.[13]   Their, attempts to discredit her were probably a retaliation against the bad publicity they received in 1934 after she turned to the Anti-Slavery Society in London begging for help. She made this desperate plea: 'The only help for our poor natives that there is comes from knowledge and public opinion in England. Australians are sensitive about that'.[14]

She was supported in Western Australia by the Women's Service Guilds and the Women's Christian Temperance Union and in NSW by the RHA. Ruby Rich (1888-1988), an Australian heiress, feminist, publicist and founding co-president of the RHA, read a paper by Bennett in London at the June 1933 British Commonwealth League Conference. It was outrageous and defamatory, according to Sydney's *Daily Telegraph* which rejected Bennett's claim that the Australian government's policies were extreme, unjustified and designed to 'separate the half-caste men from the girls and send the girls out amongst the whites and so breed out colour by adultery and prostitution'. According to the paper, Australia's honour had been 'blackened' around the world by the 'exaggerated slanders' of 'Miss Rich and her missionary friends' who 'paint a startling tableau coloured by their fervid sympathies'. The paper's outrage over this stance underlines the reality that, in spite of its name, the RHA strongly supported Aboriginal rights and vehemently opposed white men's abuse of Aboriginal women.[15]

In the 1870s Anthony Trollope (the 'Antipodean') praised 'colonial-born' Australians in London's *Daily Telegraph* and 'had no doubt whatever' that these men and women were 'superior' to those who came from England. Even 'currency lads and lasses' (the children of convicts) were described by contemporary colonial writers as 'self-respecting, moral, law abiding, industrious and surprisingly sober'.[16] Some argued that convict virtues were passed on while their faults were bred out.

Good food and a healthy climate helped to develop a 'superior' (larger and fitter), Australian type. Visitors commented on this even in convict days and more so from the 1840s. American eugenist Ellsworth Huntington identified three natural selection processes: the sick would not risk the long, hazardous journey, the timid would seek a more assured American future and the poor could not afford the trip. These factors and environmental influences explain why Australians were more homogeneous, prosperous and healthy than their stay-at-home counterparts.

Declining Birth-rates and Pronatalist Responses

The colony's first challenge was to provide food and the next was to produce a large and healthy population. Restating what the First Fleet naval officer Watkin Tench had said in 1788, a visitor in 1832 praised the 'salubrious climate' which miraculously increased the fertility of most women if they were 'below the age 42' when they arrived. Even infertile women would produce a child each year and 'beget a large family', although the author conceded that the climate had less effect on 'females of a higher class'.[17] Such observers may have believed that Australia's women and its soil were fertile and that the colony whose area was more than thirty times greater than the United Kingdom's, could support a population which equalled or exceeded that of the mother country.[18] Early views were often unsophisticated, early population records were inaccurate, and the population bulges of the 1840s, which were intensified by the gold rushes and the boom times of the 1880s, were seen as the norm. The optimistic 1880s became the depressed 1890s. There was industrial strife in the eastern states between 1890 and 1894, followed by a national drought from 1895 to

1903. Prosperity vanished after 1900 because there was also a massive withdrawal of British capital which caused extensive unemployment. Australia was moving from a rural economy to a city-based industrial one at a time of massive technological developments which were creating tensions as they transformed the western world.

During this transition period, from the 1870s to the 1930s, the size of the Australian family declined rapidly in a shift which was later called 'the most significant change in the history of Australian families'.[19] At the time, commentators could not understand the complex reasons for it, nor did they know it was experienced in most industrialized countries. The alarm was increased by statistics in 1904 which showed that the decline in births had been greatest in Queensland, where the birth rate per 1,000 population had been reduced by 23.9% between 1891 and 1900, compared with only an 8.6% reduction in England.[20] This trend was made clearer in 1920 by the British statistician George Udny Yule who told the Cambridge University Eugenics Society that the fall in the birth rate in Britain (23%) was only exceeded by that in Australia (27%) and in New Zealand (34%).

Country	Average annual births per 1,000 at all ages		Decrease % of the rate in 1901-10 on 1871-80
	1871-80	1901-10	
New Zealand	40.5	26.8	34
Australia	36.1	26.5	27
England	35.4	27.2	23
Scotland	34.9	28.4	19
France	25.4	20.6	19
Netherlands	36.2	30.5	16
Germany	39.1	32.9	16
Ireland	26.5	23.3	12
Italy	36.9	32.7	11
Denmark	31.4	28.6	9

Table 1: World Wide Decline in the Birth Rate, 1871 to 1910

Table 1 provides a summary of Yule's statistics using data from *Statistique Internationale*, which shows that the birth rate decline was 'almost universal'.

In contrast, Japan had had a 'conspicuous increase' between 1871 and 1910 and figures remained the same in some American states and South America or increased slightly, probably related to immigration.[21] From the 1890s news that Japan's population was rapidly increasing while Australia's was shrinking, fuelled anxieties about threats from the north. The medical profession shared the concerns of politicians and statisticians: on 21 November 1898 the *Australasian Medical Gazette* warned that the declining birth rate was 'a problem which legislation must deal with soon unless we are content to become a weak and degenerate country'. The view was shared by Sir James Barrett (1862-1945), Vice-Chancellor, then Chancellor at the University of Melbourne and a physician who busied himself with Empire-related movements. He was described in his obituary as a 'pioneer in all things that one could think of by which the human race might be bettered and improved'. Betterment did not include women's education which he blamed in 1901, along with women's knowledge about abortion and contraception, for having serious consequences for the British Empire and the Anglo-Saxon race, admonishing 'it is not possible to cheat God Almighty without paying a heavy penalty, both personally and racially – personally if the cases be few; racially if the cases be numerous'.[22]   Ironically, Barrett was accused of planning some cheating himself: it was widely predicted that once this authoritarian reformer arrived in Heaven, 'God would be demoted to vice president'. [23]

In 1903 the NSW Government Statistician, Sir Timothy Coghlan (1856-1926) warned that because migration had dried up, the population relied on the 'seriously diminished and still diminishing' birth-rate.   The 'satisfactory solution' was 'a national one of overwhelming importance' which would determine whether Australia would ever take its place 'amongst the great nations of the world'.[24] Coghlan's pessimism contrasted with his earlier book *The Wealth and Progress of NSW 1886-87*, in which he boasted that the 'colony' and 'all the provinces of Australia' compared favourably with any other country', that no Australians were 'born to poverty' and that the 'hereditary pauper class' had 'no existence here'. Australia was free of old world hatreds and strife 'and thus, happy in its situation and most fortunate in its wealth, it may await its future in calm confidence'. Coghlan's pessimism coincided with his statistics gathering. Havelock Ellis found the data 'specially valuable' because they gave parental age, 'period since marriage' and number of children, details which were not given in English or 'most other' records.[25] Coghlan's census material and news of Asia's increasing strength, were important stimuli for the *Royal Commission on the Decline in the Birth-rate and on the Mortality of Infants in New South Wales* – the world's first such inquiry. There were other Australian world firsts in 1904; the first Labor government in Canberra and the first Baby Health Centre in Sydney.

Rose Scott (1847-1925) was remarkable for her contempt of the Commission and for managing a few years earlier to persuade her reclusive cousin David Scott Mitchell (1836-1907) to bequeath his books to the people and finance the Mitchell Library which opened in 1910. This eminent woman was a feminist and anti-imperialist who opposed 'enforced motherhood' and contraception. She refused to be a witness and denounced the Report as a 'whirlwind' of 'superficial comment' by the 'men only' Commission which 'very contentedly' told the public that women were at fault. She was attacking twelve of Sydney's most celebrated citizens.[26] In her 1904 Presidential Address to the Women's Political and Educational League, Scott considered:

> "So long as men keep up the demand for a supply of thousands and thousands of women in every city, who are to lead degraded lives, apart from the sphere of wife and mother [they should blame themselves for the evils which influence the birthrate by] disease, selfishness and immorality. ... Quality should be placed before quantity, for population as population can be of no benefit to a country. ... It is not a question of many people or few people, but a question of what sort of people, and what sort of environment."[27]

Concerns about the 'teeming millions in Japan' were cited in the Commission's Report which attributed the blame to selfish, luxury-loving women, contraception and abortion[28] and the findings were reviewed in Australian and overseas. Dr Norman Himes, an American expert on contraceptive history, called it a 'verbose, bulky report' containing 'more opinion than science'.[29] Havelock Ellis itemised the Report's short-comings and contrasted Coghlan's conclusion, that the birthing decline was due to 'the art of applying artificial checks to conception', with that of William McLean, the Government Statistician of Victoria, who commented on the 'perfectly satisfactory' *increases* and found the decline was 'due mainly to natural causes'. McLean remarked that births were reverting to the norm after being abnormally high in the 1880s; there was no advantage in having a high birth-rate if it led to a high infant death rate because too many cradles meant too many coffins. McLean expressed it this way: 'Clearly, it is no satisfaction for any community to have a high birth-rate in order to achieve in a few years, results which are accomplished by communities with a low birth-rate at no such sacrifice of human life'.[30]

A similar point was made by the speaker who closed the 1912 Eugenics Congress – 'the greatest problem of the world is not how to bring better babies into the world, but how to take care of such as come. The tragedy of the world is spoiled babies'.[31] Edith Onians (1866-1955) also attended this Congress; she was a wealthy child-rescuer, known as the newsboys' friend and called 'Miss' by the thousands of boys she helped in Melbourne. She also made history as the first woman to be appointed to the Children's Court of Victoria. In her Report on the Congress she argued that as New Zealand (a country with a low birth rate) had the world's lowest infant mortality, it provided 'an ideal we can reach in all countries by lowering the birth-rate sufficiently'.[32] Dr Charles Vickery Drysdale (1874-1961) had made this point in *Neo-Malthusianism and Eugenics*, a 1912 pamphlet discussing birth control, although this word did not enter the language until 1914 when it was coined by Otto Bobsein, a young friend of Margaret Sanger.[33] Drysdale attacked 'ridiculous fallacies about the declining birth-rate' spread by people such as 'ex-President Roosevelt' who claimed that the 'Australian population would not double once in a century' and complained that 'several English writers' had confused birth-rates with survival-rates. Drysdale believed that in 'every country in the world except New Zealand and Australia', there was advocacy for limiting the size of the population. He explained that in Australasia, fertility was 'sufficiently restricted', food was plentiful and the death-rate was so low that 'the question of quality is now of first importance'.[34] Drysdale was mistaken or indulging in propaganda: Australia's falling infant death rate was linked with the birth rate decline of the 1890s. It was economics, not clandestine contraception nor eugenics which had made families limit their families.

Radicals and conservatives could both lie about Australia as a birth-controller paradise. In 1923 white supremacist (later pro-Nazi) Lothrop Stoddard claimed that in a few 'enlightened countries' including Australia, birth control was 'welcomed' and knowledge about it was 'freely imported to all classes'. He claimed that 'social and racial results' had been 'excellent' in 'minimizing the differential birth-rates and thus averting sudden group shifts in the population'.[35] From 1870, when free primary school education began to be provided, Australians became increasingly literate; however, few had access to supplies or self-help manuals, 'obscene' birth control books were routinely seized by Customs; and contraception was vigorously condemned until at least the 1950s.

A scathing attack on the Birth-Rate Report was made in 1923 by Neo-Malthusian Johannes Rutgers, a 'leading member of the international birth control movement'.[36] He criticised the Commission's Report for maintaining that birth control had undermined the morality of the nation and for 'its fanaticism' in maintaining that there had been an *increase* in infant deaths, while quoting statisticians from the various Australian states as witnesses, including McLean, who had declared that there had been a 'distinct *decrease*' in the death rate.[37] Jessie Ackermann, a gutsy American evangelical journalist made an astute assessment in her 1913 book about Australian life:

"Although marriage has decreased and the birth rate per family is on the decline, the increase in the population among the white race is greater than it has ever been. This is due to the diminished percentage of mortality among children, especially infants during the first year of their lives. ... The greatest advance in any science of modern times is that directed towards the conservation of infant life."[38]

The Royal Commission began their 'pronatalist theatre' in 1903, the year after women became eligible to stand for office or vote in Federal elections, but analyses of pronatalism in Australian politics have ignored the influence of the women's movement.[39] The major benefit from the Commission was the publicity it gave to babies' shockingly high death rate making the subject a 'respectable, even pressing public issue' and 'cleared the way for state involvement'.[40] In NSW the government implemented several reforms: the Infant Protection Act 1904, requiring licensing and inspection of foundling homes; the Poisons Act 1905, which required prescription-only sale of the abortifacient ergot of rye, and the Private Hospitals Act 1908, which obliged private hospitals to have licences, be inspected and to keep a register of patients, births and deaths. Similar laws were passed in other states.   However, despite the backing by politicians and patricians, there was no birthing avalanche; it is unlikely that any Australian child has been born because of its parents' sense of duty to the state. Last century, most women resolutely avoided having the large families that were common when fertility was minimally restricted.   Even so, in 1911 the 'excellent data' compiled in the Commonwealth showed that the population was slowly increasing, at a rate of less than 1% per annum.[41] The point that there *was* an increase was also made by Lyndhurst Falkiner Giblin (1872-1951), an influential and liberal-minded economist from Tasmania, who scotched a claim in the *Eugenics Review* that Australia had one of the world's lowest birth rates as a result of 'women's suffrage'.[42] Claims that votes for women led to a birth strike were similarly dismissed by the leader of Britain's Suffrage movement, Millicent Fawcett (1847-1929). She wrote in *The Times* on 5 November 1910 'that was absolutely a fatuous argument, for the birth-rate in those countries which had the vote compared most favourably with the Mother Country'. She gave figures: British women [who began their suffrage campaigns in 1866 but did not win the vote until 1918] had a birth rate of 26 per thousand, the same as the rate for Australian women who began voting in 1902, while in New Zealand, where women had been voting since 1893, the rate was 27 per thousand. Fawcett concluded that after women got the vote in New Zealand and Australia both countries had experienced 'a most satisfactory decline' in infant deaths. This made good publicity but her claim that the vote *saved* babies was as spurious as her opponents' claim that there were fewer births *because* women had the vote. Perhaps Fawcett said it in tribute to the Australians who joined in London's 1908 Women's Suffrage March.[43]

Figure 2: "Trust the Women, Mother" – Australian Suffrage Banner

Neville Hicks' *This Sin and Scandal* gives a comprehensive analysis of the 1904 RCDBR and of the debate before and after the publication of its Report, a 'masterpiece of conservative rectitude'.[44] Pronatalism, fanned by patriotism and religion, grew in response to the high death rate in World War I and peaked during the three post-war decades. In his Presidential address to the 1923 Australasian Medical Congress, Sir George Syme warned that those who urged people to 'fructify [be fruitful in the Biblical sense] and defend the country' should not forget the importance of qualitative and quantitative population increases.[45] Most only remembered quantity. For example, in 1925 Justice Piddington saw Australia as 'a dying nation' unless saved by a childhood endowment scheme.[46] Billy Hughes (1862-1952), then Commonwealth Minister for Health, intensified worries about falling numbers in his famous 1937 remark that 'Australia must advance and populate, or perish' (See **Figure 3**[47]).

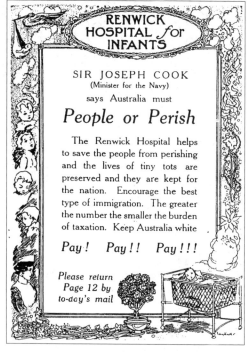

Figure 3: Populate or Perish

In his view, 'a great number of problems confront the Commonwealth, but the declining birth-rate overshadows them all. It is impossible to exaggerate its gravity. Australia is bleeding to death'.[48] It was a disaster which had to be averted thought Hughes who, fearing we were 'a white drop in a coloured ocean', 'trenchantly attacked birth control' and stressed the need for population growth.[49]   George McCleary, the British author of *The Menace of Depopulation,* seemed stunned by Australians' childbearing reluctance:

> In no country is life more sunny and pleasant. In that glorious sunshine, in view of the radiant faces that throng the great surfing beaches of the Southern Ocean, the world appears, as it appeared to Robert Louis Stevenson, 'as a brave gymnasium full of sea-bathing and horse exercise, and bracing manly virtues'. If there is any part of the world where mankind may well be expected to thrill with the joy of life it is in these two island Dominions, in both of which the reproduction rate has sunk below the rate required to maintain the present numbers of the population.[50]

But the Great Depression showed that families needed more than surf and sun and, as the world tensions erupted in 1939, couples continued to postpone child bearing in these impoverished and uncertain times. This prompted a second inquiry into the birth rate decline, conducted by the National Health and Medical Research Council in 1944. Dr Cumpston, the Director-General of Health, invited women to state the reasons for their hesitancy and 1,400 did. Many said succinctly, 'poverty'; their feelings were eloquently expressed by one woman, 'You men in easy chairs say "populate or perish". Well, I have populated and I have perished – with no blankets'. Cumpston, in his analysis of the responses found that eugenic reasons were rare; 'in a few cases' the decision was made 'because of mental or other disorders which might appear in the children' and some women refused to have children with an alcoholic or syphilitic husband.[51]

During the war the ABC bravely launched an innovative radio program, *The Nation's Forum of the Air,* to discuss public questions of major importance.   There was uproar during a panel discussion, 'Australia: Unlimited?'[52]   Catholics and pronatalists felt the matter should not be questioned and reprimanded the ABC for engaging the birth control advocate Dr Norman Haire as a speaker. They were also furious because Haire, himself an eleventh child, had talked about his mother's sufferings as a result of unfettered childbearing.

White Australia

> "Unconsciously, the White Australia Policy was one of the greatest eugenic laws ever passed in Australia. A greater piece of legislation could not have been secured for this country. The types we are bringing into it are not coming from the classes we should breed from. They are not people who, mentally and physically, are capable of filling the higher positions in life. Most of the types are domestics and miners and not the intelligentsia."[53]

Dr Richard Granville Waddy said this at the 1929 Australian Racial Hygiene Congress and there is no denying that the policy has eugenic aspects. James Curle, a yellow press writer of 'yellow peril' scares, took a different view. He claimed in the 7th edition of *To-day and To-morrow: The Testing Period of the White Race* that 'no racial idealism' prompted Australia to be a 'pure-white people', the decision was 'economic, not eugenic'. In a review of this 1928 edition of Curle's book, Leonard Woolf rejected the author's views as the 'hallucinations of high fever'.

Australians boasted of being 'more British than the British', 'bound together by that crimson thread of kinship that can never perish', to quote the 'Grand Old Man of Australian Politics', Sir Henry Parkes (1815-1896). He made this famous remark on 13 June 1891 while addressing an immense crowd at Sydney's Gaiety Theatre. The wish to be British to the bootstraps was utterly racist but, while it operated, there was no need for other measures to maintain racial purity. Consequently, racism played a lesser role in Australian eugenics than in other countries, such as America and South Africa.

Ironically, the proposal that Australia should be maintained as a white colony was made by a British lawyer who in 1833 had prepared an anti-racist bill which was crucial to the abolition of the slave trade. The 1841 proposal was made in London by the Colonial Office's Sir James Stephen (1789-1859) and the idea took hold in Australia. The notion grew in the 1850s and 1860s and, following widespread anti-Chinese riots during the gold rush, the 1880 Australian Intercolonial Conference agreed to restrict Chinese immigration. The NSW Chinese

Restriction Act became law in 1893 and three years later the ban was extended to all Asians. This portal-guarding aim was a major stimulus for bringing together the Australian Labor Party and Federation.

The new century's new nation was ceremoniously launched by Australia's first Prime Minister, Sir Edmund Barton (1849-1920) who was praised as the country's noblest son and scorned as Toby Tosspot, because of his fondness for food and drink. Despite the heatwave on New Year's Day 1901 he was suitably alert and noble in his Federation day speech about 'a nation for a continent, and a continent for a nation' which he delivered to a crowd of thousands from an ornate pavilion in Sydney's Centennial Park. The invitation for the event showed the States as allegorical maidens sailing into the dawn of a new era.[54] Embarrassingly now, the new Commonwealth embraced racist legislation which was rushed through parliament by our founding fathers to capitalise on citizens' dreams of a white Australia. The Immigration Restriction Act was signed on 24 December 1901 (after much hesitation) by Lord Hopetoun (1860-1908), Australia's first Governor General. It was a Christmas present for the people, really to keep Asians out but ostensibly aimed at all non-Europeans, who were not allowed to settle permanently after failing dictation tests in any European language of the testing officer's choice. Few efforts were made to disguise this method of excluding 'undesirable' aliens: a 1906 recruitment campaign in Britain reassured potential immigrants to Australia that the dictation test had 'never yet been applied to a white man'.[55] These tests were abolished in 1958 but remnants remained until the 1970s, long after support for eugenics had vanished. Eugenic beliefs did not initiate this policy, nor were they its sole or strongest influence.

Doctrines of social Darwinism spawned by theories of 'race and stock' and 'blood and breed' were intensified by a heady mix of nationalism, Anglo-Saxon imperialism and Caucasian racism.[56] Historians disagree about the 'genesis and growth' of the White Australia Policy. Was it economic, arising 'from a labour-oriented desire to conserve high living standards and trade union solidarity'? Was it fear of the unfamiliar or 'a primordial instinct' to keep the race pure originating from the numbers of Chinese gold miners and an awareness of 'the vast human reservoir' from which they came?[57] Now it is impossible to unravel the amalgam of racist, imperialist, eugenic, economic and patriotic views. Then it was widely seen in a positive light, as 'race purity not jobs, a natural instinct not selfishness, became the moral justification for exclusion'.[58]

The words 'White Australia Policy' were first used in June 1888 by the radical Brisbane weekly, *Boomerang* and in Sydney the policy was supported by the *Bulletin*, popularly known as the 'Bully' or the 'Bushman's Bible'. When it began in 1880 this iconoclastic but 'extremely readable' weekly, which disrespectfully wrote about the 'British Vampire' and 'Union Jackals', had for its banner headline 'Australia for the Australians'. This changed in 1908 to 'Australia for the White Man' and astonishingly, the *Bulletin* threw out this challenge until 1961 when Donald Horne became editor.

At Federation the central problem facing Australia was 'the task of holding the continent – peopled, white, an outpost of European civilisation' – because 'at the very core of nationalism was the demand to control the composition of the society. "White Australia" was no meaningless term to the small and isolated society apprehensively aware of the ever-increasing population to the north. However unfortunate a term in its choosing, it was one which aroused passions and embodied convictions'.[59] In the nineteenth century, non-whites, such as Afghan camel drivers, were allowed to stay for pragmatic reasons and by 1901 Australia's population of 3,782,943 included about 55,000 'coloured' aliens. Aboriginals were not counted in the Census. Curiously, it was believed until the 1970s that a century ago Japan was asked, but refused, to colonise the Northern Territory despite the bait of a free travel offer for the first 200 settlers. There is hard evidence about others attempts; in 1862 the Queensland Government passed the Coolie Immigration Act but after sugar plantation owners rejected the terms for employing these Indians, the Act was repealed. That same year Queenslanders began importing, often kidnapping, Pacific Islanders as indentured labourers and this continued until 1906.

All the while, the dream of a snow-white country increased, particularly after the 1893 publication of *National Life and Character: A Forecast* which was 'discussed from St Petersburg to Tennessee'.[60] The egalitarian and progressive author was Charles Henry Pearson (1830-1894), an Oxford don who settled in Australia in 1871 where he became a distinguished journalist and subsequently the Victorian Minister of Education.   Pearson, who paradoxically promoted educational opportunities for women and low-paid workers, prophesied danger 'for the higher races everywhere, if the black and yellow belt encroaches upon the earth'.[61] The views were based on temperate regions because, he argued, the tropics were out as whites might be overpowered by blacks or assimilated by them. However, it is doubtful whether 'the first effect of this powerful and original book was to carry to victory the "White Australia Policy", and with that to make racial exclusiveness a leading feature in the self-governing portions of the British Empire'.[62]

Labor politician Sir Henry Parkes, whose introduction of the Chinese Restriction Bill in the NSW Parliament in 1888 initiated the White Australia Policy, praised Pearson as 'an academic radical' and the 'Professor of Democracy'. Pearson's gloomy prophecy about white prospects was believed and President Theodore Roosevelt encapsulated this view in the phrase 'race suicide', warning Australians to 'fill up your cradles and throw open your gates. Beware of keeping your North empty'.[63] Pearson's book was read by 'most of the leading public men' who accepted it as a 'sophisticated exposition' of the 'Yellow Peril'. In 1901 Prime Minister Barton quoted Pearson as showing 'that these trends *would* be inevitable unless something was done to prevent them'. The casuistic Barton did not think that the core of the 'doctrine of equality' was 'really ever intended to include racial equality'.[64]

Myra Willard's *History of the White Australia Policy* is the pioneering text. She was one of the 238 high-achieving honours students who studied under the liberal-minded George Arnold Wood, an inspiring teacher who in 1892 became the foundation Challis Professor of History at the University of Sydney. As a new history graduate Willard began a three-year study of Australian migration which 'Woody' saw as 'the *central* Australian idea'. [65] With his encouragement, she turned some of her findings into an essay which won the Nathan prize in 1921; in 1923 Melbourne University Press produced it as their first 'real book'. Willard concluded that the main objective of the policy was to preserve 'British-Australian nationality'.[66] She quoted Australia's second Prime Minister, Alfred Deakin (1856-1919), who deserves most credit for the recognition the Commonwealth received in the first decade of last century as a social laboratory. Deakin, in turn a spiritualist, journalist, theosophist, eugenist, an 'intellectual disciple' of Charles Pearson, and 'the silver-tongued orator of Australia', stated in his speech on the Immigration Restriction Bill:

> "A united race means not only that its members can intermarry and associate without degradation on either side, but implies one inspired by the same ideals, and same general cast of character, tone of thought – the same constitutional training and traditions – a people qualified to live under this constitution, the broadest and most liberal perhaps the world has yet seen reduced to writing – a people qualified to use without abusing it, and to develop themselves under it to the full height and extent of their capacity."[67]

This self-styled 'independent Australian Briton' was as paradoxical as this description: he enjoyed the tag 'affable Alfred' and is the only Australian Prime Minister to receive a summons for riding a bicycle on the footpath.[68] However, he committed worse sins while in office. For instance, he secretly wrote for London's *Morning Post* as their anonymous Australian correspondent and used this and other newspapers to reveal confidential government information and laud his own achievements. Also, he hypocritically wanted to exclude the Japanese on the grounds of their superiority, saying 'we fear them for their virtues'. Naturally, the Japanese were outraged. Individuals in Australia who opposed this policy of exclusion included Edward William Cole (1832-1918), famous for his book arcade and *Cole's Funny Picture Books*; the geographer Thomas Griffith Taylor (1880-1963), popularly known as 'Grif' and William Macmahon Ball (1901-1986), Professor of Political Science at the University of Melbourne. The Communist Party was also opposed and Richard Dixon, Assistant

Secretary of the Australian Party wrote in 1945 'we must associate with our coloured allies in peace as in war, as equals'.[69]

The old order ceased with Queen Victoria's death in 1901 and Australians began to wonder if Britannia still ruled the waves. After empire troops suffered humiliating defeats, Britain won the Boer War in May 1902 and then, in January 1903, signed a treaty with Japan. Military and sporting defeats continued to shake white nations; in 1905 the Japanese victory in the Russo-Japanese war marked the first victory of a coloured nation against a white one and in 1908 a black competitor won in the first world title fight between a black and a white boxer. Two years earlier, a visit to Melbourne by three Japanese warships posed a diplomatic challenge as Australia had no fleet of its own, could not rely on Britain's navy for defence and had offended the Japanese by excluding them.

Now, only sporting buffs remember it but as Richard Broome has clearly shown, Australia's 1908 black versus white boxing match shook the world.[70] Because America's racial laws prevented such contests, a Sydney boxing promoter, Hugh D ('Huge Deal') McIntosh, decided to profit from this by building an open-air 16,000 capacity stadium for the match in Sydney's Rushcutters Bay. There was massive pre-match publicity aided by the influential and charismatic Norman Lindsay (1879-1969) who is now remembered for his nude paintings, his fights against puritanism and philistinism and for writing Australia's most loved children's book, *The Magic Pudding*. His dramatic illustration of the two boxers (**Figure 4**) – appeared on billboards, telegraph poles and on the cover of the high-circulation monthly *Lone Hand*.

McIntosh filmed the event and, 'to make a few bob from the sailors', held it on Boxing Day 1908 a day when America's Great White Fleet was in Sydney. It was there at Deakin's invitation and the visit, and his suggestion that Australia should ask the United States for protection, offended British sensitivities and horrified homegrown Empire loyalists.

The history-making match began mid-morning so that the light would enhance the filming. In a stunning result, the witty, flamboyant African-American Jack Johnson broke the 'colour line' by defeating the white Canadian champion Tommy Burns. There were 20,000 in the stadium and an even larger crowd outside, including the visiting American sailors. As well as the film, the match was reported by world notables including H L Mencken (1880-1956) for the *Sunday Times* and Jack London (1876-1916) for the *Sun*.[71] On the day before the match, the *Argus* reported that history would be made by London's wife, Charmian Kittredge, the first woman to be admitted to such an event. The news gave courage to six others who discussed their outfits and came to watch. Seven women were not news; instead Sydney's *Sunday Times* wrote 'A woman at title. Mrs Jack London's impressions. Excited throughout the contest. "Everything was nice and proper"'. She must have had a strong stomach because the fight had to be stopped by police in the fourteenth round. This defeat of a white boxer, like the military defeat at Gallipoli, focused the world's attention on Australia.

Figure 4: 1908 Boxing Match

Invasion fears prompted predictable and bizarre responses. In 1909 Dr Alan Carroll (c1823-1911) suggested that an Aboriginal army should defend the tropical north from intruders.[72] In January 1910 the *Eugenics Review* praised Australia for recognising the 'menace of the yellow races', as this could only be a 'healthy influence', since 'the proximity of powerful and threatening neighbours has more than once in the world's history produced a nation of more virile and even heroic men'. Reassurance came from Jessie Ackermann who had the quaint honour of being 'the first lady to circumnavigate Australia'. This American believed 'until the science of child-life is equally understood among the dark races there is little danger of the white races being swamped'.[73]   Dr Francis Pockley, the President of the 1911

Australasian Medical Congress, feared that the prolific 'dark races' would dominate white 'ancestral domains' and become 'formidable competitors' once tropical diseases were eradicated. He advised whites to avoid parasites and the tropics but more often, Australians were reminded of Imperial obligations to fill the continent. In 1925 British politician, Sir Leo Chiozza Money (1870-1944), gave his clichéd views in *The Peril of the White*. He expected Australia to stand as a bulwark against Asia which was overflowing with people who were looking this way. His views were criticised privately by Cora Hodson, the Secretary of the Eugenics Society, in a letter to the Society's chief benefactor, Henry Twitchin who is discussed in Chapter 2. She wrote in her 28 July 1928 letter to him 'I am not surprised that you are disturbed by the most dysgenic writings of Sir Chiozza Money' and she wondered how someone with so little understanding had received so much attention.[74]

The White Australia Policy was supported in 1926 by two Labor politicians, H V (Bert) Evatt (NSW) and William Kitson (WA), who were in London for a migration conference. They stressed that attempts to remove Australia's trade and labour self-determination would be resisted. The Nationalist Coalition Prime Minister Stanley Bruce (1883-1967), who was also in London, tactlessly told Imperial Conference delegates 'unless we can populate and develop these Dominions, I do not think anyone can look forward ... to the future of the British Empire'.[75] This Melbourne-born Anglophile who wore spats said in 1928 that Australia intended to 'maintain the British character of its population by friendly arrangements, rather than by throwing out defiance to the whole world'.

British-born Meredith Atkinson (1883-1929) was described by Stuart Macintyre as a 'grandiloquent self-promoter whose irregularities were notorious'. In 1920, as Melbourne University's first professor of sociology, Atkinson complained that 'few outside the Commonwealth' really understood the White Australia Policy, which had as its main objective 'the preservation of the Australian standard of social welfare'.[76] He supported this argument by quoting from Billy Hughes' speech to Federal Parliament. This was the famous 1919 speech in which Hughes, in his role as Australia's delegate to the Peace Treaty in Versailles, defended the White Australia Policy:

Honourable members who have travelled in the East or in Europe will be able to understand with what difficulty this world assemblage of men, gathered from all the corners of the earth … were able to appreciate this ideal of 5,000,000 people who had dared to say, not only that this great continent was not theirs, but that none should enter in except such as they chose. … Perhaps the greatest thing we have achieved, under such circumstances, and in such an assemblage, is the policy of a White Australia. On this matter I know that I speak for most, if not all, of the people of Australia.[77]

Paraphrasing Hughes' speech, Atkinson continued 'this is the foundation of all that Australia has fought for. This is the only part of the Empire or of the world in which there is so little admixture of races. … We hold firmly to this great principle of a White Australia because we know what we know, and because we have liberty and we believe in our race and in ourselves, and in our capacity to achieve our great destiny'. Atkinson added that Australia had 'provided the socialists and the eugenists with strong proofs of their contention that we can cultivate a super-race, if we will but furnish the social conditions of its development'.[78] By his choice of words he was treating eugenists and socialists as the other, indicating that by 1920 Atkinson was trying to disassociate himself from such undesirables. This was a speedy change of heart as the WEA had promoted eugenics while he was their Director and he had been invited to a high-level meeting on eugenics in 1918.[79] The right to inhabit an exclusively white Australia was accepted by the distinguished but unassuming Wilfred Eade Agar (1882-1951), who succeeded Walter Baldwin Spencer in 1919 as professor of zoology at the University of Melbourne. They both became Presidents of the Eugenics Society of Victoria. In 1918 Agar received a request from Leonard Darwin (1850-1943), who was Charles Darwin's son and the President of Britain's Eugenics Education Society, asking for information about Australian studies on 'inter-marriage between races'.

After a trip to Baltimore in 1926, Agar contacted Raymond Pearl, professor of biometry and vital statistics at Johns Hopkins University, asking for statistics about Japanese births. His surprising justification for the request was on the grounds that Australians were keenly interested in the 'possible results of admitting the yellow races'.[80] Agar wrote in a November 1927 to thank Pearl for his efforts but said that the requested data 'do not exist'. In the same month, Pearl severely criticised the 'biology of superiority' which lay behind such questions, asserting that eugenics had 'largely become a mingled mess of ill-grounded and uncritical sociology, economics, anthropology, and politics, full of emotional appeals to class and race prejudices, solemnly put forth as science, and unfortunately accepted as such by the general public'.[81] Terms such as 'race' and 'racial hygiene' are defined in the **Appendix**.

In 1928 Agar dismissed the idea of mixed-race marriages as 'somewhat academic' because the White Australia Policy was so 'firmly rooted in sentimental, economic and political ground'.[82] Dissenters included the geographer Thomas Griffith Taylor, who debunked the 'Nordic question' as a 'fetish', and the anthropologist A P Elkin, who dismissed dreams of 'pure Nordic supermen' as 'fiction'.[83] The fantasies were stimulated by Count Joseph-Arthur de Gobineau's *Essay on the Inequality of Races* (1853-55) in which he argued that white races, especially northern Europeans, were superior and would degenerate if they bred with others.[84] Professor Stephen Roberts, who as a German-speaker had correctly interpreted the clues when he visited Germany as Hitler was gaining power, warned in a book, which became an international best-seller, that Germany's use of Gobineau's theory threatened world peace.[85]   Twenty years later the geneticist Sir Macfarlane Burnet (1899-1985) urged Australians to 'collect the bonus of exceptional vigour that hybridization offers'.[86] In America, too, the image of migration as the crucible for the 'fusion of all races, perhaps a coming superman', was central to Israel Zangwill's play *The Melting Pot* (1908) and still sparks a powerful national response.

However, racial purity was extolled by many, including an Australian psychiatrist, Ralph Noble (1892-1965), who defended the White Australia Policy at a 1933 meeting of the International Committee of Mental Hygiene in Washington. Noble claimed that the policy had saved Australia from many problems experienced by multiracial societies. His view was bolstered by an American professor of public health who argued Australia's 'strengthened mental and physical purity of race' was because it had not mixed races. As a result, the professor argued, Australia was likely to avoid the American rates of suicide, which had quadrupled in 70 years and divorce, which had trebled in 50 years.[87] In the same year Agar made similar statements about 'miscegenation' (mixture of races), a term coined in the 1864 American Presidential elections by the Democrats' Dirty Tricks Department which alleged that the Republicans advocated the practice. Agar was sure that:

> Most of the coloured races would not make a desirable contribution to a population living under a civilization which has been slowly wrought out by the white race in conformity with their own particular genius. Nor does the experience of other countries with a large half-caste population encourage us to try the irrevocable experiment.

The 1930s were the sad years when 'there was no future any more', as Gertrude Stein put it. Bigotry was rife; the American eugenist Charles Davenport is credited with the unintentionally comic statement that people of mixed race origins would have 'the long legs of the Negro and the short arms of the white which would put them at a disadvantage in picking up things from the ground'.[88] Views of that kind have a long heritage, such as the great Swedish naturalist Carl Linnaeus (1707-1778) who, after classifying plants, classified people as Europeans highest, followed by Asians, with Africans at the bottom of the scale; and in 1869, Francis Galton claimed that Anglo-Saxons far outranked African Negroes who, in turn, outranked Australian Aborigines who did not outrank anyone.[89]

Agar claimed the 'blue-eyed Nordic' was 'unsociable and mystical' while the 'dark-eyed Mediterranean' was 'sociable, practical and subject to hysteria'. According to this logic, dark-eyed immigrants had more to offer but Agar explained that the clamour for 'Nordic' immigrants from Anglo-Saxon countries came the belief that they were superior and because they were our 'kith and kin'. Agar justified the 'Nordic cult' on the grounds that it had been upheld by many European and American writers, whose were influenced by the (now notorious) American Army Intelligence Tests in which the foreign-born recruits from the Nordic countries had higher scores than the others.[90]   He said nothing about the many other researchers who dismissed it as a racially prejudiced fantasy. In 1948 when Melbourne's *Herald* asked 'representative spokesmen' for their views; Agar 'the Eugenist' was adamant that the White Australia Policy should be enforced 'at all costs'. Nor did he change his views or remain silent, as so many others eugenists did, when these views were no longer popular. While the conservative Agar remained unreconstructed, liberals who revised their views about the White Australia Policy produced some shaky reconstructions. For example, in 1945 Professor A P Elkin wanted to keep the policy but disguise it by removing the word 'white' from the title.[91.]

Professor (later Sir Keith) Hancock (1898-1988) made things worse when he tried to correct the mistake he made in his 1930 classic, *Australia*. Initially, as a young man, he had said 'the Policy of White Australia is the indispensable condition of every Australian policy'.[92] However, in the preface of the book's 1961 reissue, he was principally concerned about a semantic fall from grace, explaining that he had used words carelessly by declaring that 'economic and "racial" necessity were the foundations of the White Australia Policy'. He continued, 'Today, no writer with any scientific or political sophistication would use the word "racial"'. Using careful code words he dismissed the White Australia Policy as 'only a popular slogan', which he said, 'has never been embodied in legislation nor has it ever precisely determined the administration of the immigration laws'. This fence-mending possibly hypocritical response, is the way an acclaimed historian responded to the embarrassment of his former, now discordant, views.   Many erstwhile eugenists have used similarly disingenuous tactics.

The softening of the White Australia Policy shows in the *Australian Official Yearbook*. In 1960 it deleted the mention of Asians being forbidden permanent settlement; in 1964 preference was to be given to 'European migrants who would be able to integrate readily' and this preference was removed in 1965. While recently released Cabinet papers reveal that in 1964 the Federal Liberal Government rejected proposals to relax the White Australia Policy, the Australian Labor

Party was more progressive. In August 1965 the ALP deleted the words 'White Australia Policy' from its immigration policy, adding that the Party would support and uphold an expanded immigration program which would be administered with 'sympathy, understanding and tolerance'. Any suggestion of Labor Party support for the White Australia Policy was 'finally buried' at the 1971 Conference, at which the amended policy stipulated 'the avoidance of discrimination on any grounds of race or colour of skin or nationality'. Paradoxically, while eugenics was declining by the 1930s, the exclusionist policy remained until the Commonwealth Racial Discrimination Act was passed in 1975.

Populating the Tropical North

Although it needed twentieth century medicine to guarantee the safety of tropical settlement, there were many earlier advocates who passionately believed that the nation's survival depended on filling the north with a healthy white population. Most politicians believed it was their patriotic duty to promote this great experiment of White Australia. There was some spirited opposition: the 1846 convict colony of North Australia (the Gladstone Colony) had soon failed from privations and attacks, and a Townsville surgeon Joseph Ahearne (1852-1926) told a scientific audience in 1895 that the tropics were harmful to adult Europeans and made their children a 'more nervous, slighter and less enduring type'.[93] In 1904 a witness at the Birth-rate Commission hesitantly agreed that children born in North Queensland were not as healthy as those born in Hobart, that it might be caused by the children's 'inherent weakness' and that 'the more rapid fermentation of food in the warmer climate' might be responsible.[94]

The following year, John Simeon Elkington (1871-1955) considered the problems in *Tropical Australia: Is it Suitable for a Working White Race?* and recommended ways to make sure it was, particularly measures to improve public health and prevent children degenerating. In 1906 two field researchers, the naturalist and anthropologist Dr Ramsay Smith (1859-1937) and a German anatomist Herman Klaatsch, produced reports which favoured white settlement of the Northern Territory. However, in 1907 Matthew MacFie disputed this in his paper for the

Australasian Association for the Advancement of Science, maintaining that white people could not stand the heat, saying that 'a third generation of pure whites in the tropics is a feeble rarity, and a fourth is unknown'. He quoted NSW Statistician Coghlan, who wrote in *Seven Colonies of Australia, 1899-1900*, that 'a considerable area of the continent is not adapted for colonisation by European races'. MacFie said the opinions of the politicians Barton, Deakin, Reid, Kingston, Forrest 'and other self-interested partisans of the "White Australia" movement' were 'visionary and unscientific absurdities'.[95]   Not surprisingly, Ramsay Smith disagreed with MacFie.

In 1912 the eugenist Dr Richard Arthur (1865-1932) asked what others thought. Singapore's Senior Medical Officer had no doubt that European settlement in tropical countries was impractical; white women's health deteriorated and their children would become degenerate and, in his opinion, neither British nor Italian labourers could work in a climate such as Singapore.[96] Surprisingly for a eugenist, in 1912 Arthur opposed solely-British immigration on the grounds that 'the general proposition that all white men can live in the tropics is very different to the limited one that some white men can live there'.   He believed the ideal of an all-British Australia was unattainable, and persistence in such a goal would be disastrous.[97] Unless Southern Europeans worked in our tropical north 'we must keep it empty till the Japanese and Chinese come and occupy it'. Arthur's proposal was to extend current practice; Northern Europeans migrated to Queensland from the 1880s and Teddy Roosevelt suggested in 1907 that Australia should bring in Spaniards, Italians and Portuguese to help fill up the north.

Plans for Establishing an Australian Institute of Tropical Medicine

Views about life in the tropics were polarised, but those who favoured settlement succeeded as they shared the government view. The need to study tropical medicine was stressed by Dr Frank Goldsmith of Palmerston (now called Darwin) in a paper he presented to the Intercolonial Medical Congress of Australasia in 1902. Congress delegates endorsed this need for research. Support was provided by the Queensland Governor, Sir William MacGregor, and the Anglican Bishop of North Queensland, who had discussions with authorities in three Australian universities. Sir Thomas Anderson Stuart, from the University of Sydney, backed the proposals and in 1907 appealed to the Royal Society of NSW for support. He explained that a school of tropical medicine would ensure that northern Australia and New Guinea could be colonised, occupied and kept healthy. The proposals became a reality in 1909 with the creation of the Australian Institute of Tropical Medicine in Townsville. It had political significance as one of Australia's first medical research institutes.

The Institute's work was outlined by its Director, Dr Anton Breinl (1880-1944), at the 1911 Australasian Medical Congress. The delegates showed their appreciation of its importance by voting for more staff and funding and recommending that the principal subject to be discussed at the next Congress should be white settlement in the tropics. This recommendation played an important part in the decision to increase the scope of the Institute: from 1921 it was administered by the Commonwealth Department of Health as its second major national project. In the year before becoming the first director-general of this Department, Dr J H L Cumpston complained that 'it was all very well to have a white Australia, but it must be kept white'.[98] He explained in a book written in 1927-28 but not published until 1978, that developing the north and eradicating tropical diseases played a key part of this goal. He was ambivalent and even wondered if such interventions had been 'biologically disastrous' in interfering with 'Nature's scheme for the survival of the fittest'.[99]   Other public servants such as Cilento, Elkington and Wickens had no such doubts. However, their optimism was questioned in the Presidential address to the 1911 Australasian Medical Congress and in one of the discussions in which Dr Tom Nisbet reminded delegates of the warning by the previous Governor-General, Lord Dudley, that having a solely European labour force 'would probably have to be reconsidered'.[100] A British doctor warned a year later that as Queensland had failed to eradicate hookworm, it would be unwise for Britain to send 'her most virile and enterprising sons for a political experiment which is fore-doomed'.[101]

In a history of this parasite, John Thearle discussed the role played by Dr T F MacDonald who wrote to the *Brisbane Courier* in 1903 warning about hookworm, which he called the 'earth-eating' disease.[102] MacDonald's sensational claims three years earlier had been refuted in the Queensland Parliament. MacDonald also featured in Australia's history of eugenics and, possibly in veterinary history as well, if his claim to be able to 'cure roaring in horses' is true. From 1896 until 1906, New Zealand-born 'Dr Tom' ran a 30-bed hospital, which he grandly called the Bureau of Tropical Disease and Cottage Hospital, in the North Queensland town of Geraldton, which in 1911 was renamed Innisfail. In January 1905 he wrote to Sir Francis Galton at the Eugenics Record Office in the University of London to apply for a Eugenics Fellowship, boasting that Prince Kropotkin (1842-1921), who denounced his Russian aristocratic heritage to become an anarchist, was his 'intimate friend'.[103] In outback Queensland in 1904 MacDonald read about Galton's fellowship in a newspaper – he may have had access to British newspapers or this 1904 advertisement may have been the first time eugenics was mentioned in an Australian newspaper. In his application he mentioned giving a conference paper on evolution and sociology[104] and said that 'more important as bearing on Eugenics' was his discovery of a disease [hookworm] causing 'perversion of moral senses' in which anaemia, caused by a parasitic worm, created 'vicarious appetite not only physically, but morally and mentally as well' with symptoms including 'lying, sexual perversion, excess and intemperance'. He operated his Bureau of Tropical Disease and Cottage Hospital to 'meet the ravages of this terrible plague' and boasted of 'doing single handed what the state and federal government should undertake'. He added that the possibility of having to 'live by his pen' in London, prevented him from 'going into views upon Eugenics' because, he said, 'new ideas are marketable'. MacDonald's strange application has been preserved in the archives with a note attached from Galton to Edgar Schuster, the first Francis Galton Research Fellow, instructing him to 'take such steps about it as you like, if any'. MacDonald had more success in 1907 when Britain's Society of Tropical Medicine and Hygiene invited him talk about hookworm.[105] Those whose lives were shattered by the disease, and tropic disease specialists in Australia, received help from a totally different quarter – in November 1908 John D Rockefeller donated one of his millions to combat hookworm.   It was a rare gesture of philanthropy from this union-hating feudal industrialist who excluded books such as *Origin of Species* from his company towns to prevent seeds of unrest being planted in his workers.

Unlike his entrepreneurial compatriot MacDonald, Griffith Taylor was a reputable scientist but he too, received very little recognition. Taylor lamented that after 20 years as 'almost the sole professional geographer in the Commonwealth', the result of years of research in tropical problems, beginning in 1906, was 'one long period of continuous disillusionment'.[106]   His work at the Commonwealth Weather Service convinced him that climate was crucial but few accepted his hypothesis – now verified – that Australia is the smallest, emptiest, driest, most infertile continent with a low and unpredictable rain fall which severely limits farming and settlement. He drew maps of rainfall, temperature and climate in an effort to prove that much of the arid interior was almost useless and that future generations of Australia would continue to inhabit the coastal fringes in the lands already known by 1865. Australia's empty lands were no asset he said; rather, they were a burden as 'their vast potentialities exist only in the mind of the ignorant booster'. Moreover, Australia was not a 'dog-in-the-manger' for keeping 'other folk out' because the land only remained an 'unused paradise' because there were no attractive unused areas left.[107]

Figure 5: Empty Australia: Practically Uninhabited[108]

By 1947 Griffith Taylor had become a confirmed determinist and a believer in environmental control, after his studies convinced him that the environment, not 'providence, priests, potentates and politicians', would determine the country's future settlement.[109] He disputed the propaganda of the 'boosters' who argued that, if you just added water, the land could sustain a population of more than 60 million. He expected Australia could support 20 million people 'when the land is developed to the same extent as the United States'.[110] He was right to add this qualification and probably knew that it was an impossible goal.[111] When Griffith Taylor described the tropical north as 'a white elephant', the University of Western Australia responded by banning one of his books. Most controversial of all were his views supporting Chinese-European marriage and debunking racial purity – views which outraged a *Telegraph* cartoonist (**Figure 6**).

WILL SOMEBODY TELL HIM?

Professor Griffith Taylor (Sydney University) asks: Why are we so horror-stricken at any suggestion of marriage with Mongolians?

Figure 6: "Will Somebody Tell Him?"

In 1921 the editor of Melbourne's *Stead's Review* complained about the costly, futile efforts to settle the Northern Territory. He concluded that rail links could not make the climate cooler nor improve living conditions; thus successful white settlement in the tropical north was impossible no matter how great the inducements offered. Griffith Taylor was also adamant that rapid settlement would not follow the building of a railway and wanted the desert to be left to its loneliness. A similar conclusion was reached by Ellsworth Huntington, a political geographer at Yale University and from 1934 to 1938 the President of the American Eugenics Society. His views were formed after a seven-week trans-Australian tour and were published in 1925 in *West of the Pacific*. He praised Australia as 'a most desirable community, marked by great homogeneity, good health and a high level of energy and intelligence' but warned that this would not continue if the country had a population of 100 million. When his friend Griffith Taylor reviewed the book, he disputed only one 'important point'; he did not agree with Huntington's argument that (provided money was spent on cooling) 'a sort of special eugenic race can be developed which will find life in our tropics profitable and pleasurable'.[112] Griffith Taylor could not see the point of all this effort when there was space for people to lead fuller lives in the temperate regions. However, he was not opposed to eugenics and had been an exhibitor in 1921 at the Second International Eugenics Congress. Australian expansion would occur in the 'fertile margin of the continent flung like a garland around the arid interior'.[113] These words of Griffith Taylor's also flung a challenge to the Million Farms plan for filling Australia's empty spaces which was promoted by Sir Joseph Carruthers (1856-1932), a one-time member of the Labor Party and former Liberal Premier of NSW. In August 1921 Carruthers and Griffith Taylor published their opposing views in the *Sydney Morning Herald* and Carruthers kept up his attack: 'A Professor of Geography in Sydney University has rashly assumed, and has recklessly broadcast his assumptions, that the unsettled portions of Australia are practically desert lands, unsuitable for settlement'.[114] Ironically, his foe called him 'professor' but the University refused to upgrade his position to full professor.

Fortunately, Griffith Taylor had at least one highly-placed ally: the brilliant Tasmanian-born economist L F Giblin whose support for suffrage was mentioned earlier. He had also prospected in the Klondike, been a Labor parliamentarian, had twice been decorated for bravery in World War I and then served as Tasmania's Government Statistician. He endorsed Griffith Taylor's findings and judged the million farms' settlement slogan 'so mad that it should have laughed its author out of public life into an asylum'. Unfortunately, while the dissident Griffith Taylor was logical, many believed his opponent's arrant orthodoxy and the speculative development scheme was backed by Sydney's allegedly apolitical Millions Club, whose membership included National Party supporters William A Holman, Richard Arthur, Henry Braddon, Thomas J Ley, Owen Cox and Arthur Rickard. In 1919 the Club began publishing the *Millions* magazine with the slogan 'a million migrants for Australia', whose patriotic aims were to keep Australia 'white, contented and prosperous and providing a steady stream of vigorous migrants', including children.[115] Carruthers was notorious for his 'colour-scare', 'here comes the Bogey man' philosophy. While Carruthers, in 1922, acknowledged that his scheme was based on the need to keep Australia white', in private he hypocritically complained that his migration scheme was hindered by the 'rabid White Australia Policy'. The scheme fell through in 1923 before vast amounts money and energy had been wasted on it.

That same year Griffith Taylor bravely questioned three items of holy writ at the ANZAAS Congress: tropical settlement, white superiority and the White Australia Policy, boasting that he was the only government official to oppose these icons. In 1924 he was censured in Parliament and called 'Doctor Dismal' and a 'Modern Jeremiah'. Recently, Nancy J Christie discussed Taylor's 'evolutionary views' in which he had 'expanded his Darwinian umbrella to cover anthropology, philology, sociology, history and urban planning'.[116] She argued that his umbrella did not shelter eugenics, using a quote in which he called it a 'faddish and unscientific palliative in an age of social stress'.[117]   However, his friendship with eugenists and his participation at the 1921 Eugenics Congress show that he had sporadically 'sheltered' eugenics. He was not alone in this, as many intellectuals had shifting and ambivalent thoughts about eugenics. The fact that Griffith Taylor did not join the Eugenics Education Society of NSW is not significant because, even if he had wanted to join, the Society would have been unlikely to welcome such a controversial member. After enduring years of hostility, he left, becoming professor of geography, first at the University of Chicago from 1928 to 1935, then in Toronto until he retired in 1951.

1920 Medical Congress

The 1920 Medical Congress in Brisbane played a significant part in the drive to develop the tropical north. Griffith Taylor urged people to read the full Report which showed that:

> Of the 16 doctors whose opinions are quoted at length, eight pointed out grave disadvantages which were directly due to the climate. For instance, Dr Tom Nisbet stated, 'The death rate of

North Queensland was one of the lowest in the world; but the ever-present desire of the inhabitants to get away from the north during the autumn of their years kept the death rate low'. ... the reason why the infantile mortality was lower than in the south was because there were no slums in the north, and many women went south before their babies were born.[118]

Twenty years later Griffith Taylor still fumed about the boosters and optimists who had misquoted the data. While their trickery had won the debate, there were dissenters. Dr Richard Arthur who in 1927 became the NSW Minister of Health, was equally sceptical about Congress' conclusions, complaining that the voting had been 'a put-up job' in favour of white settlement. In the 23 April 1921 issue of the *Medical Journal of Australia* he criticised this as 'neither scientific nor in accordance with common sense and reason'. A third critic was Dr David Hastings Young, a former Native Health Officer in New Zealand, who complained that the white settlement resolution was passed at the Congress 'in spite of much contrary evidence' in which 'even Professor W A Osborne' recommended that the attitude should be one of 'don't know-ism' as:

Malaria, yellow fever and other diseases may be contributory factors of greater importance than climate, but this question is open to dispute. ... The conclusion arrived at is that the tropics are not suitable for the permanent settlement of a white race. ... That the white man cannot live and flourish permanently in the tropics ... may be accepted as an established fact, the excessive heat, humidity, and dazzling sunlight making it impossible for the white race to thrive and settle there.[119]

Young complained in *A White Australia: Is it Possible? The Problems of the Empty North* that until Australia was prepared to induce coloured labour to develop the tropics, she endangered her own safety and the Empire's.[120] In this book which appeared in 1922, Young did not mention that this experiment had failed in the stormy years from 1863 to 1906, when Pacific Islanders worked as indentured labourers in Queensland. The reality of this opposition to the White Australia Policy was that he, and other like-minded people (particularly cane farmers), wanted a source of cheap labour. Young dedicated his book to Henry Barwell, the Premier of South Australia, calling him the 'acknowledged principal advocate of coloured settlement in tropical Australia'. Critics pointed out that Barwell had no expertise in this area and were outraged to hear that he had spread these views as often as possible in 1922 during his stay in London. David Lindsay, who explored the Northern Territory in the 1880s, asked 'What is Mr Barwell's object in defaming Australia as a white man's country?' Sir Joseph Cook, the Australian High Commissioner in London, was forced to combat these 'mischievous' views. However, minority views such as this had no impact on policy or administration, nor did they hurt Barwell's career; he was knighted that year and later worked in London as the Agent-General for South Australia.

Although it was often argued that British stock could not thrive in the tropics, eugenists believed it was imperative that they should, because in Elkington's words, 'the tropics was a prize for the fittest' – a view which was promoted by Sir Raphael West Cilento (1893-1985) who shared the racist views on population issues which were held by his colleagues Elkington and Harvey Vincent Sutton (1882-1963) but he went further than they did in his open support of regimes in Mussolini's Italy and Nazi Germany.[121] Griffith Taylor claimed that Cilento took 'an unduly optimistic view' of tropical settlement. Cilento then emphasized the importance of preventive medicine, using information about temperate zones to support his argument for settling the tropics, and dismissing the importance of climate – his rival's special field. Cilento wrote:

> It is amusing to-day to read the dire predictions of 1827-31 and earlier regarding the people of NSW. It was obvious, said the general opinion of the day, that they could never establish themselves as a people, and absolutely imperative that at the age of 8-10 years children unfortunate enough to be born in Australia must be hurried to England if their lives and their health were to be safeguarded. Six generations of healthy Australians have proved the absurdity of the contention.[122]

This example about temperate NSW was irrelevant to the debate about the tropics. Ellsworth Huntington also complained about Cilento's lapses in memory and his dire confusion when quoting from the report of Huntington's 1923 research trip. Huntington had revealed the unpalatable truth that Queensland's population was young, migratory, and select and, as a result had been fiercely attacked by the boosters, particularly Cilento and the statistician Charles Henry Wickens (1872-1939).[123]   Huntington commented 'perhaps Dr Cilento's position as Director of the Division of Tropical Hygiene in the Commonwealth Department of Health of Queensland justifies him in putting an extremely optimistic interpretation upon everything connected with tropical Australia'.[124]   Not only did Cilento's hagiographic biographer omit such criticism, she approvingly repeated the views of a researcher who had described Cilento's study, *The White Man in the Tropics*, as a masterly piece of social investigation.[125]

Academic and bureaucratic brawls continued until officials lost interest in populating the tropics. In 1930 the Commonwealth Government closed the Australian Institute of Tropical Medicine in Townsville and gave a secondary role to this field at the newly-opened School of Public Health and Tropical Medicine in Sydney. Many preoccupations in Australia during the first half of the last century were ephemeral: fears of invasion now cause less concern, the pressures to 'populate or perish' have eased, questions are rarely asked about national fitness, most tropical disease can be controlled and there is no longer anxiety about populating the north.

This is the soil in which the eugenics seed was planted.

---

[1]Charles Darwin, *Origin of Species* [1859], Richard Leakey, ed. (London: Faber and Faber, 1979), 66.

[2]Peter J Bowler, 'The role of the history of science in the understanding of social Darwinism and eugenics', *Impact of Science on Society*, 40 (1990), 273-78; Hofstadter (1955), Roy MacLeod and Philip Rehbock (eds.), *Darwin's Laboratory: Evolutionary Theory and Natural History in the Pacific* (Honolulu: Univ of Hawaii Press, 1994).

[3]Cited by William F Mandle in 'Cricket and Australian nationalism in the nineteenth century', *Journal of the Royal Australian Historical Society*, 59 (December 1973), 234.

[4]Rusden, 'Labour and capital', *Melbourne Review*, vol 1 (1876), 82.

[5] Quoted by Laurent in MacLeod and Rehbock (1994), 476.

[6]Butcher, 'Darwinism, Social Darwinism, and the Australian Aborigines: A Re-evaluation', in MacLeod and Rehbock (1994), 389.

7 *Petition to the Government of Victoria ...,* London, [1901], quoted by G Serle in *From Deserts the Prophets Come: The Creative Spirit in Australia 1788-1972* (Melbourne Heinemann, 1973, 149.

8'Preliminary Report on the Aboriginals of the Northern Territory', W Baldwin Spencer, 20 May 1913, CPP, 277.

9In Roy MacLeod and Richard Jarrell (eds), 'Dominions Apart', *Scientia Canadensis*, 17 (nos 1 and 2), 1994, 173.

10Alexander Yarwood and Michael Knowling, *Race Relations in Australia: A History* (Ryde: Methuen, 1982), 252.

11Emily Scott, quoted by Stuart Macintyre, in *A History For A Nation: Ernest Scott and the Making of Australian History* (Melbourne: MUP, 1994), 132.

12A P Elkin, 'The practical value of anthropology', Morpeth Review, 9 (September 1929), 39.

13'Memo from the Commission of Native Affairs, WA, to the Minister for Native Affairs, 21 February 1938', quoted by Kay Daniels and Mary Murnane (comps.), in *Uphill All the Way: A Documentary History of Women in Australia* (St Lucia: UQP, 1980), 89.

14 Anti-Slavery Papers, Rhodes House, Oxford, MSS British Empire, S22, 10 February 1939, quoted by Henry Reynolds *in Aboriginal Sovereignty: Reflections on Race, State and Nation* (Sydney: Allen & Unwin, 1996), 156.

15See 'The Aboriginal question' in RHA Annual Report (1932), 8 and 'Racial Hygiene Association work among Aborigines', *SMH*, 16 February 1932, 4 (e).

16Ken McNab and Russell Ward, 'The nature and nurture of the first generation of native-born Australians', *Historical Studies*, 10 (1962), 289.

17John Henderson, *Observations on the Colonies of New South Wales and Van Diemen's Land* [1832] (Adelaide: Libraries Board of South Australia, 1965), 21-22.

18The UK has 244,103 square kilometres compared with Australia's 7,668, 300.

19Quoting Peter McDonald and Patricia Grimshaw, in G Aplin et al. (eds.), *Australians: A Historical Dictionary* (Sydney: Fairfax, Syme and Weldon, 1988), 147. See also Lado Ruzicka and John Caldwell, *The End of Demographic Transition in Australia* (Canberra: ANU, 1977), 1

20*Royal Commission on the Decline of the Birth-Rate and on the Mortality of Infants in New South Wales* (Sydney: Govt. Pr., 1904), vol 1, Appendix, 61, 'Exhibit no 1: Births – Rates per 1,000 of Population – Countries of the World'. Subsequently cited as RCDBR.

21 Yule, *The Fall of the Birth-Rate: A Paper Read Before the Cambridge Eugenics Society*, 20 May 1920 (Cambridge: CUP, 1920), 11-12.

22Barrett, *ICMJA*, 1 (20 January 1901), 2.

23Geoffrey Serle, *Sir John Medley: A Memoir* (Melbourne: MUP, 1993), 21..

24Coghlan, *Childbirth in NSW: A Study in Statistics* (Sydney: Govt. Pr., 1900), 69.

[25]Havelock Ellis, *The Task of Social Hygiene* (London: Constable, 1912), 147, footnote 1.

[26]*RCDBR*, iii, lists the 'Trusty and Well-beloved' Commissioners, most of whom were probably chosen by its President, Dr C K Mackellar, a graduate in medicine from the University of Edinburgh, an expert on child welfare, President of the NSW Board of Health in 1882 and from 1885, a member of the NSW Legislative Council. The other eleven, who had strongly meshed business, medical and Board of Health links were: Sir Henry Normand MacLaurin [physician, company director, strongly linked to the University of Sydney], Octavius C Beale (President of the NSW Chamber of Manufactures); Timothy Augustine Coghlan (Government Statistician); Joseph Foreman [the first man to specialise in obstetrics and gynaecology in Australia); Edmund Fosbery (Inspector-General of Police); William Arthur Holman (Barrister-at-Law); The Right Hon Thomas Hughes (Lord Mayor of Sydney); Edward William Knox (General Manager, Colonial Sugar Refining Company); George Stanley Littlejohn (President of the Sydney Chamber of Commerce); The Hon John Brady Nash (a member of the Legislative Council and active in the NSW Branch of the BMA) and Robert Thomson Paton (Government Medical Officer).

[27]Scott, quoted in Daniels and Murnane (1980), 131-32.

[28]*RCDBR*, vol 1 (1904), paragraphs 53, 83, 173 and 174.

[29]Himes, *Medical History of Contraception* [1936] (New York: Schocken Books 1970), 326-27.

[30]Havelock Ellis (1912), 161-62 quoting *ICMJA* (20 March 1904), 125.

[31]Samuel G Smith, 'Eugenics and the new social consciousness', in *Problems in Eugenics: Papers at the First International Eugenics Congress* (London: EES, 1912), Appendix, 486.

[32]Edith C Onians, *The Men of To-morrow* (Melbourne: Thomas C Lothian, 1914), 258.

[33]Archival references quoted by Ellen Chesler in *Woman of Valor: Margaret Sanger and the Birth Control Movement in America* (New York: Simon & Schuster, 1992), 97, footnote 14.

[34]Charles V Drysdale, *Neo-Malthusianism and Eugenics* (London: William Bell, 1912), 14 and 3-4. He was the Malthusian League's President, following his father was first President from 1878.

[35]Stoddard, *The Revolt Against Civilization: The Menace of the Under Man* [1923] (New York: Garland, 1984), 118.

[36]Comment by Sheila Faith Weiss, *Race Hygiene and National Efficiency: The Eugenics of Wilhelm Schallmayer* (Berkeley: University of California Press, 1987), 137.

[37]Johannes Rutgers, *Eugenics and Birth Control*, R A Giesecke (trans.) (Dresden: Coudray, 1923), 132.

[38]Ackermann, *Australia: From a Woman's Point of View* (London: Cassell, 1913), 95.

[39]Judith Allen, *Sex and Secrets: Crimes Involving Australian Women Since 1880* (Melbourne: OUP, 1990), 67-68.

[40]Milton Lewis, *"Populate or Perish": Aspects of Infant and Maternal Health in Sydney, 1870-1939'* (PhD thesis, Canberra: ANU, 1976), 125.

[41]R A Fisher, 'The actuarial treatment of official birth records', *ER*, vol 18 (1926-1927), 105.

[42]L F Giblin, 'Discussion. Endowment of motherhood', *ER*, 3 (1911-1912), 265 quoting R Murray Leslie, *ER*, 2 (1910-1911), 291.

[43]Australian women supported the British suffragists by marching with a banner (Figure 2) painted by Australian artist Dora Meeson (1869-1955). It showed young Australia appealing to Britannia to: 'Trust the women, mother, as I have done'. The banner was returned to Australia during the 1988 Bicentennial Celebrations and now hangs in Parliament House, Canberra.

[44]*Population and Australia: A Demographic Analysis and Projection. National Population Inquiry* (Canberra: AGPS, 1975), 176.

[45]G A Syme, *MJA* (16 February 1924), 5.

[46]'Birthrate decline. Piddington takes a gloomy view', *Labor Daily*, 2 March 1925, 4 (d) and *Smith's Weekly*, 15 March 1941, 4 (a).

[47]Appeal in the *Charities' Gazette and General Intelligences* (25 September 1919), 11.

[48]NHMRC. Report of the First Session, February 1937, 4.

[49]Billy Hughes, 'A danger. Birth rate. Government Action?', *Sun*, 29 February 1936, 3.

[50] McCleary, 'Population problems in the British Commonwealth', *ER*, 30 (April 1938), 49.

[51]Annexure G, NHMRC, 18th Session, 22-24 November 1944, 70.

[52]*The Nation's Forum of the Air*, 1 (no 2), 'Population Unlimited?' 23 August 1944.

[53]Waddy, 'Eugenics' in AHRC (1929), 63.

[54]The Invitation (AA, PP608/2), in *Federation: The Guide to Records*, compiled by S G Foster, Susan Marsden and Roslyn Russell, (Canberra: Australian Archives, 1998).

[55]Australia. Department of External Affairs advertisement, 'Australia and the Immigrant: The Commonwealth Immigration Laws Summarised', *Australia To-Day*, Special Number of the *Australasian Traveller*, (8 December 1906), 6.

[56]Douglas Cole, 'The crimson thread of kinship: Ethnic ideas in Australia, 1870-1914', *Historical Studies*, 14 (April 1971), 511 and 522.

[57]Yarwood, Attitudes to Non-European Immigration (Melbourne: Cassell, 1968), 1.

[58]Cole (1971), 512 quoting *Bulletin*, 12 July, 1902 and 4 February, 1904.

[59]Gordon Greenwood (ed), *Australia: A Social and Political History* (Sydney: Angus and Robertson, 1955), 199 and 204.

[60]John Tregenza, *Professor of Democracy: The Life of Charles Henry Pearson, 1830-1894*: Oxford Don and Australian Radical (Melbourne: MUP, 1968), 238.

[61]C Pearson, *National Life and Character: A Forecast* (London: Macmillan, 1893), 96.

[62]Tregenza (1968), 234-35.

[63]Theodore Roosevelt, quoted by Richard Arthur in the *Westminster Gazette*, 20 October 1908.

[64]Tregenza (1968), 234 quoting Edmund Barton in CPD, 4 (1901), 5233.

[65]Brian H Fletcher, *History and Achievement: A Portrait of the Honours Students of Professor George Arnold Wood* (Sydney, Braxus Press, 1999), 123.

[66]Myra Willard, *History of the White Australia Policy* (Melbourne: MUP, 1923), 189.

[67]Deakin, Speech in CPD, vol 4 (1901), 4807.

[68]J A La Nauze, *Alfred Deakin: A Biography* (Sydney: Angus & Robertson, 1979), 146.

[69]R Dixon, *Immigration and the "White Australia Policy"* (Sydney: Newsletter Press, 1945), 15.

[70]Richard Broome, 'The Australian reaction to Jack Johnson, Black Pugilist, 1907-09', in *Sport in History: The Making of Modern Sporting History*, Richard Cashman and Michael McKernan, eds, (St Lucia, Qld: University of Queensland Press, 1979), 343-63.

[71]Isadore Brodsky, *The Sydney Press Gang* (Sydney: Old Free Press, 1974), 163.

[72]*Science of Man* (1 January 1909), 144.

[73]Ackermann (1913), 96.

[74]Secretary ES to Twitchin, 28 July 1928, SA/EUG C87.

[75]Imperial Conference, 1926. Appendices (London: HMSO, 1927), 58.

[76]Atkinson (ed.), *Australia Economic and Political Studies* (Melbourne: Macmillan, 1920), 11.

[77]Hughes, CPD vol 89 (1919), 12165-66.

[78]Atkinson (1920), 3-4, 55.

[79]The WEA's organising committee proposed including a paper on 'the value of eugenics in teaching sex hygiene' in their *Teaching of Sex Hygiene Conference*, WEA Minute Book, 21 July 1916, 92.

[80]W E Agar to Dr Pearl, 18 Aug 1927, Raymond Pearl Papers, B/P312, American Philosophical Society Library Archives.

[81]Pearl, in the *American Mercury*, November 1927, quoted by Kevles (1985), 122.

[82]W E Agar, 'Some eugenic aspects of Australian population problems', in P D Phillips and G L Wood (eds), *The Peopling of Australia* (Melbourne: Macmillan in assoc with MUP, 1928), 144.

[83]Griffith Taylor, 'Racial misconceptions. Showing that a mixture of races is always advantageous', *Home* (1 October 1927), 336-37, Taylor (1937), 461-62 and Elkin (1929), 34.

[84]Griffith Taylor (1927) from RHC Papers.

[85]Stephen H Roberts, *The House That Hitler Built* (London: Methuen, 1937), 51-53, 359-64.

[86] F E Macfarlane Burnet, 'Migration and race mixture from the genetic angle', *ER*, 51 (July 1959), 93-97. Puskin, Tolstoy and Gorky have been hailed as examples 'proving' hybrid vigour.

[87] 'Racial purity our aim. "White Australia" policy will save country', *Guardian* (Sydney), 9 May 1930, 16.

[88]Attributed to Davenport, cited by Elazar Barkan, in *The Retreat of Scientific Racism: Changing Concepts of Race in Britain and the United States Between the World Wars* (Cambridge: CUP, 1992), 204.

[89]Mark Haller, *Hereditarian Attitudes in American Thought* (New Brunswick, New Jersey: Rutgers UP, 1963), 11, quoting Galton, in *Hereditary Genius* (1869), 325-37.

[90]Agar (1928), 138.

[91]A P Elkin, in 'Speech to the Labour Club, University of Sydney', *Union Recorder*, 5 July 1945, 120-21.

[92]W K Hancock, *Australia* [1930] (Brisbane: Jacaranda Press, 1961), 59.

[93]Joseph Ahearne, 'Effect of the Queensland Government educational regulations on the physique of the present and future North Queenslander', *AAASR* (Brisbane, 1895), 797.

[94]RCDBR (1904), vol 2, page 150, Paragraphs 4473-75.

[95]Matthew MacFie, *How Can Tropical and Sub-tropical Australia Be Effectively Developed?*, ANZAAS, January 1907, with discussion (Adelaide: Govt. Pr., 1907).

[96]Dr F B Croucher to Dr Richard Arthur, 17 September 1912 letter, Arthur Papers.

[97]Arthur, *Telegraph*, 22 February 1912, 9 (d) and 6 June 1912, 4 (f).

[98]*MJA* (18 September 1920), 293.

[99]J H L Cumpston, *The Health of the People: A Study in Federalism* [1927-28] (Canberra: Roebuck, 1978), 49-50, 130.

[100]AMCT, vol 1 (1911), 91 and 533.

[101]Dr Lieper, quoted by A Graham Butler, *MJA* (17 December 1921), 562.

[102]Thearle, in John Pearn (ed.), *Pioneer Medicine in Australia* (Brisbane: Amphion Press, 1988), 83.

[103]Galton Papers. University College Library, London. Item 133/5A. Dr T F MacDonald's Bureau of Tropical Disease and Cottage Hospital, Geraldton, Queensland, 7 January 1905 letter to Galton Re: Eugenics Fellowship.

[104]The paper was given at the Medical Congress in Rome in 1903 and 'again in Sydney before the Society for Advancement of Science'. *AMCT* (September 1905), 487-90 lists MacDonald's paper as 'Medicine and sociology'. He graduated from the University of Glasgow in medicine and surgery, 1882 and in veterinary science, 1892.

[105] Thearle (1988), 85. MacDonald's paper was in the *Journal of Tropical Medicine*, vol 11 (1908), 25-29.

[106] Griffith Taylor (1947), 411.

[107] Griffith Taylor, *Australia: A Study of Warm Environments and Their Effect on British Settlement*. 4th edn. (London: Methuen, 1947), Taylor (1947), 7.

[108] 'Map of Australia showing distribution of population', in Griffith Taylor *Environment*, Race and Migration: Fundamentals of Human Distribution with Special Sections of Racial Classification and Settlement in Canada and Australia (Toronto: University of Toronto, 1937), 379.

[109] Griffith Taylor(1947), 444.

[110] Griffith Taylor (1947), 444.

[111] Australia's population reached the 19 million mark on 18 August 1999, a million short of Griffith Taylor's estimate but almost five times the size it was at the time of Federation.

[112] Griffith Taylor, 'The Pacific: An Australian Discusses Australia', *SMH*, 13 February 1926.

[113] *New Outlook* (19 April 1922), 10.

[114] Quoted by Stuart Macintyre in *The Oxford History of Australia, vol 4, 1901-1942*. (Melbourne: OUP, 1986), 239.

[115] *Millions* (15 January 1930), 13.

[116] Christie, 'Environment and race: Geography's search for a Darwinian synthesis', in MacLeod and Rehbock (1994), 437.

[117] Christie (1994), 440, quoting Griffith Taylor.

[118] Taylor (1947), 412 and *MJA* (18 September 1920), 290-99.

[119] Young, *A White Australia: Is it Possible? The Problems of the Empty North* (Melbourne: Robertson and Mullens), 1922, 16-17.

[120] Young (1922), 111.

[121] Gillespie (1991), 35.

[122] Cilento, in Phillips and Wood (1928), 228-29.

[123] C H Wickens, 'Vitality of the White races in low latitudes', *Economic Record*, 3 (1927), 117.

[124] Ellsworth Hungtington, 'Natural selection and climate in Northern Australia', *Economic Record*, 5 (1929), 186.

[125] Fedora Fisher, *Raphael Cilento: A Biography* (St Lucia: UQP, 1994), 44, quoting Douglas Gordon, *Health, Sickness and Society* (St Lucia: UQP, 1976), 264.

2. Four Distinctive Eugenists

Eugenics is defined in the Appendix and the concept, like those other turn-of-the twentieth century catchwords 'efficiency' and 'progressivism', has a large and shifting range of meanings – like Lewis Carroll's character who said scornfully, 'when I use a word it means just what I choose it to mean'. The confusion grew in the 1990s when more and more historians became interested in the topic. This trend had already been evident for several years in 1981 when English history professor Geoffrey Searle commented that eugenics comes up 'whenever one picks up a new book or article on politics, social policy or political thought in Edwardian Britain'. He found this an 'absurd situation' and feared that the 'eugenist' label would be 'placed around the neck of nearly every major political thinker' of that era.[1] Reacting to this imprecision and the 'bewilderingly variegated list' of eugenists, Searle compiled this classification to 'discriminate more carefully between different kinds and levels of commitment to eugenics.' Because Australian studies have similarly blurred boundaries, I decided to be as precise as possible with the aid of his classification:

1. **'Strong' eugenists:** those for whom eugenics provided a total explanation of history and the only means of escape from national collapse and decay. In England, Leonard Darwin, Karl Pearson and Caleb Saleeby belonged in this group.

2. **'Weak' eugenists**: those who were attracted to aspects of eugenics and, while retaining their initial political beliefs, grafted it onto their underlying but unaltered political creeds. These included libertarian progressives who also supported goals such as utopian socialism, vegetarianism or rational dressing.

3. **'Medical' eugenists**: mainly doctors and health workers who considered eugenics was not a political belief but a branch of public health or hygiene which, with government support, could improve people's health or reduce disease and suffering. Dr C P Blacker, was a prime example.

4. **'Career' eugenists**: academics and practitioners in such fields as genetics, statistics, education or psychology, who were dubious about the value of eugenics but sympathised with the underlying objectives and welcomed eugenics because it stimulated interest in their field of study.

5. **'Opportunist' eugenists**: those who were prepared to use eugenic phrases and ideas to promote unrelated causes. People with minimal or unwitting associations with eugenics belong in this group. I haven't considered people in this last group such as the 2,358 young Australians who entered the 1950s Mitchell Bequest without knowing the bequest had eugenic aims.

No eugenist is typical and some defy classification or straddle categories. It also helps to consider whether a eugenist had radical or conservative political beliefs, favoured heredity or environmental eugenics, or expressed lay or scientific opinions. There were probably fewer than 50 people in Australia who contributed significantly to the eugenics movement and they were isolated from the world and from each other. Australia had only one 'strong' eugenist and most were professionals with moderate views who fitted the 'medical' or 'career' categories – all factors which helped to determine the direction and strength of the movement.

The following four eugenists were interesting for a number of reasons: they were born before 1880, made their main contribution in later life and revered overseas eugenic thinking. None had significant scientific training and all occupied separate, sometimes competing, spheres of operation. They have received little or no recognition and all of them were involved in the movement's development. These four representative eugenists were:

1. **Marion Louisa Piddington** (1869-1950), a 'strong' eugenist with radical politics who endorsed heredity eugenics, promoted both positive and negative eugenics and made almost solo contributions to early sex education and eugenics debates.

2. **John [Jack] Chambers Eldridge** (1872-1954), a 'weak' eugenist with radical politics who promoted positive and environmental eugenics. He was a public servant, unionist and briefly a politician,

who contributed to the movement from 1912 until 1922 as the secretary and chronicler of the first eugenics society in NSW.

3. **Lillie Elizabeth Goodisson** (1860-1947), a 'medical' eugenist who was politically conservative, endorsed birth control and was the driving force behind the Racial Hygiene Association.

4. **Henry Twitchin** (1867-1930), a 'career' eugenist, who was conservative politically and advocated heredity eugenics. He was a pastoralist who contributed to eugenics as a financial benefactor.

1. Marion Louisa Piddington: Loose Cannon

Figure 7: Piddington in her 60s[2]

Marion Piddington's credentials as a 'strong' eugenist are irrefutable: to her, eugenics provided a total explanation of history and the only way for Australia to avoid decay or collapse. She was born in Sydney in 1869, the youngest child of Thomas O'Reilly and his second wife Rosa. Marion inherited her clergyman father's determination and passion for honesty. One of her brothers was the poet and author Dowell O'Reilly (1865-1923) who, in 1894, after election as a NSW Labor politician, introduced a women's suffrage Bill which was passed in the Legislative Assembly but defeated in the conservative upper house. Dowell's daughter was the novelist Eleanor Dark, Marion's niece. The O'Reillys lived at the boy's school which her mother ran and Marion inherited her mother's educational flair. In 1896 she married Bert (Albert Bathurst) Piddington (1862-1945), whose reputation for liberal reform may have been influenced by a term in the 1890s as Justice Windeyer's associate. Piddington was described in an obituary as the State's most colourful legal identity and a man who had been fearless and brilliant as an advocate, judge, politician and controversialist.

The Piddingtons were well-matched in their courage and drive. When they attended the 1912 International Eugenics Congress in London it was Bert (not one of Australia's official delegates) whose comments appeared in the *Times*. The audience had laughed when Piddington said that although war was 'incontestably race-deteriorating, militarism was a good training for young men so long as they never went to war'. He called it eugenic madness to preserve the unfit and offer the fit to the enemy. Within two years, the world was engulfed in global war, a dysgenic catastrophe which stirred Marion to start her life-long eugenics crusade.

Since her death in 1950 Marion Piddington has been ignored or praised with faint damnation as a correspondent with Freud, as the mentor of the novelist Jean Devanny, or as a prominent man's wife. Kay Daniels found her a strange sexual radical whose complexity of character probably explains her neglect by biographers and historians. Michael Roe conceded that while Piddington had her qualities, he thought she took a rather eccentric turn and, 'the more Marion thought about sex, and she did so increasingly, the more confused she became'.[3] Ann Curthoys was kinder in the *Australian Dictionary of Biography* and in an article in which she attempted to make the connections between Piddington's feminism and eugenics clearer.[4] Piddington herself was ambivalent and while she ran study circles at the Feminist Club she only approved of women who were 'motherhearted' and disparaged feminists who criticised unmarried mothers, calling these critics the 'un-mother married'.[5]

'Conscription of the Virgins'

In 1916 Piddington began her campaign to provide child-hungry women, who had been denied motherhood because of the war, with

the possibility of what she delicately called scientific motherhood –
artificial insemination from a eugenically-desirable donor. Eugenic,
celibate or facultative [optional] motherhood (and later, eutelegenesis)
were used as synonyms for this scheme which is now called artificial
insemination. She introduced this controversial proposal in *Via Nuova
or Science & Maternity*, giving it a scholarly touch with Latin words in the
title (meaning 'new way') and masking her identity with the pen name
'Lois'.[6] The tract was a thinly-veiled parable about Kathleen, 'one of
many' who had been bereaved by the war. A sense of duty and
religious obligation finally suggested a way for this woman to satisfy
'love to the individual, duty to the nation, and obedience to the Divine
Command, "Increase and multiply"'. Gratified, Kathleen 'invoked the
aid of Science' to perform the 'bee-like task of conveying the gift of life
to the secret sanctum of its expectant seclusion'. She died 'clasping'
the miniature of her fiancé, surrounded by her children and
grandchildren. Piddington added a postscript which listed reassuring
reasons for endorsing her campaign: the 'new way' would benefit
'individual and national destiny after the war', it was 'in accord with the
principles of modern eugenics', and it would not debase morals. The
unspecified 'method' for achieving this was 'well-known medically' she
said and had sometimes been used 'in the case of a man and his wife
whose union would otherwise be childless'.

Her plan caused such an uproar that it was mentioned 30 years later
by 'Dr Wykeham Terriss' (Dr Norman Haire), a controversial advocate
of sexual reform and contraception:

> Before the end of the last war a well-known Sydney woman
> published a little book, called 'Vita [sic] Nuova', in which she
> advocated artificial fertilisation as a means of enabling unmarried
> women anxious to have children to do so artificially. Many people
> were inexpressibly shocked at her suggestion.[7]

While Michael Roe criticised Piddington's 'highly emotional prose'
he was even more emotive, describing her scheme as 'anticipating
Aldous Huxley and Adolf Hitler'. It was the biologist Sir Julian
Huxley, not his brother Aldous, who proposed eutelegenesis in the
1930s and Hitler never did. Roe made another claim which is wrong,
romantic and sensational: 'Mary Booth was among Mrs Piddington's

followers, possibly her guiding star. The two ladies agreed that Edgeworth David – scientist, explorer, academic – would be an ideal sire.'[8] There is no evidence for this: Piddington was a loner who sometimes quoted the anti-VD and pro-sterilisation campaigner, Angela Booth (1869-1954), also known as Mrs James Booth, but *not* Dr Mary Booth (1869-1956). While neither Angela nor Mary was a follower, we know from the Stopes Papers in the British Library that Dr Marie Stopes (1880-1958) had Piddington among her followers.[9] According to Piddington, Stopes was not just the greatest living physiologist but one of the greatest living women. Piddington initiated their 21-year correspondence after Stopes became a best-selling celebrity with *Married Love* which burst on the world in 1918. The friendship meant more to Piddington than to Stopes although they had much in common; both were stern, prickly outsiders who had flowery, highly-coloured writing styles and shared sorrows. Each of these devoted mothers had lost her first son at birth and each later produced a son who survived but remained an only child. As well as the motherly exchanges about 'Bunnykins' Stopes and 'Boy' Piddington, the letters reveal Piddington as a well-intentioned woman who was obsessive and lacked judgement. Although she was trying to improve humanity, her efforts usually produced discord.

Piddington worked unflaggingly; in her first letter to Stopes in March 1919 she sent the Scientific Motherhood campaign kit, pointedly saying that she had sent another kit to Dr Charles Davenport of the United States Eugenic Record Office.[10] The package included letters to eminent people asking them to support her call for government finance of a Eugenic Institute to ensure that eugenic mother-child duos would be independent for life. Piddington boasted that girls had told her that as long as they knew that their child came of good stock and *free from disease* they would be quite content.[11]

A more realistic assessment was given by her brother, Dowell O'Reilly, who wrote in 1916 "Dear Marion, I thought of you this afternoon! I fear, from what you tell me, the meeting didn't support you, but if you had your say – that somehow is on the record".[12] Piddington and her undaunted sympathisers wrote letters in May 1918 asking doctors and the happily married to consider what the state could do to help these Spartan sufferers in the conflict, and warned them not to allow Australia to suffer the double disaster of losing its finest daughters as well as its splendid sons. A pamphlet outlining her scientific motherhood proposal was also considered by the Women's National Movement Association, a temperance group which opposed alcohol and supported the war. According to a lambasting article in *Truth*, in June the meeting agreed with the motion by the literary icon (Dame) Mary Gilmore (1865-1962) for the Association to reject the 'theory or practice' of Piddington's pamphlet.[13]

A few days after this rejection she noted that her band of about 30 had progressed during 17 months of propaganda, including the production of a pamphlet by 'Dr Swan' who had the interests of women and race improvement at heart.[14] She was referring to *Facultative Motherhood Without Offence to Moral Law*, published in 1918 by 'Dr Henry Waterman Swan'. This was literally a pen name — Waterman and Swan were popular brands of fountain pen. The author was Dr Ralph Worrall (1859-1942), later identified by Piddington as the gynaecologist who had backed the Eugenic Celibate Motherhood scheme for nine years but had been prevented by medical etiquette from speaking out. Her word was corroborated by a mysterious J Westone, from Canberra, whose 16 March 1981 letter was hand-delivered to Sydney's King George V Hospital. The writer was old, with a spidery note 'my sight is poor so please excuse the scrawl', no doubt a woman and a Piddington sympathiser, possibly a doctor, because only an insider could have been so well-informed. The letter began:

> Dear Doctor, While listening-in on the ABC I learned of the existence of your clinic at the KG [King George V] Hospital, and it made me wonder if you are acquainted with the early practice of AI [artificial insemination] in this country. It is known to me that the late Dr Ralph Worrall twice performed AI shortly after the turn of the century — 1901-04 on the same woman whose husband was impotent (sexually infantile). The first child, a boy, died in infancy, but the second, also a boy, passed away only a few years ago. ...[15]

As deaths from the war and subsequently influenza increased, Piddington expanded her efforts and, considering the pandemonium of war and its aftermath, her attempts are understandable. Australia, from a population of less than 5 million, had raised an army of 300,000 resulting in 60,000 deaths with twice that number injured. Shortly after the armistice the world was swept by an influenza epidemic, which in a matter of months, caused 20 – possibly 40 – million deaths, more than twice the number of people killed in four years of global war. The epidemic reached Australia in October 1918 and by the following February face masks were compulsory and public buildings were closed. There were 11,552 Australian deaths and unlike other types of influenza which struck the young, the weak and the elderly, the pandemic of 1918-19 principally killed fit young men and pregnant women.

Piddington acknowledged her reverses. Her 28 June 1918 letter to 'Mr' Stone began, I am very sorry that neither you nor any of the women doctors in Melbourne will have anything to do with Scientific Motherhood.[16] She persevered, sending this letter on 30 August 1919 to Dr Felix Meyer, a lecturer in Obstetrics and Gynaecology at the University of Melbourne:

> I am in touch with women in Western Australia and Queensland. The Misses Golding and their sister Mrs Dwyer, who represent the working factory girls here are with me. Men and women in the professions and in business, unmarried women of advanced years … are keen on the subject. … The head of our Women's College, several heads of large schools are with us but we realise that they must keep quiet for the present. Then too, we have some young women supporters. When in Melbourne I also spoke to Lady Helen Ferguson (this in confidence) who was interested and sympathetic.[17]

She had sent her letter to Meyer on the day when she was in Brisbane at a Women's Political Association (WPA) meeting, asking them to support her mission. It was reported in the women's pages of *Figaro*, a Queensland broadsheet incorporating the *Bohemian*. The debate lasted for several months, starting with an editorial which described Piddington's 'revolutionary – no, evolutionary' work and stressed her courage, delicacy and self-sacrifice despite receiving very little encouragement, and a lot of abuse.[18] For her, valour was the better part of discretion. The chief opponent of the scheme was a socialist poet and author, Mary Elizabeth Fullerton (1868-1946), the Vice-President of the WPA and a prominent feminist campaigner. Piddington's sympathisers were outraged by Fullerton's reference to conscription of the virgins and her claim that bastardy under the hedge was preferable.[19] The besieged Piddington boasted to *Figaro* readers in 1919 that Marie Stopes would mention the scheme in *Married Love*. Stopes did this although she was 'still very doubtful' whether it could work 'really well'.[20] Although she rejected further 'importunings' because the 'time was not ripe' for her to 'say anything more' the harm was already done. Its mention in a book 'broadcast to old and young' was used by a Chief Justice to discredit Stopes in the well-publicised court case of 1923.

Piddington had promoted her campaign in Brisbane's *Daily Mail*, emphasising that education before procreation was of paramount importance. In her view, extramarital births were just as important as those in marriage, 'if the eugenic ideal is to permeate our national life', because science could 'bestow on the child-hungry [single] woman the happiness she longs for'. This news was selectively reported in the *Eugenics Review*. It noted her despair at the lack of suitable healthy males for women to marry and her support for segregation, or a 'slight surgical interference with nature', to eliminate the unfit, assisted by birth control to stay 'the hideous result of reckless procreation'. But it was silent about scientific motherhood, apart from a vague reference to 'the eugenic ideal' of encouraging the 'finest specimens of womanhood … to pass on their gifts and characteristics'.[21] Privately, Piddington thought that flappers were 'not the sort we should breed from'.

We know that Piddington tried to interest Sigmund Freud in her plans because of his devastating reply. In June 1921 'Prof Dr Freud' barely softened his comment by saying that it was 'the private opinion of an individual who can claim no authority for it'. He doubted whether eugenics had advanced sufficiently to warrant 'practical measures' and was 'unsympathetic' to her proposal that 'childless women should procure children by artificial anonymous fecundation'. He saw 'lurking behind this device that tendency to sex-repression which will do more for the extinction of the race than war and pestilence combined'. He prophesied that lone children without a father to balance the 'undiminished weight of motherly tenderness', would be 'likely to work under heavy psychological odds, compared to the other ones'.[22] He concluded, 'I pray you will neither be annoyed by my reactionary opinions, nor by my bad English'.

Humphrey McQueen reprinted all of this important letter because it was written at a significant period in Freud's career and because of the information it provides about the eugenics movement in Australia, which 'has not been documented let alone analysed'.[23] By 1921 the 65 year old Freud was renowned in the English-speaking world so that Piddington's cause would have benefited enormously if she had gained his support. Freud replied because he was a 'conscientious' correspondent who 'answered every letter he received'.

Five years later Piddington fought back in her book *Tell Them!*, noting in Chapter 11 that Freud failed 'absolutely' in his 'over-emphasis of sex' and in his 'inability to understand the maternal instinct as separate from the mating instinct'. Stopes 'warmly' agreed with her that Freudians who, 'on the whole had done infinitely more harm than good', had underestimated 'the maternal influence and feeling in women'. Stopes despaired for their sanity, describing their writing as 'prodigious filthiness' which made her feel she had eaten a bag of soot. She reassured Piddington 'I think your Chapter 11 very excellent and sound'.[24]

While Piddington was forced to abandon her public crusade for celibate motherhood, her private resuscitation attempts show that it remained her goal. In August 1929 she asked Dr Davenport to help, arguing that 'the mere extension' of the practice to a few 'fit strains' of women outside marriage 'ought not to be considered a very marked step' and made this strange but revealing proposal:

> I have safeguarded all details in my proposal and if you could bring about the formation of a Eugenics Institute in Australia with me with your leading Biologists at the head it would be a magnificent gesture on the part of America and strengthen in eugenic control the hands across the sea. I passed through years of disesteem and have had to give up my advocacy of celibate motherhood and

worked only quietly while I taught sex education. Now the public is beginning to forgive me and I hope before long to renew the subject and bring about the sequel to rendering the unfit sterile – that of making the fit fertile.[25]

When Davenport was unresponsive Piddington tried again. She asked for his views on her paper 'Maternal repression and the new psychology' and suggested that if Davenport 'could bring Dr Jung's case [studies] before the public I think it would be of use' to get it published, adding that it could be done without mentioning the motherhood scheme if he preferred.[26] Eight years later her paper was finally published in Australia.[27] Her last letters to Stopes show that she continued to think about celibate motherhood. In 1937 when her sight was failing she wrote, 'I am nearly 70 years of age and it is just to thank you and to ask you with your dynamic power to give the world the hope of a eugenic race through scientific insemination. A crowning act from you to the race'.[28] However, in her 1940 letter to Stopes there were no more calls for help, only an admission of defeat:

> We never forgot your generous encouragement years ago when we sought after the last war to bring eugenic motherhood outside as well as within marriage. Scientific Insemination is going well for married people in Australia considering its stormy passage. I am in touch with a doctor in the USA who has scientifically inseminated two unmarried women so it is actually an accomplished fact. I am 72 years of age and shall go out of life after spending eight years and hundreds of pounds on the work, *a failure*..[29]

Despite her gloomy assessment, forty years later there was a sympathetic addendum written by J Westone, the woman who had revealed Dr Worrall's pioneering role in the history of artificial insemination [AI]. In the second part of her letter she wrote:

> So far as I know the first time AI was given broad publicity in Australia was when a judge's wife, Mrs Marion Piddington published a pamphlet on the matter during the first World War. In view of the terrible losses suffered by our forces on the Western Front in France, Mrs P thought that many women, desirous of marriage would have to remain single in the post-war world. ... You many find it difficult to realise the humbug and hypocrisy then

prevailing in sexual matters. Mrs P thought that AI should be available to those women who, although denied husbands, should not have to forego motherhood also. The publication of the pamphlet mentioned, produced much ridicule and was highlighted by *Truth* with the headline "Doing without father". Many years later, Brian Penton, then editor of the *Daily Telegraph* became interested in the subject and invited Mrs Piddington to call upon him at his office where they had a long discussion. ... [Her views] scandalised many, especially those Enemies of Joy the Roman Church. You have no idea what she had to put up with.

The World War I scheme was revisited in World War II and proposals for 'artificial births' again caused uproar. Possibly Piddington was secretly involved, with help from Brian Penton (1904-1951) who became the editor of the *Telegraph* in 1941 and bravely opposed excessive war-time censorship. *The Rationalist* noted in August 1943 that an Anglican Cannon called AI adultery by proxy and in July 1945 parliamentarians said it would treat women like stud ewes and was anti-Christian, anti-human, wicked and abhorrent. In a long letter to the *Telegraph* (29 November 1944) a correspondent recommended it on the grounds that modern developments made it quite legal, moral and practicable. He proposed it for those who did not marry or have children because they lack physical attractiveness. Not surprisingly, Lillie Goodisson found his idea obnoxious. The controversy continues even though artificial insemination and invitro fertilisation have been available since the 1980s but now the most widely-expressed concerns are about providing the service for single or lesbian women.

Links with the Workers' Educational Association (WEA)

The Workers' Educational Association was an English movement imported into Australia in 1914, following the visit of its founder, Albert Mansbridge. In July 1916 Sydney's Organising Committee for the *Teaching of Sex Hygiene* Conference recommended that one of the eight or nine papers should be on the value of eugenics in teaching sex hygiene.[30] However, three months later, the eugenics paper did not appear in this daringly radical conference. Despite this wariness about eugenics, the WEA provided a wonderful platform for Piddington, a friend of the indefatigable Henrietta Greville (1861-1964), the WEA's first female President, who continued to run their sex hygiene study group when she was in her 90s. In October 1921 Greville announced that 'Mr Ingamels (sic) of Sydney Hospital' was providing the Circle's first lecture.[31] Rumours of Loris Ingamells' involvement in the scandal relating to Ledbetter and little boys at the Sydney lodge of the Theosophical Society probably explains why the first lectures were given instead by Jack Eldridge, whose eugenics career is examined in the next section.[32] While Piddington was launching her eugenics career, reminding readers that eugenics was a 'vast subject' which encompassed all areas of WEA activity,[33] Eldridge was giving his final lectures.[34]

Women were the most avid members of the WEA Eugenics Circles which ran from 1922 to 1924 and after this, the WEA library's books on eugenics remained popular until the 1930s. As well, their newsletter, *Australian Highway*, gave publicity to eugenics. Piddington had contacted 'hundreds of mothers' through WEA sex education lectures and claimed that the wishes of the President, her friend Mrs Greville and the mothers 'led' her to publish *Tell Them!*[35] She used it to encourage women who had learnt about infant care, to progress to 'the second stage of mothercraft', by teaching the child about sex in an honest way, while remembering that 'the little mind is no more to be overfed than the little body'. The newsletter noted that Piddington was a missionary with a fine message which captivated audiences and that her book was selling well, with half the profits going to the WEA.[36]

Michael Roe was only partly right to claim that she thought 'chemico-medical prophylaxis against infection was vile, morally and physically'.[37] Although in 1926 she rejected condoms, which she called medical prophylaxis, in their place she recommended racial prophylaxis to 'see the curse of venereal disease removed for ever from the human race'.[38] Joseph Pugliese also misunderstood *Tell Them!* saying that she planned to solve the eugenic problem by 'maintaining "racial purity" through socially sanctioned forms of breeding'. He claimed that she advocated 'racial prophylaxis', disguised as children's sex education, 'to prevent white Australia "acquiring the characteristics of racial inferiority" in which 'the products of misalliances are marked by the stigma of "miscegenation"'.[39]   Piddington was thinking about the stigmata of VD, not the 'stigma of miscegenation'.

Both men misunderstood that, instead of condoms, Piddington had promoted 'parental metaphylaxis' (or 'after-guarding') for use if children made 'just one slip'. She proposed that the techniques used in army blue-light clinics should be used in the family bathroom: 'a disinfectant in the possession of parents, applied within an hour to that part of the body which has been exposed to infection will save the boy or girl from venereal disease'.[40]   She had again exposed herself to ridicule because the scheme was a foolish fantasy which disregarded privacy and relied on parents being intrusive and their children being confiding and compliant. When she tried to interest Britain's Eugenics Society they said tactfully that as they did 'no anti-VD work' they could not find a 'wider use of her excellent pamphlets'.

Founding the Racial Hygiene Association

In 1926 Piddington conducted study circles at the Feminist Club and told Stopes she wanted to start a race improvement centre modelled on Stopes' birth control clinic.[41]   Conversations at home might have been tetchy because her husband opposed birth control, fuming that its propaganda had 'achieved a vast and alarming success in Australia'. The subject was not mentioned when Piddington asked Ruby Rich to become the first joint-president of what was to become the Racial Hygiene Association. Rich remembered the maid saying 'There's a Mrs Piddington, an old lady, who says she *must* see you' and found her 'absolutely delightful', with a maturity which 'carried a lot of weight'. Piddington wanted a person who 'could talk about sex in a nice clean manner' and not shock listeners. She wanted Rich and a 'young doctor' (Dr Worrall junior, whose father was the ghost writer of the 'scientific motherhood' booklet) to launch a society to teach the public about 'the terrible scourge of venereal diseases'. Rich reluctantly agreed and Piddington arranged for her to meet Worrall and set up a committee.[42]

The new, unnamed, society was formed on 27 April 1926 and 'the subjects of venereal disease and sex hygiene were dealt with by Drs Dick and Sydney Morris (Health Department), and Dr Hamilton (clinical aspect), and Mr Cresswell O'Reilly (Film Censor), [on the] educational and positive aspect'.[43]   The next month the newly-appointed committee of nine (including Piddington) began to plan a constitution.   In June they called it the Race Improvement Society with Piddington as treasurer but factions were already mobilising within the infant Society.   One member questioned the word 'eugenics' in the third object of the Society but after a defence by five speakers (including Piddington) the constitution was adopted and Piddington became leader of the sex education group.   She had an eight-hour Pyrrhic victory because a public meeting that same day agreed to drop the original name, which had been synonymous with eugenics, and renamed it the Racial Hygiene Centre of NSW (RHC).   The President, Ruby Rich softened the blow by thanking 'Mrs Piddington for her strenuous efforts and wonderful work in the city'.[44]   However, these soothing words did not calm her.

Piddington had poor eyesight and her comments about the RHC in a June letter to Stopes show that she also had poor insight.   She said in pique 'my earlier work for celibate motherhood failed here and those who did not and would not understand it would never listen to me on anything'.   She had wronged them by forming an organization with set objectives while secretly scheming to use it as a front for her totally unrelated lost cause.   The RHC fought back.   At their first annual meeting on 11 July members supported a motion to replace the explicit third object of the constitution, 'improvement of the race on eugenic principles', with the more abstract 'education of the community on eugenic principles'.   The RHC battle was over by 16 September but the minutes of that hectic RHC Executive meeting only noted 'correspondence from Mrs Piddington in which the suggestions made were declared constitutionally impossible'.   For the RHC it was the storm before the calm.   On 24 November they accepted her resignation and then distanced themselves from Piddington and eugenics.   Surprisingly, Piddington continued to hold classes for the RHC and informed Stopes in 1928 that she held a special class to defend Stopes' name after Goodisson and a member of the RHC Committee asked Piddington, to 'say nothing about Stopes'. Neither woman was medically literate but while Piddington blindly supported Stopes (who was very often wrong), she bluntly rejected the better-informed RHC as 'working on old lines, wasting time and money, while we without financial assistance are doing the real work of teaching thousands'. 'I declined to be President of the Racial Hygiene Centre', said this woman scorned.[45]   A few months later, she forgetfully embellished this highly unlikely tale, telling Stopes that she had declined this invitation '*twice*'. She warned Stopes not think that the President 'Miss Rich', who was going to England, 'has anything to do with our work'. The RHC founder concluded petulantly 'even with all their prestige and backed up by a few doctors with government subsidy' the RHC was 'futile and inefficient'.[46]

Figure 8: Next Generation Calls the Eugenics Number[47]

Piddington turned her attention to *Herself*, a short-lived woman's magazine which was launched optimistically in June 1928 by the 'Hon Dr Arthur, Minister of Health and Friend of Women'. A special eugenics issue in April 1929 included advertisements for eugenics study circles and Piddington's article about raising boys emphasized that 'early training must be eugenic'.[48] Five months later *Herself*, now called *Herself: Her Present, Past and Future and Australian Affairs*, appealed to both religious and secular audiences by informing them 'of the many things that eugenics *was not*, including sex hygiene, birth control, prenatal culture, public health, free love, trial marriage, scientific love making, a vice campaign, "government made marriage", physical culture, Spartan infanticide, or a plan for producing "genius to order" or supermen'. The tract – identical to the American Eugenics Society's 'Eugenics Catechism' and reprinted without acknowledgement – was followed by advertisements for Piddington's study circles.

Piddington, in her hunt for 'opinions', told Stopes and Davenport that the eugenist David Starr Jordan, the progressive pacifist president of Stanford University, had been 'wonderfully kind'.[49] Although she may have been exaggerating, she certainly impressed Henry Tasman Lovell (1878-1958), who in 1921 became one of the first Australian-born senior academics the University of Sydney appointed after it had received a large bequest from the Irish-born pastoralist and philanthropist, Sir Samuel McCaughey (1835-1919). 'Tas' Lovell was a superb teacher who brought credit to the new home-grown appointment policy and progressed from associate professor to full professor of psychology in 1929. He enthused about Piddington's 'objective method' for teaching racial health', commenting in the *Sun* (13 December 1931) that she was 'an influence for good' and 'training mothers' was 'undeniably right and necessary'. Unfortunately, few others responded in this way. For instance, apart from a flurry of correspondence, nothing was done when she sent a reply-paid telegram to the Prime Minister on 10 April 1931 asking 'will you grant use of War Memorial Museum, Sydney, for shelter unemployed men during winter?'[50] Remembering the living as well as the dead in this masterpiece of Art Deco was a good idea and some American states still make National Guard armories available to the homeless during winter.

Although Piddington made exaggerated claims and was promoted as the great authority on eugenics and sex education, she made 'no pretension of being anything but a woman of long experience having devoted years to the work'.[51] As an isolated amateur, it is hardly surprising that she praised cranks and dubious scientists from overseas. For example, on 13 March 1930 the *Sydney Morning Herald* reported that 'prominent Austrian radiologist' Dr Wolfgang Wieser had reduced the extent of feeble-mindedness in children by X-raying their heads and bodies. Piddington bragged about his 'most courteous' reply and of her contacts with the American eugenists Goddard, Davenport, Johnson, Gosney and Popenoe, whose views influenced Nazi sterilisation and eugenics policies.

The Piddington couple fought perennial censorship battles and in 1923 Stopes thanked them for their 'gallant' efforts to allow her books to pass through Australian customs. The RHA 'got to work again' in 1930 and prompted the police to confiscate Stopes' books, declaring some were obscene. Piddington promised to do what she could, adding that associations did more harm than good and attracted a type of mind that does infinite harm.[52] Piddington was obsessed with 'the terrible Racial Hygiene Association' and fumed 'the type of mind that controls organization work is hopeless and very unclean'. At the same time Dr Edith How-Martyn, a Life Fellow of Britain's Eugenics Society, sent her a copy of *The Birth Control Movement in England* and asked about Australian progress. She had to admit 'there was nothing to tell!'.[53]

The Institute of Family Relations

Piddington abhorred a vacuum and formed her own society. In January 1931 she told Stopes that Lang's (NSW) Labor government was 'likely to grant' her facilities so that she might 'succeed in forming an Institute of Family Relations.' She enclosed this leaflet:

> Arrest of Racial Decay. The Hon W Davies, Minister of Education, has granted the use of the Assembly Hall, Education Building, Bridge Street, Sydney, to a group of social workers who propose to carry out, under the direction of Mrs Marion Piddington, a campaign against the dangers of promiscuity and 'the menace in our midst'. ... The classes, which are an extension of the

work carried out by Mrs Piddington and others during the past eight years, will follow her special 'impersonal' method.

The 'menace' was VD and she may have had this support because William Davies (1882-1956), like the Piddingtons, was a loyal Lang supporter. Davies was minister for public instruction in Lang's second ministry in 1927 and he retained the education portfolio in Lang's 1930-32 government. He also maintained good relations with the Teachers' Federation and Davis, with Piddington's husband, A B Piddington, fought to prevent the dismissal of married women teachers. However, in an attempt to gain credibility Marion may have overstated the claim about Davis' support as the hall she mentioned was available for hire and many groups rented it.[54] She may not have used the hall because she mentioned working in 'a small room', probably her flat, when she wrote to Stopes using the 'letter paper' of the Institute of Family Relations on 12 August 1931, admitting that it was only an extension of the previous ten years' sex education work and that the 14 Directors were working in a voluntary capacity. The Institute was to operate 'under a Directorate of Working Directors. Trustee: Dr Bradfield, ME, DSc'. In the four-page entry for civil engineer John Job Crew Bradfield (1867-1943), the *ADB* mentions the central roles he played in Sydney's railways, constructing the Harbour Bridge and founding the Institution of Engineers, but it says nothing about this role which Piddington claimed he had. Her stationery was donated by 'Public and Private school teachers' and the Directors were:

> Rev P J Bothwell; Mrs Bowering; Mrs Butler; J T Dingle, Esq BA; Mrs Greville, JP; R H Greville, Esq AICA, AAIS; A D Hope, Esq, BA; Mrs Roy Jones; Mrs Carrie Tennant Kelly; Mrs Marion Piddington; Rev H M Riley; Mrs Elsie Rivett; Miss M Terry; Mrs Trevenna, A Inst P I.

Some were well known: Mrs Butler could have been Janie Butler who gave money to the Eugenics Society of Victoria; J T Dingle was the Institute's psychologist; A D Hope (1907- 2000), 'Phallic Alec' to his friends, became a conservative force in Australian culture and the Grand Old Man of Australian poetry; Mrs Greville was labour organiser Henrietta Greville MBE (1861-1964); R H Greville, her husband Hector and Mrs Elsie Rivett (1887-1964) was a social worker.

They would be assisted by 'Eminent Honorary Specialists: biologist, physician, urologist, gynaecologist, psychiatrist, venereologist, obstetrician and psychologists'. Piddington fantasised that in 1932 'a scientist' would work with her as President and, after her death, the IFR would become a Scientific Institute for Research.[55]

The Piddingtons became friendly with Jean Devanny (1894-1962) a struggling novelist from New Zealand who said she valued this 'friendship deep and lasting' which began in 1929 when she was in gaol and during her difficulties with the Communist Party. According to Drusilla Modjeska, the 'difficulties' related to Devanny's efforts to develop a Sydney-based front organisation for leftist writers and artists several years before this became Communist Party policy.[56] Marion made their Blue Mountains holiday house available to the impoverished and hard-pressed author who assisted Piddington with her classes at the Institute of Family Relations. Unfortunately, in 1930 Devanny's propaganda was even more excessive than Piddington's:

> Sterilization is the logical extension of birth control, to include those stocks whose feeble-mindedness or degeneracy precludes the use of ordinary methods. Voluntary birth control among the superior types must be offset by enforced birth control among the uncontrolled, the bestial, the simple.[57]

In October 1931 the IFR undertook this 'logical extension' to the disgust of the Sydney magazine *Smith's Weekly*, (1919-1950) whose readers were mostly returned soldiers and workers. *Smith's* warned about the crankiness of IFR apostles of social hygiene and eugenics – 'clergymen, literary ladies, scientists and psychologists' – who wanted to 'alter fatherhood and motherhood'. They said the IFR had indulged in 'astounding activity' by sterilizing a 'pioneer patient' for no charge, who was 'poor, sickly and on the dole'.[58] *Smith's* then interviewed the 'brave wife' as she held the hand of the 'stricken' man 'whose inherited taint had been a lifelong nightmare'.[59] John Dingle, described as the IFR's official psychologist, discussed another patient as being typical of the need for sterilisation. He was one of 18 children with a low mental calibre mother and an epileptic pensioner father. Of the nine living children, two were married, four were at school and three were below school age. Two moron sisters were described as being dirty, untidy and illiterate and never likely to make useful citizens or healthy mothers.[60] Another paper, the *Sun*, noted that the IFR had 'supervised the first case of sterilisation in Australia' and was 'tackling the problem on purely scientific grounds'.

In 1932 the Piddington family suffered a crisis. Ironically, for a couple who frequently won their battles against book-banning, they could not save their only son Ralph from academic censors who forced him to leave Australia. Ralph had been granted a Rockefeller Fellowship while he was in his early twenties and, on completion of his field trips, created a storm by claiming in a Sydney newspaper that 'Aborigines on cattle stations are in slavery'.[61] He blamed pastoralists, police and a 'callously indifferent' Western Australian government, for creating this 'plague spot of European oppression', which was 'a national disgrace'. Officials retaliated and ultimately banished him from Australia in a shameful episode which has recently been described as the 'first of several blatant denials of academic (and civil) freedom to anthropologists'.[62] It is likely that this injustice led her to change the way the IFR operated; by March 1933 the letterhead listed only her name, 'assisted by eminent honorary specialists'.

The Margaret Sanger papers, now in the Library of Congress, include scathing reports about Piddington's venture with the first criticism coming from Dr Edith How-Martyn in London, the Director of Margaret Sanger's Birth Control Information Centre. How-Martyn warned the Centre's Head Office in New York that Piddington was 'rather unbalanced', tried to 'cover far too much ground', and had 'made the movement look rather foolish by her strong advocacy of artificial insemination'.[63] She warned against 'bothering about Mrs Piddington' and was concerned because the IFR sold Stopes' occlusive cervical caps by mail, for a 'heavy' charge of 21 shillings, without fitting each woman or knowing whether the cap would fit. How-Martyn said Piddington's lone and lay approach contradicted the movement's policy to 'get this matter of birth control methods into the hands of the doctors'. Piddington's involvement in sex education and advice on marriage and 'abnormalities of sex' were 'far better left to other societies and not mixed up with birth control'.[64] The condemnation continued. In 1934 Alice Hicks, a midwife and member of Sanger's

Birth Control International Information Centre, visited 'M P' (Marion Piddington) several times. She reported that M P was 'individualistic' and described an 'atmosphere of mystery' about the IFR which had no advisory committee, because Piddington believed that 'the machinery of organization retards the work of an individual'. Neither would M P ally herself with any other organisation and she refused to name her assistant specialists. Hicks warned that Piddington made abortion referrals and had reluctantly conceded that the 'perfectly reliable' contraceptive method she claimed to have invented was only a sponge which she sold with a home-made spermicide recipe. Hicks concluded that '*M P was the Institute*' which had been set up as a money-making concern.

Unintentionally but undeniably Piddington's activities hindered the work of the birth control pioneers, although in the 1930s there was no public condemnation of the problems associated with her Institute's inexpertly delivered care. When the IFR placed an advertisement in the WEA's magazine, *Australian Highway*, the Executive of the WEA's Victorian Branch wanted to ban such advertising on moral grounds. Ironically, knowing nothing of the IFR's dubious reputation, the more liberal-minded Executive of Sydney's WEA overruled this complaint and defended Piddington's right to continue advertising. Much later Dr Norman Haire criticised the cost but not the quality of a service which, while not named, was clearly hers.

On 23 October 1937 the very conservative Joseph Lyons became the first Australian Prime Minister to win a third consecutive general election and in that same week, Piddington appealed to Professor Agar for support. 'Our Institute has completed almost the first cases of voluntary sterilization', she said, 'we have had grateful letters from those who have had this very simple operation, and also the major operation for women'.[65] It is hard to believe her claim that 'more than 41,000' had attended her classes or that the IFR performed female sterilisations, and least likely of all is the 'accolade' she claimed to have received from Lord Horder, the President of the British Eugenics Society, "Tell Mrs Piddington that sterilisation is the first thing to do."[66]

Piddington was dogged but deluded with her strategy: eugenics was her goal, with sub-goals of celibate motherhood, birth control (to protect the health of fit mothers and to reduce or eliminate the births of the unfit) and the sterilisation of the unfit. She believed that sex education was essential because informed children, as adults, would avoid prostitutes and promiscuity and, as a consequence, be protected from VD. Piddington longed for a totalitarian utopia in which only fitness for motherhood would be considered, little boys would not have trouser pockets so that they would not become sexually precocious and the unfit would happily forgo parenthood for the good of the nation. She promoted honest communication between parents and children and it was not prudery that made her disapprove of condoms but a fear that they encouraged profligacy and vice. When the country's only unswerving eugenist died, her brief obituary in the *Sydney Morning Herald* on 6 February 1950 did not mention eugenics:

> Mrs Marian [sic] Piddington, who died in a Sydney private hospital last week, aged 81, was a pioneer in the work of marriage guidance. For 30 years she carried on, almost unaided, the Institute of Family Relations from an office in Phillip Street, Sydney. In a period when people were suspicious of any frank advocacy of sex education, Mrs Piddington was educating parents in the art of wise parentcraft. She gave personal interviews, lectured to classes, and sought support for her cause from politicians and leaders in the community. Mrs Piddington's only son, Dr Ralph Piddington, is a reader in social anthropology at Edinburgh University.

Almost certainly, it was written by her friend Jean Devanny who misspelt this enigmatic woman's first name and said nothing about her driving passions. In 1950 eugenics had become disreputable while Marion's other passions, artificial insemination and birth control, were not yet respectable.

2. John [Jack] Chambers Eldridge: Labor Politician

Eldridge was a 'weak' eugenist who grafted eugenics onto political beliefs for ten years but when he shed eugenics, his politics emerged unscathed. Eldridge was born in 1872 to Australian parents who were living in Calcutta. After attending state schools in Australia, he began a

38-year career with the NSW public service in 1889. Starting as a junior draughtsman with the Sewerage Department, earning £50 a year, he rapidly progressed to senior positions and, by the time he resigned to enter Federal Parliament in 1929, his annual salary was more than £560.[67] This was a secure, well-paid position, unlike that of most workers at the outset of the Depression. Although unemployment was over 30% in the darkest days of this period, when politics ousted Eldridge in 1931 he was able to resume his career in the public service.

Figure 9: Eldridge at 59[68]

Eldridge was also a union member and pioneered the Australian Labor Party speakers' classes. He was a florid and forceful speaker, broadcaster and pamphleteer who was a described as a 'stalwart' by his supporters and a 'militant' by his detractors. From 1912 to 1922 he supported eugenics and became the prime mover and only chronicler of NSW's first eugenics society. It began in July 1912 when Eldridge was 40, sparked by a broadside in Sydney's *Telegraph* against the 'so-called science of eugenics' with a reminder that 'people, like race horses, could win and lose in all shapes and sizes'. 'Marriages' it said, 'should be controlled by sentimental impulses not eugenics'. Eldridge counter-attacked in eugenics' defence, calling it 'the youngest assuredly the greatest of all sciences which had no involvement in matrimonial selection, and had merely proposed segregation of the hopelessly unfit'.

The Eugenics Education Society of NSW was launched in Sydney on 11 December 1912, with Dr Richard Arthur the President, Robert Francis Irvine (1861-1941), Australia's first Professor of Economics, Vice-President and Eldridge the Honorary Secretary. Eldridge also applied for membership of the London-based Eugenics Education Society (EES), informing them he was the Secretary of the State Labour Bureau of NSW and falsely claiming to have qualified in economics from the Sydney University.[69] Eldridge told the EES that the newly-established Sydney Branch shared the parent body's objectives.[70] He was motivated by the news of that New Zealand had established eugenics branches and explained 'that as a result of perusing a splendid series of articles appearing in Harmsworth's *Popular Science* on the subject of Eugenics, I wrote to the Editor of that section asking him to be good enough to furnish me with some information concerning your organisation'. He meant the Edinburgh-trained Dr Caleb Saleeby (1878-1940) whose eugenics activities appropriately matched his surname, which is Arabic for crusader.[71] While Arthur Mee (1875-1943), the English journalist and educator, was the overall editor of the illustrated and illustrious *Children's Encyclopaedia*, Saleeby wrote the 36 instalments on eugenics which appeared in *Popular Science's* seven volumes. Eldridge's choice of hero was unfortunate as the maverick Saleeby had switched from a being strong supporter of the Society to become its chief irritant and opponent. In 1909 Saleeby embarrassed his colleagues by claiming that eugenics was going to save the world and in 1910 he was removed from the EES Council because of his bumptiousness and his championship for such causes as temperance and divorce law reform. In 1913 the egalitarian Saleeby had criticised the Society's class prejudices after it had spurned his offer to read a paper.

On 3 June 1913 Sydney's *Sun* reported that Eldridge, in his address to a large gathering of the Rationalist Association of NSW, explained that eugenists wanted to make people consider the race, not just themselves.   Eldridge's new eugenics society colleagues shared Saleeby's distaste for class eugenics, which he had called the 'better dead' school – genetic determinists who aimed to eliminate the unfit. Nurtural eugenists such as Saleeby were sometimes called euthenists because they prompted euthenics, the science of bettering the environment by improving living conditions.   While they did not use the term, it aptly described the social reform orientation of the decision-makers, Eldridge, Irvine and Arthur. Although initially sharing the (hereditarian) objectives of the parent EES, the NSW group now turned away from the parent body and supported Saleeby's nurtural (environmental) perspective. This reversal is apparent in the Society's new statement about eugenics, modelled on Saleeby's proposals. Sydney's *Telegraph* had also modified its anti-eugenics stance by 5 March 1914 when it decided to publish Eldridge's EES eugenics manifesto:

1. Natural or Primary Eugenics: Biology, Heredity, etc

(a) Positive – encouraging worthy parenthood

(b) Negative – discouraging unworthy parenthood

(c) Preventive – opposing the racial poisons (venereal diseases, alcohol, etc)

2. Nurtural or Secondary Eugenics: Sociology, Environment, Education, etc

(a) Physical – including nurture from beginning (not just the cradle) to the grave

(b) Psychical – including education, etc

(c) Social and moral – home, school and nation.

Professor Irvine was Chairman of the Public Service Board who from 1905 had lectured public servants on economics and commerce and Eldridge was Irvine's disciple on matters of eugenics, economics social sciences and low cost housing. For example, Eldridge applauded Irvine's statement that the problem of how to produce a superior civilisation is both biological and sociological and found this in total accord with eugenic principles.[72]   He also recycled parts of Irvine's 1913 *Report of the Commission of Inquiry into the Question of the Housing of*

Workmen in Europe and America two years later in a union report on the economic origins of housing troubles.[73]

Eldridge, in the first progress report to the parent EES in October 1916, outlined 'press work on eugenics', most of which he had written, including an epic of 35 instalments in *Navvy*, a union broadsheet produced by the Railway Workers and General Labourers' Association of NSW. He correctly judged that the workers and the masses were bored or suspicious about eugenics, and told EES Secretary Mrs Gotto that he taken the subject to an important, hard-to-reach quarter. He then made the unlikely claim that his message was attentively received and had received active support.

Eldridge defended the unorthodox style he had used to gain the attention of this audience. Unfortunately, the war or workers' distaste, proved fatal to his convoluted conversion attempts. The editor ambiguously noted in the final September 1916 issue that the educative value of Mr Eldridge's articles will not cease with the circulation of *Navvy*. Eldridge informed the EES that progress in Australia's efforts to limit VD had been slow, despite the work done by the Commonwealth government and voluntary organisations such as the EESNSW. Some appreciated the threat but ignorance, prejudice, sectionalism and a lack of co-operation between organisations, had all delayed progress despite the efforts of Dr Arthur. Although they were political opponents, Eldridge generously described Arthur as an able advocate and champion of this subject. In a farewell report Eldridge (who had enlisted for active service) apologised because the Sydney Branch had not achieved more, although members had done their best, constantly informing the public about the importance of eugenics. He hoped for better results in the future years.

After his demobilisation, Eldridge sent a progress report to the EES on 9 November 1921 outlining the group's renewed activities. He rather pointedly thanked the EES Secretary for her courtesy and kindness but regretted that his visits to their London office in 1918, 1919 and 1920 had not been mentioned in the *Eugenics Review*. He followed this with a blunt question – did EES find the current economic system essentially dysgenic?[74] His questions related to the position he held briefly as the Under-Secretary for Motherhood in the office of J J G (Greg) McGirr, a crash-through-or-crash Irish Catholic politician who was the first and only Minister for Motherhood in the 1920-1921 Storey (NSW) Labor Government.[75] While Eldridge claimed that McGirr's Motherhood Endowment Bill would be paid for with money saved by abolishing the State Children Relief Board, others later claimed that the proposal lapsed because of objections to a child support scheme being funded by a State lottery. On 16 November 1921, after the second reading of 'Mother McGirr's Bill', Eldridge noted the Opposition MP, Dr Arthur's in principle approval which showed the Bill's eugenic origins:

> We owe to the child, if possible, that it should have good parents. I believe that in the future far more attention will be paid to the science of eugenics than is done at the present time. We will seek to prevent persons who are suffering from some disease which may be handed on to their offspring from propagating their kind. … But once a child is here we must regard it as our primary duty to supply it with the necessaries of life. The first essential is an abundant supply of good and wholesome food, adequate clothing, housing in hygienic surroundings, and ample opportunities for education.[76]

Truthfulness is something politicians are rarely accused of, but Arthur's claim to be the 'earliest and most persistent advocate of child endowment' *was* true.[77]

Eldridge's next letter to the EES summarised McGirr's proposed legislation and asked the *Eugenics Review* to give it publicity. Curiously, he wrote 'although the subject has no direct eugenic significance, I feel sure that on general grounds it will be of interest to members of the Society, as well as to the general public'.[78] When it appeared, the review was merciless:

> In our last issue we printed a proposed scheme for the Endowment of Motherhood in NSW. On consulting the Parliamentary Debates, … we find considerable opposition in Committee to this measure. In his opening statement Mr J J G McGirr (Lab), Minister for Motherhood, remarked that the measure was practically noncontentious as it aimed at 'benefiting

the class of people who of all are the most deserving – the mothers
who are rearing large families, and whose husbands are the poorest
paid men in the community'. The 'cult of incompetence' could
hardly go further![79]

McGirr had described the scheme as an unprecedented and
innovative attempt to provide a benefit, initially to families on the basic
wage, and later to assist every mother who is doing her duty to increase
the best class of immigrant Australia can have – the Australian child.
Its pronatalist intention was emphasized by Arthur in platitudes about
the ominous impact of the birthrate on white Australia.   The Bill
lapsed and so did Eldridge's faith in eugenics.   While no letter
announced the Sydney Society's death, Leonard Darwin was being
fanciful in 1923 when he mentioned his members in Australia.[80] The
next year the EES Secretary told a Queensland paper merchant there
was not yet any well organised Society in Australia or New Zealand.[81]
It seems that the first Eugenics Society in NSW had meant very little to
the parent group.

Eldridge later expunged eugenics from his political bio-data. Five
years after the schism, he supported Lang's Family Endowment Bill
(1927), which *was* passed. One of Eldridge's pamphlets for this Bill
began with this unfortunately-worded sentence, 'The human race
marches forward on the feet of little children'. He was elected as the
Labor Member of the House of Representatives for Martin (NSW), in
the 1929 swing to Labor and entered Federal Parliament aged 57, a
sombre time to enter Parliament.[82]   However, indiscretion, not the
Depression, killed Eldridge's political career which was brief but
included some arresting moments, for instance, his 'thunderous
declaration' on 18 November 1929 that an Australian, 'possibly even a
woman', should be chosen as the next Australian Governor-General.
Manning Clark noted that on hearing this, both sides of the House
collapsed into hilarity.[83] They should not have laughed; Scullin's Labor
government was soon to win the first battle (overcoming royal and
religious prejudices). On 22 January 1931 Sir Isaac Isaacs became our
first home-grown Governor-General but women are still waiting.

Eldridge was part of the faction which supported NSW Premier
Lang's finance plan and refused to pledge their acceptance of federal

policy but he really blasted his political career two months later by calling the Church 'Harlots of Mammon'.[84] He made another mistake in 1941 by paying a cordial tribute to the Japanese Consul, signing himself as 'one who wishes you to know that an Australian citizen respectfully approves of your just and valued contribution to current thought on the situation in the Pacific'.[85] The diplomat replied that the 'Japanese Government desires only the friendliest relations with Australia, and looks to Australia for co-operation in the preservation of peace in the region of the Pacific'.[86] Eldridge's death in 1954 was scarcely mentioned in Lang's newspaper, suggesting that he played a minor role in Labor's history. He was described as a keen student of social problems and a keen propagandist who had trained young Labor speakers and given them a grounding in economics. In his long retirement he had survived being hit by a tram. Paradoxically, while nothing came of Eldridge's attempt to write a history of early Labor politics, he provided a useful record of NSW's first eugenics society.

3. Lillie Elizabeth Goodisson: Team leader

Figure 10: Goodisson, probably in her 80s[87]

Lillie Elizabeth Goodisson, who was intimately connected with the Racial Hygiene Association (RHA), used eugenics in her goal to improve women's health and fight VD and is one of the two eugenists listed by the *Australian Dictionary of Biography*.[88]   Welsh-born Lillie Elizabeth Price came from a medical family, her father was a doctor and she became a trained nurse. At the age of 19 she married Dr Lawford David Evans and the couple migrated to New Zealand, where their son Brooke was born in 1881 and daughter Evelyn in 1883. Evelyn, perhaps the product of her mother's nature and nurture, was described as a handsome, intelligent and forceful woman, with conservative political views who disliked trade unions.[89]

Details are sketchy about Goodisson's early life. She was living in Melbourne by 1895 and became the matron of her own private hospital; in the early 1900s she moved with her family to Western Australia. She was widowed in 1902 and, a year later, her misfortunes continued when she married Albert Goodisson without knowing he had syphilis. She continued with her political work and in the summer of 1912 made the long trip to Hobart where she gave a paper at the 5th Commonwealth Conference of the Women's Liberal Leagues.[90] In September the following year Albert went to an asylum in Batavia for 'health reasons', suggesting that his advanced symptoms were now impossible to hide. Five months later he died of 'general paralysis' and dementia, the unmistakable features of untreated tertiary syphilis. VD was infectious, feared and fatal in those pre-penicillin days and if a hospital matron had been deceived when she married, so had many others. Lillie's response, much later, was to educate women about the dangers.

Goodisson returned to Melbourne where, during the 1914-18 war, she received financial and emotional support from Ivy Brookes, whose husband was the wealthy businessman and political power-broker, Herbert Brookes. Ivy's father was Prime Minister Alfred Deakin and she had links with organisations related to women, education, music and politics, and became the foundation secretary of the Women's Division of the People's Liberal Party. Goodisson took over from her as the Division's Secretary, writing letters to the Melbourne *Argus* in 1915 and 1918. She was also active in the Empire Trade Defence Association and ran a small library which Brookes had helped fund, but when Goodisson became ill and the business failed she moved to Sydney in 1926 to be near her daughter. That year Goodisson joined the Crows Nest Branch of the Women's Reform League on Sydney's north shore and these women, with her activism and help from the

Women's Service Guilds, launched what became the Racial Hygiene Association of NSW. She had begun her life's work. The year buzzed with initiatives; in NSW Lang's Labor Government introduced widows' pensions, the Nurses' Registration Act was proclaimed and electric trains and radio 2GB began operating in Sydney; the Commonwealth could deal with political agitators and communists; the *Canberra Times*, Myer's Emporium, Hoyts moving-picture cinemas and General Motors car assembly plants were established; the noxious Prickly Pear weed was brought under control by the *Cactoblastis* caterpillar, and electricity and the now-defunct *Miss Australia* contests transformed suburbia.

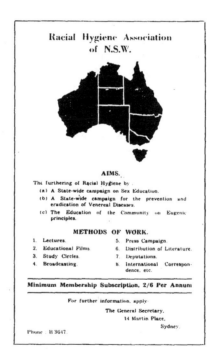

Figure 11: Aims of the Racial Hygiene Association (RHA) [91]

At the age of 66 Goodisson found her niche as General Secretary of the RHA whose three aims were to provide sex education, combat VD, and promote eugenics. In spite of community opposition, she established racial hygiene on a firm footing, becoming the leader of the band of six women who ran the RHA.[92]   But Ruby Rich gave most credit to Marion Piddington and Anna Roberts (the President of the Women's Reform League of NSW) who had asked her to help them found the Association. While Goodisson *was* the RHA, Rich would only concede that 'dear Goody', a 'wonderful, wonderful person' had begun the RHA's birth control work.[93] Goodisson gave stability to the RHA, unlike the various patrons, presidents and executive members who were chosen for their name, influence and interest but never stayed long. Members said she was the Society and without her there would be no Society'.[94] The President, Victor Roberts, called her a 'brick' and appreciated her 'very strenuous work'. Dr John Cooper Booth agreed she had 'been the driving force ever since the Association has been in existence. When Mrs Goodisson goes on the warpath you have to give in in the end. She usually gets her way'. In Melbourne Sir James Barrett commented, 'Mrs Goodisson thinks that Racial Hygiene is the most important work of all'. This seemed self evident to her. She asked, 'what work can be greater than morals, health and education?'[95]

Theosophy

Historian Jill Roe, in *Beyond Belief: Theosophy in Australia, 1879-1939*, documented the influence of this movement in Australia after the charismatic Annie Besant (1847-1933) established it on a firm footing in the 1880s.[96]   It was a shadowy movement which also infused feminist, rationalist and artistic groups. Organizations such as the RHA, WEA and the Peace Society often had theosophist members although many prominent Australians preferred not to reveal that they were theosophists. The secrecy may have related to the 1922 scandal in Sydney's Theosophical Society which caused Besant to hurriedly end her Australian tour and it could explain the Society's silence about their Good Film League which they established in 1922 to promote ethical, artistic films and encourage people to complain about foreign, particularly American, films if they offended women, decency or

British civilization. The first objective was taken seriously; from 1930 Sydney audiences could enjoy plays at the theosophist Savoy Theatre or watch quality films at their North Sydney cinema. The Theosophical Society was a staunch supporter in the 1930s; they published Goodisson's articles in their magazine, made the Savoy theatre available for the RHA-sponsored play *Just One Slip* and, for seven years allowed her to give weekly radio broadcasts on their station, 2GB. She did not reveal the station ownership when she thanked the station's manager and acknowledged that 99% of the correspondence and interviews was generated by her weekly radio program.[97] Perhaps Goodisson was a member but she or the RHA did not want this revealed; possibly she was respecting the Society's protocol as theosophists were very secretive about the station's origins and their mission to theosophise Australia.[98]

RHA Publicity

Goodisson gave frequent radio broadcasts, wrote for the *Progressive Journal*, used the WEA magazine *Australian Highway* to publicise RHA work and ensured that press publicity was maintained. She was also involved with the RHA's Vice-Regally endorsed funding appeal which amply demonstrates the organisation's initial prestige and respectability.[99] However, some booklets, and posters such as **Figure 12** and **Figure 13**, were reproduced without giving any credit to their American or British sources. Goodisson lectured, showed films, arranged Health Week exhibitions, organised the Australian Racial Hygiene Congress in 1929 and repeatedly tried to establish a national network of RHA branches. She also co-ordinated various deputations and represented the RHA on numerous women's and welfare bodies including the Mental Hygiene Society, the National Council of Women, the American Social Hygiene Association, the Parks and Playgrounds Movement, the Good Film League, the 2GB Happiness Club and the Standing Committee on Maternal Mortality.

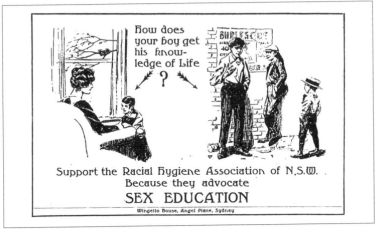

Figure 12: Sex Education: Mother's Knee or the Gutter?[100]

Figure 13: RHA – 'We Say: "Knowledge means Safety. Give Them Light"'[101]

Censorship

Initially the RHA supported censorship but then drew back from this. From Goodisson's account in the RHA's 1929 annual report, she was trying to distance herself from the RHA's ill-judged alliance with hard-line book banners. For example, her carefully chosen words about the deputation to ban salacious literature do not reveal the pro-censorship stance of the Good Film League nor the links she and Cresswell O'Reilly had with the theosophist League:

> At the request of several persons, who do not belong to our Organisation, we called together a Committee of those who were taking a keen interest in the matter. [It met four times and a meeting of interested parties was addressed by] Mr O'Reilly, Rev R B S Hammond, Mrs [Mildred] Muscio and the Rev Victor Bell. Unfortunately, there was some division of opinion as to the best methods to be used.[102]

RHA efforts to dam floods of objectionable literature were short-lived. The *Sydney Morning Herald* gave details on 10 July and on 17 September 1929 after the police responded to calls from the Council of Churches, the Salvation Army, the Education Department, the Young Men's Christian Association and the RHA. There was a report in January 1930 of police 'being seriously inconvenienced by thousands of people who surged round them during a bookshop raid in Martin Place while police confiscated about £1,000 worth of allegedly indecent material'. The crowd was huge and so was the value of the seized material at a time when a fibro house in the outlying Sydney suburb of Bankstown cost about £580 and a brick or stone one in harbour-side Mosman might fetch £1,700. The RHA's lobbying forced Parks Brothers to close their bookshop and after the January raid, Shakespeare's *Venus and Adonis*, Erich Remarque's best-selling war novel *All Quiet On The Western Front* and some of Stopes' books, were banned. While the RHA revealed in its 1930 Annual Report that many of those books were 'quite harmless and even good', the *Herald* found it 'an amusing instance of how hope may be too generously realised'.[103] In this hypocritical climate, even the most reputable books on birth control were not displayed because booksellers had been driven to this self-censorship to avoid being overwhelmed with protests from 'purity' fanatics.[104]

The RHA's zealotry came in tandem with one of the 1929 Vice Presidents, Walter Cresswell O'Reilly (1877-1954). He was Sydney's blue-pencil wielding, high priest of censorship; from 1925-28 as the Commonwealth Censor, then as the Commonwealth Film Censor. He next became Ku-ring-gai's Mayor, for five consecutive terms from 1929-1933, enriching this district of Sydney's north shore with recreation areas and conservation plans. Unfortunately, his eugenic efforts were less benign. For example, in a radio broadcast on 'Race Improvement', reported in the *Sydney Morning Herald* on 16 October 1931, O'Reilly claimed the cream of the country's men and women had been skimmed off and did not adequately beget its kind. To prevent 'the lower strata, the subnormal and the undesirable' from populating the world, he urged society to embrace eugenic principles, which he said would result in progressive evolution and the production of a 'super race with God-like power'. Fortunately, his influence on the RHA was brief and he was their only member who promoted censorship *and* eugenics.

The RHA also had a troublesome radical in their midst, George Southern, a psychologist who tried to form a NSW branch of the World League for Sexual Reform in 1932. At their meeting on 7 June, the RHA Executive was divided on whether he should be asked to resign. Southern responded by writing, publishing and distributing a book with the subtitle 'A broadside attack on sexual morality, likely to make wowsers[105] yell and thinkers think' and an added note that 'the PMG [postal authority] banned this book'.[106] To modern readers, the best thing about Southern's peculiar book, *Making Morality Modern*, is the picture of the author at work by the celebrated photographer Max Dupain (**Figure 14**) and the funniest is Havelock Ellis' comment that 'communism might not be the best way to produce a sexually enlightened society'. In 1933 Southern referred to the RHA as a small club to which be belonged and dismissed them as wowsers because, after he had tried to arrange for them to hear his paper, they had developed chilblains and had suffered from cold feet ever since.

Figure 14: George Southern and his Printing Press

Southern was unfair because by 1933 the RHA were strongly *opposing* censorship and had even made history that year by their defence of free speech. In a test case, two RHA Vice-Presidents gave expert evidence to support Robert Storer, a doctor in Sydney's prestigious Macquarie Street and former RHA Vice-President. While other aspects of Storer's life were sinister,[107] on this occasion he had innocently but naively asked a policeman in the street if he wanted to buy a copy of his book, *Sex in Modern Life: A Survey of Sexual Life in Adolescence and Marriage.* He was charged under the Obscene Publications Act but the farce had a happy ending because, according to Peter Coleman, it was the first obscenity trial in NSW where expert witnesses were allowed to testify. Harvey Sutton (a professor of medicine) and Rev T E Ruth (a Congregational minister) were RHA members and the third witness was Rev Heathcote (a Unitarian minister). Their evidence convinced the Magistrate and Appeal Judge that Storer's book was not obscene.[108]

> Despite early censoriousness, the RHA helped promote discussion about taboo topics. In 1928 the RHA affiliated with the National Council of Women and Goodisson became Convener of their Equal Moral Standards Committee. Although no prude, she once

objected to nude female figures being dressed in shop windows
and to the advertising and display of sanitary towels.

Goodisson: The Woman

Goodisson achieved more for birth control than Piddington but has
received less attention, probably because she was quietly efficient and
her achievements were often indistinguishable from those of the RHA.
Most information comes from Goodisson's own writing and, while
much of it was RHA propaganda, it provides some glimpses of her
personality. For example, she generously reviewed Piddington's book
Tell Them! even though it was published after Piddington's
acrimonious rift with the RHA. Goodisson, in a review published in
the January 1927 issue of *The Dawn*, said the book was well written and
a wonderful help to mothers and described Piddington as an advanced
thinker and writer. She rarely expressed her private opinions because
community disapproval of the RHA was widespread.

However, in the RHA's Annual Report she mentioned spending six
months of 1930 in Hobart helping her sick elderly mother. She
combined this with political campaigning which resembles
Piddington's, complete with tallies of audience sizes:

> I gave 15 addresses in the Domain on Sunday afternoon. The
> attendances range from 150 to 500 making an aggregate of between
> 3,000 and 4,000. ... I also addressed the Theosophical Society and
> attended a good many political meetings, the State elections being
> in progress, ... questioning candidates as to whether if returned
> they would 'press' for the provision of adequate facilities for the
> treatment of venereal disease.

The flamboyant Ruby Rich uncharitably called her a 'very cautious
person' who thought it was better not to have the birth control pioneer
Dr Norman Haire (1892-1952) as a member because he 'wasn't very
popular'.[109] This would have been a group decision made from
prudence not timidity. Goodisson was often bravely controversial in
her defence of the RHA. For example, in a 1931 Health Week radio
broadcast, she tackled Sydney's Roman Catholic Archbishop of
Sydney, Dr Michael Kelly, saying that he showed ignorance of
biological facts by calling birth control murder. Adding that, 'if failure

to give life was equivalent to taking life were true, then self control, which was the method he advocated, was also murder'. When much later Kelly wrote abusively about her, she sent this response via a Sydney paper; 'Neither the Racial Hygiene Association nor I personally believe in companionate or trial marriages, or in any illegal unions, though we know they exist; and I have been able on several occasions to dissuade girls from entering into such agreements'.

In 1932 Goodisson unsuccessfully contested the Newcastle seat as a Social Reform candidate in the NSW state elections. She said she did this in an attempt to stir a sense of public responsibility about VD and to 'write the need for such reforms across the political sky'. She 'had two good meetings' and was able to 'spread more propaganda in two weeks than was usually possible in three years'.[110] That year she mentioned experiencing an undercurrent of criticism. Possibly it was related to her political campaign, and tensions increased after the RHA's Birth Control Clinic opened on 1 December 1933. Goodisson may have been hinting at this in a letter she wrote to Professor Harvey Sutton on 8 July 1933. As well as inviting him to make a speech at their annual meeting, she asked him to give his opinion and 'help to unravel some of the knots which always come up'.

Marion Piddington was the toughest knot. Although Goodisson was politically conservative and Piddington was affiliated with the Labor Party, they had similar views about promiscuity, sex education, VD, birth control, and sterilisation of the 'unfit'. Both lectured, gave advice, ran classes, published and distributed literature, went on promotional tours, sought support and used the press in their efforts to educate the community about eugenics. However, these powerful women were competing in the same city; they provided similar services and preached similar messages. Goodisson was remarkably restrained when she said that the RHA's Martin Place birth control clinic in the centre of Sydney was 'the first properly constituted' one in Australia. Only outsiders would miss the inference that Piddington's clinic which opened two years previously, two blocks away in Phillip Street, was not. Goodisson's clever use of language is understandable, but it is hard to understand how Australian National University demographers Lado Ruzicka and John Caldwell could say:

Although a small [birth control] clinic was established in a private house in Sydney in 1926, it sought to avoid attack until the 1960s by its eugenicist name, 'The Racial Hygiene Association of Australia'.[111]

They were wrong about the place, date and name: the clinic was on an upper floor of an imposing life insurance office building at 14 Martin Place, the heritage-listed facade of which now encases an office tower; the clinic opened in 1933; the RHA never expanded to become the Racial Hygiene Association of Australia and the name was chosen in 1928, five years before their birth control clinic opened and, in any case, a eugenicist name would not have deflected attack.

Figure 15: Lillie Goodisson's Address to Women Voters

Goodisson, like Piddington, continued crusading into old age and **Figure 15** shows an elderly Goodisson addressing the Australian Federation of Women Voters in 1936. She continued to spread the message in magazines, stressing that 'we want migration, we want babies, we must have both, but let us have them of good quality'. As she put it, the healthy ancestry of the parents, not their marital status, was the prerequisite for breeding a healthy race.[112] During 1936 the Eugenics Society of Victoria began in Melbourne, much to Goodisson's disgust, Australia's National Health and Medical Research Council was established in Canberra and, in Britain, King Edward VIII abdicated. Goodisson was only once quoted as 'a eugenist', in the

Telegraph on 8 December, when she gave her views about the proposed abdication:

> He has every right to make a personal decision. A man should choose his own wife. The woman of a man's own choice is likely to be a better wife racially than the wife forced on him by others, particularly when the latter is chosen from the intermarried ranks of European royalty. Personally, I would like to see him give up the marriage and remain King, but he has the right to choose.

While Goodisson's argument was logical, it was eugenically unorthodox as the conventional view would have been to consider the needs of the nation, not the man, as the deciding factor.

As well as the financial difficulties during the Depression, Goodisson alluded to RHA internal antagonisms when she commented in the 1939-40 Annual Report that she had retained the support of some of the RHA Executive who had faithfully backed her when she had been 'placed in a very difficult position through the unwarranted action of a small section of the Committee.' Perhaps she had clashed with the socialite Comtesse de Vilme-Hautmont (1881-1962), a former Gilbert and Sullivan star known as Vinia de Loitte who was a newly-appointed member of the RHA Executive Committee. Goodisson defended the RHA's birth control clinic from unfair criticism and denied that it had anything to do with the falling birth rate. She also accepted that resignations and slights, such as being left off guest lists, were an inevitable consequence of defying convention. Unfortunately, there was such an acute rubber shortage during World War II that the RHA clinic could no longer supply their custom-made 'Racia caps'. In Sydney Goodisson was trying to ensure that the RHA would survive, a task which became even more difficult in 1940 after the NSW Government grant was again withdrawn, placing the organization in a perilous financial position. No further RHA reports were published during the war although Goodisson continued to be quoted in the newspapers. Despite the Melbourne clinic's closure in 1940 because of rubber shortages, she and Dr Victor Wallace continued to correspond and in 1945 she confided that, although at 85 she was getting too old for the job, she had held on because of the RHA's 'run of bad luck with secretaries'. She also continued as

National Council of Women's Equal Moral Standards Committee Convener until 1946 when she asked to be replaced by Portia Geach (1873-1959) the affluent artist, known as the housewives' friend, who was only 73.

When Goodisson died on 10 January 1947 at the age of 87 the *Sydney Morning Herald* reported that for 20 years she had been General Secretary of the RHA which she started and that she was 'greatly interested in political affairs all her life, had contributed to the success of Health Week and would be mourned by all who were associated with her in this and other activities to improve the health and well-being of the people'. Phyllis Cilento, in her 1987 memoir, *Lady Cilento: My Life*, looked back on her medical career which began in the 1920s when birth control was 'not quite nice'. She believed that attitudes had changed rapidly as a result of Mrs Goodisson's efforts. In reality, it took time and, as other birth control pioneers have acknowledged, the secret of success was the union of like-minded people which helped in forming and moulding public opinion.

4. Henry Twitchin: Benefactor

Henry Twitchin, who viewed eugenics as an extension of the stock breeding techniques he employed on his animals, left most of his fortune to London's Eugenics Society. This made the Society financially comfortable, ensured its archives were saved and gave it an influence far beyond its small membership.

Strangely, the EES Archives do not contain a picture of Henry Twitchin and most details about him come from his own letters. After his death in 1930, biographical information was supplied by a close friend, possibly a lover, from Berkshire, who had kept in touch with him and had been the sole helper with his outfit and packing when the 21-year-old Henry emigrated to Western Australia in 1890.[113] She described his childhood on a white elephant of a farm where life was difficult for the hard-working but indulgent mother and three children. They were dominated by the church-avoiding father who, despite his reputation for holding advanced views, insisted on sealing the house to avoid draughts and imposed a cloistered life on Henry's two 'delicate' sisters who died young from TB. She said that his irritable father was not in sympathy with the kind, gentle boy and this, together with his very reasonable fear of TB and his desire to see the world, explains why he left home.[114]   Twitchin probably escaped his housebound sisters' fate because he was allowed to ride a bicycle and attended the local grammar school. He then went to an agricultural college where he became the 'livestock prizeman' in 1888 and met like-minded students who stimulated him to think about emigration. His family strongly opposed the trip, but he raised the money, included a dress-suit in his luggage despite his father's jeers, and arrived in Albany, Western Australia on 17 May 1890. Ten years later, he was well established and a humane employer, according to a Travelling Inspector of Aborigines who commented on conditions at Twitchin's Towera station:

> No natives on relief here. One old man 60, blind and one woman about 55 nearly blind are fed and kept by Mr Twitchin, who considers it his duty to keep these old people, they having no near relations working for him, neither does he ask for blankets for them but finds them himself. It is quite refreshing to meet a gentleman with such views. I am sorry there are not more like him.[115]

Twitchin's properties were near the Exmouth Gulf on the remote north-western coast of Western Australia, where the United States' naval communications station was built in 1963. After losing sheep in the 1891-1903 droughts, the enterprising young farmer had returned to Britain and managed to raise capital for sinking artesian wells on his land. As a result he became wealthy and by 1923 he described himself as the largest land holder and stock owner in the State.[116]

In 1921 the *Eugenics Review* announced that it had received a substantial bequest from Peter Mitchell, a pastoralist from Albury, NSW.[117]   Probably this prompted Twitchin to make formal arrangements about his bequest to the Eugenics Education Society – as a member he received the *Review* – and, because mail is precious in remote areas and he was interested in eugenics, he would have thought about Mitchell's 1921 bequest. The following year, Twitchin explained to the EES Secretary, Major Leonard Darwin, that he had resolved in 1911, when he joined the Society, to send donations and leave them his estates (valued at between £57,000 and £160,000) for use in promoting eugenics.[118] As a stockbreeder in the 1890s, he became convinced that racial improvement would only occur if the same techniques used on animals were applied to people. He had discussed his extreme eugenics views with one or two of his neighbours and was in favour of the 'immediate introduction of legislation in all civilised countries prohibiting the propagation of the unfit from any cause'. Fortunately, he was never more than a front-porch philosopher because *his* utopia would have been a nightmare of 'pedigree' people, with ugliness banned.[119]

He sent the first of his many letters to Leonard Darwin on 26 March 1922, saying he was born of unsound parents and had inherited their weaknesses. He contradicted himself by commenting that he had never married 'although better fitted to do so probably than fully one-half of those who do' which raises questions about his 'unsoundness'.[120] Twitchin may have feared that he would die from the disease that killed his sisters. Twitchin's questionable self-diagnosis was accepted by his beneficiaries who portrayed him as a flawed personality and a 'queer being', an assessment which subsequent researchers accepted.[121] In his next letter, in 5 September, he told Darwin that one of his inherited handicaps was a difficulty in explaining himself in writing and speech, particularly when he was worried. Ironically, a reviewer said of Leonard Darwin's own writing that it 'lacked literary facility' and showed 'heaviness of touch', flaws which did not seem to have troubled him. The self-doubting Twitchin, on the other hand, was a thoughtful man who posed questions which Darwin had to get his colleagues' help to answer. For example, Twitchin asked if the acquired inheritance theory was discounted, how could you explain an untrained sheep-dog pup's ability to round up chickens. He also wondered which eugenic methods Plato proposed.[122]

The obituaries, and the publicity resulting from his 1930 bequest, emphasised Twitchin's nervous delicacy and his hereditary defects and one writer made the extraordinary claim that Twitchin had made the donations anonymously to avoid 'winning any notoriety for himself'.[123] Leonard Darwin, an octogenarian ex-army man with no empathy for

Twitchin, made these snide comments in *Nature*, the *Times* and the *Eugenics Review*. In a tasteless eulogy to the Society's 'most generous benefactor', Darwin made the contradictory claims that Twitchin suffered 'constantly' from 'periods' of depression, and his private conversations were totally disparaging. Snobbery about dealing with a wealthy man who had made a fortune in the colonial outback was a factor – reviewers found the social smugness in Darwin's books was appalling. Darwin's behaviour was boorish and unprincipled in the way he managed Twitchin to ensure the donations would continue 'with certainty'.[124] Even more disturbing is Darwin's disclosure that Twitchin signed a codicil on the day of his death, leaving the Society his French properties.

While Twitchin was alive, Leonard Darwin and Sir Ernest Allen – the joint executors of the will – sent effusive and obsequious letters to their backer. Sometimes Darwin used other strategies to help safeguard the legacy. For example, Twitchin told Darwin that as an experienced livestock breeder he knew 'the utter madness of going on breeding up when the Ranch is fully stocked and there is no, or insufficient, outlet for the surplus'. Darwin paraphrased this statement about over-breeding in *What is Eugenics?* (distributed at Twitchin's expense), commenting that managers of large stock farms in the Dominions had learnt this. However, the negative assessments were accepted by Lord Horder who repeated these comments about Twitchin's hereditary tendencies to unsound health in a public lecture on eugenics he gave in Melbourne which was reported in the *Medical Journal of Australia* in October 1935. Perhaps in an attempt to flatter his Melbourne audience and justify why Britain rather than Australia benefited from Twitchin's legacy, Horder said:

> It was not in the older countries so much as in the new, where deep-rooted prejudice was not so strong, that [Twitchin] placed his hopes for the success in eugenic propaganda; at the same time he realised that it was in the older countries that eugenic reform was most needed.

Recently, a medical researcher thought Twitchin's name might indicate a familial link with Huntington's disease.[125] This was not evident in the sisters (who died from TB) and his parents died in extreme old age, although people with this disease rarely survive for so long. As the name 'Twitchin' relates to location, not behaviour, this disease hypothesis is as unlikely as the mentally unstable image of him which the Eugenics Society created. After his retirement at 57, Twitchin lived on the French Riviera in the coincidentally named Villa Eugène until, at the age of 63, he died unexpectedly after an appendix operation. Twitchin's death was reported on the front page of the *West Australian* on 29 March 1930:

> Twitchin, on March 19, at Villa Eugène, Fabron, Nice (France), after operation, Henry Twitchin, late of Kennett House, Newbury, England and Towera and Lyndon Stations, Yanarie, Ashburton, [north-western coast of Western Australia], aged 63 years.

Twitchin's achievements cast further doubt on the Society's claims that he suffered from depression and mentally instability. On 19 May 1923 Twitchin wrote from Perth, where he was having medical treatment for pneumonia, asking Allen to come out after all, all expenses paid, if he was still free to do so. On 2 December 1923 he informed Ernest Allen about changes in his fortunes affecting the bequest to the Society. Twitchin explained that he had been very sick when he left his property for medical treatment in Perth and had had to leave his papers behind. Because of his illness, and because of the volatility of the property market, he could not remember what he had previously written and his recollection of recent events was also very hazy. He suggested meeting in Perth where he was staying during the summer and emphasised the need for confidentiality about his bequest, adding 'it will be time enough when a majority in the world can see the truth and importance of its teaching – and I trust that you will take every precaution to keep it secret'. Allen had been chosen for the negotiations because of his engaging manner, perseverance and foresight.[126] However, Allen reneged on his 1923 offer to visit Twitchin and asked for Darwin to help him deal with this 'nervously unstable' man.[127] This manipulative twisting of Twitchin's words is Allen's justification to withdraw:

> He writes of his strength giving way, so much so that he could not write. He is 'very sick'; his recollection is very hazy, even of *recent* happenings!! His affairs have undergone so many changes that he

hardly knows what he has written. He is very suspicious of everyone – a hampering secrecy is all important. He wants me to start not later than the middle of January 1924!! I got his letter on the 31st of December 1923.

Darwin replied on 19 January: 'In the first place I do not see such marked signs of mental instability in Mr Twitchin as you do'. Twitchin was almost 20 years younger than Darwin and the other Society members he contacted and, apart from their similarly conservative viewpoints, eugenics was probably their only shared interest.[128] In his will, Twitchin described Allen and Darwin as 'friends', yet their behaviour towards him appears cold and mercenary. The woman who supplied Darwin with biographical details noted her scepticism about his claims that Twitchin had inherited bad health. She concluded:

> At last, when he sold his estates the money paid represented the largest turn-over ever known in the Australian colonies. But his success was built up at the expense of his health. I think he was perfectly sound and healthy when he first went to Australia … but the long years and the hard life of the tropics wore him out.[129]

She may have been the person who pressed for positive aspects of Twitchin's family history to be published in the *Eugenics Review*.[130] This was done and a pedigree written by a Fellow of the Royal Historical Society who traced Henry's probable descent from a schoolmaster who attained some note in the sixteenth century, via generations of sound stock who blossomed unseen until Henry's appearance as 'a man of note' in the twentieth century. As enthusiasm for eugenics was ebbing in the 1930s, it probably suited the Eugenics Society to accept Twitchin's self-assessed 'unsoundness' and to add embellishments of their own about his mental instability. They may have felt that the messianic appeal of a selfless but doomed colonial hermit sacrificing himself to save humanity would provide dramatic publicity and rally support to their cause. The Berkshire friend was understandably sceptical about the picture promoted by the Society. However, Twitchin did have some alarmingly undemocratic views. For instance, on 13 May 1924 Darwin informed Sir Ernest Allen that Twitchin found the Society too academic. As most people were not ready for 'such a revolutionary change' as he envisaged, Twitchin suggested a

Machiavellian scheme: the EES should 'educate the masses to see the inestimable advantage of adopting the principle and gradually enforce control'.

While three Western Australian research institutions held very little information about Twitchin,[131] two other sources did: Alison Drake-Brockman's appeal to Twitchin's Executors, indicating that he had 'expressed his intention of providing for her and her children' and had been paying her '£50 every three months'. She said Twitchin was 'very fond of [her] and her late husband who was his oldest friend in Australia' and that the men had been school friends in Britain. She claimed that the 'whole' of her husband's and her money 'went towards Towera and Lyndon Stations'. The Public Trustee employee 'never quite understood' how *Alison* Drake-Brockman 'came into the matter' as Twitchin's two stations were bought by a syndicate of four including *Alice* Gertrude Drake-Brockman and her husband, Alfred Howden Drake-Brockman. The Public Trustee noted that 'it may be that Mrs [Alison] Drake-Brockman had claims of more than a superficial nature against Mr Twitchin' but suggested that the Executors had no power to provide her with an allowance unless it had been stipulated in Twitchin's will.[132] Secondly Sally Morgan, in her best-seller *My Place,* recorded a conversation with Alice Drake-Brockman who confirmed that Howden had bought Towera. *My Place* reveals his relationships 'of more than a superficial nature' with Sally's destitute Aboriginal grandmother and mother who had never revealed their 'white family secrets'. They received no assistance from this pastoralist progenitor in life or death.

The four eugenists in this chapter were important as individuals and because they represented four distinctive eugenic styles. Personal experiences influenced Twitchin (his 'inherited bad health') and Goodisson (her syphilitic husband). Australian-born Eldridge and Piddington and Welsh-born Goodisson attempted to further the cause of eugenics in Australia. English-born Twitchin (a 'career' eugenist) gave his money to further eugenics in Britain and had the longest-lasting commitment to eugenics, although he told few people about it.

Eldridge, Piddington and Goodisson were middle-aged or older before they embarked on their very public campaigns of eugenic education. However, while neither of the women faltered in their commitment, Eldridge's loyalty only lasted ten years. Eldridge (a 'weak' eugenist) embraced eugenics while it helped his political career, but the women's aims were humanitarian and their political activities were aimed at furthering their eugenics-related causes. Piddington (a 'strong' eugenist) believed that human history could be explained in terms of eugenics and she crusaded energetically for a eugenic utopia. Goodisson (a 'medical' eugenist) made pragmatic use of both eugenics and politics to further her public health goals. Eldridge and Piddington were affiliated with the Labor Party, but while he favoured an environmental approach, she espoused hereditarian eugenics. Goodisson and Twitchin were politically conservative, but while she focused on women's health, he focused on the eradication of the unfit. These brief biographies reveal the confusingly complex appeal of eugenics which could attract such a heterogeneous group of followers. The style of Australian eugenics reflects the fact that its members were drawn almost exclusively from those in Searle's 'medical' and 'career' groups. Having established the different kinds and levels of commitment to eugenics in Australia, the following chapter considers the dynamics in which these diverse groups interacted in the development of eugenics in various states and in three international eugenics congresses.

---

[1]Geoffrey Russell Searle, 'Eugenics and class' in Charles Webster (ed.), *Biology, Medicine and Society 1840-1940* (Cambridge: CUP, 1981), 239-40. The quote about Humpty Dumpty's meaning of words comes from Lewis Carroll's *Through the Looking-Glass and What Alice Found There* [first published in 1871], (New York, Peter Pauper Press, 1941), 123.

[2]Portrait of Marion Piddington in her 60s, *Smith's Weekly* (16 January 1932), 16.

[3]Michael Roe, *Nine Australian Progressives: Vitalism in Bourgeois Social Thought, 1890-1960*, (St Lucia: UQP, 1984), 214, 232.

[4]Ann Curthoys, 'Eugenics, feminism and birth control: The case of Marion Piddington', *Hecate*, vol 15 (1989), 73.

[5]M P, *The Unmarried Mother and Her Child* (Sydney: Moore's Bookshop, 1923), 14-15.

[6]Jan Roberts said in *Maybanke Anderson: Sex, Suffrage and Social Reform* (Sydney: Hale & Iremonger, 1993), 132, 128-29, 170, 178, that Maybanke Anderson (1845-1927) had adopted the name 'Lois' in 1901 which Piddington used 'coincidentally' in 1916.

[7]*Sex Talks*, by Dr Wykeham Terriss, (Sydney: Vanguard Publications, 1946), page 241. The mistake is understandable as *Vita Nuova* translates as 'new life'.

[8]Roe (1984), footnote 43, page 242, was to 'Letter of 16 February 1917 (and others of period more generally), O'Reilly papers'. There are no references to Edgeworth David or Mary Booth.

[9]British Library, Department of Manuscripts, Additional Papers 58572. Stopes Papers. Piddington-Stopes correspondence 1919-1940. The first letter was Marion Piddington to Marie Stopes, 24 October 1919, folio 3. Subsequently cited with folio numbers and the women's initials, MP and MS. This correspondence in Stopes' papers provides valuable insights to Piddington's private thoughts which would have been lost otherwise, because these letters are not included in her papers which are held in Australian archives.

[10]M P, 'Breffny', Glenbrook NSW to M S, 10 March 1919, 3.

[11]M P to M S (10 March 1919), 6.

[12] Dowell O'Reilly Papers, MSS 231, vol 3, 28 July 1916, 339.

[13]'"Pure" parentage and "scientific" motherhood…', *Truth*, 23 June 1918, 10.

[14] M P to Mr (sic) Stone, 28 June 1918, 6.

[15]This letter was sent to gynaecologist and medical historian Dr Frank Forster by the hospital's Clinical Superintendent, Dr Susan Fleming. Forster thanked her on 23 April 1981 for the letter with its mine of information said he could not find 'Mr' Westone in the Canberra telephone book. Frank Forster Collection, The Library, Royal Australian College of Gynaecologists, Melbourne.

[16]M P to Mr Stone, 28 June 1918, 1. 'He' was probably Grace Clara Stone (1860-1957) a doctor at Melbourne's Queen Victoria Hospital, operated by women for women. In 1891 Grace was one of the first women to graduate in medicine in Australia. Her sister Constance studied overseas and in 1890 was the first woman to be registered as a doctor in Australia.

[17]M P to Dr Meyer, 31 Aug [1919], 4-5. M P told M S on 16 September 1919, 8, that 'Professor Berry' and 'many gynaecologists' were earnestly considering the scheme. The five women Piddington mentioned were: **Katherine Dwyer** (1863-1949), who in 1916 was the first woman appointed to the Senate of the University of Sydney; in 1907 the *Cyclopedia of New South Wales* described **Annie Golding** (1855-1934), as a pioneer suffragist, educationist and social reformer who assisted in forming the Teachers' Association and **Belle Golding** (1864-1940) as one of the 'foremost advocates' for the emancipation of women. Scottish-born **Louisa Macdonald** (1858-1949) arrived in Sydney in 1892 after being appointed Principal of the University of Sydney's Women's College (the first women's college in the British

Empire to be fully affiliated with a university), and **Lady Helen Munro Ferguson** (1861-1941) was the 'able and imperious' wife of the Governor-General, Sir Ronald Munro Ferguson.

[18]'Something new', *Figaro*, 30 August 1919, 8. Further items about Piddington appeared on 6, 13, 20, 27 September, 18 October and 8 November 1919.

[19]'Mater no 4', *Figaro*, 8 November 1919, 7.

[20] M S to M P, 9 July 1919, 1, ML.

[21]*ER*, 12 (1920-21), 475.

[22]Freud to M P, 19 June 1921, in Marion Piddington Papers. MS 1158 (Canberra: NLA).

[23]McQueen, 'Freud: Letter to our subcontinent', *Bowyang*, no 4 (September-October 1980), 142.

[24]M S to M P, 19 May 1926, ff. 63-64.

[25]M P to C D, 22 August 1929, 6-7.

[26]M P to C D, 19 September 1929, 2.

[27]Piddington, 'The frustration of the maternal instinct and the new psychology', *AJPP*, 15 (September 1937).

[28]M P to M S, 14 September 1937, f.125.

[29]M P to M S, 11 June 1940, f.126.

[30]WEA Minute Book, vol 1 (Sydney: Trades Hall, 21 July 1916), 92.

[31]Greville, 'The Women's Organising Committee', *AH* (1 October 1921), 6. Ingamells was the hospital's Chief Dispenser in 1921 and he became the first NSW President of the Pharmacy Guild.

[32]Jill Roe, *Beyond Belief: Theosophy in Australia* (Kensington: UNSWP, 1986), 263 & 271. David Stewart, *AH* (1 December 1921), 3-4, noted Eldridge's 5 and 17 November 1921 eugenics lectures. Ingamells was the hospital's Chief Dispenser in 1921 and he became the first NSW President of the Pharmacy Guild.

[33]'Breffny', (the name of the Piddingtons' holiday house), 'Eugenics', *AH* (1 Dec 1921), 11-12.

[34]'The Eugenics Circle is continuing its meetings and the dates for February are the 4th and the 18th, with Mr J C Eldridge as leader', *AH* (1 February 1922), 6.

[35]Marion Piddington, *Tell Them! Or the Second Stage of Mothercraft* (Sydney: Moore's Book Shop, 1926), 17. It was dedicated to the feminist Dr Lilian Helen Alexander who in 1887 had persuaded Melbourne University to admit female medical students.

[36]*AH* (10 September 1928), 226.

[37] Roe (1984), 232

[38] Piddington (1926), 156.

[39] Joseph Pugliese, 'Language and minorities', in Shirley Fitzgerald and Garry Wotherspoon, (eds.), *Minorities: Cultural Diversity in Sydney* (Sydney; State Library of NSW Press and the Sydney History Group, 1995), 208.

[40] 'Parental metaphylaxis', *HPC* (September 1930), 10, 44 and 46-47.

[41] M P to M S, 1 June 1926, f.65. The BMA was 'a mighty curse' which prevented Women's Hospital doctors from giving contraception to diseased mothers or ones 'overburdened with children'.

[42] Rich, 12 Dec 1976, Hazel De Berg (Canberra: Oral History Unit, NLA), tape 955 and 994.

[43] Women's League of NSW Annual Report, June 1926, 11.

[44] Ibid, these 23 June 1926 minutes were signed by Ruby Rich on 11 October 1926.

[45] M P to M S, 20 February 1928, f.80.

[46] M P to M S, 22 June 1928, f.88.

[47] *Herself*, April 1929, cover.

[48] *Herself*, September 1929, 16.

[49] Ibid and M P to M S, 24 August 1924, f.55.

[50] AA. AWM No: 38, Item 3DRL 6673/689, 'Circular letter to the Board of Management and a copy of a memorandum for the Department of Home Affairs relating to a request by Marion Piddington for the Australian War Memorial in Sydney to be used as a shelter for unemployed men in winter'.

[51] M P to C D, 22 August 1929, 5.

[52] M P to M S, 20 February 1930, f.105.

[53] M P to M S, 11 March 1930, f.107.

[54] Mary MacPherson, from the Education Department's School History Unit, consulted their archives which did not have information about this, Pers comm., 4 July 1995. After World War I, the WEA held classes in the Education Department's building and it was also used by the Race Improvement Society in 1926. See also Jane Tabberer, *The Times of Henrietta* (Sydney: Union of Australian Women, 1970), 198, and article, 'The Society [which became the RHA] will meet at the Assembly Hall, Education Department, on Wednesday at 8pm', *SMH*, 19 June 1926, 10 (e).

[55] MP to M S, 12 August 1931, ibid.

[56] Drusilla Modjeski, *Exiles at Home: Australian Women Writers, 1925-1945* (Sydney: Sirius Books, an imprint of A & R, 1981), 102-03.

[57] Jean Devanny, 'Eugenic reform and the unfit', *Stead's Review* (1 May 1930), 22.

[58] 'Made sterile by surgeon at his own wish. Sydney man's act staggers social opinion', *Smith's Weekly*, 10 October 1931, 1, 13.

[59]'Sterilised man tells reason why. Inherited taint was his lifelong nightmare. Brave wife joins hands with stricken husband', *Smith's Weekly*, 17 October 1931, in RHC papers.

[60]*Smith's Weekly*, 10 October 1931, 13. Dingle's employment was listed in *AJPP*, vol 7 (1927), 227-33, as the 'Psychological Laboratory, University of Sydney'.

[61]*World*, 14 January 1932 and 7 July 1932.

[62]Mulvaney, in MacLeod and Jarrell (1994), 178-182.

[63]Dr Edith How-Martyn, London to Miss F Rose, National Committee on Federal Legislation for Birth Control, New York, 30 May 1933, Sanger Papers, vol 22.

[64]How-Martyn (1933).

[65]M P to W E Agar, 27 September 1937.

[66]Lord Horder, the ES President from 1935 to 1948, was a moderate eugenist who did not advocate sterilization in 1937, a time when Nazi excesses were becoming known.

[67]The *NSW Public Service Lists* record Eldridge's career from 1890 (aged 17) until 1928 (aged 56).

[68]'J C Eldridge, Labor MHR for Martin (NSW)', *Bulletin* (10 June 1931), 13 (a).

[69]'Membership application', Eldridge to EES, 17 December 1912, EES Archives (London), SA/EUG, E2, 'Eugenics Education Society in NSW'. Subsequently cited as Eldridge to EES. Records at the London School of Economics mention a 'Certificate in Economics' from the University of Sydney, but he did not graduate. He received paid leave from the Australian Imperial Force Educational Section to attend the London School of Economics from May until December 1919. His war dossier states that in May 1920 London University awarded him a Certificate in Social Science and Administration.

[70]*ER*, (July 1912), 107-14.

[71]Caleb William Saleeby was listed in *Popular Science* credits as one of the contributing staff, but on page 5145 he was acknowledged as the author of the work's eugenics section.

[72]J C Eldridge, 'Eugenics', *Telegraph* (5 March 1914), 4 (e).

[73]J C Eldridge, *The Housing Problem* (Sydney: Worker Trade Union Print, 1915), 3. See also Eldridge's endorsement, in the 9 May 1916 issue of *Navvy*, of Irvine's 'illuminating' 1914 publication, *The Place of the Social Sciences in a Modern University*.

[74]Joint Hon Sec to Eldridge, 3 February 1922. The EES replied 'I think we as a Society mean by the term "poverty" or "lower class" to refer to those who are of so inferior a stock that they are non-self-supporting. ... our Society exists for two purposes; (1) for research work (2) to focus interest and inquiry into fields of knowledge in as much as they affect the science of heredity'.

[75]John Joseph Gregory McGirr (1879-1949) was a pharmacist, land-dealer and father of nine. He left the Labor Party to establish the Young Australia Party but lost his seat in 1925 and then made a fortune from country hotels.

[76]Eldridge to EES, 14 November 1921, 3, and 16 November postscript. NSWPP, Second Series, 84 (Session 1921), 1713.

[77]Roe (1984), 170-71, noted Arthur's proposal on 12 December 1916 was 'probably his most important speech to Parliament' and that child endowment remained his primary goal until 1927.

[78]Eldridge to EES, 18 November 1921.

[79]'E.I.C', 'Endowment of Motherhood', *ER*, 14 (1922-1923), 134, reviewing Eldridge, 'Motherhood Endowment in Australia', *ER*, 14 (1922-1923), 54-58.

[80]On 17 November 1923 Leonard Darwin urged Commonwealth representatives to promote 'race propagation' studies, SA/EUG, D.166, Premiers: India and Colonies 1923-27.

[81] Sec, Eugenics Society, London to Joshua O'Brien, Brisbane, 25 February 1924, SA/EUG, C 255.

[82]Eldridge stood for the Senate in 1925, and in 1931 unsuccessfully contested the seat of Barton (in Kogarah, a suburb in Sydney's south). Martin (which he held from 1929-1931) covered many of the city's northern suburbs, mainly in the Ryde and Ku-ring-gai municipalities.

[83]C M H Manning Clark, *A History of Australia, vol VI, 1916-1935* (Melbourne: MUP, 1987), 332 quoting CPD, 122, 20 November 1929, 6-8. Also *SMH*, 18 November 1929, 12.

[84]'"Harlots of Mammon" says Eldridge', *Labor Daily*, 30 May 1931, 1; also *SMH*, 30 May 1931, 13 (e); J T Lang, 'Three words blasted a politician's career', *Truth*, 6 April 1958, 37 (a).

[85]Eldridge to Akiyama, Consul-General for Japan, 18 Feb 1941, AA (NSW), Series C443, Item J 19.

[86]Ibid, Akiyama to Eldridge (undated, March 1941?).

[87]This picture of Goodisson was presented to the RHA after her death at 89 in 1949.

[88]Marion Piddington was the other person listed by the *ADB* as a 'eugenicist'.

[89]Goodisson's son, Brooke Price Evans, lived in Perth and her daughter, Evelyn P Evans, lived in Sydney where she was secretary of the Australian Trained Nurses' Association from 1917 to 1946 and the Australian Nursing Federation 1924 to 1951. See Mary Dickenson, *An Unsentimental Union: The NSW Nurses Association 1931-1992* (Sydney: Hale and Iremonger, 1993), 37

[90]*The Liberal Woman*, no 78 (1 March 1912), 85. Representing the WA branch of the League, Lillie stressed the need for 'careful selection, proper training and strict medical examination' of immigrants. Goodisson may have combined the trip with

a visit to her mother. The RHA Annual Report (1931), 4, noted she spent six months in Hobart in 1930 because of her mother's illness.

[91]RHA Annual Report (1938-39). The RHA's dreams of expansion are suggested by their use of a map of Australia. Goodisson wrote in her 23 March 1936 letter to Captain Bracegirdle, Military and Official Secretary, Government House, Canberra: 'At present the Association only exists in this State and in Queensland. Our Adelaide branch will be revived shortly, and we are making arrangements to form an Australian Association'. AA (ACT) A2880/2, Item 20/6/24, 'Associations, Societies – Patronage. Racial Hygiene Association of NSW, 1936'.

[92] Dr Lotte A Fink, in *Third International Planned Parenthood Conference Proceedings*, Bombay, November 1952 (Bombay: FPA of India, 1953), 207.

[93] Ruby Rich (1976), tape 13, 359 and 369. The Birth Control clinic did not start until 1933.

[94]Reverend W Stewart, RHA Annual Meeting, 18 July 1932, 3.

[95]RHA Annual Report (1934), 9.

[96]Jill Roe (1986), 53.

[97]RHA Annual Report (1933), 7.

[98]2GB began in 1926 and the call-sign was the initials of the freethinker Giordana Bruno, a 16th century martyr who, theosophists thought, was a previous incarnation of their leader, Annie Besant. Alfred Edward Bennett (1889-1953) was the station's manager from 1926-1936.

[99]'Racial Hygiene Centre', *SMH*, 21 February 1928, 6 (d).

[100]RHA Annual Report (1928-29).

[101]RHA Annual Report (1928-29). Di Tibbits reproduced a slightly different version of this poster, as illustration 29 in her 1994 Monash University PhD thesis, *The Medical, Social and Political Response to Venereal Diseases in Victoria, 1860-1990*. The illustration was included in exhibit material listed in the *Catalogue of Social Hygiene Books, Slides, Exhibits, Accessories and Other Approved Educational Material*, issued by the American Social Hygiene Association Inc, circa 1922. The RHA used a wide range of overseas materials in this manner.

[102]'Salacious Publications, Postcards etc', RHA Annual Report (1929).

[103]'Book censorship. Results of police activity', *SMH*, 16 October 1930, 12 (f).

[104]Haire (1942), 28.

[105]John Norton, the founder of the scandal-rag *Truth*, claims to have coined the term wowser, meaning killjoy, an insult which was first used as a headline 1899. It's origins are disputed with some saying it is an acronym for 'We Only Want Social Evils Remedied'

[106]George W R Southern, *Making Morality Modern* [Mosman, NSW: Southern 1934].

[107]In 1933 Storer was censured by the BMA in Melbourne for advertising a 'premarital health laboratory, privately endowed clinic for venereal research (no

fee)'. In 1935 he was struck off the Medical Register in Britain and Australia for advertising for his London clinic, the Cavendish Institute of Pathology. Melbourne's *Truth* linked his name with boys and in July 1938 Storey won a farthing's damages from *Smith's Weekly* for libel. He was arrested that September (in a car with a 15 year old boy) and sentenced to 12 months gaol. His application for medical re-registration was refused in April 1939 on the grounds that he was not of good character.

[108]Peter Coleman, *Obscenity, Blasphemy, Sedition: Censorship in Australia* (Brisbane: Jacaranda Press [1963], 81-82.

[109]Rich (1976), tape 13, 368.

[110]RHA Annual Report (1932), 4.

[111]Ruzicka and Caldwell, *The End of Demographic Transition in Australia* (Australian Family Formation Project Monograph no 5), Canberra, Department of Demography, Institute of Advanced Studies, Australian National University, 1977), 31.

[112]'The Racial Hygiene Association. Australia's want of population', *Progressive Journal* (10 April 1936), 7.

[113]Twitchin's correspondence is in the Wellcome Institute for the History of Medicine, Eugenics Society Archives: SA/EUG, C87, '[Twitchin's] 1922-1930 correspondence with the Eugenics Society'; C343, 'H Twitchen (sic) correspondence (1922-1930)'; H and I. Copies of files C343 and H are in the Mitchell Library, M2565.

[114]H1, 1-3

[115]State Archives of WA, Acc 255, File 500/1900.

[116]H T to Allen, 2 December 1923, C87.

[117] 'A squatter's will', *ER*, 12 (1920-1921), 428.

[118]Twitchin said his properties were valued at £160,000 in 1922. The bequest estimates varied: 'about £100,000 net', *Times*, 5 April 1930, 16 (c); '£70,000 to £80,000', *ER*, 22 (July 1930), 87 and 'about £57,000', *ER*, 60 (1968), 149.

[119]H T to L D, 4 April 1922.

[120]H T to L D, 26 March 1922.

[121]Daniel J Kevles, *In the Name of Eugenics* … (NY: Knopf, 1985), 172 and Richard A Soloway, *Demography and Degeneration: Eugenics and the Declining Birthrate in Twentieth-century Britain* (Chapel Hill, NC: University of North Carolina Press, 1990), 163, 195, 218.

[122]H T to L D, 26 August and 14 Dec 1927. LD to HT, 13 September 1927 and 6 January 1928.

[123]1930 obituaries in *Times*, 5 April, 16; *Nature*, 19 April, 610 and *SMH*, 2 May, 12.

[124] Sec, EES to Allen, 13 May 1924, C343; Allen to Sec, 26 June 1926, C343

[125]I provided material about Twitchin to Associate Professor Garth Nicholson from the Molecular Medicine Laboratory, Concord Hospital, including the information that the name Twitchin comes from the old English word for 'road-fork' or 'cross-roads'. Nicholson presented a paper, 'Henry Twitchin: An Australian contribution to the eugenics movement', at the Australian Society of the History of Medicine Conference, 2-9 July 1995.

[126]Sir Charles Stewart to L D, 2 January 1923.

[127]Sir Ernest Allen (knighted after retirement from the Public Trustee Office) gave health and financial reasons for wishing to end the negotiations, Allen to L D, 18 January 1924.

[128]Twitchin's conservative views are indicated by such examples as his distaste in having to pay £28,000 tax on the sale of his properties 'to support the Australian parasitic majority', 20 December 1926, and by his remark about 'socialist governments in Australia', 26 August 1927.

[129]Pedigree and Family, H1, 3, 5.

[130]W T J Gun, (from material supplied by Leonard Jessop Fulton), 'Henry Twitchin: Some notes on his family history', *Eugenics Review*, vol 23 (April 1931-January 1932), 117-118.

[131]Archivists at the University of WA could not find information about Twitchin and the J S Battye Library of WA History supplied his death notice. An archivist at the State Archives of WA told me on 2 September 1992 that 'our research confirms [the Battye Library's] conclusion that there is little documentary evidence available on Twitchin's life in this State'.

[132] H6. Correspondence re Estate Claims of Mrs Drake-Brockman. Extracts from letters from the Public Trustee to Major Darwin, 29 July 1930 – 1 August 1930.

3. Organised Eugenics

This chapter examines seven attempts to establish eugenics groups and Australian involvement in the three International Eugenics Congresses. While the first such congress in 1912 was hailed as an important scientific event, the third one in 1932 was greeted with scepticism. There was a similar switch in Australia: a high-level delegation attended the first congress but officials declined the invitation in 1932.

The Language of Eugenics

The words used by British, American and Australian eugenists were similar to the strident language of their predecessors, the degeneracy theorists. There are numerous examples but the *Australasian Medical Gazette* report of an October 1913 speech by the Bishop of Riverina is typical. He warned a Brisbane audience about the 'dark blot of race suicide', calling it a 'plague-like evil which infected most Christian nations'. As a result, he said, 'the West was undermining her strength by luxury, lack of seriousness and infidelity, while the East, by self-denial, alertness, adaptation and numbers, was prospering and becoming conscious of her strength'.

Proposals for environmental or 'nurtural' eugenics were made for the collective good, couched in abstract and uplifting terms such as those used by Sir John Macpherson (1858-1942), who, on his retirement in 1921, left Scotland to become the founding Professor of Psychiatry at the University of Sydney. He gave this enthusiastic endorsement in 1924:

> Eugenic principles are carried out in many ways and embrace all those legislative and municipal measures which aim at good housing and drainage, better conditions of labour, pure food regulations, general hygiene, the abolition of dangerous drug habits, and increased facilities for early and efficient medical and surgical treatment to those in need of them.

In contrast, proposals for negative eugenics were usually subjective, derogatory and restrictive, with the intention of controlling individuals. Those targeted were people affected by 'racial poisons', particularly prostitutes, consumptives, epileptics, the mentally ill and those with inherited conditions. Eugenists judged what was good and bad, desirable and undesirable, fit and unfit. Having done this, they wanted people of 'good stock' (the fit) to have large families and hoped to make people of 'bad stock' (the unfit) have few children or none. Eugenics created its own code words but the jargon still exists, such as this 1995 gem: 'Eugenics is a discourse of surveillance designed to patrol the reproductive capacities of women's bodies'.[1]

In 1914 the ANZAC Commander General Birdwood warned troops training in Egypt about the dangers of alcohol, prostitutes and VD, urging them to abstain 'in the interest of our children and children's children' and keep Australia 'clean and white'. Three years later, Professor David Welsh said it was criminally negligent to allow immigrants with 'strains of criminality and feeble-mindedness to be grafted onto our imperial stock'.[2] The theme of moral purity continued in the 1920s when audiences were often asked if they wanted a White Australia: not merely white in skin, but white at heart – a really good, clean Australia? Good, clean and pure were synonyms for white, with its unfailingly positive image, while black images were always negative. As Susan Sontag (in *Illness as Metaphor*) puts it, words describing diseases often indicate disapproval, horror or revulsion. Blood is the old metaphor for heredity and a person with bad blood, contaminated by germs or genes, was himself contaminating. Alcohol was the black terror, venereal disease was called the pox, the great pox, a social disease, the social evil, the scourge or the terrible peril. It was also called the red plague to distinguish it from the black (bubonic) plague, the white plague (TB) and the yellow plague (smallpox). Words for racial poisons were frightening and negative, while reformers delicately tried to avoid them by the use of neutral terms. For instance, anti-VD workers said they were engaged in social hygiene.

Eugenic arguments often recycled a limited range of ideas and some, such as Arthur Hayes' 1915 tract against degeneracy, were incoherent.[3] They could also be moralistic and melodramatic as in the 1920s description of heredity and alcohol as having the 'unenviable distinction of being the princes of blight producers'.[4]   Frequently eugenists and other social reformers used alarmist language and quoted (or misquoted) experts in their efforts to convince.   William Little asked rhetorically:

> Does it not matter that King Alcohol's besotted army dares invade your home, and by its tainted breath curse future generations? ... battalions of spectral silent generations, with inherited taints, unfairly penalise the innocent, and force them to erect asylums, jails and homes for the poor and sick, as well as to maintain their fleets and armies, and custodians of life and property.

Little's allegory, *A Visit to Topos, and How the Science of Heredity is Practised There*, published in the gold-rich Victorian city of Ballarat in 1897, claimed to contain proofs that maternal impressions would harm unborn children and the assertion that Darwin considered that 'forms of disorder, malformation, and even maiming are transmissible'.[5] These campaigners' florid use of melodrama and pathos reminds a modern reader of Oscar Wilde's quip about needing to have a heart of stone to read about the death of Little Nell without bursting out laughing.   This nineteenth century genre continued into the twentieth century.   For instance, *Eugenics and Sex Harmony*, written in 1935 by American eugenist Dr Herman Rubin, warned that 'blood always tells' causing 'people of degenerated or deteriorated blood' to produce 'scrub children, defective children, degenerated children'.[6]

Sometimes eugenists gave words a new meaning.   For instance, Australia's National Fitness movement provided wholesome activities such as sport and recreation camps for children.   However, as Arnd Kruger noted in the Spring 1991 issue of *Journal of Sport History*, darker aspects of 'national fitness' occurred in Germany, where 'naturism' (physical culture, nudism, dance, natural healing), at first used to achieve fitness, evolved into theories of Aryan superiority.   In Australia in the 1920s and 1930s fascist ideals were promoted in fringe magazines such as *Better Health and Racial Efficiency Through Diet, Hygiene, Psychology, Physical Culture* and *Health and Physical Culture*, which in 1930 announced a series on world-famous physical culturalists, starting with Mussolini.[7]   For 40 years eugenists used the word betterment: the first editorial in the *Eugenics Review* announced that its noble purpose was for the betterment of the Human Race.[8]   It also had darker connotations with the betterment aim being linked with activities such as sterilizing the unfit or confining Aboriginals to reserves when it was used as a euphemism, just as ethnic cleansing became the code word for genocide in the 1990s Balkan war.

In 1917 Professor David Welsh admonished students in a magazine produced by the University of Sydney Society for Combating Venereal Diseases, warning them to avoid 'nights of sin, because 'it is the wild asses who sow the wild oats'. The same year the Australian Catholic Truth Society published a salutary tract, *Factors in National Decay*, by Rev Eustace Boyland. In it the author presented an unintentionally amusing image of Ancient Rome's downward slide: 'Race suicide broke the arm which had held the world in its grip'. There were numerous examples of this pessimism, such as the 1924 complaint by Professor Berry in a Melbourne newspaper that 'the unfit breed like weeds and are just about as useful'. Warnings about fallen grandeur and gardening images were perennials.[9]   In 1926 the seeds/weeds metaphor was used in an important Nazi film, *Erbkrank* (in English, *Hereditary Defective*). The closing shot shows people planting seeds while an editorial voice-over emphasises the film's message, 'the farmer who prevents the overgrowth of the weed promotes the valuable'.[10]

In 1940 the Secretary of the Eugenics Society of Victoria wrote to the Australian Prime Minister urging his support for 'a better world with better – biologically better – people to live in it'.[11]   He was repeating a phrase which the *Eugenics Review* used in 1937 and 1938.[12] They were no doubt unaware of its ugly origins – the German slogan 'National Socialism is nothing but applied biology', which Fritz Lenz coined in 1931 and was adopted by the Nazis to give their activities scientific respectability.[13]

Figure 16: Only Healthy Seed must be sown[14]

Lenz was the likely propagandist behind the light-hearted political spin which appeared in London's newspapers, informing the world about Germany's new sterilisation law. At that time, as Geoffrey Searle has noted, Australian newspapers mainly published Imperial and world news filtered through Reuter's cable-service and on 25 October 1933 this London cable appeared without comment in the *Sydney Morning Herald*:

> It will apply to sufferers from chronic alcoholism, feeble-mindedness, insanity, epilepsy, St Vitus Dance, blindness, deafness, dumbness and deformity. Dr Lenz, Professor of Eugenics, extolled Herr Hitler as a teetotaller and non-smoker. He said that the banning of drink and tobacco would greatly increase public health and efficiency. Only 10 out of the 100 concentration camps in Germany are now occupied. These will be closed as soon as

circumstances permit. Most of the workmen who were detained for political reasons have already been liberated, although many undisciplined Nazis remain ... Nazis in Vienna are intensifying their propaganda activities. They are even fixing contrivances on the backs of dogs, with sausages fastened in front of their noses, so that every time the animals attempt to seize the sausages they operate a jack-in-the-box, out of which pops a swastika.[15]

Professor Lenz was a member of Germany's Society for Racial Hygiene and a Hitler apologist who skilfully listed serious and feared disabilities to persuade the world that only medically justified sterilisations would be performed. Hitler was presented, not as a teetotalling totalitarian but as a benign reformer, in the hope that people would find his unspecified plans as acceptable as his plans to ban smoking and drinking. Fears about concentration camps and Nazi excesses were calmed with the news that under-filled concentration camps would be closed once order was restored among unruly Nazis, and he concluded with a joke, implying that they resembled fun-loving children so there was no need to worry about their pranks. In reality, by March 1933 some 4,821 communists and Social Democrats were already incarcerated in Dachau, the concentration camp near Munich, which was the first to be opened.[16]

W J Thomas, who had been Secretary of the Australian Association for Fighting Venereal Disease, warned in 1940 of the 'sinister fact that Hitler and his associates have exploited the primitive sex urge as a political weapon'. 'Under the guise of "liberty" they had broken down all moral barriers and deliberately pandered to the primitive in man. In order to stimulate the birthrate at all costs, the Nazis had reduced sexual relations to the level of the stud farm'. He added that women who were 'obeying the Führer' were called 'army mattresses' by Nazi soldiers.[17] Startlingly, Professor Harvey Sutton continued to write approvingly of eugenics in *Lectures on Preventive Medicine*, a book for Australian medical students in 1944:

> The aim is human betterment: first the progressive improvement of inherited worth in its broadest sense – the best seed in the best soil. Second, the guarding against degeneration of the race by greater numbers and proportions of duds – (a) deficient,

disordered or deviated mentally, deformed and disabled, drunkards and dope addicts, (b) degraded morally, (c) degenerate sexually, (d) delinquent, (e) destitute, especially where these are capable of handing on their defect or the tendency of the defect to their children – the worst seed in the worst soil.[18]

Eugenics fascinated some of our leading writers and Professor Edmund Morris Miller (1881-1964) included four of their eugenics-influenced books in his seminal survey, *Australian Literature from its Beginnings to 1935*.[19] These were *The Modern Heloise* (1912), by Alfred Buchanan (1874-1941); *The Wider Outlook* (1925) by Agnes Considine; *Murder by the Law* (1932) by Paul McGuire (1903-1978) and *Prelude to Christopher* (1934) by Eleanor Dark (1901-1985). Eugenics provided a fashionable frill to the book by Buchanan who also worked as a journalist and lawyer. However, while it was more central in Considine's domestic story which included evangelistic discussions about eugenics, it was peripheral for McGuire, who used a eugenics conference at an English resort as background in one of his crime mystery books, *Murder by the Law*. He was a prolific writer, poet and scholar who, after a 1937 visit, praised Franco's 'peaceful, industrious and Catholic Spain', lectured on international politics and became Australia's first Ambassador to Italy. Dark was for 20 years a best-selling author who knew depression and whose aunt was the redoubtable Marion Piddington; vital clues to her 1934 'exploratory novel' in which the central characters agonised about eugenics and hereditary madness.

Curiously, Morris Miller did not mention the interest shown by other writers, such as Jean Devanny[20], William Baylebridge (1883-1942) and Erle Cox (1873-1950). A major part of Noel Macainsh's *Nietzsche in Australia* considered Baylebridge's writing, particularly his *National Notes* which were written from 1909 to 1913.[21] As historian Michael Roe noted, Baylebridge was advancing a thoroughly fascist regime for Australia *before* 1914 and had absorbed Nietzsche's philosophy second-hand, as interpreted by eugenists. New editions of Baylebridge's 'blood and soil' manifesto appeared in 1922 and 1936. Dorothy Green wrote, in the 1984 revision of *A History of Australian Literature,* that Baylebridge's vitalist philosophy showed only superficial resemblance to Nazism and fascism, but warned that 'it would be unwise to underrate the appeal of his rhetoric to irrational minds'. The danger seems exaggerated: boredom or mirth are more likely responses.

Erle Cox, one of Melbourne's best-known journalists, published three novels including one with a eugenic theme, *Out of the Silence*. This science-fiction saga, about a super-woman's plans to make the world perfect, was published in the Melbourne newspaper the *Argus* as a serial in the 1920s, then as a book, and again in the newspaper in the 1930s, followed by editions in America, Britain, Russia and France with unexpurgated versions appearing in 1947 and 1976. The lasting popularity of these books by renowned writers shows the interest in eugenics during the 1920s and 1930s. Dark's novel won the Australian Literature Society's gold medal and received many glowing reviews. The topic was also popular in literary, current issues and women's magazines such as Sydney's *Triad* (1915-27), *New Outlook* (1922-23) and *Progressive Journal* (1935-36) and Melbourne's *Stead's Review* (1892-1931).

Feminists skilfully used the language of eugenics to promote their causes: it gave birth control a respectable cloak so long as women said they only wanted to eliminate the unfit, and it was also a forceful tool in women's fight against 'racial poisons' such as VD, alcoholism and prostitution. Eugenics gave new status to motherhood because it encouraged healthy, genetically-fit women to fill their national and imperial obligations as 'mothers of the race'. Feminists, by adopting eugenic rhetoric to achieve rights for women, knew long before the invention of the 1970s slogan, that 'the personal is political'.

The International Eugenics Congresses

The 1912 Congress in London

The first eugenics Congress marked the spirit of a new era – as Virginia Woolf observed, 'in or about 1910, something changed'. Galton, the revered eugenics elder, had died in 1911. A historic plaque on the London house where he lived for more than 50 years reflects current sensitivities by describing his achievements in this order: 'Explorer, Statistician, Founder of Eugenics'. He was also a versatile anthropologist who introduced the classification and forensic use of fingerprints, he invented the term 'anticyclone' and provided the *Times* with its first weather map in 1874.[22] This first congress occurred when the audience was receptive to the papers being given to promote Galton's last great cause. Eugenics enjoyed great prestige and respectability in 1912. As evidence of its impeccable status, the invitation to attend the congress was sent from 10 Downing Street to Andrew Fisher, the (Labor) Prime Minister of Australia.[23] Fisher asked Lord Denman, the Governor-General, to advise the Secretary of State for the Colonies that the Commonwealth Government would be represented by Sir John Cockburn (1850-1929). Australia's other official representatives were the NSW Government Statistician 'the Hon T A Coghlan (New South Wales), the Hon A A Kirkpatrick (South Australia) and Professor A Stuart (University of Sydney)'.[24]

Cockburn, in a 1905 letter to Francis Galton, said he was deeply interested in eugenics.[25] Anderson Stuart (and probably Coghlan) were sympathetic, but there is no record of the views held by the pioneer Labor politician Andrew Kirkpatrick (1848-1928). The guest list appears to have been politically determined: Sir Newton James Moore, formerly the Liberal Premier of Western Australia, was there but the Premier of Victoria declined to send a representative. The Piddingtons and Edith Onians attended but not as delegates and Onians was the only Australian at the Congress to write a report.[26] Australia's press gave several positive reports[27] and *The Liberal Woman,* a Sydney magazine, praised Sybil Gotto for her unique feat in getting the Congress papers (in English, French, Italian and German) printed *before* the opening meeting. No one took credit for the inadvertently apt title: *Problems in Eugenics.*

The 1921 Congress in New York

Australian newspapers did not mention Thomas Griffith Taylor who was one of the 126 contributors to the exhibition held in conjunction with the Second International Eugenics Congress.[28] However, the press lavished praise on the other Australian exhibitor, whose affiliation was listed as 'Commonwealth Bureau of Census and Statistics'. This was Sir George Knibbs (1858-1929), a genial man with an unchallengeable position in the esteem of the world of science and learning. The *Sydney Morning Herald* announced in the Personal Column on 15 October 1920:

> Mr G H Knibbs, Commonwealth Statistician, has been nominated by the National Research Council of the United States of America as a vice-president of the Second International Eugenics Congress, to be held in New York City, September 21-28, 1921. ... Dr Charles B Davenport ... of the Eugenics Committee, stated that it was [in] appreciation 'of Mr Knibbs' work on demography'. He also stated that the nomination was approved by the Eugenics Education Society of London of which Major Leonard Darwin, son of the late Sir (sic) Charles Darwin, is president.

Knibbs was described as a 'nimble scientist' and a 'versatile mathematician' and praised for 'the excellent *Official Yearbook of the Commonwealth* issued under his direction [which] is the amazement of the world's experts in figures'. His nomination was supported by Davenport who hoped he would accept the appointment and Leonard Darwin urged him to contribute a paper. Knibbs accepted, although he was not sure he could attend because 1921 was Census year. He did not go, although in 1919 he had been on the International Eugenics Committee in London. However, Knibbs' acceptance of the Congress appointment and his role as a Congress exhibitor indicate that the Australian government still found eugenics respectable, as Knibbs acted in his official capacity as Commonwealth Statistician and his appointment was publicly announced.[29] In contrast, overseas reporting about eugenics had become less respectful by this time.

The 1932 Congress in New York

By the time the third Congress was held, the status of eugenics had deteriorated to such an extent that on 28 August 1932 the *New York Times* reported that eugenists had been 'losing ground ever since genes ... were discovered'. The wording of the official invitation to the Congress in New York, and the Australian response, indicate that feelings about eugenics had changed so dramatically that the Australian and American Governments now wished to distance themselves from the Congress. The Australian Archives have a copy of the March 1932 invitation which was sent to the Attorney General and Minister for External Affairs by the American Consul, who noted that 'the Congress is not held under the auspices of the United States and that it has no official connection with the Government of the United States'.[30] The former Labor politician Joseph Lyons, newly elected as the (United Australia Party) conservative Prime Minister of Australia, diplomatically replied 'The Commonwealth Government, while appreciating the kind invitation of the Management of the Congress, regret that they are unable to see their way to arrange for representation'.[31] There are other signs that enthusiasm for eugenics had dwindled: no record exists of Australians at the Congress and it did not receive any Australian publicity, even from the RHA. An ex-RHA member spoke of 'the fallacy of eugenics' and said 'the stupidity of these reformers is grotesque'.[32]

Congress	Place	Numbers of 'officers, committeemen and delegates'	Numbers of 'members'[33]
First 24-30 July 1912	University of London	324	99
Second 22-28 September 1921	American Museum of Natural History	312	401
Third 21-23 August 1932	American Museum of Natural History	73	400

Table 2: Attendances at Eugenics Congresses

Estimates of the individuals and countries attending the three congresses vary widely. For instance, the proceedings of the third congress listed 400 delegates while a delegate who attended said that enrolment was 'less than 1,000' and in 1985 Kevles made an unsourced claim that it 'attracted fewer than a hundred people'.[34] A comparison of the countries who were members of the International Federation of Eugenics Organizations in the 1920s and 1930s shows that considerable changes took place in this period.[35] One explanation is that the counting was imprecise and this seems likely because membership tallies produced by eugenics organizations in Britain and America were quite different. However, in Europe, after the Habsburg Empire disintegrated as a result of World War 1, the redrawing of national boundaries might explain why Hungary was not listed in 1929, but it was in 1932. In the case of Russia, which had been a member of the international eugenics body since 1922 but was not listed in 1932, the reason is unequivocal: after Tromfin Denisovich Lysenko (1898-1976) resurrected the old Lamarckian myth which promised to deliver Stalin a quick solution to the agriculture crisis, the eager acceptance of this ideologically driven pseudo-science meant that genetics was denounced, eminent scientists were arrested and eugenics was officially banned in 1930.

In 1921 Australia *was* eligible for representation at the International Commission of Eugenics[36] but in 1932 Australia *was not* one of the 22 countries represented at the Federation.[37] The insignificance of Australia as a contributor to world eugenics in 1932 was emphasized in the *Eugenic Review's* pre-congress report: 'Eugenics is now alive in India, China, Japan and Java. Africa and Australia are also stirring'.[38]

Robert Cook from Washington, DC provocatively called his 1932 congress paper 'Is eugenics half-baked?' and while he did not think so, many did.[39] It was Cook who had said that less than 1,000 had attended and he added that 'unless eugenics congresses were as well attended as political conventions, eugenists have failed their mission'. Cook's comment was perceptive: the utopian vision for eugenics had failed by 1932.

Establishing Eugenics Organisations in Australia

There were seven eugenics groups which operated, sometimes shakily, in all mainland states except Queensland. **Table 3** summarises these organizations, their members of note and key eugenics activities from 1911 to 1961.

To help place Australian eugenics in context, **Table 4** identifies significant Australian, British, American and world events from the 1850s until the 1940s.

Table 3: Eugenics Organisations in Australian States, 1911-61

Years of operation	State	Organisation	Notable members and activities
1911 to 1916 (but mainly in 1911)	SA	S A Branch of the British Science Guild, Sub-Committee on Eugenics	William A Magarey, Dr Edward Angas Johnson, Dr Robert Marten, Sir Henry Newland, Dr Robert Pulleine, Dr Charles Reissman, Thomas Smeaton and Sir Fred Young. In 1911, the eight Sub-committees each produced a *Race Building* report which was reprinted in Adelaide's *Mail* in 1916
From 11 December 1912 until February 1922	NSW	Eugenics Education Society of NSW	Dr Richard Arthur (Pres), Prof Robert F Irvine (Vice-pres), J C Eldridge (Sec), H A Bell (Treas), R L Baker, Dr Andrew Davidson, C C Faulkner, A W Green, Rev R B S Hammond, Peter McNaught, Prof T P Anderson Stuart, Colin Smith, David Stead, Misses Fraser, Cotton and Von Hagen
Some time between 1913 and 1920	WA	Eugenics Society	Professor William Dakin tried to establish a society in the University of Western Australia, but it 'failed due to lack of public support'
From July 1914. In February 1915 in 'suspended animation'	Vic	Eugenics Education Society of Melbourne	Prof Baldwin Spencer (Pres), Dr W Ernest Jones (Vice-pres), Mr G H Knibbs, Ada Mary à Beckett, S A Burrows, Alfred Deakin, Carlotta Greenshields, W Groom, Alec Hunt, Julia Lavender, A McDonald, Dr Felix Meyer and Dr Harvey Sutton
From 27 April 1926 onwards	NSW	Race Improvement Society of NSW, then Racial Hygiene Association, then the Family Planning Association from 1960	Ruby Rich and Dr Ralph Lyndal Worrall (Presidents), Lillie Goodisson (Sec), Marion Piddington (briefly Treas), Dr Phillip Addison, Dr Richard Arthur, Sir Henry Braddon, Florence Liggins Elkin, Sir Benjamin Fuller, Walter Cresswell O'Reilly, Judge Alfred E Rainbow, Anna Roberts, Victor Roberts, Miss MacCallum.
From July 1933. By 1937 it had 'gone into recess'	WA	Eugenics Society, University of Western Australia	Muriel Marion (Pres), Mr D Stuart (Sec), Mr L Snook (Vice-pres), Mr C Thiel (Treas), Mr G Bourne, Mrs Farleigh, K C B Green and R E Parker, supported by Prof E Nicholls, Dr Everitt Atkinson, Dr H J Gray, Dr Roberta Jull and Dr R G Williams
From 12 October 1936 until 1961	Vic	Eugenics Society of Victoria	Prof Wilfred E Agar (Pres), Dr Victor H Wallace (Sec), Dr Pierre M Bachelard, Angela Booth, Rev William Bottomley, Prof George S Browne, Dr William Bryden, Mrs Janie Butler, Dr Kenneth Cunningham, Dr John Dale, Dr Fritz Duras, Dr Reg Ellery, John Alexander Gunn, Prof Peter MacCallum, Sir Keith Murdoch, Dr Clive Faran Ridge, Sir David Rivett, Sir Sidney Sewell, Dr George Simpson, Dr Georgina Sweet, Mr Frank Tate

Table 4: Events with Significance for Eugenics, 1850s to 1940s

Date	Australia	Great Britain	United States	World
1850s to 1870s	• 1788 to 1868 convict era • 1850s to 1880s gold rushes • Anti-Chinese riots • 1875 Aust Health Society founded	• 1780+ Industrial Revolution • 1859 Darwin's Origin of Species • 1860s Contagious Diseases Acts • 1876 Knowlton birth control trial	• 1869-79 Oneida Community • 1877 Dugdale's 'The Jukes': A Study in Crime, Pauperism, Disease and Heredity	• Theories of de Gobineau 1850s Weismann 1860s • 1877 Degeneracy theories • Births slump in west, rise in Japan
1880s	• Boom 1860 to 1890 • Immigration wave • Free education	• Galton coined the word 'eugenics' • Social Darwinism widely accepted	• Comstock laws aim to suppress vice and contraception	• Works by Ibsen, Zola, Lombroso and Nietzsche were influential
1890s	• Depression • National drought • Decline in births • Invasion fears ('yellow peril')	• 1898+ Havelock Ellis' sex studies • 1899-1902 Boer war	• 1890 to 1915 Progressive era	• Depression • Freud's theories from 1895 • 1899 to 1900 Boxer Rebellion in China
1900s	• 1900 Bubonic plague • 1901 Federation • 1901 to 1960s 'White Australia' • 1904 Royal Commission on the Birth-rate Decline • Pronatalism	• 1900 Mendel's paper rediscovered • 1904 Inter-Dept Royal Commission on the Care and Control of the Feeble-minded • 1907 Eugenics Education Society	• 1903 immigration restrictions • 1907 Indiana sterilisation law • Eugenics Record Office, Cold Spring Harbor, New York • 1912 Goddard's The Kallikak Family	• 1904 Binet's IQ tests • 1904-05 Russo-Japanese war • Ehrlich develops VD treatment • 1907 German Society for Race Hygiene
1910s	• 1912 £5 baby bonus • 1911-14 second immigration wave • 1916 'Scientific Motherhood'	• 1912 First Eugenics Congress • 1913 Mental Deficiency Act • 1918 Stopes' Married Love	• Charles Davenport assembles family pedigrees • 1913 to 1933 Prohibition era • 1917 Margaret Sanger jailed	• Development of town planning • 1910 first birth control conference • World War I • 1917 Russian Revolution

1920s	• 1921 C'wealth Dept of Health established • 1925 Royal Commission on Health	• Lidbetter's 'pauper pedigrees' • 'Big Brother' movement sends adolescents to Australia	• 1920 start of radio broadcasting • 1921 Second Eugenics Congress • 1924 Johnson Act bans 'unfit' migrants	• Switzerland, Denmark, Finland and Alberta, Canada pass sterilisation laws • 1929 to 1933 world Depression
1930s	• Birth-rate at lowest point • 1936 NHMRC established • 1938 blood transfusions	• 1930 Lambeth Conference, Anglican Bishops back birth control • Sterilization Bill defeated	• 28 states with sterilisation laws • 1932 Third Eugenics Congress • Geneticists disown eugenics	• 1930s and 40s Papal encyclicals ban eugenics, birth control • From 1933 Nazi sterilisations
1940s	• 1941 Federal child endowment • National Fitness Councils	• 1946 start of British £10 migration scheme to Australia	• McCarthyism • Cold war • 1948 Kinsey Report	• World War II • 1943 Penicillin used to treat VD

Checking the Bona Fides

In the 1912 and 1938 the British parent eugenics society took a critical interest in the development of its antipodean offspring. In the first instance, the Eugenics Education Society checked Australian credentials after Jack Eldridge announced pompously on 17 December 1912, 'I have pleasure in notifying you that on the 11th instant the Eugenics Education of NSW (Australia) was formed in Sydney, the capital of this, the Mother State of Australia'.[40] He also applied for membership of the Eugenics Education Society of Great Britain. While they accepted him, a member of the Society had added this note on the back of Eldridge's application requesting both letters to be brought to the EES Council: 'Eldridge, Labour Department, Public Service; Arthur, MD about 40, rather an enthusiast. *Public Service List* to be sent'. Written after this was the name 'Dr Ashburton Thomson' (sic).

The Society's informant was the NSW Government's Medical Adviser, an English-educated public health expert, Dr John Ashburton Thompson (1846-1915), who from his 1884 appointment had played a key role in the state's public health service. For example, his work in tracing the source of a typhoid outbreak to a contaminated milk supply resulted in the Dairies Supervision Act (1886); he formulated pure food laws and the Public Health Act (1896), and in 1900 advised the government that fleas from infected rats transmitted bubonic plague to humans, writing reports on observations which were internationally recognised, though not all of the research was his own work.[41] Ashburton Thompson had impressive contacts in Sydney and Britain.[42] This austere humourless man held a prestigious position as NSW's Chief Medical Officer and Permanent Head of the Department of Public Health but his snide comment about Dr Richard Arthur revealed his unflattering view of colonials. He returned to England when he retired in 1913.

In 1937 the parent society did not initially respond to Dr Victor Wallace's 'greetings from a little sister organisation in Australia', sent a year after the Eugenics Society of Victoria was established.[43] However, the British Society undertook another secret and more extensive check in 1938 after Wallace asked for money:

> We are the pioneers in this country and it is probable that the Victorian Society will later become an Australian one, for we have had many enquiries from the capital cities of other states. ... We were interested to learn that Mr Henry Twitchin, who left your Society such a substantial legacy, made his fortune through sheep farming in *Australia*. Would it not be appropriate if a Eugenics Society in Australia were to be assisted by you in its infancy? If your Society in its wisdom, sees fit to assist us in a small way financially, the grant will be 'thankfully received and faithfully administered'.[44]

Dr C P Blacker (1895-1975), the Society's Secretary, suggested to Clifton Chance, a wealthy Manchester investment consultant, that 'it would be graceful if we made them a grant of £100'.[45] Chance warned him about the Society's 'very unfavourable' accounts and suggested that 'before making a grant to people in Australia, I think we ought to satisfy ourselves that the people concerned are really satisfactory and that there are no rival groups to whom we should be equally obligated to make grants'. Chance said he knew the Australian economist Colin Clark and offered to ask Clark to check on the society's credentials.[46] Blacker informed the EES President Lord Horder that, subject to his approval, the Committee would make a grant of £25.[47] Horder had not met the Society's officials on his Australian visit in 1935, indicating that these Melburnians had only recently acquired their enthusiasm for eugenics. As a result, EES Committee members decided to 'hold back the grant' until they knew more about the new group.[48]

THE EUGENICS SOCIETY OF VICTORIA

Syllabus of Lectures 1937

Five public lectures, each dealing with some aspect of the Science of Eugenics, will be given at Scots Church Hall, Russell Street, at 8 p.m. on the following Thursdays:—

July 29th.—"The Menace of Depopulation"
by Mr. Colin Clark, M.A.

August 12th.—"The Principles of Heredity"
by Dr. W. Bryden.

September 9th.—"Mental Deficiency and Insanity"
by Dr. Reg. S. Ellery.

September 23rd.—"Birth Control and Eugenics"
by Dr. V. H. Wallace.

October 7th.—"The Eugenic Outlook for the Future"
by Professor W. E. Agar.

Admission to each Lecture, 1/-.

Members of the Society will be admitted free to all the lectures. The Annual Subscription is 10/- for Full Members, 2/6 for Associate Members. Persons wishing to become members should communicate with the President, Professor W. E. Agar, The University, Carlton, N.3., or the Secretary, Dr. V. H. Wallace, 61 Collins Street, C.1.

Figure 17: Eugenics Society of Victoria – 1937 Syllabus[49]

Their first informant was Colin Clark who had given the very first of the Eugenics Society of Victoria's lectures, on *The Menace Of Depopulation*, a preoccupation of this Catholic convert with nine children (**Figure 17: ESV**). He often railed against birth control and, in a 1944 national radio broadcast, said it involved acts which were 'filthy, vicious and disgusting'.[50] Clark reported to Blacker, 'Agar is a first rate man and I do not think there is any chance of a rival group arising in Victoria. He is planning to get some population research done under university auspices. Wallace is good too'.[51]

The Society also asked Dr Zebulon Mennell, an Australian-educated Harley Street doctor who obtained the information by contacting Dr Geoffrey Kaye in Melbourne. Kaye provided the EES with information from three anonymous but easily identifiable 'informants'. It is not clear whether they knew of Kaye's purpose or, if they did, whether they intended to help or hinder the Eugenics Society of Victoria. This is part of the report from information which Kaye supplied:

> **Informant A** (senior university professor; virile type; positive views; great admirer of the achievements of National Socialism).
>
> Has no personal knowledge of Melbourne Eugenic Society ... but recognises your 'Dr Agar' as Wilfred Agar, professor of Zoology in this university – he is, of course, a perfectly reputable man and it speaks well for the Society that he is its President.
>
> Regards Dr Wallace as a dubious personality but is not disposed to explain or amplify this opinion.
>
> **Informant B** (locally-eminent psychiatrist; young, literary; a disciple of Freud; far-travelled; rather communist in opinions – until he went to Russia and found there, not communism, but National Socialism!).
>
> Had lectured to Eugenics Society soon after its formation ('Eugenics and mental disease'). Small gathering; about 70 people. Of these, many were 'abnormal types' such as delight to attend public meetings, especially those of slightly sexual character. Believes the really serious members to number about 30-40. Is himself in sympathy with the aims of the Society. ...
>
> Knows Wallace – regards him as a genuine, if unstable, enthusiast in the cause of contraception. ... Does not know of any particularly 'prominent people' in the Society, apart from Professor Agar and Dr Wallace.
>
> **Informant C** (high official of local BMA; forceful, rather dictatorial; necessarily involved in medical politics, but more concerned with paediatrics and medical history; an admirable organizer and a pillar of the Army Service).

Confirms much of the two previous informants' opinions. Regards the Society as a small but earnest body engaged in propagating the latest ideas and literature on contraception. BMA was notified of its foundation and has no quarrel with it, although equally no interest in its activities.   Regards the organisers as genuine enthusiasts, while deploring their publicity campaign.

Considers Dr W as a sincere and ethical, but rather unstable, enthusiast. Rather neatly, says that his character is conveyed by his Christian names, which are Victor Hugo! [52]

The informants were **A**: Professor William Osborne,[53] **B**: Dr Reg Ellery[54] and **C**: Sir James Barrett.[55] The Eugenics Society, it might be thought, was less concerned about informants' or society members' extremist political affiliations than about their status. The critical tone suggests that the Society wanted an excuse to say no. Yet six months after the request, Blacker sent £25 and some second-hand books and pamphlets. Wallace nevertheless was grateful for this small grant and thanked the parent body for its 'interest and confidence' in the fledgling society.

First Attempts

Eugenic organisations and individual eugenists often fought. Professor Richard Berry and Sir James Barrett were members of the University of Melbourne's Council who were famous for their rivalry. Dr Wilfred T Agar, the son of another eugenist, Professor W E Agar, recalled details for me in 1995. When he was a child in the 1920s, Berry was the next door neighbour when the Agars lived in the University grounds. He said that every morning Berry would rush to collect the newspaper and search the obituary columns for Barrett's name. Berry's own obituary, in the *Medical Journal of Australia* on 23 March 1963, contained a revealing anecdote: Berry had informed a colleague that he was prepared to 'bury the hatchet' in a long-running feud with Barrett but the colleague was sure that Barrett would have preferred to 'hatchet the Berry'.   There is also evidence to suggest that a dispute with 'that bugger Barrett' precipitated Berry's abrupt resignation from Melbourne University in 1929.   Eugenics organisations were not exempt from such feuds which explains the otherwise strange tactics that some groups adopted.

The first eugenics group was established in South Australia in 1911. Dr William Ernest Jones, Victoria's Inspector-General of the Insane, was in England in 1913 for the BMA meeting which discussed eugenics and in January 1914, listed five antipodean Eugenics Education Society branches in his report to the *Australian Medical Journal*:

> Affiliated Branches have been established in New South Wales, and in New Zealand there are four in the cities of Dunedin, Christchurch, and Wellington and in the town of Timaru. There is also a society in South Australia, but at present I understand it is not affiliated with the Eugenics Education Society. There should be, I think, a society in Victoria, and it seems highly desirable that this society should be affiliated with the London one.

The Australian attempts are discussed chronologically in the next sections. Despite New Zealand's eager start, all four branches closed because the 'spirit of destruction dampened the ardour of those who used to be full of enthusiasm'.[56] Jones differentiated between eugenics groups and those promoting pronatalism, such as Melbourne's Race Preservation League, which was formed in 1912 to educate 'all people to a recognition of their paternal and maternal responsibilities with a view to the preservation, expansion and improvement of our race, and to encourage purity of life and conduct'. Doctors and the clergy praised the League in a series of addresses on social evils.[57] Politicians kept reminding women about the sacred duties of motherhood, and a member of the British aristocracy warned that recalcitrants would kill off the Empire.[58] These pronatalists were not concerned about fitness but urged *all* women to be fruitful and to avoid the sins of contraception and abortion.

South Australia

South Australia, which boasts of being the only state which was not sent convicts, was also proud of its reputation for social reform and religious freedom. Jill Roe noted that the state's wish to uphold this distinctiveness made it act in 'conformity with what were thought to be the best British practices'.[59] South Australia formed the first eugenics group in Australia in 1911 as a sub-committee of the South Australian Branch of the (pure or 'hard' science) British Science Guild, rather than a branch of the (social or 'soft' science) Eugenics Education Society. The former might have been easier to establish in South Australia where there was less opposition because the state had fewer Roman Catholics and there was more interest in science because of the Lutheran colonists' German heritage. Competitiveness also played a part as the settlers wanted to 'be the first of the Australian States to recognise that racial energy, endurance, and health are at stake'.[60]

The catalyst was probably Sir John Cockburn, the state's former premier who took office in London as the South Australian Agent-General in 1898. He had represented Australia at the 1912 Eugenics Congress and became chairman in Britain of the Guild's Committee on Education. The Guild's Sub-committee released its eugenics report on 19 October 1911, published by eight eminent citizens, with the assistance of a doctor and two preachers.[61] Their recommendations, which they moderated in the hope of winning public acceptance and implementing legal changes, were for a Board of Health to maintain a register of eugenic diseases. Marriage licences were to be withheld from sufferers with any of a long list of diseases or tendencies because, they reasoned:

> Habitual criminals and sex perverts should be segregated permanently in specially administered institutions. Our suggestions are not new, save in scope and detail. The Eugenic idea, with varying modifications, has apparently been already adopted by the legislatures of Austria, Italy, Servia (sic), the Argentine Republic, and a number of the American States. We advocate the application of the Eugenic method as an effective means of abolishing much of the suffering and poverty which oppress society.[62]

Such plans were usually given this humanitarian justification. Eight reports on race building – the Guild's 'great work' – were produced in 1911[63] and one on VD was published by the *Medical Journal of Australia* in July 1914. However, despite support from Australian-born Professor Thorburn Brailsford Robertson (1884-1930) 'of the

California University' (Berkeley), nothing came of the request for a national research institute. [64]

Dr William Ramsay Smith (1859-1937) expressed qualified support for eugenics. This Scottish-educated physician, naturalist, anthropologist and 'literary thief' was a public servant who, after two career setbacks, became the Permanent Head of South Australia's Department of Public Health.[65] In 1899 he complained that sociologists' blind acceptance of nature's biological laws was like the fatalistic acceptance of the ancient Israelites' chant, 'Thus saith the Lord'.[66] In a 1910 Peace Day address, he mentioned eugenics which, he hoped, might remove the need to study war.[67]

His *On Race-Culture and the Conditions to Influence it in South Australia* which appeared in 1912, summarised British and Australian developments and concluded that most studies were really about race-deterioration. Fearing the Science Guild's zealotry, he warned against 'going beyond what the scientific facts warrant, and of going ahead of public opinion'.[68] Britain had its zealots too, such as a Science Guild member who requested a national stock-take because 'the character and physique of the British must be changing rapidly on account of the draining of the picked men to the colonies'.[69] The irony of this suggestion was lost on the speaker or he had forgotten the period when Britain picked men to send to Australia for their country's good.

Ramsay Smith made the point that in Britain, Francis Galton's work had 'been extended both scientifically and popularly, and medical gentlemen who have either devoted themselves to journalism and authorship, or who combine extensive practice with effective preaching, have done a great deal to awaken general interest in the subject of race-culture'.[70] In Australia, Ramsay Smith argued that although eugenics' influence would be felt globally as part of a general scientific and popular movement, other unique influences were at work in Australia. As a result, 'the type produced by a thousand years of inter-breeding, that seemed unalterable, appears to have become radically changed in the course of two or three generations'. In addition to the social laboratory image, Australia qualified as the world's anthropological laboratory. As early as 1909 its significance was emphasized by Knibbs in the first *Official Year Book of the Commonwealth of Australia*, indicating the official backing and central importance of this question:

> The population of Australia is fundamentally British ... The biological and sociological significance of this will ultimately appear in the effects of the physical and moral constitution produced by the complete change of climatic and social environment ... It will not be possible to point to a distinct Australian type until three or four generations more have passed. Even then ... with our great extent of territory and varying conditions ... a variety of types are to be expected.

> The Australian at present is little other than a transplanted Briton, with the essential characteristics of his British forebears, the desire for freedom from restraint, however, being perhaps more strongly accentuated. The greater opportunity for an open-air existence and the absence of the restrictions of older civilisations may be held to be in the main responsible for this.[71]

Although at this time 90% of Australians (or their forebears) came from Britain, they differed substantially from those who stayed behind. A very high proportion of these immigrants were working class or Roman Catholic – many were Irish, Scottish or Welsh – and there were fewer middle class, Protestant or English people than in Britain itself. This had later implications for Australian-style eugenics but initially Ramsay Smith's concerns were to increase Australians' natural advantages with public health measures such as medical inspections of school children. He warned of the need to proceed cautiously because there was the danger that 'while trying to do a little good scientifically, we [may] do a great deal of harm socially'.[72] However, he was totally in favour of environmental measures such as housing, sanitation, the control of TB and the implementation of subsidiary influences including:

> School education and all that it includes, proper home-life and all that it implies, should embrace all that is necessary for the well-being of the individual, the family, and the State. Where children are orphans, and where for any reason they require other care, then the State Children's Department supplies such by means of foster

parents and school privileges. If all these matters were faithfully attended to, little else would require to be said in connection with the subject of race-culture … The supply of the unfit would stop naturally.

Ramsay Smith made the pointed comment that as these improvements would take several generations, 'it [was] desirable to notice some other matters and to refer to other methods and agencies, in case anyone may think that his panacea for social evils has been neglected or is unknown'.[73] He may have been thinking of the Guild's Eugenics Sub-committee which published its abridged Eugenics report in 1911. Extracts from their full report show their fanaticism:

> The study of heredity is of recent growth. … It follows, therefore, that complete absolution must be given to those past generations who have unwittingly handed down their imperfections, but the same absolution cannot be given to those of the present and the future. All that is necessary in the people is a national outlook – a recognition that social science cannot be complete until the propagation of the species ceases to be a personal licence and becomes regulated as a branch of an enlightened national life. … The recognition by [unfit people of] the necessity for restraint is, we need hardly say, the highest form of patriotism.[74]

Ramsay Smith, in his 1913 Presidential Report to the Anthropology Section of the Australasian Association for the Advancement of Science Congress, considered how a 'white population foreign to the soil' would achieve 'its destiny'.[75] He envisaged 'infinite possibilities of good for Australia and no known or suspected dangers that need influence the country's present immigration policy'. He stressed that education would ensure that environment maximised a person's heredity, as opportunity determined whether a boy with 'the bump of acquisitiveness' would become a thief or the curator of a national museum. He considered that marriage, childbearing and pensions were aspects of positive eugenics and 'as far as we are warranted to go in advising or in restraining' because 'beyond this we have no real knowledge'.

Eugenics remained dormant in the state until the 1930s when the RHA again tried to establish a branch in South Australia. After

Goodisson spent two months in Adelaide, she had initial success and reported in the 1934 RHA Annual Report: 'After many setbacks, with Councillor A J Barrett as President and Mrs Davis as Hon Secretary', 'some of the leading men and women' had been enrolled on the committee which had framed their ideals and constitution on RHA NSW lines. The 1935 Report revealed that the RHA had heard 'little' from their SA branch and, finally, the 1936 Report noted that the branch had 'been closed down from lack of interest and funds'.

The next attempt to start a branch is described by the forerunner of the Australian Security Intelligence Organization (ASIO), then called the Security Service, which kept a wartime dossier on the RHA. In 1943 the South Australian Branch of the Service received information from its offices in the eastern states that Mrs Charles Helman, a Jewish 'refugee alien', had contacted Mrs [now Dr] Winifred Mitchell, a 'leading member of the South Australian Communist Women's Committee, arranging for their meeting to discuss plans for the formation of a Racial Hygiene Association in this state'.[76] The letter from RHA President Ruby Rich, to Mrs Helman shows that she may have known about the surveillance:

> I went to the Racial Hygiene with Mrs Mitchell and Mrs Dugood and saw to it that both of them took away a good deal of literature. ... I think it best if all correspondence goes through the office at 14 Martin Place, Sydney. Do not think me non-co-operative if I urge that this be done.[77]

In 1995 Dr Mitchell told me that while this 1943 attempt to establish a clinic in Adelaide failed, she had positive memories of the RHA's Martin Place birth control clinic in the 1940s when their emphasis was on women's health, not eugenics. After a fourth RHA failure in 1967 – a clinic in the industrial city of Whyalla – the Family Planning Association of South Australia was established in 1970.

New South Wales

By 1911 the gloom of the depression and drought had lifted and Australia was becoming modern; telephone and telegraph systems were starting, the film industry was developing, migrants were flooding in (the largest intake since the 1850s) and there was a £5 baby bonus. In this time of prosperity and hope the Commonwealth agreed in May 1912 to send delegates to London for the first International Eugenics Congress in July. Jack Eldridge responded to press reports about the Congress but in New South Wales the momentum built slowly; on 2 November Miss C E Montefiore, an Executive of the conservative Women's Reform League, gave the state's first public address on eugenics in the Blue Mountains town of Lawson.[78] The 12 December founding of the Eugenics Education Society of NSW has already been discussed.

The 'volatile' Rev George Walters who gave lectures for the NSW Eugenics Education Society, had different values from those of Society stalwarts, Arthur, Eldridge and Anderson Stuart which became irreconcilable. In the Society's very first week, Walters gave a sermon on socialism, over-population and the 'extremes of eugenics':

> One is a misnamed 'charity', based upon exaggerated humanitarian ideas, which would 'coddle' the unfit, and leave them free to propagate their undesirable kind. The other which Dr Saleeby rather forcibly denounces as the 'beasthood of Nietzsche' and his disciples, along with their 'mad misconceptions of the Darwinian theory'.[79]

Walters called for limits to the world's population because, while some of Europe's millions might emigrate to America or Australia, the 'teeming millions' 'will not be able to emigrate to another planet'. He was adamant that crime, unemployment and feeble-mindedness would not disappear, despite 'philosophic socialism's' aim to improve the environment by providing appropriate housing, work, wages, and recreation. He aimed to form public opinion as this was 'pretty well our only comfort just at present', suggesting there was little support for eugenics, even at the outset.

Despite their differences, Walters gave a sermon in 1916 which the Eugenics Society published. In Walters' view, war would force people to consider healthy parentage. 'By destroying many of the best fitted' it would teach people 'to prevent the indiscriminate reproduction of the unfit' and would 'convince rational men and women that what is deemed necessary in the breeding of horses and dogs may be even more necessary in the case of human beings'.[80] Considering eugenics as a sort of higher-cattle breeding was anathema to the society's mainstay, Eldridge, so Walters' heretical views would explain why the society crumbled after Eldridge withdrew in 1922.

In 1926 the Race Improvement Society's aims (as shown in Figure 11) were to teach sex education, eradicate VD and educate the community along eugenic lines and its founders came from the politically conservative Women's Reform League.[81] In 1927 the society became the Racial Hygiene Centre of NSW and in 1928, after a third name change, the Racial Hygiene Association of NSW. Thirty-two years later it became the Family Planning Association of NSW.

In 1950 the Association requested the Prime Minister to include a British medical authority as one of the six eminent scientists the government planned to invite to Australia for the Commonwealth Jubilee celebrations.[82] They offered five experts for consideration: Drs Helena Wright, Dr C P Blacker, Edward Griffith and David Mace, and Mr Cyril Bibby.[83] All had eugenics links and the first three were strong birth control advocates: Wright was a pioneer in the field and one of Griffith's books on the subject had been seized by the Queensland Customs in 1938. However, the RHA's request was refused because of birth control, not eugenics.[84] After examining the Society's annual reports, Dr Cumpston informed the Prime Minister 'doubt is expressed as to the desirability of inviting a British medical authority to lecture on racial hygiene during the celebrations'.[85] The Premier of NSW was told to advise the RHA that their suggestions would be added to a list and that the British Medical Association had been asked if it wanted to be associated with such visitors.[86] Cumpston rightly assumed that matter would be shelved because the BMA would not support the RHA's request.

Curiously, although Edith How-Martyn and Thistle Harris were advocating eugenics in Sydney in the 1940s, neither knew about the other. Nor was their presence acknowledged by the RHA whose Newsletters now emphasized talks and bridge parties. This change had taken place after Goodisson's death and it would explain their silence about British-born Mrs Edith How-Martyn who became a member of

Britain's Eugenics Society in 1927 and whose pioneering achievements in women's suffrage and birth-control were honoured in her obituary in 1954. She spent the last ten years of her life in Australia and made this lament in a letter to Miss Faith Schenk, who later became the Eugenics Society's General Secretary:

> This extra copy [of the *Eugenics Review*] I shall pass on each month hoping to get a few new subscribers. I wish I could do more but there is not the interest in Eugenics in Sydney I should like to see.[87]

This lack of interest explains why the Sydney Teachers College biology lecturer Thistle Harris (1902-1990) sent her articles on eugenics to London where they appeared in Norman Haire's *Journal of Sex Education*. In 1938 she had written *Wild Flowers of Australia* which became a perennial favourite, just as Professor William Dakin, a zoologist and fellow eugenist had won a loyal audience of listeners with his 'Science in the News' talks which he gave on ABC radio from 1938 until 1944. Dakin's *Australian Seashores*, which was published after his death, and Harris' *Wild Flowers in Australia,* were much-used reference books, even in non-bookish families. In her February 1949 article for the *Journal of Sex Education* Harris argued that questions about the desirability of cousin marriages presented 'another strong case for the establishment of eugenics centres collecting data from generation to generation'.[88] Three months later she expressed frustration about the lack of enthusiasm for such centres:

> The shortness of human life makes institutions, which take generations to accumulate data, of little public appeal and, no doubt in part for this reason, eugenics centres do not receive the significance they deserve. When added to this they have no political value for the same reason, it is understandable that it is not easy to sell the idea to the public [even though] it is of very great significance in the advancement of genetics itself.[89]

There were no further proposals for eugenic legislation from the RHA or the ESV after the 1930s. The Victorian Society closed in 1960, the same year the Sydney Association changed its name to the Family Planning Association. Dr Laira Perry, a RHA Medical Officer from the mid 1940s until 1968, explained in the March 1960 *Racial Hygiene Association Monthly Bulletin* that 'from as far back as 1952' the

International Planned Parenthood Federation (the Sydney Association's 'roof organisation') had been urging them to change the title and 'fall in line with the other organisations the world all over'. Mary Howard (who became their General Secretary after Goodisson's death) said that Margaret Sanger had asked her in 1955 to agree adopting the new name of 'Family Planning Association'. Howard added 'since that was one of the main objects of our work now' and because 'many of the objects which were responsible for the choice of our present name have fallen by the wayside'. The newsletter mentioned that VD and TB were then curable, although fighting TB was not one of the RHA's objectives. She did not mention eugenics, despite its significance in the Association's name and its inclusion as the RHA's third objective. The part eugenics had played in the Association had become invisible.

Eugenics was only marginally relevant to the RHA but it sounded scientific and, as Ruby Rich explained years later, it served as the 'large umbrella' which gave the RHA an excuse to do 'lots of things' outside their charter.[90] The RHA's eugenics clause, number 3(e) in the Articles of Association, remained for a generation because no one noticed it or thought that it should go. However, after a takeover of FPA NSW by feminists, eugenics was an archaic embarrassment and the reference to it was deleted in 1975 when the new Board revised the FPA's Articles of Association. The offending word was removed from the national family planning body's constitution in November 1989.

Western Australia

The University of Western Australia opened on 13 February 1913 and has the distinction of being the first free university anywhere in the British Empire. A eugenics society was launched in its pioneering 'tin shed' years and a second society began operating in the 1930s. Information about both was provided by Miss Muriel Marion, who told Britain's Eugenics Education Society in August 1933 that a eugenics society had been formed 'during the last few months'.[91] She said that an attempt was made 'about twelve years ago' by Professor William Dakin, but failed 'owing to lack of public support'. She is probably the author of this account in the university newspaper:

Scarcely more than a decade ago Professor Dakin and some of his contemporaries endeavoured to interest a phlegmatic public in this vitally important subject, but all was unavailing – he was subjected to ridicule by all and sundry. The momentous question now is will the younger generation prove as unintelligent as their forebears and as easily frightened by the discussion of recognised social evils.[92]

The story is strange for several reasons: there are no other accounts of a furore and, as Dakin had travelled from England to the wilds of Western Australia in 1913 to become the founding biology professor, he would have been welcomed during its early years, both as an overseas expert and as an experienced speaker. Given his interest in eugenics, he probably started a group but, even if he did suffer 'ridicule', it is unlikely the memory of it would survive for 20 years.[93] Perhaps Dakin proselytised during the war when concerns about immediate survival made people angry about his plans for improving the race. Marion had an unreliable memory herself, making no mention of the eugenics benefactor Henry Twitchin, whose death made headline news in the 29 March 1930 issue of the *West Australian*, three years before she started the group, even though this news from the west was so significant that it had also been reported in the *Sydney Morning Herald*.

According to Marion, the new group began well. Even before its first meeting in July 1933, the Eugenics Society of the University of Western Australia had 'a very representative membership' and support from the Biology Professor, E Nicholls and the Commissioner for Public Health, Dr Everitt Atkinson. Three lectures were given by 'leaders in the medical profession': Mr G Bourne, with a Masters degree in Science; Dr R G Williams, a 'Brain Pathologist to the Asylum for the Insane'; and Dr Roberta Jull, the first female doctor in Perth.[94] The *West Australian* reported that Williams supported the Society 'whole-heartedly' but feared that its members might be caught 'between two fires': the 'semi-scientific circles' who felt they could cure 'sub-normals', and the 'lay public'.[95] This may explain why the group did not last very long. Even so, the group is interesting because it is different from other Australian eugenics groups in two respects: it had no famous members and the group was 'rather youthful'; students in fact, although membership was open to the community.[96]

In 1936, the Sydney RHA entertained Bessie Rischbieth from Perth, a theosophist feminist who was strongly identified with the Women's Service Guilds of Western Australia. In the 1936 RHA Annual Report, Goodisson reported giving her a 'good deal' of information in the hope that she would start a branch in Perth, 'where already the Women's Service Guild has a Racial Hygiene Committee'. The Guild had called for laws to deal with mental defectives and in 1933 some of its members were interested in eugenics. The Guild does not appear to have contacted Marion's society and no action followed any of these initiatives.   Finally, in 1971, the Family Planning Association of Western Australia was established.

William Dakin's story has a post-script.   His eugenics allegiance evolved though various transitions after 1929 when he was appointed Professor of Zoology at the University of Sydney.   An August 1935 article in *The Sunday Sun and Guardian* began with the sensational headline, 'Sterilise unfit: Would End Evil in Generation, says Professor.' He sent mixed signals here, concluding with the equivocal claim that 'the blunders of early eugenists', religious and medical opposition, and the belief that the 'notion that eugenics was an unwarrantable intrusion' were the reasons for its 'tardy growth'. However, in July 1938, despite his early passionate support, he was highly critical of eugenics in his ABC talk *Science in the News*, saying 'the first scientific interest' in population decline 'was aroused in connection with eugenics when some folk, more ardent than wise, were greatly concerned about the decline in the birth rate of what they called the upper classes'.

Victoria

On 1 November 1912 *Australia To-Day* published *The Hopes and Fears for Australia* by the pioneering essayist Walter Murdoch (1874-1970), who subscribed to 'the sacred duty of growling' and attacked pretension and the 'suburban spirit'.[97] While he was unsure if we were breeding good citizens, he rejected positive eugenics as being 'starkly impossible', although we 'may be among the first countries to adopt at least some negative system of eugenics'. He said he knew little about eugenics but honoured it as 'one of the most important subjects that could engage our attention'. Although he believed the Australian race is physically one of the fittest in the world, he questioned its mental and moral fitness. He did not mind 'conceit, complacency and bumptiousness' in Australia's youth but hated their frivolity and apathy towards great public questions, characteristics which, he believed were 'diseases at the very roots of citizenship' and democracy. Murdoch then became the University of Western Australia's founding Professor of English.

Melbourne's interest in eugenics was revitalised in January 1914 when Dr Ernest Jones mentioned it in a medical journal and reaffirmed his support in an address on *The Science of Man-Breeding* in March. The meeting was backed by the Criminology Society and held in the break-away Australian Church which the 'outstanding and outspoken' Rev Charles Strong had been forced to establish after offending an extremely orthodox congregation by describing the book of Genesis as a 'Creation myth'. His new church, which was influenced by American radicalism, was a forum for writers, poets and others who wanted to improve society. After the eugenics meeting, Carlotta Greenshields wrote to Mrs Sybil Gotto, the Secretary of the Eugenics Education Society in London, on behalf of a few people who wished to start a similar society in Melbourne.[98] Mrs Gotto, an admiral's daughter and widowed at 21, was a founding member and prime mover of the British Society. The Victorian group believed that this part of her reply was a directive:

> The approval of Professor Spencer at the University would, I think, be almost essential to any Branch founded in Melbourne as he is one of the recognised authorities on Biology and is already in touch with the Society. I would suggest your communicating with him and asking him if he could assist to form a governing body composed of leading medical men and members of the Staff of the University.

A small but enthusiastic meeting decided on 13 July 1914 to form an Eugenics Education Society of Melbourne, as an affiliated branch of the society in London, with Spencer the president and Jones the senior vice-president. On 14 July Melbourne's *Argus* published an impressive list of provisional committee members: 'Mrs Lavender, Dr Jean Greig, Mrs T à Beckett, Dr Felix Meyer, Dr Harvey Sutton, Mr G H Knibbs, the Rev W Closs, Mr S A Burrows, Mr W Groom, Mr Alfred Deakin, Mr A McDonald, and Mrs R P Greenshields'.[99]   The list did not include Sir James Barrett, nor did he subsequently join any eugenics society. It was not a good time to begin and Dr Ernest Jones had to inform Mrs Gotto:

> I am afraid that the Victorian Eugenics Society is in a state of suspended animation. The war put the *coup de grace* to it whilst it was yet in a shaky condition owing to the fact that your society intimated that they would like to see Professor Baldwin Spencer as its first President. This gentleman was so busy that he was quite unable to give us any assistance.

Jones told Mrs Gotto that he hoped that others would help him form a new substantial, society towards the end of 1915 but there was no action for three years. In May 1918, Leonard Darwin wrote to Frank Tate, Victoria's Director of Education, asking how to secure the best possible stock to populate the Empire.[100] In August, Tate's office issued this file note: 'Inform received letter from Darwin. As the Melbourne Eugenics Society has ceased, and action seems desirable in certain directions, Director would like to confer with you and others. Meeting 27 August 1918'.[101] Prominent people were again approached including eugenists James and Angela Booth, Ernest Jones and George Knibbs and members of Melbourne's medical and teaching professions.[102] The following year, Alec Hunt told Tate that 'a long time had elapsed since the Eugenics Education Society matter' which had been 'relegated to a constitution-drafting sub-committee' consisting of Cumpston, Knibbs, Osborne, Gates and himself. The task was then left to Hunt who said on 3 April 1919 that he was 'too obsessed with his official work to continue'. This third attempt had also failed.

Fifteen years later there was a fourth attempt. In 1934, as part of the RHA's expansionist dream, Goodisson spent two months in Melbourne attempting to get the one remaining society (Barrett's) to enlarge its ideals and change its name. Dr John Dale (1885-1952), who later achieved the unique distinction of having 'died in a car accident in Venice'[103] was then the City Medical Officer. Goodisson enthused that Dale was 'keenly interested, and I am sure they will arrange the alterations necessary to enable us to … form an Australian Association'. She was referring to the Australian Health Society, which Sir James Barrett ran on 'similar lines' to the RHA from 1920 to 1937. As Barrett disapproved of contraception, this reduced the likelihood of a merger between his Association and the RHA. There was no merger. News that Barrett's group had disbanded prompted Goodisson and Ruby Rich to visit Melbourne in October 1936 to arrange a meeting in the hope of forming a Victorian branch of the RHA. Professor Agar, a noted eugenist, chaired it with help from Dr Wallace and Dr Maurice Schalit. The plan failed, as Goodisson noted in her carefully worded statement in the year's Annual Report:

> At the first committee meeting [on 12 October 1936, the Victorian group] became a Eugenic Society, which I venture to say, will not touch the people we want to help. Our hope, therefore, of forming an Australian Federation of Racial Hygiene, has, at any rate for the present, expired, but we have by sad experience realised the reason thereof. It is necessary for the organiser of any new Branches to spend some months in each State to prepare the way for a big meeting and to remain until a capable secretary and a good committee are appointed.

The Victorians had ruined any chance of forming a national association when they established the Eugenics Society of Victoria (ESV) as a branch of Britain's Eugenics Society. It was ironic that the Victorians, who did not want to be dominated by NSW, agreed to adopt the objectives of the British group. Goodisson expressed her outrage in her 18 November 1936 letter to Wallace, the Secretary of the new Victorian society:

> I do think it is most shockingly bad taste for anyone to go on a Provisional Committee of an Association, and then turn it into another. … I feel that it is the end of my work in any other State … There is the end of our Federation … I am afraid Professor Agar's Association will be all talk and no work … probably the

methods which you are going to take up, are too vague to appeal to the ordinary citizens. One wants deeds not words.

Mrs Janie Butler provided words, deeds and donations. In 1997 a former ESV member told me of her vivid memories of Butler: 'She was a wealthy over-enthusiastic member who embarrassed us by bailing up pedestrians in Melbourne's fashionable Collins Street, insisting they should read the Society's very important leaflets'. A pedestrian-stopping precedent had been set in 1928 when Collins Street became the first street in Australia with traffic lights. In 1939 Mrs Butler donated £100 for a clinic which the ESV planned to open in a Melbourne slum. The Melbourne *Sun* reported on 24 April 1939 that Sir John Harris, the Minister for Health, was heartily disapproving and the Roman Catholic Archbishop of Melbourne, Dr Daniel Mannix, was reported as being 'astounded to read that certain busy bodies propose to establish a birth control clinic to help people send Australia all the faster tobogganing down into disaster'. The ESV thanked Marie Stopes for sending a liberal donation (in reality £10) after hearing about the tumult. The controversy was rekindled in 1940 by Dr Halliday Sutherland (Stopes' Catholic adversary[104]) who made an extensive Australian lecture tour in which he had pointedly attacked eugenics and made vigorous onslaughts against birth control.[105] There was also internal division between Wallace (who from 1934 had been the director of Melbourne's first birth control clinic) and Agar, the ESV President who only wanted contraception for 'eugenic reasons'. But as this was rarely sought, the ESV abandoned the birth control idea. Instead, Wallace formed a Social Hygiene Society (to withstand criticism more easily than individuals could) and 'quietly' established a clinic, not as planned in a Melbourne slum, but in down-town Collins Street.

Eventually Goodisson's prophecy that the ESV would be all talk and no work was confirmed. In 1945, Agar looked back on eight years of operation.[106] It was 'not a very imposing total', consisting of only two pamphlets and from 1937 to 1939 (the ESV's peak years) 17 poorly-attended public lectures which attracted 'very few of the influential section of the population of Melbourne'. Agar gloomily noted that only overseas countries had done research on ways in which eugenic or dysgenic trends were operating and that, as the ESV could not sponsor such work, it was impossible to discover whether similar conditions existed in Australia and they could only alert appropriate bodies of the need for such research. He suggested that the National Health and Medical Research Council's Committee on Social Services Research might consider eugenic problems such as the size of families from which mentally deficient, backward and clever school children come, and 'follow up of past pupils from special schools for defective or backward children'. Nothing came of this suggestion although Agar said the Committee agreed that these were 'suitable subjects' for their interest.[107]

Agar also deliberated whether the Society should stick rather rigidly to eugenics in its strictest sense, or include issues such as welfare, VD, housing and alcoholism. Despite conflicts with other members on this issue, he backed pure (hereditary) eugenics because 'an improvement or deterioration of the inborn, inherited, qualities of the race is permanent'. As well, 'nearly all of these problems immediately become involved in medical questions, and without a strong and active medical representation' in the membership, the Society was not 'in a position to study these questions in an expert manner'. They were also politically naive and despite the horrors of the Nazi death camps, in 1949 Dr Wallace asked Dr C P Blacker why Professor Francis Crew from Edinburgh did not once use the word 'eugenics' in his two Melbourne lectures. Blacker said he was not in the least surprised by this, explaining that he 'would sooner explain it orally than in writing'. In 1957 the British Society formalised this tactic by adopting a policy of 'crypto-eugenics' in which they promoted eugenics 'by less obvious means'.[108]

Comparison of the NSW and Victorian Groups

Other reasons have been offered for the ESV failure: women's organisations had backed the RHA and formed a reserve which could be enlisted as RHA members, with back-up support from medical and other experts. In addition, while in Melbourne, 'Goodisson approached the "experts" (medical, academic and professional) first, expecting that a unified group would result'.[109] Sydney had

Goodisson's 'energy and the financial support of wealthy patrons' and it was not possible to transplant her zeal to another state.[110]

There are some problems with this reasoning; while initially the RHA had eminent patrons and wealthy subscribers, this ceased with the Depression. In the 1930s the high-level RHA patrons lent only their names; finances were tight and the lack of private or government backing caused panics when the RHA ran out of money. During her Victorian mission Goodisson would not have had the local knowledge of Melbourne's rich and powerful – the list seems to be a standard list of Melbourne's elite, similar to the lists compiled by Victoria's earlier groups. The RHA also repeated the mistake of enlisting people who were known for their name, influence and position, but not for their support and staying power.

Unfortunately for the RHA, support became *over-involvement* in the case of one eminent patron, Lady Enid de Chair whose husband, Sir Dudley de Chair, was the NSW Governor from 1924 to 1930. In 1927, the couple endorsed the new Racial Hygiene Centre 'heartily' in a fund-raising appeal in a newspaper advertisement, giving their signatures and the Government House address.[111] However, in 1929 the RHA ruefully thanked Lady Enid with this cryptic rider: 'Although some of her remarks gave rise to much newspaper criticism, she kept up her interest'.[112] Sydney's *Daily Guardian* relished this spat in which Vice-Regal enthusiasm to fight VD had been so contentious that a public meeting had voted in an attempt to silence her. The sport-and-scandal paper listed her 'notable' supporters who won the vote and not one was an RHA member, despite their anti-VD mandate.[113]

A comparison of the Sydney and Melbourne groups also needs to consider the changed attitudes to eugenics in the decade separating each group's vital early years, and consider their different mandates and styles. For instance, in the late 1930s the ESV was primarily interested in eugenics and for them, birth control was secondary. Agar's group had a formal style with lectures and booklets which contrasted with Goodisson's lively use of booklets, film screenings, tours, talks and, most importantly, radio shows to promote RHA services. From the 1920s Goodisson was an asset and the ESV had no similar figure but the RHA won out because they chose birth control. Even if there had been a Victorian 'Goodisson', the ESV would probably still have failed because, in Goodisson's words, eugenics was too vague to appeal to ordinary citizens. Even so, neither state could point to many achievements and the RHA was always worried about its small membership and the difficulties of attracting presidents and office bearers. Goodisson persevered even after the rift with the ESV; while holidaying in Melbourne she visited prominent medical men and women, making 'two good contacts with people in somewhat similar societies'. These were Dr Victor Wallace of the Eugenics Society and 'Dr R [George] Simpson' of the Australian Health Society. Agar had identified the key difference between the ESV and the RHA which determined their fates: the ESV strove for an unattainable abstract goal and had little popular or medical support, while the RHA had popular and medical support because birth control was a tangible health service which many people wanted.

Thirty years later, Dr Wallace gave this valediction for the ESV:

> Some [groups] have had a brief existence, some have become firmly established as permanent institutions in our society, and some occupy a borderline position which means that their survival or their dissolution and subsequent revival are determined by fluctuations in popular interest and support. It would seem that eugenics belongs to the last class. ... It is difficult to assess the exact influence of any particular group on the life of a community. The Eugenics Society of Victoria did have an impact upon public opinion. In certain respects we were pioneers in this country and the subject which we presented to the public stimulated discussion and aroused controversy.[114]

Goodisson's successors repeated her mistakes when they tried to establish a branch clinic in Melbourne; after the opening in August 1961 in Melbourne's St Kilda Road, the clinic closed from lack of support a year later. Judge Alfred Rainbow, president of Sydney's Family Planning Association of Australia (the renamed RHA) blamed Melbourne doctors for the failure.[115] However, Melburnians said that it failed because the site was unsuitable, there was poor publicity and it lacked local roots, having been set up and administered from the

Sydney office.[116] In the 1960s, as in the 1930s, volunteers' attempts to
clone a branch in another state failed because it ignored logic, logistics
and state rivalry. In 1970 the local community successfully established
FPA Victoria.

A postscript is provided by a man who, like Twitchin did not belong
to a eugenics society, but left his money to further eugenics. In 1949
the will of Mr John Nicholas Peters, 'gentleman' of St Kilda, gave a
£33,000 bequest to the University of Melbourne 'for the purpose of
establishing a lectureship in Eugenics'.[117] Dr Wallace, who wanted the
position, sent Eugenic Society's Dr Blacker extracts from Peters'
bequest which was

> To further the investigation into the laws of heredity in man, the
> influence of heredity and environment on human characteristics on
> the actual position in Australia in regard to the birth rates of feeble-
> minded or other defectives and other work of a similar nature with
> a view to finding some means to ensure that future generations
> shall be descended mainly from persons of good stock and thus to
> assist nature in producing a more highly evolved type of human
> being which should be the ultimate aim of all human endeavour.

No eugenics lectureship was established and, in response to my
queries to the University of Melbourne, this is the slow saga of the
bequest.   In 1949 a geneticist from Canada declined a position in the
Department of Experimental Medicine and from 1951 to 1955 the
University again failed to attract a Cambridge researcher to the
Statistics Department. In 1960 Wallace tried again to get support from
the Eugenics Society's new General Secretary, Dr G C L Bertram.[118]
John A Goodwin, Council Secretariat Officer (on behalf of the Vice-
Chancellor) confirmed that in 1961 the University had recommended
the establishment of a Readership in Human Genetics, which had 'in
fact happened' and that the capital from the bequest, valued in 1996 at
over $400,000, has been used to promote research in genetics and
human biology.

Evidence in this chapter refutes orthodox views about eugenics in
Australia before 1914.   For example, Alison Turtle wrote 'the
organized eugenics movement gained little ground, and almost none at
all until after the [1914-18] war'[119] and, in a similar vein, Stephen

Garton stated that the eugenics movement was weak prior to 1914.[120] The fallacy of these statements is shown in the descriptions of seven attempts from 1911 to establish eugenics organizations in four states. Australia reacted positively to this new ideology and in addition to this intense activity, it was also the formative, training years for health administrators such as J H L Cumpston, Sydney Morris, Ernest Jones, Harvey Sutton and Anderson Stuart. They were all influenced by eugenics before 1914, and this left a legacy in their subsequent careers which had a substantial influence on the nation's health.

---

[1]Pugliese, in Shirley Fitzgerald and Garry Wotherspoon (eds.), *Minorities: Cultural Diversity in Sydney* (Sydney: State Library of NSW and the Sydney History Group, 1995), 208.

[2]Sir Charles Mackellar and David Arthur Welsh, *Mental Deficiency: A Medico-sociological Study of Feeble-mindedness* (Sydney: Govt. Pr., 1917), 62.

[3]Arthur W Hayes, *Future Generations: Woman*, the Future Ruler of This Earth. If This Earth was a Stud Farm and the Men and Women Thereon Represented the Stock, Three Quarters Would be Rendered Incapable of Reproduction (Sydney: typescript, 1915), ML.

[4]James Eastman, in *Happy Marriage* (Melbourne: McCubbin, [193-?]), 21, warned that 'the least valuable strains – the diseased, the degenerate, the mentally defective, the alcoholic – show the most marked tendency to multiply and pass on their undesirable characteristics to their swarming progeny'. See also John Bostock, 'Mental deficiency: causes and characteristics', *MJA* (5 March 1927), 325.

[5]William Little, *A Visit to Topos, and How the Science of Heredity is Practised There* (Ballarat: Berry and Anderson, 1897), 18 and 25.

[6]Herman Harold Rubin, *Eugenics and Sex Harmony: The Sexes, Their Relations and Problems*, 2nd edn (New York: Pioneer Publications, 1942), 24. First published in 1933. Dr Cumpston tried to ban the book in 1935 because the subject might be 'objectionable' for lay readers.

[7]'Benito Mussolini. World famous physical culturalists. No 1', *HPC* (June 1930), 29, 38.

[8]*ER*, 1 (1909-1910), 3.

[9]It continued into the 1940s, in articles such as 'Dr Noel M Guttridge's, 'Human Gardening', *New Horizons in Education*, vol 2 (no 5), April, May June 1942, 21-24.

[10]Quoted by Stefan Kuhl in *The Nazi Connection: Eugenics, American Racism, and German National Socialism* (New York: OUP, 1994), 48-49.

[11] Victor Hugo Wallace, 26 May 1940 to the Prime Minister's Department, Canberra, AA/ACT, A461, Item T347/1/1.

[12] *ER*, 30 (October 1938), 31, 163 and (October 1939), 151-52.

[13] Kuhl (1994), 36. The career of Fritz Lenz (1887-1976) is analysed by Sheila Faith Weiss, in *Medizinhistoriches Journal*, 27 nos 1-2 (1992), 5-25.

[14] A poster reproduced by Lesley A Hall in 'Illustrations from the Wellcome Institute Library. The Eugenics Society Archives in the Contemporary Medical Archives Centre', *Medical History,* 34 (1990), 327-33, Plate 3, CMAC: SA/EUG/G/G. Poster ' Healthy Seed' [1930s].

[15] 'Germany. Sterilization of the unfit', *SMH*, 25 October 1933, 13 (a). See also Robert N Proctor's 'The anti-tobacco campaign of the Nazis: A little known aspect of public health in Germany, 1933-45', *BMJ*, 7 December 1996, 1450-53. This whole issue of *BMJ* is devoted to the Nuremberg Doctors' Trial: 50 years on', 1445-1470, 1475.

[16] Modern concentration camps were first used by the Spaniards in Cuba during the Spanish-American war of 1898 and, during the Boer War (1899-1902), more than 20,000 (mostly women and children) died in the camps which the British established in South Africa. Forced relocation and corrective labour camps were a feature of Russia's history, starting with the camps established by the Bolsheviks in 1918 and intensifying until Stalin's death in 1953.

[17] Thomas, *Plain Words: A Guide to Sex Education* (Sydney: F Johnson, 1942?), 21, 23.

[18] Harvey Sutton, *Lectures on Preventive Medicine* (Sydney: Consolidated Press, 1944), 25.

[19] Edmund Morris Miller, *Australian Literature from is Beginnings to 1935: A Descriptive and Bibliographic Survey of Books by Australian Authors in Poetry*, Drama, Fiction, Criticism and Anthology with subsidiary Entries to 1938 [1940], (Sydney: SUP facsimile, 1975).

[20] See Carole Ferrier's *Jean Devanny: Romantic Revolutionary* (Melbourne: MUP, 1999), 35-36, 62, which explored the eugenic themes in her novels, the 1930 rejection by Angus & Robertson of her layperson's guide to eugenics and her three magazine articles on the topic.

[21] Noel Macainsh, *Nietzsche in Australia: A Literary Inquiry into a Nationalistic Ideology* (Munich: Verlag fur Dokumentation und Werbung, 1975), 105, quoting Baylebridge.

[22] Peter Medawar, *Memoir of a Thinking Radish: An Autobiography* (Oxford: Clio Press in Assoc with OUP, 1989), 129.

[23] The dispatch issued 'Two invitations to Ministers and Heads of Government Departments to become Honorary Members of the First International Eugenics Congress. Two invitations to Government Departments and Boards to appoint delegates to the above Congress', Downing Street, L Harcourt, Sec of State for the Colonies, Dispatch 210, 10 May 1912, AA (1912).

[24] 'Delegates' in *Problems in Eugenics*. Papers communicated to the First International Eugenics Congress, University of London, July 24-30, 1912 (London: EES, 1912), xv-xvii.

[25]University College London, Galton Papers, 133/5N, 22 March 1905, 'Sir John Cockburn deeply regrets that an engagement in the north will prevent him from being present on October 30. He is deeply interested in Mr Galton's researches in Eugenics and trusts that some further opportunity may present itself for conferring on the subject'.

[26]Edith Onians, *The Men of To-morrow* (Melbourne: Lothian, 1914), 258. This was part of an account of her two-year study of child rescue work in England, America and Europe.

[27]In 1912, positive responses were published in *AMG* (20 April), 414-15, *Argus*, 20 June, 11; 26 July, 7; 24 August, 18; 5 September, 14; 7 September, 9 and *SMH*, 29 July, 9.

[28]H H Laughlin, *The Second International Exhibition of Eugenics 22 September to 22 October 1921* (Baltimore: Williams & Wilkins, 1923), Exhibitor 112, Professor Griffith Taylor, Associate Professor of Geography, University of Sydney. Exhibition. 'One wall-diagram dealing with racial variation'.

[29]Knibbs' letters to Davenport were on the letterhead paper of the Commonwealth Statistician, Melbourne. The congress was reported in a favourable light in the *Argus*, 24 December 1921, 4.

[30]Wilbur Keblinger, American Consul, Sydney, forwarding the 1 February 1932 invitation from the International Federation of Eugenic Organizations, Cold Spring Harbor, Long Island, New York to J G Latham, Attorney General and Minister for External Affairs, Canberra, 23 March, 1932, AA/ACT, Item A981, Conferences 103 (1932).

[31]J A Lyons, Prime Minister and Acting Minister for External Affairs, Canberra to the Consul-in-Charge, Sydney, 27 June 1932, AA (1932). On 30 June, Albert M Doyle, the American Consul, informed Mr Lyons that his response had been 'forwarded to the Secretary of State at Washington for transmission to the Secretary of the Congress', *ibid*.

[32]Robert Storer, *Sex in Modern Life: A Survey of Sexual Life in Adolescence and Marriage*, 2nd edn. (Melbourne: James Little, 1933), 70. He was on the RHA Board from 1928-1930.

[33]*A Decade* of Progress in Eugenics: Scientific Papers of the Third International Congress of Eugenics … held at the American Museum of Natural History, New York. August 21-23, 1932 (Baltimore: Williams and Wilkins, 1934), (1934), 13-14, 522-26. In a summary of attendances at all three congresses, Harry H Laughlin stated that 200 of the delegates made the trip to Cold Spring Harbor, ibid, 8. Problems in Eugenics (1912) listed 99 delegates, four from Australia.

[34] Daniel Kevles, *In the Name of Eugenics* (New York: Knopf, 1985), 169.

[35]The 1929 International Federation of Eugenic Organizations membership list, in *The Eugenical News*, XV (January 1930), 11-15. This American newsletter also published a list in 1932.

[36]Item 7 of the 'proposed rules' of the Second International Eugenics Congress (1923), quoted in *ER*, 13 (April 1921 – January 1922), 524, listed 'co-operating countries' as 'In Europe: Belgium, Czechoslovakia, Denmark, France, Great Britain, Italy, the Netherlands, Norway, Sweden; In America, Argentina, Brazil, Canada, Columbia, Cuba, Mexico, Venezuela, United States of America. Also Australia and New Zealand'.

[37]*A Decade* (1934), 522-26, listed representatives from 22 countries. Those joining in 1912 were Argentina, Belgium, Cuba, Denmark, France, Germany, Great Britain, Italy, Norway, United States of America; in 1921-1923 Czechoslovakia, Finland, Hungary, The Netherlands, Sweden, Switzerland; in 1924-1928 Austria, Estonia, Poland, South Africa, and from 1929-1932 Canada and the Dutch East Indies.

[38]'International Eugenics Congress', *ER*, 22-23 (April 1930 – January 1932), 241.

[39]Robert Cook, in *A Decade* (1934), 441-46.

[40]Eldridge to Secretary EES, 17 December 1912, Wellcome Institute, Eugenics Society, SA/EUG, E2, Eugenics Education Society in NSW 1912-1930. Formation of EESNSW.

[41]At the History of Medicine Conference, Sydney, 7-10 July 1999, Peter J Tyler presented evidence showing that it was not Ashburton Thompson but NSW's first microbiologist (Dr Frank Tidswell (1867-1941) whose finding about rats were reported first, in April 1900, to the Board of Health.

[42]In 1902 Ashburton Thompson became a brother-in-law and close friend of Sydney University Anatomy Professor James Thomas Wilson (1861-1945) who career in Australia and Britain is traced by Patricia Morison in *J T Wilson and the Fraternity of Duckmaloi* (The Wellcome Institute Series in the History of medicine) (Atlanta, Ga: Rodopi, (Clio Medica 42), 1997, 133.

[43]V H Wallace to Sec ES, 2 June 1937, E3, Victorian Eugenics Society 1914-1939.

[44]Wallace to Sec, E3 ibid, 15 February 1938.

[45]Blacker to Chance, E3 ibid, 21 March 1938.

[46]Chance to Blacker, 22 March 1938.

[47]Blacker to Lord Horder, 6 April 1938.

[48]Blacker to Mrs E E Potton, 13 April 1938, who suggested that Dr Zebulon Mennell would check the credentials of the Eugenics Society of Victoria.

[49]The ESV published a syllabus from 1937 to 1939 and in 1945.

[50]Colin Clark, in *The Nation's Forum of the Air*, vol 1 (no 2), 23 August 1944, 10, *Population Unlimited?,* published as a pamphlet by the Australian Broadcasting Commission in Sydney.

[51]Clark to Blacker, 2 May 1938.

[52]Kaye to Mennell, 3 June 1938. Geoffrey Alfred Kaye, MB BS 1926, MD (Melbourne 1929), Honorary Anaesthetist Alfred Hospital Melbourne and Dental Hospital, Lecturer in Anaesthetics, University of Melbourne, 1937.

[53]William Alexander Osborne (1873-1967), obituary, *MJA* (16 December 1967), 1144. He was Professor of Physiology at the University of Melbourne, 'a typical "Nordic" – tall, robust, blue-eyed, strikingly handsome. His manner was concise and rather chilling. This Irish-born academic was a leader-writer for the *Age* in 1912-13 and made broadcasts in 1915 on the need for national efficiency and the need to develop scientific research in Australia. The person who helped me by identifying Osborne as 'Informant A' asked not to be identified.

[54]Reginald Spencer Ellery (1897-1955), qualified in medicine and psychiatry from Melbourne University, worked in the State's Lunacy Department and ran a 20-bed hospital. Ellery travelled overseas to learn about insulin shock therapy for people with schizophrenia and was one of the first Australians to advocate the therapy. He published the results of his work in the *MJA* (vol 2, 1937), 552-64) and (with D C Lear) in the *MJA* (vol 2, 1938), 779-81.

[55]Sir James William Barrett (1862-1945) was an ophthalmologist and publicist and an exponent of national efficiency who maintained 'a voluminous writing to the press, especially the Argus'. He had links with the University of Melbourne, as vice-chancellor in 1931, deputy chancellor in 1934 and chancellor in 1935-1939.

[56] McGregor Walmsley, St Kilda, NZ to Sec EES, 25 June 1933, SA/EUG, E19.

[57] Charles Bage, 'Race suicide', in *Social Sins*. A Series of Sermons and Addresses on Social Evils, St Paul's Cathedral, Melbourne. *Church of England Messenger*, 1912, 17-28.

[58] Viscount Wolmer, a British MP and father of seven, told the League of National Life that 'the pernicious doctrines of birth control will cause the eventual downfall of the British Empire', *SMH*, 1 November 1929, 14 (e). William Matthew Palmer Wolmer (1912-1942) was educated at Oxford and served in the Hampshire Regiment.

[59] Jill Roe (ed.), *Social Policy in Australia: Some Perspectives 1901-1975* (Stanmore, NSW: Cassell, 1976), 13.

[60]'Physical Culture' (no 3), 26 April 1911, in British Science Guild. South Australian Branch, *Race Building*. Reprinted from *The Mail* (Adelaide 1916), 10.

[61]British Science Guild, SA Branch, *Eugenics* [Adelaide: 19 October 1911]. Dr Charles Reissmann, consulting surgeon; Dr Robert Pulleine, obituary in *Transactions of the Royal Society of South Australia*, 59 (1935); Thomas Hyland Smeaton (1857-1927) architect, writer and politician was president of the SA Temperance Alliance; Sir Frederick William Young (1876-1948), a Liberal politician who supported state sponsorship of British migrant youths to work on the land and became the SA agent-general in London; Sir Henry Simpson Newland (1873-1960), surgeon and President of the Royal Empire Society from 1935-55; Dr Robert Humphrey Marten, in 1901 the first in SA to remove a cerebral tumour with the largest and most lucrative practice in Adelaide; Dr Edward Angas Johnson, a physician at the Royal Adelaide Hospital, and lawyer William Ashley Magarey. Their assistants were Dr Michael Henry Downey, Joseph Coles Kirby (1837-1924) a fanatical

Congregational minister and prohibitionist with extremist views about sterilization, and Rev Henry Howard (1859-1933), a Methodist minister.

62 *Eugenics* (1911), 3.

63The Guild examined: Puericulture [infant nurture], Scientific nutrition, Physical culture, Graduated ethics, Science in schools, Negative eugenics, Venereal diseases and the establishment of a Research institute.

64Brailsford Robertson, an idealistic and brilliant professor of physiology and biochemistry who in 1907 gained a PhD from the University of California, provided 'very full and valuable' details of the cost and scope of the proposed Federal Institute, *Race Building* (1916), 26-27.

65These setbacks are documented in John Mulvaney, Howard Morphy and Alison Petch (eds) '*My Dear Spencer: The Letters of F J Gillen to Baldwin Spencer* (Melbourne: Hyland House, 1997, 273 and 468-69, as follows: In 1896 Smith was expelled from the SA branch of the BMA and never readmitted. In 1903 he was suspended from his duties as coroner following charges of misusing human bodies. He was later cleared. The claim about Ramsay Smith's literary plagiarism was made by Drs Adam Shoemaker and Stephen Muecke and reported by Luke Slattery, in 'How our $50 hero was robbed of his mythical tales for £150', *Australian*, 22 October 1998, 1. The researchers claim that '70 to 90% of Ramsay Smith's 1930 book, *Myths and Legends of the Australian Aborigines* (reprinted in 1996 as *Aborigine: Myths and Legends*) was based, without acknowledgment, on the unpublished manuscript of David Unaipon, the man on the $50 note.

66Ramsay Smith, *The Practical Aspect of Heredity and Environment* (Adelaide: Whillas & Ormiston, 1899), 21.

67Ramsay Smith, *Peace: An Address Delivered at the University of Adelaide on Peace Day, 9 November 1910.* (International Peace Society, Adelaide Branch, 1910), 5.

68Ramsay Smith, *On Race-Culture and the Conditions to Influence it in South Australia* (Adelaide: Govt Pr., 1912), 7.

69Ramsay Smith (1912), quoting Sir Lander Brunton at a 1907 deputation to the British Prime Minister. The Science Guild membership came from these prestigious organizations: Royal Anthropological Institute, Sociological Society, Childhood Society, Royal College of Surgeons, Royal Society and Royal Statistical Society, but not religious groups.

70Ramsay Smith (1912), 10.

71George H Knibbs, *Official Year Book of the Commonwealth of Australia* .. 1901-1908 (Melbourne: Commonwealth Bureau of Census and Statistics, 1909), 158. The title varied.

72Ramsay Smith (1912) 12, 14.

73Ramsay Smith (1912), 20.

74*Race Building* (1916), 19-20.

[75]Ramsay Smith, 'Australian conditions and problems from the stand point of present anthropological knowledge', AAAS Congress (Sydney: Angus & Robertsons, 1913), 3, 10.

[76]Deputy Director of Security, Sydney to Director General of Security, Canberra, 10 December 1943, AA/SA D1915, Item 22063.

[77]AA/SA, ibid, Ruby Rich, 'The Astor', Etham Ave, Darling Point, NSW to Mrs Charles Helman, 137 Henley Beach Rd, Torrensville, SA, 1 December 1943. Mrs 'Dugood' was probably Phyllis Duguid, the second wife of Dr Charles Duguid. From 1940-1947 he was a member of the SA Government Aborigines Protection Board.

[78]The Liberal Woman, 1 December 1912, 47. Miss Montefiore's continued support for eugenics and sterilization is shown in a letter in The Woman's Voice (formerly The Liberal Woman), 1 June 1918, 12.

[79]Eugenics; or Scientific Race Culture. A lecture delivered by the Reverend George Walters, Hyde Park Unitarian Church, Sydney, NSW, 15 December 1912, 10.

[80]Eugenic Problems and the War, a lecture by George Walters, Hyde Park Unitarian Church, Sydney on 27 August 1916 and published by the Eugenics Society on 29 September 1916.

[81]The Women's Reform League (formerly the Women's Liberal League) was founded by Mrs Molyneux Parkes in December 1902. In 1917 the League united with the Nationalist Party.

[82]AA/ACT, A1658, Item 200/2/48, 'Racial Hygiene delegates, Premier to Prime Minister, 31 October 1950'.

[83]Helena Wright was also a ES member; C P Blacker, the ES general secretary, advocated birth control as did Edward Griffith. David Mace was an authority on marriage counselling and Cyril Bibby, the British editor of International Journal of Sexology, wrote sex education books which the NSW Dept of Education used.

[84]The Catholic Church told women to avoid the RHA's clinic, banned books about contraception and in 1942 supported the National Security (Venereal Diseases and Contraceptives) regulations which prohibited contraceptive advertising.

[85]A J Metcalfe, Director-General of Health to Prime Minister's Department, 7 December 1950 (?), AA/ACT, Item 200/2/48.

[86]Ibid, Prime Minister to Hon James McGirr, Premier of NSW, [18 December 1950?].

[87]Mrs Edith How-Martyn to Miss Schenk, Eugenics Society, London. 12 September 1950 (Eugenics Society Archives (London), SA/EUG – C176).

[88]Thistle Harris, 'Should first cousins marry?', Journal of Sex Education, vol 1, February 1949, 213.

[89]Thistle Harris, 'Eugenics and Society', Journal of Sex Education, vol 1, June 1949, 234.

[90]Ruby Rich interviewed by Hazel De Berg (Canberra: National Library of Australia, Oral History Unit, 12 December 1976), tape 995, counter no 13,357.

[91]SA/EUG, E5, Muriel Marion to Pres, EES London, 12 August 1933, 1,2.

[92]'Eugenics Society', *The Pelican*, 16 June 1933, 2, [Muriel Marion ?].

[93]While Muriel Marion said in 1933 that the upset was 'about twelve years ago' it could have been longer as Dakin taught at the University of WA from 1913 to 1920.

[94]Marion (12 August 1933), 1-2. Papers: Bourne, 'The scientific basis of eugenics', Williams, 'The selective breeding' and Dr Roberta Henrietta Jull (1872-1961), 'Heredity and environment'.

[95]'Community welfare. Importance of eugenics', *West Australian*, 6 July 1933. This and 'Eugenics Society. Lecture at University', ibid, [13 July?] contained in SA/EUG. E5.

[96] The Univ of WA Eugenics Society was registered on 6 July 1933. The Committee was: Miss M Marion (Pres), M L Snook (Vice-pres), Mr D Stuart (Sec), Mr C Thiel (Treas), Mrs Farleigh, Mr G Bourne and Mr K C B Green. In 1936 it had nine shillings and by 1937 it had 'gone into recess'.

[97]Geoffrey Searle described Sir Walter Logie Forbes Murdoch, as being the best known 'literary man' of his day, witty and the most liberal of conservatives. He was the uncle of Sir Keith Murdoch (who was a member of the ESV) and the great uncle of the media mogul Rupert Murdoch.

[98]Carlotta Greenshields, Glenferrie, Melbourne to Mrs Gotto, EES, 3 March 1914, SA/EUG, E3.

[99]Committee members included: Ada Mary *A'Beckett* (1872-1948), biologist, demonstrator and assistant lecturer in biology at the University of Melbourne from 1901 and closely involved with the kindergarten movement; Alfred *Deakin* (1856-1919), Prime Minister of Australia in 1903-04, 1905-08 and 1909-10; Dr Jean *Greig* (1874-1939), a founder in 1896 of the Queen Victoria Hospital 'by women for women' and Medical Inspector, Education Department; as the politician *W H Groom* died in 1901, it must have been one of his sons; George Handley *Knibbs* (op cit); Julia Margaret *Lavender* (1858-1923), rationalist, feminist, teacher and the first female graduate from an Australian university; *Arthur Stephen McDonald* (1891-1955), a radio engineer who became prominent in establishing broadcasting; Dr Felix *Meyer* (1858-1937), Lecturer in Obstetrics and Gynaecology at the University of Melbourne and Dr Harvey *Sutton* (1882-1963), Medical Officer, Victorian Department of Public Instruction.

[100]Leonard Darwin, EES to Frank Tate, 'Steps taken for Australian racial purity', 4 May 1918. Education Dept, Special Case files, Public Record Office of Vic. SP 1106 Sex Education in Schools

[101]Letters re Eugenics meeting sent on 21 August 1918 from Tate to 17 people.

[102]Invitations were also sent to Meredith Atkinson, R J A Berry, Dr J H L Cumpston, Dr Eileen Fitzgerald, Dr Jean Greig, Alec Hunt, James McRae, William Osborne,

Stanley Porteus, Dr John Smyth, Drs Stephens and Collins and the Reverend Charles Strong.

[103]Noted in Dale's obituary in the *University of Melbourne Gazette* (October 1952), 82.

[104] Stopes had foolishly sued him for libel and in her famous 1923 trial, Sutherland won.

[105] *The Rationalist*, April 1940, 136 and May 1940, 158.

[106] W E Agar, *History of Our Past Activities* [1945], supplied by Wilfred T Agar, 12 March 1994.

[107]Agar (1945), 8.

[108]Quoted by Faith Schenk and Alan Parkes, ER, 60 (1968), 154.

[109]Grant McBurnie, *Constructing Sexuality in Victoria 1930-1950: Sex Reformers Associated with the Victorian Eugenics Society*, (PhD thesis, Monash University, 1989), 94.

[110]McBurnie, ibid, 94-95, interview with Mrs Ethelwyn Wallace-Dawson, September 1988. She with her first husband Dr Victor Wallace were prominent members of the ESV.

[111]Their Vice-Regal appeal issued from Government House in Sydney, *SMH*, 5 November 1927, 17. The RHA Annual Report of 1928-29 listed around 100 individual and corporate subscribers, including heiresses Ruby Rich and Dame Eadith Walker, businessmen R M Marcus Clark, Sir Samuel Hordern, Sir Arthur Rickard, Edward William Knox (whose father founded CSR), Sir Henry Braddon, Sir Owen Cox, Sir Arthur Meeks, James Dunlop (the tyre manufacturer) and the Tattersall's Club. Financial difficulties are listed in the RHA Annual Report (1933), 1.

[112]RHA Annual Report (1930), 5. See also 'Governor's wife speaks mind' and 'Vice-Regal pair publicly join controversial movement', *Daily Guardian*, 24 July 1929, 1.

[113] 'Combating red curse. Sydney notables praise Lady de Chair', *Daily Guardian* (Sydney), 26 July 1929, 1. Those in favour were Rev W J Grant, Sir Arthur Cocks (NSW President YMCA), Grace Scobie (Professional Workers), Mr P J L Kenny (Father and Son Movement), Matron Kirkealdie (Royal Alexandra Hospital for Children) and Mrs Edmund Gates (Women's League).

[114]V H Wallace, 'Eugenics Society of Victoria (1936-1961)', *ER*, 52-53 (Jan 1962), 215, 218.

[115]Alfred E Rainbow, in 7th Conference of the International Planned Parenthood Federation, 10-16 February 1963, Singapore (Amsterdam: Excerpta Medica Foundation, 1963), 643.

[116] John Leeton and Janet Peterson, 'Family planning in Melbourne', *MJA*, 8 March 1969, 540.

[117] Wallace to Blacker, 18 March 1961 and Peters' death notice, *Argus*, 3 September 1946, 2.

[118] Wallace to Blacker, 15 August 1949, SA/EUG, E4 and 14 September 1960.

---

[119] Alison Turtle, 'Anthropometry in Britain and Australia: technology, ideology and imperial connection', *Storia della Psicologia*, 2 no 2 (1990), 134.

[120] Stephen Garton, 'Sound minds in healthy bodies: reconsidering eugenics in Australia, 1914-1940', *Australian Historical Studies*, 26 (October 1994), 164.

4. Boosting the Population

Positive Eugenics

Motherhood and migration have always mattered in this isolated continent and governments have promoted both in the belief that Australia's wealth and progress depended on an ever-increasing population. While some fantasised about positive eugenics, the mainstream preoccupation was about population growth and national fitness.

Figure 18: Positive Eugenics – Perfect Pair Produce Four[1]

In 1912 Dr Charles Vickery Drysdale (1874-1961) believed that the goals of eugenics and neo-Malthusianism (birth control) were united as far as negative, educative and preventive measures were concerned, but vehemently opposed eugenists' goals for 'so-called' positive eugenics because:

> We do not want an aristocracy of fitness any more than any other aristocracy to dominate us, and a general high level of happiness and vitality can better be produced by the agricultural method of weeding out the unfit and mixing the remainder than by the horticultural method of breeding from selected stocks.[2]

On the grounds that it was 'brutal, unscientific and immoral', Drysdale and his fellow birth control campaigners 'unreservedly' rejected the notion that the 'fit' should reproduce as much as possible in order to eliminate the 'unfit'. Women's role in this, as 'merely the passive instruments of unlimited maternity, without any rights to higher education or participation in public affairs,' was an aspect which he found 'particularly objectionable.' His preferred method was birth control which he said 'would soon result in the elimination of all those who are insufficiently endowed with the bump of philoprogenitiveness', leaving 'the recruiting of the race' to lovers of children.

Drysdale (inaccurately) argued that in 1912 Australia and New Zealand were neo-Malthusian, feminist and infant-death-eliminated utopias:

> in which women are the freest in the world, and in which the diffusion of neo-Malthusian practice is the most widespread, have seen the most rapid fall in the birth-rate but their general and infantile mortality is the lowest in the world, their rate of increase of population is the highest, and it has recently accelerated.[3]

However, while many doctors cheerfully talked about eliminating the unfit, most rejected plans for positive eugenics to increase the numbers of fit people. For example, in August 1913 the *British Medical Journal* scoffed at two such schemes; in the 1700s, Frederick William, King of Prussia, tried to 'propagate procerity' [height] by marrying his gigantic guards to tall women. A spirit of religious socialism inspired the 1870s scheme in which John Humphrey Noyes established the Oneida Community in New York, hoping to produce superior babies (many of which he fathered) through scientific propagation. Twenty one years later the Community's *Handbook* regretted the consequences of 'this terrible combination of two very good ideas – freedom and love'.[4] The Prussian plan also backfired, because the King was too fond of his guards to let them fight. However, the Roman poet Ovid (43 BC – 17 AD) described do-it-yourself eugenics with a happy ending. In his poem *Metamorphoses* (transformations) an adaptation of a Greek myth, the sculptor Pygmalion made a statue of his ideal woman and fell in love with it; in answer to his prayers, the goddess Venus brought the statue to life. George Bernard Shaw's *Pygmalion* and the 1950s version, *My Fair Lady* are similar heaven-on-earth fantasies. They might work in myths and musicals but in real life, New York's 'remarkable eugenics experiment' was ridiculed in a 1913 issue of the *Australasian Medical Gazette*. Doctors would choose a perfect couple who would be rewarded if they married and had children. Mrs William Kissam Vanderbilt, a wealthy member of the selection committee, said that the eugenically-fit couple would receive $100 at their wedding and another $100 on the birth of their first child.

In theory, eugenists supported the twin aims of increasing good births and reducing or eliminating bad births. However, from the outset eugenists acknowledged the difficulties of trying to encourage the finest types to have larger families. Dora Russell mentioned a difficulty faced by those who pay rent – 'Bishops and generals like babies but landladies don't'. In practice few eugenists promoted positive eugenics, which H L Mencken ridiculed as 'the augmentation of the teachable minority'. Eugenists would have found it hard to be persuasive because many of them, including Francis Galton and Leonard Darwin, were themselves childless. What is more important, critics such as the influential Sydney journalist Linda Littlejohn (the President of the Women Voters' Association and the Vice President of the Feminist Club of NSW) pointed out in 1929 that, even if science could improve the race, the choice of the 'fit' would always be a problem. Should the model be 'a Mussolini or a Gandhi, a Darwin or a Ford – a tall man or a short one, a giant in brawn or a giant in intellect – a prohibitionist or an anti-prohibitionist'?[5] This quandary underpins George Bernard Shaw's apocryphal conversation with an actress (Isadora Duncan or Mrs Patrick Campbell) who wanted a child to inherit his brains and her beauty. He replied, 'but what if it had *my* beauty and *your* brains?'

While Nazi Germany's Lebensborn ['fount of life'] experiment to produce perfect Aryans is the most infamous attempt, other positive eugenics schemes still operate. For example, since the 1980s, the Singaporean government has tried to tempt tertiary-educated women to marry and raise large families. In the 1970s American consumers could choose designer babies in addition to a range of cosmetic surgery such as breast augmentation and penile implants. In 1979 an elitist program was financed in California by Robert Graham (1906-1997) who made his millions by manufacturing shatterproof spectacles. His Repository for Germinal Choice, dubbed the Nobel Sperm Bank, boasted of four laureates who gave sperm and status. They were not saying how many of the 200 children were fathered by these four men and only one Nobel Prize winner spoke up, William Shockley. His admission did not allay suspicions about the venture as he had already attracted criticism for publicising IQ tests purporting to show that blacks are less intelligent than whites. Graham denied any plans for a super race, saying that he wanted a better society populated by children who met his criteria for health and emotional stability.

Mitchell Bequest

Two Australians passionately believed in positive eugenics and devoted money and energy to support their causes. The first was Peter Stuckey Mitchell (1856-1921) from Albury, who was described in the *Australian Encyclopaedia* as 'a grazier and philanthropist, a race horse breeder, a good judge of stock and an admirer of strength and efficiency'. A nephew said that his uncle fancied himself as a second Cecil Rhodes.

Mitchell's idiosyncratic will, which has been 'criticised, cursed and chronicled'[6] began with a 1,153-word sentence which specified that prizes for eugenics competitions were to be awarded from his £500,000 estate. In 1921 Britain's *Eugenics Review* discussed his bizarre scheme, explaining Mitchell's belief that, instead of assisting the weak, more lasting good could be accomplished by assisting the healthy and strong to develop their natural advantages. There were to be annual prizes for unmarried females not exceeding 30 years of age, British subjects and *bona-fide* residents of the Commonwealth, of a white race and not the offspring of first cousins. Female applicants had to sit for a written exam and were selected according to physical excellence, freedom from hereditary taint or disease, particularly of the intellect, brightness and cheerfulness of disposition. Their ability to bear and rear normal healthy children and their knowledge of history, geography, English literature and the 'Protestant Bible' were all important. Other prerequisites were swimming, horse riding, housekeeping, domestic economy and infant care. Male contestants had to shoot well, have an excellent physique and have honourably fulfilled any military obligations. There were also prizes for the Army, Navy and Police.

Figure 19: Mitchell Bequest – Hunt for Perfect Men and Women[7]

Although Mitchell died in 1921, the bequest lay dormant for 33 years until his widow died.[8] On 28 June 1954 'one of the strangest wills in Australia's history' was the lead article in Sydney's *Sun*, under the heading 'Hunt for perfect men and women. Strange £160,000 bequest'. The paper continued 'Mitchell [who was] not an eccentric' had ensured that 'once a year from now on a first prize of about £500, second of £250, third of £125 and 12 others of about £60 must be given to 15 unmarried women under 30'. The *Australian Women's Weekly* sponsored the contests and a selection panel was announced in March 1955. It was taken so seriously by this high-circulation magazine that the competition essays were to be judged by Education Department-approved examiners. The selection panel was led by Adolphus P Elkin, the University of Sydney's professor of anthropology, assisted by Miss Fanny Cohen, former headmistress of Sydney's Fort Street Girls High, Dr John Fulton, medical superintendent of the Royal Alexandra Hospital for Children and Mrs Charles Tilden, described as a wartime administrator of the Country Women's Association Girls' Hostels, now a 'practical housewife and mother'. There was extensive publicity, more than 2,358 people applied, 200 completed examinations and £10,000 in prizes were awarded.

In the 1950s, the winners were announced and I managed to contact two doctors, a man and a woman, who had won Mitchell bequest prizes 40 years before. Both had entered the contest on an impulse when they were 21-year-old medical students and they confirmed that eugenics was never mentioned. The woman who had won a minor prize in 1955 told me in the 1990s that Mitchell wouldn't have approved because she had married three times and had produced only one child, although she also has adopted three and has many grandchildren. The man who had won the first prize of £634/18/6 in 1956 told me that his family had helped while he stayed up late writing the essay on the night before the competition deadline. He spent the prize on a holiday and a car, is married and has had six children, one of whom died in infancy. The *Women's Weekly* discontinued its involvement in 1959 because it was too expensive. There have been legal wrangles for 50 years and sponsors were deterred by the stipulation that applicants must be white. On 24 October 1971, the *Sunday Australian* announced that the Mitchell bequest competitions

would again be offered, this time with prizes of $6,750 for Army and Navy personnel. By this time there was no hint of eugenics – one prize was for an essay on Soviet naval power in the Indian Ocean – and the competitions may still continue.

Hopewood House

Another scheme for positive eugenics flourished in Bowral in the southern highlands of NSW from 1942 until the 1960s. It was the dream of Leslie Owen Bailey (1891-1964), the millionaire owner of the Chic Salon dress shops, who was determined to prove his theories about child welfare. He bought a Victorian mansion on a 750 acre farm and established Hopewood House as an orphanage for the 'betterment of society'. 'Daddy' Bailey and his business associate 'Aunty' Madge Cockburn provided love and wholesome food to the children, 43 boys and 43 girls, who had been born under 'unfortunate circumstances'. He urged supporters of his haven to 'work together to show Australia what fine children Bowral can produce'. By 1955 Bailey had invested more than £650,000 and other donors included the child management educator Zoe Benjamin, biscuit makers William Arnott Ltd, retailer David Jones, Murrumbidgee Dried Fruit Sales, the 2GB Happiness Club and the Theosophist-linked Order of the Star in the East. Bailey's fanaticism about 'natural health' and 'rational eating', and his rejection of conventional medicine were influenced by Dr Alan Carroll (c1823-1911) an anthropologist and paediatrician with faddish beliefs about links between diet and longevity. Bailey kept meticulous records of the children's health which showed that, while Australia's infant death rate was 6.8% in 1941, Hopewood did not have a single death, even though the mothers were 'distressed' (code for single women whose babies were fathered by servicemen) and the infants were bottle fed. Bailey made his purpose clear, 'when we are able to demonstrate about 100 children with sound teeth and health records well above average, and a mortality rate which is a record low, we will be in a position to encourage others to pay more attention to our child welfare methods'.

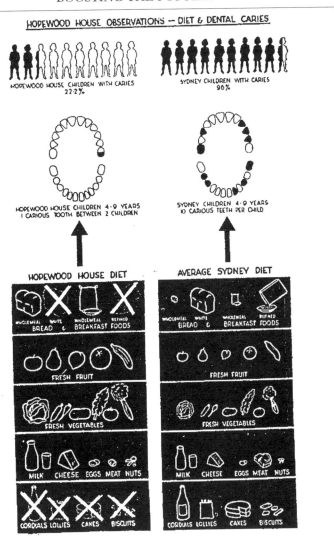

Figure 20: Environmental Eugenics – Good Food Produces
Great Teeth[9]

Bailey, the son of a dentist, believed that teeth are a barometer of health and he arranged for dentists to examine the children's teeth regularly. The findings were impressive, particularly a five-year study by Sydney's Institute of Dental Research which was published by the *Medical Journal of Australia* in June 1953. This study showed that Hopewood children (aged from four to nine) had better teeth than children in other areas of Australia, New Zealand, Canada and three New Guinea villages. Significantly, the dental decay of Hopewood children was 95% less than that of Sydney children's teeth.

My father was a dentist who once combined a 1950s family holiday in Bowral with a visit to Hopewood House. He carried out dental inspections while I played and helped the children to feed their animals. I was nine and envied the children's excitingly free life. They seemed like a large, happy family; the 'baby', aged three, proudly showed me how he could make his own bed and the older ones boasted that they were taken to school in the home's own bus. I remember having snacks of carrots and dried fruits and being allowed to use my teeth to open nuts. A similarly benign picture was given in a 1953 *Medical Journal of Australia* article:

> The type of life led by the children is what is generally described as 'healthy'; that is to say, they are well housed and well clothed, and have regular meals and regular exercise under supervision. Those of school age attend school; the younger ones attend a kindergarten within the home itself. As far as possible, the children are made to feel that they are a large family living in what is virtually their own home.

On 5 February 1994, the *Sydney Morning Herald* gave a very different view of the life at Hopewood. It was written by journalists after interviewing almost 40 people who had lived there as children. The title, 'Blind vision: The Sydney kids who were to breed a super race', might sell newspapers but it was misleading as the emphasis was on the children's health, not on their inter-breeding. Bowral was *not* a latter-day Oneida community and the children (like most who were raised in a kibbutz) did not inter-marry as adults. Certainly, Bailey complained about staffing problems and some children must have resented the rigid regime of wholesome food and water-only fasts when they were sick. Even in the most child-friendly home, life would never be a *Sound of Music* idyll. However, it is unfair to criticise his humanitarian aim to provide children 'deprived of the normal father/mother relationship with an opportunity to reach their maximum potential'. It is impossible to know whether or not the Hopewood children received this benefit. At the very least, they began their adult lives with good health and superb teeth.

Baby Bonus

In Australia, child or maternity allowances have always received strong public support.[10] These benefits were introduced in 1912 and formed an important social welfare initiative. They were implemented in response to demands (starting in the nineteenth century) by socialists, feminists and eugenists, for the state to provide financial assistance to mothers in recognition of the social benefit they provided.[11]

Figure 21: The Australian Baby – Australia's Greatest Asset[12]

They were liberal, almost revolutionary, because the benefits were provided without means testing to both married and unmarried women. It was an early and significant government investment little more than a year after Australia had held is first Commonwealth Census in April 1912. The bonuses began in an era, as the ABC's Dr Norman Swan is fond of quoting, when it was riskier to go and see a doctor than stay at home and hope for the best. However, although general medical care improved after 1912, pregnant women were still at risk for several more decades.

While Marie Stopes enthused about radiant motherhood, others worried because there was too little of it. William Jethro Brown (1868-1930), a law professor at the University of Adelaide, said that in 1912 much was heard about introducing a tax on bachelors and the childless.[13]   During the year Andrew Fisher's (Labor) Federal Government introduced a 'Baby Bonus' (or maternity allowance) in which £5 was given to white mothers after the birth of each child. This was more than two week's pay for many unskilled workers and some critics believed the allocated £600,000 could be used more efficiently in other ways to improve mothers' health and increase births.[14] The intent of the bonus has been debated: some claimed it should pay for doctors or midwives to attend births, and Billy Hughes claimed that it would provide a 'wholesome antidote' to the 'national poison' of birth control.[15] It raised strong emotions and some people still believe, like churches groups in the 1910s, that 'out of wedlock' mothers should not receive encouragement.[16] The *Australasian Medical Gazette* thought the government should exclude wealthy people who 'really do not want it' and, in 1936, the National Council of Women urged payments to be made to Aboriginal mothers.[17]   The egalitarianism rationale for the bonus exasperated the *Eugenics Review* which hoped 'that some effort will be made to direct such funds towards the parents of good stock who are likely to produce fit and healthy children, and that the state is not offering a reward of £5 for the birth of mentally deficient and unemployable of pauper stock!'[18]

Dr Arthur was motivated by equality and eugenics in the family endowment policy he proposed in 1919, commenting that the one-child family was often the result of VD; that children who were 'semi-

starved' could not benefit from free and compulsory education; and
that the two-child family would mean 'racial and national suicide'.[19]

> It is the people who [raised more than three children], by sacrifice
> of the comforts and pleasures of life, who are the true patriots, and
> they should be recognised as such, and their extra children
> regarded as a national charge. [His proposal was not meant to
> increase the birth rate] – offering five shillings a week to a woman
> who did not want children would not induce her to do so. [It was]
> for the welfare of the children who are already here, and are not
> getting enough to eat to-day, and who are not getting enough
> clothes and a proper start in life.

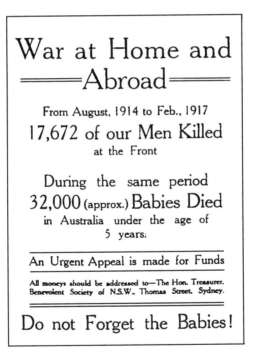

Figure 22: Infant Deaths in Australia: 1914 to 1917[20]

Dr Edith Barrett, Secretary of the Victorian Branch of the National Council of Women and Sir James Barrett's sister, gave a paper at the 1923 All Australian Women's Conference on the Maternity Bonus.[21] She told delegates in Melbourne that in the ten years the Bonus had operated, the birth rate had steadily and seriously declined and it had failed to protect the lives of the mothers or seriously reduce infant mortality. She said it was an act of folly to allow infants to die from preventable causes, such as VD, while spending large sums on migrants. She admitted that the bonus was a boon for doctors as many more of them were now employed than formerly. Her doubts about doctors' efficacy were confirmed by the federal government's 1925 Royal Commission on Health which examined VD, the falling births and the high maternal and infant deaths, and in 1929 when it was shown that the risks *increased* when doctors, rather than midwives, delivered babies.

Barrett's concern about the bonus was shared by Muriel Heagney (1885-1974), a trade unionist who described herself as a 'gradualist socialist' and fought for equal pay for women.[22] Heagney did not agree with Barrett's suggestions that the yearly £700,000 spent on the Bonus should be used for antenatal clinics, maternity hospitals, visiting nurses and domestic aids. Heagney wanted to keep the Bonus and give it directly to mothers, as the money spent on it was 'insignificant' in comparison with the £80,000,000 a year spent for five years on the war, the huge interest being paid, and the vast spending on immigration.[23] Quoting from Eldridge's 'Motherhood Endowment' paper and from Saleeby, she stressed the environmental causes of the high death rate:

> In 1918, one in every 219 married mothers died from puerperal [childbirth] causes, and one in every 123 unmarried mothers. This shows the relation between economic and social conditions and the high death rate. Bad industrial conditions prior to marriage, unhealthy homes, lack of proper food and rest, financial anxiety and worry, ignorance of physical conditions are all admitted to be contributory factors.

> If we are to get to the root of the evil, we must ensure for every mother in the community good housing, continuous income,

freedom from arduous toil, medical care and attention, and everything else that is conducive to the production of healthy children, whilst retaining her own health and vigour. Only by these means can we wipe out the blot of which we are speaking.

This angered Britain's Eugenics Education Society which argued that Australia's policies would increase the size of the 'less valuable' classes. They criticised the Australian £5 Bonus in 1912; in 1922 they rebuffed Eldridge for his 'Endowment of Motherhood' proposal, and Leonard Darwin's address to the Second International Eugenics Congress contained a thinly-disguised criticism of A B Piddington's proposals in *The Next Step: A Family Basic Income*. Darwin was clearly dismayed by Australia's egalitarian approach:

> It follows that to increase the taxation on the more fit in order to ease the strain of family life amongst the less fit would do a double dose of harm; that is by decreasing the output of children where it should be increased and by increasing it where it should be diminished! ...
>
> In regard to all proposals such as that recently made in Australia, for directly and indirectly taking from all workmen a proportion of their earnings and for distributing the money thus obtained amongst the parents in proportion to the number of their young children, here again the racial effects will be good if, and only if, the benefits received from each couple are proportionate to the contributions made by members of the same group to which they belong, a condition almost certain to be neglected.[24]

In 1927 NSW Labor Premier Jack Lang's Family Endowment Act was passed, a year after the first child allowance in the world was pioneered by New Zealand. A B Piddington, who was Marion's husband and the Premier's friend and supporter, had won his battle for child endowment to become an adjunct of the basic wage. Lang was guarded about their relationship when he recalled the endowment victory in *I Remember*, which, he said, aimed to avoid 'personal reminiscences' because he 'never had any time for such trivialities'. Ironically, Lang (the brother-in-law of poet and story teller Henry Lawson) committed these sins in his tale which was decidedly flowery – in both senses of the word. After hearing the good news, Lang ran into Piddington who was carrying 'a large bunch of flowers' and 'dancing with delight' because he had 'realised the ambition of a lifetime'. The 'Big Fella' ('Mad Dog' to his enemies) complained 'he thrust the flowers into my hand, scattering them all over me in the process of throwing his arms around me' and then 'garlanded me with flowers in the middle of Macquarie Street'. Lang was embarrassed by this 'Gallic' display. A more apt book title might have been *I Forget*, because while Lang magnified this joyful moment, he said nothing about the public humiliation he suffered at the 19 March 1932 official opening of the Sydney Harbour Bridge. Painfully for him, the images were captured by Newsreel cameras as fascist New Guard member Francis de Groot (1888-1969) galloped past Premier Lang and the official party to slash the ceremonial ribbon with his sword.

Child endowment continued to be an issue. In 1928 a Sydney newspaper published an item about Julian Huxley's 'notion for a Ministry of Eugenics', and a response by John Charles Lucas Fitzpatrick (1862-1932), a journalist and politician who had held posts in Sir George Fuller's ministries, who mused 'so many strange and fanatical ideas are being propounded just now that one hardly knows whether to treat them seriously or otherwise'. He took Dr Arthur seriously enough to propose that 'the little doctor' would be well qualified to lead such a Ministry as 'no harm and a lot of good might come out of it'.[25]

An indication of the escalating economic troubles is shown in the statement, by the Commonwealth's 1928 Royal Commission on Child Endowment or Family Allowance, that a national endowment scheme would only be acceptable if the benefits it produced were greater than the disadvantages of the needed additional taxation to fund them.[26] The Commissioners proposed to only assist children of the 'right kind of stock' because, to justify public spending, 'eugenic considerations which have not hitherto been regarded must be taken into account'.[27] Dr Cumpston noted that 'there may be a large difference of opinion as to how far eugenic control could safely be carried out at present' and the Commissioners concluded:

A logical consequence of the establishment of a Commonwealth scheme of Child Endowment would be the creation of some form of eugenic control.

Expert witnesses appeared unanimous that up to a certain point, such control is both practicable and desirable. The unmistakably feeble-minded, and persons tainted with serious and transmissible diseases or defects, should be prevented from reproducing their species. Within such limits, in our opinion, eugenic control should be established, whether or not Child Endowment be accepted as a feature of national policy.

While the 1929 Depression killed the scheme, British health expert Dame Janet Campbell was commissioned to report on maternal and child welfare in Australia.[28] The *Times* reported on 15 May 1929 that because of the special importance to the Empire as a whole, Britain's Minister for Health had agreed that she could undertake her special mission in Australia. Dr Arthur, the NSW Minister for Health, objected to this news, saying that she would find more in Australia than she could teach and insisting it was unnecessary to have another Royal Commission on the matter. Prompted by the controversy, the National Council of Women astutely asked the Commonwealth Government to provide state funding so that obstetrics could be taught in university medical schools.[29] Millicent Preston Stanley (1883-1955) used the slogan 'horses' rights for women'. She was a member of the Nationalist Party and the first woman to be appointed to the NSW Legislative Assembly and wanted the University of Sydney to establish a chair in midwifery rather than one in horse obstetrics. The slogan was first used by an American judge, Ben Lindsey (1869-1943), who supported human rights and 'companionate marriage' and argued that women's rights should at least be equal to horses'.[30] Dame Janet's findings, in her 1930 Report to the Australian Parliament, confirmed Edith Barrett's view that women's preference for doctors rather than midwives had caused the high death rate during childbirth.

In 1938 and 1944, two ESV members proposed startling measures to encourage the 'fit' to have more children. On 7 July 1938, German-born physician Dr Fritz Duras gave a lecture on 'Eugenics in Germany today' which Melbourne's *Age* reported.[31] Duras, the Director of

Physical Education at Melbourne University, described the Nazis race improvement as one of the most interesting biological experiments in the world. In October 1938 he reminded the Federal Government of the importance 'of enlisting the help of the health authorities and the medical profession' in the national fitness campaign.[32]   In 1944 Professor Agar, the ESV President, proposed that families with above average incomes would be encouraged to have more children and the childless would provide money for a family 'equalisation' allowance by 'sharing out' their incomes.[33]   Agar's elitist scheme was unusual for Australia and he seemed surprised when it was 'turned down very contemptuously by Mr Chifley', the Labor Prime Minister.[34]

Dr Norman Haire, who returned to Australia in 1940 after more than 20 years in Europe, also expressed a contentious view.[35]   In an ABC radio forum in 1944, Haire provocatively suggested that the government should provide a 'No-Baby Bonus' to parents of bad stock as an incentive for them to remain childless and, in addition, the baby bonus should only go to healthy and otherwise desirable parents. This, he hoped would dissuade the births of children who were likely to be a burden to the community and induce parents of good stock to produce healthy children who would be an asset. In his view, the choice of suitable 'migrants from the womb' was just as important as choosing suitable migrants from overseas.[36]

Dr Wallace believed that the 'differential birth rate' which Agar sought to overcome 'was not so prominent a feature of Australian vital statistics as it is in those of older countries'.[37]   He also questioned the ability of an official body [the National Health and Medical Research Council][38] to discover the 'elusive truth' about women's reasons for limiting births, believing that an honest response was more likely in questionnaires which he had received from 530 women who consulted him about contraception.[39]   His analysis of their reasons for using contraception, compiled between 1934 and 1944, and the reasons which women gave for attending the RHA Birth Control Clinic in 1938-1939, are both shown in **Table 5**, which while unsophisticated, show a predominant pattern of economics and health, rather than eugenics, as the reasons for using contraception.

Birth Control Clinics	Financial difficulties	Health	Eugenics/ Hereditary
Dr Wallace's clinic	292	221	8
RHA's clinic	358	227	8

Table 5: Reasons for Attending Birth Control Clinics in the 1930s

The findings of these two small samples in the 1930s were validated in 1944 when financial hardship was the overwhelming reason given by 1,400 women for limiting their family size. Dr Cumpston, in an analysis of their statements to the National Medical and Research Council, stated that women only gave eugenic reasons 'in a few cases', for example where there was a family history of mental or other disorders which might appear in the children, or because the husband was an alcoholic or had VD and the 'wife refused to have children to such a father'.[40]

Kindergartens and Schools for Mothers

From the 1890s Australian social reformers worked to improve the care of mothers and young children. Feminists, led by Margaret Windeyer and Maybanke Wolstenholme (later Anderson), formed the Kindergarten Union of NSW and in 1896 launched the first free kindergarten in the British Empire, in the inner-Sydney area of Woolloomooloo. William Spence, the labour hero who founded the Amalgamated Shearers Union in 1886, took a broad view of what was required to raise healthy children. In his 1908 pamphlet *The Child, the Home and the State* he argued that to produce 'the highest type of man and woman possible' it was necessary to improve the environment, provide pure food and take better care of mothers. Spence, a tetotaller and temperance advocate, agreed with the 'eminent biologist' Dr Saleeby, that 'character-making should be the supreme aim of the legislator'. Spence continued:

> The fault is not always with the parents; it is with society ... The mother is swindled by adulterated food, and when the baby is made sick and the doctor is called the prescription is useless because of fraudulent drugs. Worry and loss to parents and loss of good citizens to a Commonwealth which is crying out for

additional population is the result. We take more care of cattle, sheep, or pigs than we do of our own flesh and blood. We call upon the women electors to help bring the remedy into operation.[41]

In a 1910 Presidential address to the South Australian Branch of the British Medical Association, William Verco suggested that such measures as female inspectors visiting each home before and after a baby was born, dairy inspection, and the supply and distribution of sterilised bottles of milk for babies would save infants and make them strong. The beneficial consequences that would flow from these measures, aimed at the mothers of the race, would amply compensate the State for the effort.[42] As well, many reformers began teaching women mothercraft, basing the instruction on the model provided by Britain in 1907 with its School for Mothers.[43] The training included large doses of patriotism in which mothers were reminded of their Imperial obligations, their duty to Australia and the need to comply with the mother-focused purity feminism. In 1913 the redoubtable American author Jessie Ackermann scoffed at the 'usual groan of the alarmist' that these Australian reforms were saving the unfit. She was sure that women believed it was better to rear three or four healthy children than to 'swell the increasing flood of poorly equipped specimens of humanity'. She was adamant that 'no railing or wailing or abuse would shake women's determination to safeguard the future generations'.[44]

Figure 23: Purity Feminism – Family Values not Debauchery[45]

Early last century, women were often lectured about their maternal shortcomings but there were positives too such as the practical advice given to mothers who attended the well-baby clinics in Sydney, started by the Benevolent Society in 1906. Valuable initiatives were undertaken even earlier by Dr William George Armstrong (1859-1941), a public health pioneer in Australia, and probably the first in the world to seriously try to reduce infant deaths and educate mothers. From 1903 Armstrong's *Advice to Mothers* pamphlet was sent to the home of every new mother.[46] Armstrong was helped by the National Council of Women which ran the Alice Rawson School for Mothers, whose motto was 'Save the children for the nation'. The first School opened in 1908 in Sydney's Bourke Street, Darlinghurst and others were established in the inner city areas of Newtown and Alexandria. This pioneering doctor began his work four years earlier than Sir Frederick Truby King (1858-1938) the New Zealand eugenist who now receives most of the kudos for pioneering infant care. In another irony, while women's groups now fight to stop government cuts to child care, in

1915 the Women's Liberal League of NSW called it 'officialdom strangling free action' when the Baby Clinics Board assumed the operation of the Rawson School for Mothers. They decried this as the State's tendency to absorb 'all voluntary effort'.

Figure 24: The Unwanted Baby[47]

In 1918 the Royal Society for the Welfare of Mothers and Babies was established to co-ordinate work of child rescue institutions such as the Benevolent Society of New South Wales, which since 1813 had provided shelter and motherly care for unwanted, often illegitimate, babies. Unfortunately, despite it's benevolent image, 100 years ago, most of the Benevolent Society's 'foundlings' died before their first birthday.

Adelaide law professor Jethro Brown acknowledged that 'a superior type of women entered the professions and were absorbed by their work'.[48] He contrasted his liberalism with the conservatism of a British professor who, in 1909 proposed that talented female chemists should be denied work in the field and encouraged to become the mothers of future chemists.[49] However, apart from domestic service, Australian women were discouraged from doing any paid work. For instance, a 1912 editorial in the *Australasian Medical Gazette* opposed girls' employment in factories on the grounds that they would become puny, anaemic and dyspeptic, making them unfit for motherhood. Equally, if girls refused to be servants, middle- and higher-class women would be unfit for motherhood, as they could not bear children and attend to household duties as well. The author, Dr Roberta Jull, thought that the remedy – 'obvious but unlikely with a Labor Government' – was to make laws banning women from trades and factories and compelling girls to serve a training in domestic economy. This feminist doctor argued that conscripting domestic servants would increase births more effectively than the proposals of the 1904 Royal Commissioners.[50]

Charles V Drysdale had argued in 1912 that race improvement did not depend on 'the sacrifice of women to passive and unlimited maternity'[51] but New Zealand's Truby King still endorsed the old womb-centred role for women. He warned delegates at the 1914 Australasian Medical Congress: if an undue proportion of women's energies and blood-supply went to the brain there would not be enough left over for the rest of the system. Such folly would result in flat-chested over-pressured girls who would never have children. Instead, King suggested that girls should be trained to become good mothers, and used memorable slogans such as 'Breast-fed is Best-fed'. He believed that giving girls a greater interest in matters connected with home life would help women and the race. He wanted a woman's hand to rock the cradle provided she only aspired to rule the nursery world.

King said he used to be 'all enthusiasm' for women's higher education but had changed after hearing a paper at a Conference on Infant Mortality and Child Welfare in London read by a Chicago doctor, Caroline Hedger. In her study of female graduates from Wellesley College, Hedger found that few of them married or had children, few mothers breast fed their babies and the children they produced were inferior.[52] At the Australasian Medical Congress, the Section in which he spoke supported King but he could not persuade the full Congress to endorse his resolution to limit girls' education to domestic science.[53] Sadly, the university-educated campaigner Dr Mary Booth, agreed with King's view. After graduating in Arts from the

University of Sydney in 1890, she followed this with a medical degree from the University of Edinburgh in 1899 and then worked in the Victorian Department of Education where she helped establish the state's first school medical service. The eugenic interests of this dynamic woman were expressed in her concerns about mental deficiency. She also joined the University of Sydney's Society for Combating Venereal Diseases and was awarded an OBE in 1918.

Despite her feminism, education and career, Booth argued that girls should not be exposed to demanding school work because this would divorce them from home interests and make them lose the taste for a contented home life. In 1936 she established a Memorial College of Household Arts and Science in North Sydney which trained girls in order to upgrade their status as housewives. In an ironic feminist twist, after it closed in 1961, College funds were used not for home economics but to endow a scholarship for female economics students at the University of Sydney. Dr Booth had not been the only university-educated 'Aunty Tom': in 1910 Dr Edith Barrett proposed to the National Council of Women that household science should be taught at university and from 1927 to 1935 Jessie Street (who was later revered as a feminist icon) operated a House Service Company to train and supply domestic workers and later suggested that the NSW Premier should provide a federal grant to train girls for domestic service.

In 1922 William Blocksidge (who later adopted the name Baylebridge), in rhetoric which preceded that of Hitler, described women as 'the sacred vessels of maternity'.[54] Blocksidge's eugenic vision was for all healthy women to find 'their highest duty and pleasure in producing and bringing up the largest number of efficient citizens that their health and means would permit'.[55] The unhappy alternative was self inflicted, according to the Reverend R B S Hammond, who had been a member of the Eugenics Society of NSW. In an address to University students, reported in the *Sydney Evening News* on 22 June 1925, he claimed that birth control caused the neurotic conditions of that time. The view that healthy married women should be mothers was the widely-accepted norm, certainly not a fringe view held by pronatalists and eugenists. Vehement opposition to contraception was expressed by people as diverse as Sir James Barrett, Billy Hughes and Octavius Charles Beale and mothers' duty to rear healthy children dominated discussions of infant mortality and child welfare, whether the focus was on quality or quantity, on the nurture of the fittest, or on the preservation of infant life. An example of this pronatalism appeared in an editorial on Motherhood, in the *Medical Journal of Australia* on 24 April 1926. It stated that 'the average woman has a period of productivity of about 30 years and Nature gives her opportunities of bringing into the world a family of 20 or more'. The author regretted that *Homo sapiens* differs from other animals in a deliberate opposition to Nature's methods. No one objected to this enthusiasm for unfettered fertility.

Because pronatalism was the norm and sacrosanct Catholic dogma, the RHA had to be cautious and stressed in 1955 that they only worked to prevent abortions or pregnancies which would 'not end happily'.[56] The RHA did not knowingly give advice to the unmarried and consistently emphasized that birth control was only used as a strategy to space births or to prevent them in cases of disease or economic hardship.

National Fitness

Plans to protect and improve national fitness began early because colonial authorities recognised the need for disease control, particularly in the tropics, and were aware that, despite being an island continent, quarantine was vitally important. In 1832 the first Quarantine Act was passed in NSW(modelled on the English Act of 1825) and in 1838 a shipload of typhus-infected immigrants was quarantined. In 1908 federal quarantine acts replaced the individual state's acts, and under the national system all ships were medically inspected and special plague protection was introduced. Sir Thomas Fitzgerald, in his Presidential address to the 1889 Intercolonial Medical Congress, warned delegates that 'fever stalks each year', although medicine continued to advance, making it imperative for good sanitation to accompany the 'educational progress and mental improvement of the people'.[57] A smallpox outbreak in Sydney in 1913 emphasised the need for greater Commonwealth involvement in health and a major step towards this goal was the establishment of the Commonwealth Department of Health in 1921 followed in 1936 by the National Health and Medical Research Council. Dr Emanuel Sydney Morris, a talented public health administrator, stressed in his 1933 Presidential Address to the Health Inspectors' Association that social progress was dependent on good hygiene which comprised the collective measures needed to safeguard the public's health.[58]

Infant deaths were decreasing by the early 1900s. However, despite progress in medical practice in the first quarter of the twentieth century, Dr Morris, then the Senior Officer of the NSW Department of Health, noted in a prize-winning essay published in September 1925 that deaths from childbirth-related infections had shown 'no noteworthy diminution' and had shown 'a very serious increase' in several states.[59]   Each year 700 mothers in their prime died in childbirth. Contraception was either unavailable or unreliable and, as a result, from 1909 to 1920 'the combined number of illegitimate births and births occurring under nine months after marriage comprise over 54% of the total first births'. Paradoxically, the risk of death was greatest for women who were attended by doctors not midwives and for births which took place in city hospitals. Morris despaired because the medical profession had contempt for their 'inferior' public health colleagues.[60]

Some of Morris' 'superior' colleagues preferred to ignore his evidence. Defensiveness, or a lack of candour, is evident in an October 1925 speech to nurses given by John C Windeyer (1875-1951), Professor of Obstetrics at the University of Sydney, in which he complained about press reports of 'alleged excessive maternal mortality'.[61] Windeyer had also boasted of founding Australia's first antenatal clinic in 1912, while not mentioning the international record set in 1904 when Armstrong launched the infant welfare movement in inner city areas of Sydney.[62] Astoundingly, the Commonwealth waited until 1936 before it made its first grant to universities for research and there was no significant reduction in the maternal death rates until the late 1930s and early 1940s which saw such advances as the introduction of antibiotics and blood transfusions.

In 1938, at the recommendation of the newly-established National Health and Medical Research Council, a National Council for Physical Fitness was established.[63]   Efforts to improve national efficiency by expanding child endowment and other public health measures intensified because of the approaching war. As well, six model child-care centres – the Lady Gowrie Child Centres – were set up by the Commonwealth Government. An example of the increasing concerns about national fitness is displayed in statements by Dr Morris who had become the NSW Director-General of Public Health.   In 1937 he wrote: 'while private medical practitioners frequently opposed Baby Health Centres, public support for them had become insistent and politically significant'.   Nevertheless, despite the public demand for such preventive services, Morris was convinced that the Australian medical profession was neither sympathetic nor tolerant towards its public health colleagues.[64] His pessimism was short-lived because, as the probability of war increased, the role of public health increased. In 1938 Morris wrote this flowery sentence: 'One of the most potent national urgings towards physical fitness has been the desire to provide a race of strong, virile, stalwart individuals who would provide an invincible bulwark for defence in times of crisis or emergency'. He noted that the renewed interest in physical education had coincided with international troubles. Although he considered physical fitness as primarily an individual responsibility, it was 'obviously a matter of direct concern to the state' as well, since it was 'an essential qualification of socially efficient citizenship'.[65]

By 1939 Morris reported: 'The State is slowly but surely taking upon itself the management of the physical life of the individual from the moment of conception until he has shuffled off his mortal coil'.[66] He contended that Australia could no longer rely on its natural advantages of sunshine, climate and good food, and that the State had to improve the 'unfit', who were an 'incubus' borne by the 'industrious and able sections of the community'.   The National Health and Medical Research Council (NHMRC) gave a careful response:

> It is a particular attribute of the British character that voluntary organizations have often shown themselves more ready to undertake activities essential to the welfare of the nation than governments have been to enforce them by legislative measures.

Thus, in the field of physical education, there are numerous bodies so engaged from the Boy Scout and Girl Guide organizations to church groups and sporting clubs and associations.[67]

However, the NHMRC became involved itself in 1939 by setting up demonstration child care centres in each state capital to 'investigate and model programs for the mental, social and physical development of children'. These centres, named after Lady Gowrie, the wife of the then Governor General, still operate.

The high priority on national fitness continued during the war; the Commonwealth National Fitness Act was passed in 1941 and National Fitness Councils were established in all states. Kathleen M Gordon, who was appointed National Fitness Officer, presented reports[68] and in 1951, Gordon and three others investigated social problems in Britain, America and Australia. The Carnegie Corporation, whose money brought about the founding of the Australian Council for Education Research (ACER) in 1930, also funded the team which recommended that Australia should co-ordinate and extend its services for youth. Their proposals followed the work of Edith Onians, who in the nineteenth century had helped Melbourne's illiterate newspaper boys, and the Police Boys' Clubs which began in Sydney in 1937. The 1951 report had significance for eugenists because the report's editor was ACER Director Dr Kenneth Cunningham who was President of the ESV from 1947 until it ceased in 1961.[69] After the war, National Fitness changed its emphasis to children's leisure activities such as national fitness camps and swimming classes.

The Women's Movement and Eugenics

Many scholars of the early feminist, birth control and eugenics movements have criticised these groups from their own 1970s, 1980s or 1990s perspectives. Don Kirschner examined the 'ambiguous legacy' of the Progressive reformers. At the time, they were portrayed 'almost as saints'. However, 'in the hands of several recent [1960s] scholars' they appear 'as detached as a group of engineers redesigning a worn-out mechanism'.[70] For some, the saints have become sinners. In Pasadena, Ellen Chesler criticised the critics at the 1992 launch of her book *The Battle for Reproductive Freedom: Margaret Sanger and Her Legacy*:

Birth control has fundamentally altered private life and public policy in this country. Kennedy found Sanger too hot. Sanger was too cool for Linda Gordon. The view of Sanger as a racist had been propagated by the New Right. Angela Davis was also critical and such criticisms have had a profound impact.[71]

Chesler did not write as a Sanger sycophant but to unmask myths promoted by these Sangerphobes: biographer David M Kennedy who claimed 'Sanger turned women's concerns back to the personal, and that the personal is not political. I believe that the personal *is* political; this is the second stage of feminism';[72] author Linda Gordon who claimed that Sanger deserted feminism and socialism to further male eugenists' aims to control the poor,[73] and Angela Davis, the black activist on the FBI's '10 most wanted list' in 1970, who claimed that white birth controllers were part of a genocidal plot to eliminate blacks. Such critics ignore the fact that Sanger was active when eugenics was a respectable scientific reform while birth control and feminism were not.

In 1993 Deborah Cohen found flaws in the accepted negative views about Marie Stopes.[74] She examined the Mothers' Clinics records of staff and patients, and found that despite historians' extensive writing about Stopes and the birth control movement, their views were remarkably lopsided: by ignoring the clinics, they had 'wrongly identified a critical *characteristic* of birth control propaganda as the most important *outcome* of its practice'. Cohen showed that Stopes' 'practical work in the clinics was governed not by her loudly-proclaimed eugenic allegiances, but by her concern for the happiness and health of the individual woman'.

In Australia Margaret Conley had launched an attack on the RHA in 1980. She wrote 'The RHA showed no interest in increasing the individual freedom of women, and despite their concern with physical and genetic transference of disease, they were primarily interested in health only as an indicator of genetic fitness. The primary concern of the RHA and the state to which they pledged allegiance (because of their economic status under its regime) was population control'.[75] Arthur's Liberal-Nationalist government provided the RHA's subsidy from 1928 to 1930, when it was withdrawn by the NSW Labor

Minister for Health, a Catholic, because the Labor Party was 'not at liberty' to support an organisation which might offend its Catholic supporters.[76] 'The Association was not the object of the hostility experienced by reformers such as Marie Stopes and Margaret Sanger' wrote Conley, dismissing the RHA as God's Police; politically conservative middle-class women bent on eliminating the unfit and controlling the poor.

There are problems with Conley's conclusions; as the RHA said, their birth control clinic was 'not responsible for the falling birth rate' in the 1930s; the RHA had no 'allegiance' to the 'regime' of 'the state' other than the usual obligation to be law-abiding.   The wish to improve women's health was the RHA's primary concern; as they wrote in 1940 'the Birth Control Clinic properly managed by expert medical women, assisted by nurses, does good work and saves many women from unwanted children, and from illegal abortions. Children who cannot be fed, clothed and educated, should not be born, and if an ordinary middle-class working pair have more than four children, it is impossible to give those children a decent chance in life'. A similar concern motivated Dr Arthur, the state's Health Minister and when his opponents claimed that he was returned to office in 1928 by the women's vote, he said this showed women's good sense, declaring, 'I'm a feminist and proud of it'.

The NSW Government gave the RHA subsidies to support their VD work, not for their 'contentious' birth control clinic and it was the Depression which caused the subsidy to be withdrawn in 1930, three years *before* the birth control clinic started. At that time the country was in 'populate or perish' mode, birth control was taboo and most people were opposed to it, not just the Catholic church. Goodisson, who had to struggle for finances and acceptance, earned her position with the 'reformers' Sanger and Stopes.

As shown in **Table 5**, most women gave health or financial difficulties as their reason for using contraception but the RHA had to disclaim such reality and adopt 'one of the standard protective tactics – providing information and services through a network of sympathetic practitioners, while appearing virtuous in public'.[77]

Anthea Hyslop preceded Chesler and Cohen in her criticism of the critics. She reported in her 1980 doctoral thesis that liberal, radical and conservative views about public health and child welfare were 'almost indistinguishable' in Melbourne from 1890-1914. She found there were surprisingly similar views about racial improvement and national vigour and all agreed on the need for a 'larger, healthier, racially pure population, and for the preventive and scientific treatment of social problems'.[78] She rejected the sterile dichotomy in which Progressivism was dismissed as a self-serving middle class attempt to manipulate workers.[79] While the 'progressive measures of the early twentieth century were chiefly instigated by middle class people', their measures and goals 'had the endorsement, and sometimes the active support of the Labor Party'. The same applied to the RHA which had both radical and conservative supporters and opponents. Retrospective judgments are risky as many factors influenced a group's public behaviour often masking their real motives, particularly in clandestine operations such as the RHA, which had to be 'careful about what they said and even more careful about what they wrote'.[80]

The relationship of birth control, feminism and eugenics is fraught with ambiguity and conflict although eugenics could provide women opportunities for social action.[81] However, Jane Clapperton, a British feminist and socialist eugenist, had no organizational backing in 1885 when she produced the first eugenic discussion of birth control,[82] a book which she called *Scientific Meliorism and the Evolution of Happiness*[83] in tribute to her 'early teacher', the novelist George Eliot who, because she disliked the word 'optimist', coined the word 'meliorist', a belief that life could be made better. Clapperton, a like-minded radical, proposed that laws should allow greater freedom in marriage and greater strictness about parentage, because marriage was a private matter, whereas childbirth touched the 'interests of the whole nation'.[84] She wanted to merge the eugenics and birth control movements to alter the 'confused sentiment, illogical thought, and disastrous action in the field of eugenics to clearness of purpose and consistency of life'.[85] Few agreed with her and, during the infancy of the eugenics movement in Britain and America, most eugenists did not share her optimism about the advantages of such a merger. A 1911 editorial in the *American Breeders' Magazine* typifies this pessimism:

> With the rapid increase of wealth a large number of women of well-to-do families go into the leisure class, producing, often, neither children nor other forms of national wealth. But the great change has been from work in the home, usually the farm home, to work as an employee. ... Contemporaneous with this stupendous economic, educational, social, and political movement of women is a very strong tendency to reduction of the birth rate. And those with splendid eugenic heredity ... use their knowledge to lessen the birthrate.[86]

Such rebukes about 'fit' women's wilful opposition to childbearing were common but in Australia social and reform movements offered women an opportunity for public activism. At the 1893 Congress of the Australasian Association for the Advancement of Science, Henry Rusden claimed that women were fortunately 'alive' to the need for an 'improved choice of mates' but he wanted the young to be 'better instructed.'[87] In 1910 the British suffragist Mabel Atkinson quoted a misogynist chemistry professor, H E Armstrong, who disparaged women's 'sterile independence'[88] and noted that 'many eugenists and men of science regard the feminist movement with critical not to say unfriendly eyes'.[89] By the 1930s the hostile interaction between feminism and eugenics had begun to thaw.

In her 1975 study of eugenics and the American women's movement, Martha Ellen Bettes claimed that most eugenists sensed the urgency of convincing feminists to become mothers as they knew that feminism had particular appeal for those women they labelled 'superior stock'.[90] The women's movement had begun a generation before eugenics and while some feminists had tailored their eugenics so that it did not conflict with feminism, most left eugenics to the men; most women who were progressives picked the women's movement *or* birth control.[91]

Bettes' hypothesis is generally correct but Marie Stopes was an exception and Margaret Sanger even more so, because she adapted eugenics to suit her primary birth control purpose, guided by her feminist belief that 'no woman can call herself free who does not own and control her body', and by her wish to improve women's health. Certainly, most Australian suffragists took the either/or approach because they were afraid that their cause would be harmed if they also supported contraception – 'appurtenances of the brothel'. In the nineteenth century Brettena Smyth (1842-1898) was probably Australia's only woman publicly to embrace both. This brave woman, who as a campaigner for suffrage and women's rights, defied convention as a 'feminist, free-thinker, phrenologist, eugenicist, self-taught health reformer, birth-control advocate, conventional moralist and political campaigner' who contributed to Melbourne's 'social and cultural life in the 1880s and 1890s'.[92] As Meredith Foley noted in her 1985 thesis on the women's movement in New South Wales and Victoria from 1918 to 1938, social and political reforms were frequently initiated by women.[93] These feminists were not faced with the suffragettes' dilemma of choosing votes or birth control; early last century some, like Sanger, Stopes and the RHA, used eugenics as a conveniently acceptable framework to provide their much less acceptable birth control services.

Suitability of Immigrants

In the nineteenth century, Malthus' theories stimulated British fears about over-population. The fears abated when people realised that a symbiotic relationship could be established in which surplus people in Britain could be sent to stock the Empire, particularly Australia. While there was no choice in the convict days, afterwards migration became a prime concern for Australian governments.

When the economy boomed between 1909 and 1913, immigration soared; after the 1890s Depression, only 3,859 assisted migrants arrived in 1901-05; this climbed to 40,932 in 1906-10 and made a spectacular jump to 150,570 in 1911-15.[94] However, despite post-Federation euphoria and the prosperity of the early years of last century, there were concerns about having to rely on migration for the country's population growth and many would have preferred the increase to be home-grown. For example, Australia's first medical Rhodes Scholar, Harvey Sutton, commented:

The child born in Australia comes into the world with many natural advantages. Hereditarily 'sprung of the earth's first blood' with 'titles manifold', belonging to one of the whitest races on the globe – 98% British – the Australian babe is widely and rightly acclaimed as Australia's best immigrant.[95]

The slogan that babies were our best immigrants was made popular in 1905 by the politician W A (Bill) Holman (1871-1934), an intellectual, an 'orator of eloquence and fire' and one of the 1904 Birth-rate Commissioners who later became the Labor Premier of NSW.[96] In 1905 the federal and state governments encouraged immigration but the Labor Party actively discouraged it, though they denied this in 1910.[97] The slogan was used again in 1919 by the shrewd but humourless Sir Joseph (Joe) Cook (1860-1947), a former Prime Minister, in a fund raising appeal for Sydney's Renwick Hospital for Infants. The 'People or Perish' slogan (shown in Figure 3) asked readers to 'Pay! Pay!! Pay!!!' to make sure that the lives of 'tiny tots' were preserved and kept for the nation.

He appealed to patriotism and economics, 'the greater the number the smaller the burden of taxation'.[98] Paradoxically, Cook used identical rhetoric two months later to support *adult* immigration.[99] This aggressive debater made another U-turn in 1925, when as the High Commissioner of Australia, he supported one of Britain's (now notorious) child migration schemes. Ironically, his plea for funds to help infants appeared in the newsletter of the Benevolent Society of NSW, whose own foundling home, as mentioned earlier, had shocking statistics which had been revealed in the first volume of the 1904 *Royal Commission on the Decline of the Birth-Rate and on the Mortality of Infants in New South Wales*, Volume 1, Exhibit number 139, with a death rate of 86% of the 'foundlings' (under the age of one) who were admitted in 1896.

Migration was favoured by the bumptiously conservative Prime Minister Stanley Bruce who told delegates at the 1926 Imperial Conference in London that the need for a better distribution of the white population was the greatest problem facing the British Empire. Not surprisingly Australian eugenists and immigration groups often shared common ground and the RHA affiliated with the New Settlers'

League in 1929. In the same year, Dr Richard Granville Waddy, a Council Member of Sydney's pro-immigration Millions Club, complained that Britain was not sending her 'thoroughbreds': being white and British was not enough. In his view Britain's unskilled labourers were not desirable contributors to Australia's national stock.[100] Changes in immigration policies increased this concern. Although immigration practically ceased during World War I, the *Eugenics Review* noted that 6,918 British women had married Australian soldiers by December 1918 and would soon settle in Australia, and welcomed this as being infinitely better than an immigration scheme.[101]

When migration resumed in 1920, officials accepted some applications from non-British immigrants. One trigger was America's eugenically-based Johnson Act which, after it was introduced in 1924 to protect the country's 'Nordic' stock, was greeted sympathetically in Australia.[102] After labourers from central and southern European were denied access to America, many came to Australia where resources were scarcely coping with the needs of returned soldiers. The usually liberal A B Piddington complained in 1924 in his *Smith's Weekly* column that Australia's standards of manhood would decline because the government was subsidising the immigration of human derelicts and paupers;[103] Australia, he said, was accepting the sweepings of the Mediterranean which American immigration officials had rejected.[104] A year later, the *Labor Daily* reported that mental hospitals were filled with insane aliens, a claim which was quickly denied by officials who said that 'about 80% of overseas inmates of these asylums originate in Britain'. Apparently, mad British inmates were acceptable but mad 'aliens' were not. Usually however, mental deficiency was considered a much greater threat than insanity. For example, Dr Ernest Jones revealed in the *Sydney Morning Herald* on 14 August 1928 that 18 years earlier he had been 'the unfortunate person who directed the attention of the Victorian State Parliament to the large number of mentally deficient people among the immigrants'.

In the *Australasian Medical Gazette* on 20 July 1910, Dr William Verco stressed the need to become the home of a virile race which would be physically fit, mentally robust, morally clean and commercially sound. In 1913 a Melbourne doctor stated that a great wave of immigration was beginning and begged the government to select immigrants from Britain and European countries that breed good colonists. He urged strict medical screening for immigrants: 'While we are prepared to extend a warm welcome to all who are in earnest to make Australia their home and add to her strength and wealth, yet we have an equal right to refuse to allow *any* to make our country the scene, either of their ineffectiveness, their follies, or their crimes'.[105]

Ernest MacBride, Professor of Zoology at Britain's Imperial College of Science and an office bearer of the Eugenic Society, proposed a bizarre scheme in 1927 for 'checking degeneracy'.[106] He doubted whether Australia's tropical sun and luxurious vegetation were suitable for white races which had 'evolved in a struggle with grey skies and invigorating climate'.[107] Despite this, he suggested

> that if numbers of British city people were transported to the wilder parts of Australia and left to their own resources they would in two or three generations again develop into quite respectable people.[108]

Coincidentally, in June 1927 the *Labor Daily* reported that Judge Walter Bevan had called for 'exhaustive mental tests' to ensure that Australia did not receive mentally deficient migrants and the following month Australian doctors were appointed in three British immigration ports to inspect immigrants.[109] The next year the RHA lobbied for a female doctor to be employed at Australia House to screen female immigrants. It is hard not to laugh at the argument which Lillie Goodisson used to justify this service. She said 'we do not want people with venereal diseases brought out here because we have quite enough of our own'.[110]

In 1928 Sir George Knibbs, the only Australian to have made a significant contribution to the world-wide debate on eugenics, was concerned about transferring 'inferior sections of humanity' to 'relatively empty countries'.[111] Knibbs assured Margaret Sanger that her work would 'bear fruit rapidly' and that Comstock's suppression of vice law, which banned birth control, would end.[112] Knibbs, who was a Vice-president of Stopes' Society for Constructive Birth Control, told

Stopes that the world was in for a very hard time unless 'we are to improve and make the lot of humanity more satisfactory by being governed by the more intelligent and altruistic (the few), instead of by the ignorant and selfish masses'.[113]   Knibbs, who was Australia's representative on the General Council of the 1927 World Population Conference in Geneva[114] had offered a paper on population and migration.[115]   He sent it to the Conference President, Sir Bernard Mallett, noting that it covered population and migration but not birth control. Although he thought it was a mistake to omit this topic, he said that he understood it had to be evaded for diplomatic reasons. Despite his self-censorship, the paper was still cut from the conference. Knibbs was similarly cautious when he offered the paper to the *Eugenics Review* – it appeared without mentioning his Australian roots and his criticism of Britain was oblique:

> If nations could be permitted to rid themselves of their very poor or derelict members, by simply sending them to other lands, such nations would escape the discipline to which they ought undoubtedly be subject, from the presence of such persons in their midst; and they would impose troubles elsewhere. The result from the world point of view, would on the whole be unquestionably disadvantageous. Communities which have built up commendable standards of living, and desirable social developments generally, will necessarily be hostile to all proposals that they should receive the moral, intellectual, economic and social defectives of other peoples. ... No community, in any way interested in building up its social life, in organising its educational system, and in moulding the ideals of its growing generations, can for a moment admit the claims of other peoples to send their surplus of population, merely on the grounds of its numerical capacity to absorb them.[116]

Previously, Australian officials were happy to accept all British applicants. Knibbs' successor as Statistician in 1922 was Charles Wickens, whose paper *was* read at the Population Conference.[117]   In 1928, Wickens colourfully observed that Australia was like the boa-constrictor which habitually bolted its immigrants and then rested until they were digested. In his view, this process of alternate gorging and inertness did not seem the best way of organising the country's development.[118]   Australia received a flood of immigrants once Britain's Empire Settlement Act (to reduce Britain's problems of unemployment and urban crowding) came into force in 1922.[119] Britain agreed to contribute up to half the expense of emigration and land settlement. However, despite government assistance, in the 1920s most of Australia's immigrant and soldier-settlement schemes failed.[120] In 1950 the Council For New Era Emigration was launched in London with the British aircraft engineer and jet plane pioneer, Air Commodore Sir Frank Whittle (1907-1996), as the Chairman. He told the *Times* (25 November 1950) that the Council's object was to ensure that Britain survived the third world war by encouraging British migration to under-populated Commonwealth countries. This body, known as the Migration Council from 1951, had branches in Australia and New Zealand and had close links with the Eugenics Society.[121] Britain habitually used its empire as a resource; for example, in 1890 Sir Charles Dilke proposed that Britain and its colonial empire should become 'Greater Britain' to solve a coming world crisis, in which all the world's English-speaking people would be marshalled against the Russian Empire.[122]

Child Migrants from Britain

Another plan involved children. Until recently, few people knew about the British children who were sent here without family support. Religious and charitable organisations sponsored them with the approval and financial support of the British and Australian governments.[123] Britain sent thousands of children from orphanages or destitute families to various colonial countries. The imperial motive was to send these little 'bricks for Empire building' under the philanthropic guise of 'a child rescue'.[124] The eugenic motive was to transplant children, rather than adults, from slums in the belief that, if taken away from their parents at an early age, they would escape slum-induced degeneration.[125]   Essentially the same motives were at work *within* Australia where children were frequently taken from mothers who were Aboriginal or unmarried.

Statistics of the children Britain sent to Australia are not accurate but it is likely that at least 30,000 arrived. They were mostly sent to remote rural areas to swell the population and boost the unskilled work-force. According to one source, 'from 1800 to 1853 Britain exported 500 to 1,000 children a year, most of them to Australia'.[126] However, as the British academic and social worker Lady Gillian Wagner noted in her 1979 best-selling biography *Barnardo*, during the Australian gold rush period (from the 1850s to the 1900s) Britain sent children to other parts of the Empire where they were considered less exposed to moral temptations. Alan Gill believes that it was this book, based on a PhD thesis, which first drew public attention to child migration.[127]   More details were provided by Margaret Humphreys (also a social worker) who in 1993 achieved a most unusual honour; although British, she was awarded an Order of Australia for her services on behalf of child migrants. She reported that:

> Between 1900 and the Depression of the 1930s, children were primarily sent to Canada, but after the Second World War the charities and agencies began to concentrate on Australia and, to a much lesser extent, Rhodesia and New Zealand. ... The last child went out in 1967.[128]

Religious and charitable organisations often deceived the children and their relations in many ways. In some cases they changed the children's names, or they told the children that their parents were dead and the relatives that the children had been adopted in Britain. In others, they destroyed the family records. Recent revelations of the hidden, negative aspects of this migration are having considerable ramifications.

In 1910 Sir George Reid (1845-1918), the Australian High Commissioner in London, appealed for young migrants to go to Australia. This proposal was endorsed by Professor Anderson Stuart who became President of the British Immigration League of Australia in 1907. Adolescent boys began arriving in NSW in 1911 under the Dreadnought Scheme and received farm training, with about 7,000 of them settling in Australia by 1930. In 1912 the South African-born Kingsley Fairbridge (1855-1924) wrote to Dr Arthur asking for details of the Pitt Town Training School, one of Arthur's schemes to give farm training to city boys.[129] In July that year, Fairbridge and his wife established the first of their farm schools, in Pinjarra, Western

Australia, on land offered by the State's Premier. The school prospered while Fairbridge was alive and the boys fondly remembered their training and a memorial plaque at another of these schools in Molong, NSW, also suggests tranquillity:

> On this 1,500 acre Fairbridge Farm from 1938 to 1973 some 12,000 British and Australian boys and girls were brought up to love the country and to learn country skills and ways in keeping with the ideals of Kingsley Fairbridge, founder of the Fairbridge Farm schools of Australia and Canada.[130]

However, some former pupils regretted their experiences at Molong where they received minimal education.[131]   Other charity-operated child migration schemes began in the 1920s. In London, the Oversea Settlement Special Sub-Committee assured delegates at the 1926 Imperial Conference there were unlimited openings overseas for British juveniles under satisfactorily guaranteed schemes. In Australia several such schemes were promoted by the Millions Club which had been established in 1919 to promote the settlement of a million farmers on a million farms. The Millions Club and the RHA had many links. For example, Dr Arthur was a Vice President of the Club and the RHA Patron in 1930.   He was also the President of the Immigration League of Australia and a strong advocate of immigration and defence. The Club President was a Sydney 'realty specialist' Sir Arthur Rickard[132] who, in 1921 with the Millions Club backing, initiated the Barnardo's scheme in Australia. Under his Chairmanship, the Club arranged passages for approximately 3,000 child migrants.[133] The Big Brother Movement was another of the Club's projects which sponsored British youth and trained them as farm hands under the direction of a 'big brother'. It was launched in 1925 by Rickard, who, like Arthur, had RHA links – first as an RHA member and then in 1928-29 as an RHA Vice President. More than 10,000 Little Brothers had arrived in Australia by 1982.

Britain's child exodus intensified in periods of intense poverty and urban overcrowding, with its associated high levels of illegitimacy and marriage failure. Many deprived and destitute children were sent to Australia which, some said, was used 'virtually as a dumping ground'.[134] However, Australia actively sought the children and on 31 October

1945 Arthur Calwell, Immigration Minister in the Chifley Labor Government, said on an ABC *Nation's Forum of the Air*, broadcast, 'we are anxious to bring a minimum of 50,000 children to Australia but Great Britain simply has not got the children to send'. While nowhere near this number arrived, after the war, child migration figures were high with the Catholic Church sending the most. The pronatalist slogan, 'the Australian child is the best immigrant', had been twisted in the 1940s to 'the child, the best immigrant'.[135]

The needs of the Empire, not of individuals or eugenics, were the primary consideration in this Anglo-Australian undertaking. Belatedly, it was acknowledged that children had been abused in West Australian orphanages operated by the Christian Brothers. From the 1980s, reports about deception and trauma relating to these schemes began to emerge in books and as a result of advocacy by the Child Migrants Trust.[136] However, most Australians did not know that such schemes even existed until they saw two harrowing television programs which were screened on the 8th, 9th and 12th of July 1992: they were the award-winning joint ABC-BBC mini-series *The Leaving of Liverpool*, and the BBC documentary *Lost Children of the Empire*. At first the Catholic Church defended its role in child migration.[137]

In July 1992 Christian Brother Dr Barry Coldrey told me that he had produced a history of the scheme 'in haste'. The Order had commissioned him as a trouble-shooter to investigate allegations of sexual abuse and he wrote two reports – one for the public (*The Scheme)* and another confidential one which was uncovered by prosecution solicitors in court hearings (*A Secret Report for the Executive of the Christian Brothers – Sexual Abuse from 1930 to 1994*), containing material omitted from the official history. In 1993, the Christian Brothers publicly admitted that they had abused some boys in their care but in 1994 forced a publisher to withdraw a book about this.[138] Following legal action against the Order in 1996, the Christian Brothers paid $3.5 million to 210 men who as children were physically and sexually abused by the Brothers. The case was described as 'one of the biggest class actions in Australia's legal history'.[139] There was another attempt to cover up and revise this history; in July 1997 an article by Brother Coldrey was published in *History*, the magazine of the Royal Australian

Historical Society, which gave no hint of Coldrey's involvement with the Christian Brothers or the scheme's dark side and later declined to publish such information.

In December 1998, after visiting Australia, the British House of Commons Health Committee's inquiry into child migration accepted that it had been a misguided policy and announced a £2.5 million support fund for these unwilling immigrants. After 18 months' consideration, the Australian Government gave its response to the British inquiry in January 2000. To the dismay of some of these former migrants, the Government decided 'to improve their current welfare, rather than undertake a large-scale and expensive inquiry about past wrongs'. In 1999-2000 the Child Migrant Trust was set to receive $120,000 to provide counselling and family research and assist reunions in addition to the $645,000 which the Department of Immigration has provided since 1990.[140]

---

[1] Eugenics Society Archives, CMAC: SA/EUG/J.18, Contemporary Medical Archives Centre, Wellcome Institute, London.

[2] Charles Vickery Drysdale, *Neo-Malthusianism and Eugenics* (London: William Bell, 1912), 9, 22. He was the son of Dr Alice Drysdale-Vickery, a pioneering feminist, and Dr Charles R Drysdale, the Neo-Malthusian League's first President.

[3] Drysdale (1912), 12.

[4] John Humphrey Noyes, *History of American Socialisms* [1870] (New York: Dover Publications, 1966), 638.

[5] Linda Littlejohn, in *Australian Racial Hygiene Congress, Report*. Sydney 15-18 September 1929, 7. The NSW Department of Public Health's Annual reports list 'Mrs Emma Linda Palmer Littlejohn' as a member of its prestigious State Board of Health, from 1930 to 1935.

[6] Helen Livsey, 'The Search for a Perfect Australian: The Strange Will of Peter Stuckey Mitchell', Albury and District Historical Society, 1988, 1.

[7] 'Hunt for perfect men and women', *Sun* (28 June 1954) 1.

[8] There was a similar delay in the case of J J W Power's art bequest to the University of Sydney in 1943. This £1 million bequest was not made public until Power's widow died in 1962.

[9] 'Child health. Diet and dental caries', *Health* (a monthly journal dealing with developments in the field of public health issued by the Commonwealth Department of Health) 3 (no 3), September 1953, 69-70.

[10]Thomas H Kewley, *Social Security in Australia, 1900-72*, 2nd edn. (Sydney: Sydney University Press, 1973), 99-116.

[11]Anna Davin, 'Imperialism and Motherhood', *History Workshop: A Journal of Socialist Historians*, Issue 5 (Spring 1978), 22-24.

[12]*The Charities' Gazette and General Intelligencer: Official Organ of the Benevolent Society of NSW*, 20 (no 7) 1 July 1918, cover.

[13]Brown, *The Underlying Principles of Modern Legislation* (London: Murray, 1912), 267.

[14] 'Eugenics and the Baby Bonus', *SMH*, 23 October 1912, 12 (d).

[15]Speech by W M Hughes, 24 September 1912, in the second reading of the Maternity Allowances Bill, CPP [Representatives], 1912, 3338.

[16]'Maternity Bonus. Mr Thomas replies to Council of Churches', *Argus*, 30 September 1912, 11. The Maternity Allowance was reduced and means-tested in the Depression and abolished in 1978.

[17]'Aboriginal women. Issue of maternity bonus urged', *SMH*, 18 September 1936.

[18]'Notes. The birth rate in Australia', *ER*, vol 4 (April 1912-January 1913), 325.

[19]*State Endowment For Families and the Fallacy of the Existing Basic Wage System.* Dr Richard Arthur, MLA to the NSW Board of Trade, 2 September 1919 (Sydney: Govt Pr, 1919), 4-8.

[20]*The Charities' Gazette and General Intelligencer* (4 March 1917).

[21]Edith Barrett, in *Health*, 1 (May 1923), 121-126.

[22]Patricia Ranald, in Bevege et al (eds.), *Worth Her Salt: Women at Work in Australia* (Sydney: Hale and Iremonger, 1982), 284.

[23]Muriel A Heagney, 'Has the Maternity Allowance Failed?', *Health*, 1 (May 1923), 135-36.

[24]'Darwin's address to the 1921 Congress', *ER*, 13 (April 1921-January 1922), 507-08.

[25]Huxley quoted by Fitzpatrick in the [Sydney] *Times*, 2 December 1928, in the RHC Papers.

[26]*Report of the Royal Commission on Child Endowment or Family Allowances*, CPP, vol 2 (1929), 1301.

[27]*Royal Commission on Child Endowment*, 'H. Eugenic Control', paras 627-633, 1359-1360.

[28]*SMH*, 15 May 1929, 15 (c).

[29]'Maternity deaths could be halved! Expert's scathing attack on to-day's obstetric methods, "Doctors lose far more patients than do midwives". Dame [Janet] Campbell also critical', *Daily Guardian*, 6 September 1929, 15.

[30]A B Piddington, *The Next Step: A Family Basic Income* (1921), 29, 'a work with a striking title was published a few years ago by the famous Judge Lindsey, *Horses' Rights For Women*'.

[31]'Marriage bonuses. Germans want more babies. Honours for mothers', *Age*, 8 July 1938, 12.

[32]Duras, 'We can be the fittest nation', *Herald* (Melbourne), 22 October 1938.

[33]W E Agar, 'Family income', *Herald* (Melbourne), 24 June 1944.

[34]Agar, 'History of [ESV's] past activities' [1945], 4.

[35]Norman Haire, *Sex Problems of To-day* (Sydney: Angus and Robertson, 1942), 14.

[36]Haire, in *The Nation's Forum of the Air*, vol 1 (no 2), August 1944, 8, 'Population Unlimited?'.

[37]Victor Hugo Wallace, *Women and Children First!* (Melbourne: OUP, 1946), 46.

[38]NHMRC Report of the 18th Session, November 1944, Appendix 1. *Interim Report of the NHMRC Council On the Decline in the Birth Rate*, 9-96.

[39]These were not the 'charitable cases' Wallace saw at clinics of the District Nursing Society or Social Hygiene Society and were 'representative of the married women of Australia', Wallace (1946), 43-44. Surprisingly, an extensive survey on birth control had been published twenty years earlier, in May 1926, in an Australian literary magazine, *The Triad*. After the editor wrote to 2000 Australian doctors he received 1,403 replies and in August published a summary of these responses which fell into five categories: in favour of birth control (the overwhelming majority), opposed, limited approval, suspended judgement and those who refused to discuss the issue (the smallest minority). The editor received only one objection on religious grounds.

[40]J H L Cumpston, (comp.), 'Statements made by women themselves in response to a public invitation to state their reasons for limiting their families', *NHMRC* (1944), Annexure G, 74.

[41]W G Spence, *The Child, the Home and the State* (Sydney: Worker Print, 1908), 5.

[42]William Verco, 'The influence of the medical profession upon the national life in Australia', *AMG*, 20 July 1910, 340

[43]Davin (1978), 38-43.

[44]Jessie Ackermann, *Australia: From a Woman's Point of View* [1913] (Sydney: Cassell Australia, 1981), 96, 98-99.

[45] Herman Rubin, *Eugenics and Sex Harmony*, 2nd edn. (NY: Pioneer Publications, 1942), 493.

[46] E Sydney Morris, 'Obituary. William George Armstrong', *MJA*, 28 February 1942, 273. See also *ADB*, vol 7, 97-98.

[47] *The Charities' Gazette and General Intelligencer*, 3 May 1919.

[48] Brown, 'Economic welfare and racial vitality', *Economic Record*, vol 3 (May 1927), 19.

[49] Brown (1912), 204-05, quoting Professor H E Armstrong.

[50]Roberta Jull (1916), quoted in Kay Daniels and Mary Murnane (comps.), *Uphill All the Way: A Documentary History of Women in Australia* (St Lucia: UQP, 1980), 133-34.

[51]Drysdale (1912), 21.

[52]Truby King, 'Education and eugenics', *AMTC* (February 1914), 85-86. See also Daniel Kevles, *In the Name of Eugenics: Genetics and the Uses of Human Heredity* (NY: Knopf, 1985), 89.

[53]*AMTC* (1914), 42-44.

[54]William Blocksidge, *National Notes*, new edn. [Sydney: privately printed, 1922], 39.

[55]Blocksidge (1922), 37, 40-41.

[56]Lotte Fink, 'The Racial Hygiene Association of Australia', in Gregory Pincus (ed.), *Proceedings of the 5th International Conference of Planned Parenthood* (London: IPPF, 1956), 289.

[57]Fitzgerald, *IMCAT*, January 1889, 16.

[58]E Sydney Morris, 'Hygiene and Social Progress', *Health Inspectors' Association of Australia, NSW Branch, 22nd Annual Conference* (Sydney, 25-30 September 1933), 9.

[59]Sydney Morris, 'Essay on causes and prevention of maternal morbidity and mortality', *MJA* (12 September 1925), 314.

[60]Sydney Morris, in NHMRC, 1st Session (February 1937), Appendix, 3, 5.

[61]Windeyer, 'Maternal mortality and measures which should be adopted in order to reduce it', *Australasian Nurses Journal* (15 October 1925), 484. 5.

[62]W G Armstrong, 'The beginnings of baby health centres in NSW', *MJA* (29 April 1939), 672.

[63]NHMRC, 5th Session (November 1938), Resolution 2, 'Physical fitness', 11.

[64]Morris (February 1937), 5.

[65]Morris, *Physical Education: An Outline of its Aims, Scope, Methods and Organization*, in NHMRC, 5th Session (November 1938), Appendix 1, 13.

[66]Morris, 'Physical education in relation to national fitness', Section I. Medical Science and National Health, *ANZAAS*, Report of the 24th meeting, Canberra (January 1939), 195.

[67]NHMRC, Session 5 (November 1938), 10.

[68]Kathleen Gordon, *Community Centres*, 7th Session, Commonwealth National Fitness Council, Canberra (29 September 1943) and Gordon, *Youth Centres* (Canberra; Govt. Pr., 1944).

[69]*The Adjustment of Youth: A Study of a Social Problem in the British, American, and Australian Communities*, Kenneth S Cunningham (ed.) (Melbourne: Published for the Australian Council for Educational Research by Melbourne University Press, 1951), 252.

[70]Don S Kirschner, 'The ambiguous legacy: Social justice and social control in the Progressive era', *Historical Reflections*, 11 (Summer 1975), 70.

[71]From my notes of Ellen Chesler's book launch at the California Institute of Technology, 4 November 1993. Daniel Kevles reviewed it in the *New York Times Book Review*, 28 June 1992.

[72]*New York Time*, ibid, 34, Chesler quoting Kennedy.

[73]Gordon, *Woman's Body*, Woman's Right: A Social History of Birth Control in America (NY: Grossman, 1976).

[74]Cohen, 'Private lives in public spaces: Marie Stopes, the Mothers' Clinics and the practice of contraception', *History Workshop: A Journal of Socialist and Feminist Historians*, Issue 35 (Spring 1993), 95-116. See also Deborah Cohen, "Marie Stopes and the Mothers' Clinics" in *Marie Stopes, Eugenics and the English Birth Control Movement* (Ed Robert A Peel) Galton Institute, London, 1997.

[75]Margaret Conley, "'Citizens: Protect your birthright". The Racial Hygiene Association of NSW', *Bowyang*, 6 (1981), 8-12.

[76]Conley, quoting from Margaret Ripper's 1977 BA thesis (1981), 9, 11.

[77]Erica Fisher, 'Opposition to family planning in Australia', ESEAOR [East and South East Asia and Oceania Region of the International Planned Parenthood Federation] Workshop, Kuala Lumpur and provided to Council members of the FPA ACT, 23 October 1987, 2.

[78]Hyslop (1980), 12.

[79]Hyslop (1980) 403, quoting Kirschner (1975), 69-88.

[80]Ruby Rich discussing the early days of the RHA, Pers. comm, 24 November 1987.

[81]Nancy Leys Stepan, *'The Hour of Eugenics': Race, Gender and Nation in Latin America* (Ithaca: Cornell University Press, 1991), 108-09.

[82]Samuel Holmes, *A Bibliography of Eugenics* (Berkeley: Univ of California Press, 1924), 342.

[83]Jane Hume Clapperton, *Scientific Meliorism and the Evolution of Happiness* (London: Kegan Paul, Trench, 1885), vii-viii.

[84]Clapperton (1885), 32.

[85]Clapperton (1885), 429.

[86]'The woman movement and eugenics', *American Breeders' Magazine*, vol 2 (third quarter 1911), 225-26.

[87]H K Rusden, 'The Survival of the unfittest', *AAASC* (1893), 523.

[88]Mabel Atkinson, 'The feminist movement and eugenics', *Sociological Review*, 3 (January 1910), 51.

[89]Atkinson (1910), 51.

[90]Martha Ellen Bettes, *A Marriage of Motives: Relationships Between Eugenics and the Woman's Movement* (BA Hons thesis, University of Pennsylvania, May 1975), 38.

[91]Bettes (1975), 23, 24, 42. For a discussion of feminism and eugenics in Britain see Lesley Hall, "Women, Feminism and Eugenics" in *Essays in the History of Eugenics* (editor Robert A Peel), Galton Institute, London, 1998.

[92]Farley Kelly, in Margaret Bevege, et al, *Worth Her Salt: Women At Work in Australia* (Sydney: Hale and Iremonger, 1982), 215.

[93]Meredith Anne Foley, 'The Women's Movement in New South Wales and Victoria, 1918-1938' (PhD thesis, University of Sydney, August 1985), 44.

[94]Wray Vamplew, (ed), *Australians: Historical Statistics* (Sydney: Fairfax, Syme & Weldon Associates, 1987), 5. Assisted immigrants are defined as those receiving assistance from Colonial funds, not the British government or from employers or land companies.

[95]Harvey Sutton, 'The Australian child and the progress of child welfare', *MJA* (14 November 1931), 612.

[96]'More people. A Labor view. "Baby the best immigrant"', *Telegraph*, 18 September 1905, 7.

[97]Joan Rydon and Richard N Spann, *New South Wales Politics, 1901-1910* (Melbourne: Cheshire, 1962), 59 and 123.

[98]Appeal in *The Charities' Gazette and General Intelligencer*, 25 September 1919.

[99]'Keeping Australia White, an appeal by Sir Joseph Cook', *Millions*, 1 (1 November 1919).

[100]Waddy, 'Eugenics' in *ARHC* (1929), 63.

[101] 'Inter-Imperial migration', *ER*, 11 (1919-1920), 49-50.

[102] Brian Murphy, *The Other Australia: Experiences of Migration* (Cambridge: CUP, 1993), 46, quoting H S Commager (ed.), *Documents of American History*, vol 2 (NY, 1968), 135-7, 192-94.

[103]A B Piddington, 'Importing human derelicts to reduce Australian manhood standard. State and Federal governments offer £11 a head for adult paupers. Australia House and its farcical "medical examinations"', *Smith's Weekly*, 27 September 1924, 9 (c).

[104]A B Piddington, 'Turn off the Mediterranean tide. What the USA dams back will flood Australia. 280,000 new voters at next Federal elections now on the alert. If Dagoes come, Mr Bruce will go', *Smith's Weekly*, 4 October 1924, 13.

[105]Albert Weihen, 'Medical inspection of immigrants to Australia', *AMCTC* (Sept 1911), 638, 645.

[106]Richard A Soloway, *Demography and Degeneration: Eugenics and the Declining Birthrate in Twentieth-century Britain* (Chapel Hill, NC: University of North Carolina Press, 1990), 176.

[107]*ER*, 18 (1926-1927), 134.

[108]'City Populations. Checking degeneracy. Professor's theory', *SMH* , 5 January 1927, 13 (a).

[109]'Migrants and health. Medical examinations', *SMH* , 27 July 1927, 15 (g).

[110]Goodisson, 'Racial Hygiene Association', *Progressive Journal* (10 March 1936), 32.

[111]Knibbs, *The Shadow of the World's Future or the Earth's Population Possibilities and the Consequences of the Present Rate of Increase of the Earth's Inhabitants* (London: Benn, 1928), 114.

[112]Anthony Comstock (1844-1915), the founder of the NY Society for the Suppression of Vice, is known for his eponymous law 'for the Suppression of Trade in, and the Circulation of Obscene Literature and Articles of Immoral Use'. According to 'Comstockery', contraception *was* vice.

[113]Library of Congress. Knibbs to Margaret Sanger, 13 December 1927, Sanger Papers, vol 21.

[114]Sanger (ed.), *Proceedings of the World Population Conference*, 29 Aug-3 Sept 1927 (London: Edward Arnold, 1927), 12.

[115]In Knibbs' letter to Stopes, 11 July 1927, BL, Stopes Papers, Add MS 38,573, f. 25.

[116]Knibbs, 'The fundamental elements of the problems of population and migration', *ER*, 19 (April 1927-January 1928), 267-89.

[117]Wickens, 'Australia and its immigrants' in Sanger (1927), 312-24.

[118]Wickens, in Phillips and Wood (1928), 54.

[119]Imperial Conference (1926), 272.

[120]On 19 October 1926 the Discharged Soldiers' Settlement Board of Australia indicated that its 1925 debts exceeded £4,000,000.

[121]Blacker to Whittle, 28 November 1950, SA/EUG, D122.

[122]Colls & Dodd (1986), 45-46. Dilke (1843-1911) was a British lawyer and a radical Liberal MP.

[123]'Report of Oversea Settlement Special Sub-Committee', Appendix X, Imperial Conference (1926), 266-90.

[124]Quoted in Philip Bean and Joy Melville, *Lost Children of the Empire: The Untold Story of Britain's Child Migrants* (London: Unwin Hyman, 1989), 1, 78.

[125]Caleb Saleeby, *The Progress of Eugenics* (London: Cassell, 1914), 113-14.

[126]Bean and Melville (1989), 37.

[127]Alan Gill, *Orphans of the Empire: The Shocking Story of Child Migration to Australia.* (Sydney: Millennium Books, 1997), 495.

[128]Margaret Humphreys, *Empty Cradles*, (London: Doubleday, 1994), 56-57.

[129]Kingsley Fairbridge to Richard Arthur, 13 February 1912 letter, Arthur Papers, ML.

[130]Quoted by David Rutherford (Molong: Molong Historical Society, 1983), 137, 140.

[131]Bean and Melville (1989), 126-29.

[132]Sir Arthur Rickard was Chairman, later President of Barnodo's in Australia from its start until his death in 1948.

[133]Reported by J B Rickard [*not* Sir Arthur Rickard], in *Millions*, 15 September 1924, 21.

[134]Quoted by Bean and Melville (1989), 110, and by Barry Michael Coldrey in *Child Migration, the Australian Government and the Catholic Church, 1926-1966* (typescript), (Box Hill, Vic: Tamanaraik Publishing, 1992), 69.

[135]Initially made by Holman in the *Telegraph*, 18 September 1905. The reversed slogan quotation is cited by Coldrey (1992), 42, 44-48.

[136]For example, Gillian Wagner's *Children of the Empire* (London: Weidenfeld and Nicholson, 1982); Bean and Melville (1989) and Humphreys (1994).

[137]Silvia Dropulic 'Church defends its child migration', *Australian*, 11-12 July 1992, 4.

[138]Graham Duncan, 'Brothers regret abuse of boys', *SMH*, 5 July 1993, 5. Robert Pullan, in 'Christian Brothers gag orphan's expose', *SMH*, 8 July 1994, 1, indicated that Harper/Collins withdrew from sale *When Innocence Trembles: The Christian Brothers' Orphanage Tragedy – A Survivor's Story*, by Kate Davies. The book was later published by Angus and Robertson and reviewed by Mary Rose Liverani, 'A childhood betrayed', in the *Australian Weekend Review*, 31 December 1994 – 1 January 1995, 4.

[139]Richard Guilliat, 'Brotherly Love', *SMH* (V), 22 July 1995, 4A, reported a legal firm's discovery that Coldrey, the official historian for the Order (*The Scheme*), had also written a separate report containing the damning material left out of this history. Matthew Russell, in 'Sex abuse: Brothers to pay $3.5m', *SMH*, 1 August 1996, 1 and 5.

[140]Amanda Vaughan, 'No inquiry into UK child migrant abuse', *SMH*, 28 January 2000, 7.

5. Combating Social Evils

This is the first of two chapters about negative eugenics, the movement's plans for the 'unfit'. It examines 'racial poisons' such as VD, TB, prostitution, alcoholism and criminality, and the plans made for dealing with society's racially contaminated unfit and misfit.

Degeneracy Theory

From the 1860s to about 1911 many psychiatrists and neurologists accepted the validity of 'degeneracy theory', a view that a person's acquired characteristics were passed on and, unless there was some circuit-breaking intervention, the flaws would increase over generations until the line died out. Degeneracy was slow but self-limiting – neurotic parents would start the biological descent by producing disturbed children; followed by paupers or criminals for grandchildren, and in the fourth and last generation the family would die out because the degenerate descendants had become sterile idiots.[1] In 1885 Dr Frederick Manning, NSW's Inspector-General of the Insane, was expressing an orthodox view when he said 'it is well known that any morbid tendency existing in each parent is transmitted with great certainty, and usually in intensified degree, to the offspring'.[2]

Steven Gelb was surprised by the studies reprinted in Nicole Hahn Rafter's *White Trash: The Eugenic Family Studies, 1877-1919,* because some were by eugenists 'with a substratum of degeneracy thinking' and others were 'prime examples of degeneracy theory'.[3] He stressed the irony of this position which 'was inherently subversive to the eugenics movement; if the propagation of inferiority was really self-limiting, one rationale the movement was based on would be undercut'. However, the theory was accepted widely; by the eugenics movement, in discussions about acquired characteristics and in nature-nurture debates. While Degeneracy Theorists believed that improving social conditions might halt the slide, eugenists believed that degeneration resulted from the 'bad' heredity and could only be reduced if affected people did not breed.

208

In 1924, Samuel J Holmes, zoology professor at the University of California, defined negative eugenics as the term 'generally employed to designate those procedures whose aim is to promote racial improvement, or check racial deterioration, by preventing the multiplication of inferior hereditary stocks' but agreed that 'there has been much discussion of the legal aspects of different proposed remedies'.[4] In fact eugenists could never agree what constituted 'fitness' or 'unfitness'. Francis Galton hesitated about this in the eugenics paper he gave in 1904 to members of London's newly-formed Sociological Society. 'Fitness was not the problem'', he said. It would be easy to compile 'a considerable list of qualities which most people apart from "cranks" would consider when selecting the best specimens of his class'. His fit list, sounding like a self-description, would include 'health, energy, ability, manliness and courteous disposition' and those chosen would have more vigour, ability and consistency of purpose, 'all qualities that are needed in a State'. He trusted the community to reject criminals and other undesirable types. Galton concluded, 'the aim of Eugenics is to bring as many influences as can be reasonably employed, to cause the useful classes in the community to contribute *more* than their proportion to the next generation'.[5]

Criticism of the lack of a 'criterion of fitness' in the 2 August 1913 *British Medical Journal* discussion of eugenics was tolerated because it came from Prince Kropotkin, a benign-looking anarchist in exile who was much admired by Britain's intelligentsia. Few eugenists were concerned about vague definitions or doubted their own fitness although I did find two references to allegedly eugenically-flawed eugenists; the first about Henry Twitchin, was made by the Eugenics Society after his death in 1930 and may relate more to their need for publicity than to his genetics. The second was made by Dr Norman Haire who said in 1949 that he had remained childless after discovering two relatives had epilepsy. Homosexuality, rather than genetics, is the more likely explanation.[6]

There was the same difficulty with definitions in Australia. In November 1912, Dr Arthur advocated 'the elimination and the prevention of being born to all those who are manifestly unfit to become future citizens of any community'.[7] The following month, the

Eugenics Education Society of NSW was established, with Arthur as President.   Secretary Eldridge favoured a broader, more liberal approach: 'encouraging worthy parenthood', 'discouraging unworthy parenthood', and 'opposing the racial poisons'.   On 24 February 1914 Robert Irvine, the Society Vice-President, was cautious in his comments to the *Sydney Morning Herald*. Two days later, he warned readers that there was insufficient knowledge to select those human qualities which would benefit society. He added 'as Bateson, a man of wise caution, says "we have little to guide us in estimating the qualities for which society has, or may have, a use"'.[8]   He was referring to William Bateson (1861-1926) who coined the term 'genetics' in 1905. Bateson had visited Sydney in 1914 and delivered the presidential address on 22 August at the British Association for the Advancement of Science Congress.   On the same day Irvine, in perhaps his last involvement with eugenics, concluded that some serious physical and mental defects, vice and criminality could be eradicated 'if society so determined'.[9]   Irvine, who had a varied and turbulent career, was the University of Sydney's first professor of economics but was later forced to resign on the grounds of adultery.   He was described as 'magnificent instructor' who had 'a zeal for the truth and a zeal for the service of the commonwealth'[10]   After he died in 1941 he was largely ignored until Bruce McFarlane wrote a major biographical study in 1966: *Professor Irvine's Economics in Australian Labour History, 1913-1933*, and in 1984 Michael Roe gave him a chapter in *Nine Australian Progressives: Vitalism in Bourgeois Social Thought, 1890-1960*. None of the studies mentioned Irvine's interest in eugenics.

In 1914 there was another attempt to define unfitness in 'Care of the Feeble-minded in Australasia', which the *Eugenics Review* described in its July issue as a 'rather disappointing report'. Based on a survey which had received few responses from school principals and answers from only 211 of the 2,450 doctors approached, it was the work of an Australasian committee delegated by the Australasian Medical Congress in 1911 to find out the extent of the problem.   The committee planned to implement a public education campaign with support from the medical profession, education bodies, eugenics societies, kindergarten unions, children's departments, charitable hospitals and homes, social workers, the National Council of Women, churches and the press.[11]

Dr John Yule, a Victorian committee member, agreed that it was a 'perfectly legitimate eugenic aspiration' for any country to encourage the fittest individuals to produce future citizens. However, it would be difficult to even think about positive measures as 'many a mental and spiritual genius would be excluded were we to mate on a basis of bodily perfection alone, and many a deplorable physical weakling included if the mental and spiritual traits alone received recognition'. The committee rejected any attempt to pass laws to stop the unfit mating on the grounds that this might lead to 'a monstrous tyranny' or a 'deeper degradation of the worst class of the population'.[12] As the editor of Sydney's *Telegraph* had expressed it in 1912, eugenics was a principle which people didn't want for themselves but readily agreed was 'all right' for 'other people's children'. In marriage selection, the paper argued, the danger posed if 'temperamentally and sentimentally incompatible' people mated was much greater than any threat posed by the marriage of the physically and mentally unfit because, despite this, the 'physique of the white race was improving, not deteriorating'.

As well as fuzzy definitions, there was confusion about the difference between insanity and mental deficiency: from the 1880s the Melbourne-based Dr John Fishbourne had been urging authorities to make this distinction, pointing out that each country had different interpretations of mental deficiency.[13] The 1908 report of the British Royal Commission on the Care and Control of the Feeble-minded had listed six categories:

> Persons of unsound mind, persons of mental infirmity, idiots, imbeciles, feeble-minded and moral imbeciles.

It was argued in the *Medical Journal of Australia* (24 June 1916) that there should be new and better definitions because the category of mental deficiency had become 'so wide it could be applied to the majority of people'.

Choosing which people to include in social problem groups was of particular interest to Richard James Arthur Berry (1867-1962), a British-born anatomist, neurologist and anthropologist whose specialty was mental deficiency and the correlation between brain size and intelligence. He researched these topics as professor of anatomy at the University of Melbourne from 1905 and published a report on mental deficiency in Victoria.[14] Berry, and his researcher Stanley Porteus proposed in 1918 that terms for mental deficiency terms should expand to include previously unrecognised feeble-minded people and those who could not play a useful part in the community because of defective will control or abnormal instincts.[15] In 1920 Porteus suggested applying this term to any person 'who by reason of mental defects other than sensory cannot attain to self-management and self-support to the degree of social sufficiency'.[16]

Shortly before his hurried departure from the University, Berry had written a second report on mental deficiency, *The Mental Defective: A Problem in Social Inefficiency*, published after Berry's return to England in 1931, Berry (with R G Gordon) noted that before 1899, the British did not differentiate between 'unsanity' and insanity. J Shaw Bolton introduced the term *amentia* (from Latin, meaning without a mind) and *moron* (from the Greek word for a fool) was coined by a now discredited psychologist, Dr Henry H Goddard.[17] Berry, then Director of Medical Services of the Stoke Park Colony For Mental Defectives near Bristol, and Gordon, the Colony's neurologist, agreed with Karl Pearson's wish to change the words 'mental defective' to 'social inefficient'.[18] William Dawson, professor of psychiatry at the University of Sydney warned about the fine line between fitness and unfitness; in the August 1931 issue of *Medical Journal of Australia* he reminded doctors, before diagnosing mental deficiency, to consider 'rheumatism, chorea, rickets, epilepsy, tonsils and adenoids, defective vision, hearing and speech, and an uneasy adolescence, environmental and social handicaps including poverty (insufficient food, clothing and sleep), overwork outside school, and unsettled or inharmonious home conditions'. Malnourished children also risked becoming 'functionally mental defectives' and were advised by Dr Arthur, the NSW Minister for Health, to eat more prunes.[19]

Annie Duncan, a Public Service Inspector of Factories and Shops (and one of the few female witnesses) told the 1904 *Royal Commission on the Decline of the Birth-rate* that Australian children were less sturdy and more anaemic than the 'home-born' [British] children'.[20] Racial decay became an obsession with one of the Commissioners, Irish-born and Quaker-educated Octavius Charles Beale (1859-1930), who claimed that feminism was a 'formidable adversary of fecundity' and had fathered 13 children in his first marriage.

His achievements were impressive as a piano manufacturer, NSW President of the National Protection League, linguist, unionists' friend, Alfred Deakin's confidant and the founding president of the Federated Chambers of Manufactures of Australia. In 1893 he opened a piano factory in the Sydney suburb of Annandale, after first making sewing machines with the motto 'Advance Australia'. His pianos won every award at the 1908 Franco-British Exhibition in Paris and by the 1920s his company employed 560 people and was the largest self-contained piano factory in the British Empire. Australian timbers were used in these superbly crafted pianos; Queen Mary had one, Lady Enid de Chair installed a Beale grand piano in Government House and the NSW Conservatorium of Music purchased at least 19.

Unfortunately, Beale was less gifted as a writer and in 1910 he had to pay for someone to publish *Racial Decay: A Compilation of Evidence from World Sources*.[21] Neville Hicks noted the 'significant fact' that although Beale had argued in favour of the orthodox pronatalist view of that time, his colleagues ridiculed his self-published book which was reduced in price and ultimately remaindered.[22] However, in 1911 the former American President, Theodore Roosevelt (1859-1919) in a long tirade about race decadence, briefly noted that although Beale's book was 'not good in form' it deserved studying more 'than any other book that has been written for years'. Six years later, a Catholic tract praised the book as a 'monumental work' which had been 'conceived in a spirit of lofty patriotism'. In 1966 Peter Fryer described it as 'quite the oddest book on contraception ever published, in a field where competition is heavy'. In reality, it was a diatribe *against* contraception.

Until the 1940s Australian medical journals often published articles about racial health, motherhood and sterilisation of the unfit. In the previous two decades, as James Gillespie demonstrated in *The Price of Health: Australian Governments and Medical Politics 1910-1960*, many of the medical profession favoured state-regulated 'national hygiene'. Public health doctors hoped that by adopting such a policy, they would build a superior race.

The preoccupation began in Britain at the time of the Boer War (1899-1902). It was prompted by the high rejection rates of medically-unfit recruits and grew as the 'tea time' war became a national disaster. The horrors were revealed in photographers' images from the front, made possible in the world's first media war, by the newly-available moving picture technology. These films, and journalists' accounts of the major defeats suffered by Britain's trained forces, who outnumbered their Dutch farmer opponents four to one, provoked public disquiet and parliamentary demands for action. Despite the rules for media censorship which were drawn up for the first time in 1879 to try and filter this information, leaked details about the massive British death toll – finally estimated at around 22,000 with 16,000 of them from preventable diseases such as typhoid – caused a massive loss of public confidence. This blow to Britain's status as a super power prompted a national efficiency drive, including the formation in 1903 of an Inter-Departmental Committee on Physical Deterioration which, in its 1904 Report, emphasized the environmental causes of some newborn babies' poor health.[23] Despite official rejection of claims that the urban poor were degenerating, the myth continued with many treating 'deterioration', 'degeneracy' and 'decadence' as synonyms.

Fears about the threats to the Empire were compounded by British fears about internal collapse, with many of Britain's well-off feeling distrust and disgust about the urban poor. While many Australians had fears for the Empire, there was little of the fear and loathing of the poor which was widespread in Britain. For example, Cecil Rhodes advised that if the British wanted to avoid civil war, they had to become Imperialists[24] and Scouting leader Baden-Powell sought to harness the rabble and 'churn out admirably obedient lads'.[25] John Carey demonstrated in *The Intellectuals and The Masses* that 'dreaming of the extermination or sterilization' of the masses was the 'imaginative refuge' for many of Britain's literary icons.[26] The President of the Eugenics Society in London, in a letter to Commonwealth Heads of

State at the 1926 Imperial Conference, warned of the 'probability that racial deterioration was now actually taking place'.[27] Two years later, prominent Eugenics Society member Dr Charles Bond called for a national stock taking.[28]

In contrast, while fewer Australians feared civil war, many were terrified about racial suicide, either before or after an Asian invasion. Archibald Brockway told the Queensland Branch of the BMA in 1910 that although city people needed to improve their fitness, Australia was never likely to reach Britain's deplorable state of physical degeneration. He considered that physical education was the most important part of girls' upbringing to ensure they were fit to become mothers of the sons of Australia, as he believed that sons, not daughters, inherited their mothers' physical attributes.[29] Dr Sydney Morris was confident that the average Australian's physique compared very favourably with other nations' but believed we should lead the world in physical fitness.[30] However, this aim was deplored by a Catholic convert, Dame Enid Lyons (1897-1981) who married at 17 and bore 12 children, becoming a politician after her husband Joe died in 1939 while Prime Minister. She criticised birth control and eugenics, claiming that Australians were as obsessed with physical beauty as the Ancient Greeks, making us 'feel that unless a child is 100% perfect it is better for it not to be born'.[31]

A quaint variation on degeneracy theory was outlined to a Sydney audience in 1893 by British Theosophist Isabel Cooper-Oakley who warned that people who did not try to improve the conditions in slums might be doomed to inhabit a slum when they were reincarnated.[32] Australian Theosophists (some of them eugenists), as well as embracing the usual health reasons for opposing VD, were also concerned because a disease-ravaged corpse would make an undesirable start in the next life.[33]

In 1897 Dr William Cleland (1847-1918) told the Criminological Society of South Australia that he supported the nurture position and wanted authorities to avoid housing children with bad heredity in barracks but instead to provide surroundings which were as natural and healthy as possible. Cleland, who had been appointed Chief

Medical Officer of the State's Lunacy Department in 1878 and Colonial Surgeon in 1896, argued that 'heredity need not be looked upon as a tyrant with inflexible power driving the offspring to destruction'. 'Acquired peculiarities' might be transmitted as 'a predisposition', which could be modified so that people had to struggle, not with fate but with 'flexible powers', thus justifying treatment and hope.[34]

Acquired Inheritance

Jean Baptiste Lamarck (1744-1829) a French naturalist and one of the first to use the word 'biology', proposed a now-discredited but once influential theory of evolution in his *Zoological Philosophy* (1809), fifty years before Darwin's classic study. Lamarck argued that animals, birds and fish deliberately use and strengthen some parts of their bodies and weaken others by disuse, and then transmit these acquired characteristics to their offspring. An 1883 American home medical guide by Dr John H Kellogg claimed that a man's finger deformity, the result of a shooting incident, had been inherited by all his descendants.[35] He believed that parents transmitted 'moral as well as mental qualities' to their children. One sceptic noted: 'wooden legs don't run in families, but wooden heads do'.[36] Stephen Jay Gould was right, however, to make the 'simple but profound' point that 'reading, writing, filming, teaching, practising, apprenticing and learning', which pass knowledge from one generation to the next 'act as Lamarckian boosters to our cultural history'.[37] It is complex, as the term 'hereditary' means different things to scientists and lay people; some took it to mean everything you got from your parents: germs and genes, habits and houses.

The argument that a more important influence is the hereditary material contained in chromosomes, was based on the work of August Weismann (1834-1914), a German geneticist. The views of Lamarck and Weismann have been hotly disputed: in 1890 Edward Stirling, professor of physiology at the University of Adelaide, tentatively approved of Weismannism.[38] In 1899 Dr Ramsay Smith said it was 'not science' and found Weismann's method 'completely wrong'.[39] In 1902 Henry Laurie, Australia's first professor of philosophy, concluded that Lamarck's theory of 'use-inheritance' was misleading.[40] Yet in 1914 Professor Dakin could 'see no reason yet for believing that acquired characteristics were not inherited'.[41] A novel twist was added by a pronatalist who argued that childless people 'die out, leaving no descendants, but only the pernicious influence of their bad example'.[42] Perhaps responding to this irrationality, a letter writer to the *Times* pointed out that 'no authenticated case has been known in which sterile parents have transmitted that quality to their offspring'. The old controversy of acquired inheritance was revived at the Second International Eugenics Congress[43] in 1921 and at the third in 1932.[44]

In 1931 Professor Agar, after lengthy research,[45] refuted Lamarckian claims and since the 1930s most biologists have tacitly accepted Weismann's theories. In 1942, after Julian Huxley gave a BBC talk on Charles Darwin, he was amused to find that his 'emotional' friend Bernard Shaw still believed in acquired inheritance. However, in 1945 he was appalled to find that this 'form of genetics which was based on an ancient superstition' had official sanction in Russia, 'backed with fraud and propaganda'. This 'strange and disturbing phenomenon' which shackled science for decades was driven by the peasant agronomist, Lysenko who Huxley correctly labelled 'a Savonarola of Science'.[46]

There were other earlier, amusing mistakes. For example, Saleeby wrote that judging from information coming from the First International Eugenics Congress 'almost nothing but nonsense was reported' and other liberal eugenists conceded that a 'great deal of rubbish' had been written about eugenics.[47] Many Australians (including scientists) believed bizarre claims if they were made by overseas experts. For example, in May 1913 the *Australasian Medical Gazette* did not criticise Professor Karl Pearson's statement that, 'if he was given a free hand, he could evolve, in a few generations, a white man from a black race, but not the reverse'. And, in an address to a WEA Eugenics Study Circle in 1922, Dr Ellice Hamilton endorsed the views of an unspecified scientist who claimed that eye colour indicated temperament and ability, after he had observed portraits in London's National Gallery and found that famous soldiers and sailors had blue eyes, while the eyes of actors, orators and clergymen were brown. She claimed to have substantiated the National Gallery finding with Australian evidence in which '40% of city folk had brown eyes', she said, 'as orators and actors naturally congregate in cities'. As well, 'the eyes of 40% of our country brothers were blue and they had been the valiant defenders of the Empire'.[48] Although she presented some very dubious science, Hamilton was no fool; in 1915 Sydney's academically-acclaimed Fort Street High School had congratulated their former pupil's 'brilliant success' on winning the NSW Government's Science Research Scholarship at Sydney University.   There are equally nonsensical examples of anti-eugenic claims. For example, Dr James Purdy, the NSW Health Department's Chief Medical Officer, stated in 1929 that the 'progeny of people united solely for the purpose of eugenic breeding, are frequently mentally defective'.[49]   Similar examples have been published more recently. The most extraordinary is an unsubstantiated claim made by Grant Rodwell at a 1992 Conference. His paper was called 'Clitoridectomies in Glass Houses: Eugenics in our Kindergartens: 1900-1950'[50] and even he admitted that 'data of clitoridectomies in Australia' was 'particularly allusive' (sic).[51]

In 1993 the prize-winning author Frank Moorhouse claimed in *Grand Days*, his fascinating and well-researched epic about the League of Nations, that Francis Galton and Florence Nightingale had together created the eugenics movement.[52] There is no evidence for this: by the time the movement was created both of them were frail octogenarian recluses. Barry Smith's 1984 biography, *Florence Nightingale: Reputation and Power*, contains two references which emphasise the unlikeliness of any such collaboration.   In the first, on page 87, Smith quotes Nightingale mentioning in an 1872 letter to her aunt, that she was glad to be childless because the prospect of it was 'immeasurably awful' in 'light of Francis Galton's recent discoveries about heredity'. On page 200, Smith notes that in 1897 Nightingale cut £2,000 from an allocation to Francis Galton for a Nightingale Professorship on Applied Statistics partly because he 'had become untrustworthy because he admitted to a belief in germ theory'. When I checked with the Galton Institute in 1998, I was sent additional convincing evidence:

> The Eugenics Society was formed in 1907. Florence Nightingale died in 1910 at the age of 90, so it is unlikely that she was ever a

member; [however in] correspondence with Francis Galton in 1891 she sought his support for the creation of a Chair of Applied Statistics at Oxford. Galton was highly critical of the proposal which came to nothing. This is discussed in Karl Pearson's *Life, Letters and Labours of Francis Galton*, vol 2, 414-24.

Rob Watts initiated a few more apocryphal eugenics stories in 1994 with his claim that Australian eugenists had proselytised for 'National Parks' and that 'it was not exaggerating to see the first half of this century as the age of eugenics'.[53] His claims are both wrong: the first half of the twentieth century is remembered as an age of disasters in which droughts, depressions, pandemics and world wars created unprecedented chaos. In addition, conservationists battled to install national *parks* while Australian eugenists tried to instil national *fitness*. The first group wanted to protect nature while the second sought to perfect human nature. Generally, the groups occupied separate spheres[54] with those interested in nature predating those interested in eugenics: Tasmania's Royal Society was established in 1842 (to foster interest in flora and fauna) but eugenics societies did not start until 1911. Australia's first national park, and the world's second, was proclaimed in 1879 in an area on Sydney's southern outskirts which is now called the Royal National Park. Others were established following pressure from conservation societies and bushwalkers such as Myles Dunphy (1891-1985), Paddy Pallin (1900-1991) and Marie Byles (1900-1979) who also pushed the frontiers for women by becoming the first female solicitor in New South Wales.

Nature Versus Nurture

The convenient jingle of words, 'nature and nurture', which Francis Galton made popular in 1874[55] are central to the eugenics debate. Ruth Schwartz Cowan's study of Galton's plan presupposed that heredity is 'omnicompetent' in determining the character of the human race, or, put simply, that nature plays a much more important part than nurture. Galton set out to prove this statistically, adding to the debate which had been growing steadily since Darwin's *Origin of Species*. In 1869 Galton summarised his attempts in *Heredity Genius* and his 1874 publication, *English Men of Science: Their Nature and Nurture*, also aimed to prove that heredity was paramount. Galton's view went against the prevailing belief from around 1860 to 1900, with the most extreme of the environmentalists likening the brain at birth to a *tabula rasa* on which impressions and abilities were imprinted throughout life. The debate was mainly between those who believe that improving the environment would have a genetic benefit because acquired characteristics would be passed on to future generations, and those who believe that nature is predominantly or solely responsible, thus making improvements to the environment futile, as advances in one generation would not be inherited by the next. Peter J Bowler expresses it very well: 'nature' in this context means genetic inheritance, which determines a person's character so that it can only be minimally changed by environmental factors and education, while 'nurture' relates to environmental factors. Biologists and psychologists emphasized 'nature' to support the claim they 'have the key to understanding how human nature may be controlled'. Social scientists such as educators and sociologists tend to support 'nurture in the belief that social rather than biological measures will help humanity.[56]

In his infamous 1855 essay, *Inequality of Races*, 1855 de Gobineau took a hardline hereditarian view and the nature-nurture controversy became a crucial eugenic consideration from 1900 to the 1940s. A researcher in 1949, who examined the writing of 24 of the chief nature-nurture protagonists from Britain and America, considered the relationship between their scientific opinions and their politics; eleven of the twelve environmentalists were politically either liberal or radical and eleven of the twelve hereditarians were conservative.[57] Eugenists have supported both sides of the debate.

In the 1990s the extent to which genes determine human behaviour is still contentious.[58] Conventionally, hereditarian-conservative links were most evident in ultra-right-wing groups such as the fascist population policies of Hitler and Mussolini which were underpinned by a belief that inequality was hereditary and 'natural'. However, in Australia, the relationship is not so clear as biological and environmental determinists can be radical or conservative and both groups can have unexpected political allegiances.

In 1897 Catherine Helen Spence (1825-1910), suffragist, feminist, reformer and journalist, was on the side of nature in an address to the Criminological Society of South Australia. This 'grand old woman of Australia' complained about the rigidity of Calvinistic teaching which was 'paralysing to human effort' but found it less harsh than the law of heredity as portrayed by the pessimists Zola and Ibsen, who claimed people 'inherit only the vices, the weaknesses, and the diseases of our ancestors'. Spence added that if this really were the case, the world would have become progressively worse.[59] She mentioned *Ghosts* (the tragedy written by Henrik Ibsen in 1881) in which the son exhibits his father's evil qualities but not the virtues of his mother who had raised him. Syphilis is the family 'ghost' which the son has acquired, either directly from his infected father, or by living in the same debauched way. Spence argued that heredity 'need not be regarded as an over-mastering fate' because everyone 'has an almost limitless parentage to draw upon'. Spence had inherited her crooked little fingers from her father's mother, but not the tuberculosis which had killed her and most of her children. She had inherited most of her good qualities from her mother, but she had inherited hope, 'which is invaluable for a social and political reformer', from her 'much too speculative father and grandfather'.[60]

Spence also considered Zola's 1871 work [the 19-volume *Les Rougon-Macquart*] which paints a terrible family history, similar to Richard Dugdale's history of the Jukes, which appeared soon after.[61] Spence noted that although people continually cited the Jukes as proof of the importance of heredity, those who had read the book attentively, 'instead of merely accepting allusions to it which are one-sided and defective', would 'see clearly that it forms the strongest argument for change of environment that ever was brought forward'. 'No helping hand removed the children from their vicious and criminal surroundings; neither Church nor school compelled them to come in'. Spence was correct and Dugdale himself had acknowledged that heredity was influenced by environment.[62] Havelock Ellis had found it 'noteworthy' in 1912 that Dugdale 'was concerned to prove the influence of bad environment rather than of bad heredity'.[63] That same year South Australia's Dr Ramsay Smith may have been responding to reviews of the book when he claimed that Dugdale's hereditarian conclusions were not justified.[64] He was not alone and 'the systematic misuse of his conclusions by succeeding generations' is 'perhaps the most remarkable aspect of Dugdale's work'.[65] Daniel Kevles pointed out that Dugdale *had* emphasised the part played by the 'degradation of their environment' in the Jukes' misfortunes but 'the misinterpretation of his work simply reflected the mounting hereditarian propensity of the day'.[66]

The man who generated this heat was Gregor Johan Mendel (1822-1884), an Austrian monk and biologist whose studies on heredity in 1866 and 1896 were discovered and publicised in the English-speaking world around 1900. Like Darwin before him, the implications of Mendel's concepts have been revolutionary. In the nineteenth century and the first two decades of the twentieth, the preoccupation with nature meant that less attention was given to the part played by income, nutrition, hygiene, knowledge and adequate pre- and post-natal care in the production of healthy children; it also 'relieved the social conscience and reinforced the moral complacency of the well-to-do in an age noted for its sentimentality and optimism on the one hand and its lack of compassion for human suffering on the other'.[67]

Dr Cumpston did not share this preoccupation with heredity and instead focused on health considerations in a lecture he delivered in Western Australia, *The Architect as a Factor in Social Progress,* which was published in Perth's *Daily News* on 19 August 1909.[68] However, Cumpston did not share the paper's 'hard-line' position on eugenics. While the editorial approved of his advocacy of larger, better designed and well-ventilated bedrooms, it added a section on 'Government and Eugenics' because the editor disagreed with Cumpston who had written:

> Why should it not be possible to alter the environment, and by improving the congenial elements and eliminating the antagonistic to produce in a short space of time those successful types which were considered desirable? Students of sociology were fully cognisant of the fact that the fitness of the individual or of the community was a quality that should be cultivated and improved so that the chance of a survival in the struggle for existence became

very much greater, and it was realised that the best, if not the only, way to accomplish this was by providing a congenial environment. In proportion as the conditions under which the individual spent his existence could be improved so would the physique, the resistance to disease, and the general well-being of the individual be correspondingly improved.

Cumpston's proposed improvements displeased the editor who commented that such actions would 'keep alive a large number of weakly individuals who, under less favourable conditions, would be eliminated.' This, he said explained the 'remarkable increase in insanity during the last 100 years. Eugenics must go hand in hand with social improvements. Something must be done sooner or later to encourage the multiplication of the best and to discourage the multiplication of the worst, if the human race is to enjoy permanently the full benefits of improved environment'.

In 1980 Carol Bacchi, in a wide-ranging paper which kindled interest in eugenics, argued that in Australia the pre-1914 political and social climate influenced the preference for environmentalist eugenics and that as a result 'hereditary determinism had found fewer adherents than in England or America'.[69] She stressed the importance of the nature-nurture debate in Australia and her views were widely accepted in the 1980s.[70] However, in the 1990s scholars gripped by postmodernism began to blame Bacchi for leading numerous historians into 'the bog of this oppressive dichotomy'.[71]

Alison Turtle noted that a strong environmentalism flourished in Australia at the turn of the nineteenth century in which the nature-nurture debate 'was remarkable neither for the logic nor the consistency with which individuals expounded their views, any more than for a clear understanding of the scientific position to which such views related'. While this was true, Bacchi rightly argued that the debate *was* important in the early years of Australia's eugenics movement.

Because it was so hotly disputed,[72] Leonard Darwin had urged eugenists to 'avoid such phrases as the relative influence of heredity and environment' and instead 'pay attention to methods of doing good by attending to both'.[73]   The fledgling birth-controllers argued that 'good heredity and good environment, or eugenics and eutropics [from the Greek words for good rearing] were equally important for the advancement of the human race'.[74] Sanger was irritated by the age-old discussion because the forces could not be disentangled, in the same way that a mother was 'environment' and 'heredity' to her foetus.[75] But Charles Davenport maintained there were fundamental differences of view between euthenists, who wanted to improve living conditions, and eugenists, who wanted to improve people.[76]

In 1926 Agar warned students at Melbourne University that endless discussion about the importance of heredity or environment in 'moulding the chromosomes of man' could never head anywhere; while environment was 'very important socially and individually' it had little relevance for eugenics: 'good environment allows the inborn patent of individuals to develop to the utmost but the next generation starts independent of the environment to which their parents were subjected'.[77]   The debate was kept alive by work, much of which has been hotly disputed, by scientists such as Sir Cyril Burt, Raymond B Cattell, Hans J Eysenck and Arthur R Jensen.[78] These controversies were recently re-ignited, particularly by the late Richard J Herrnstein and Charles Murray, with their 1994 best-selling book, *The Bell Curve: Intelligence and Class Structure in American Life*, continued in 1996 by Richard Lynn's Dysgenics: *Genetic Deterioration in Modern Populations*, and set off again in 1998 by *Brave New Worlds: Staying Human in the Genetic Future*, a pessimistic summons to resist 'scientism' by *Sunday Times* journalist Bryan Appleyard.

The debate had important ramifications for the eugenics movement. Despite the high-level political affiliations and the clout of many prestigious individuals who belonged to the Eugenics Society in Britain, as an organization, the Society had surprisingly little political impact in Britain before or after 1914 because of its hereditarian stance. Dorothy Porter takes this view and, as evidence, notes that their membership never exceeded 700 and, unlike eugenists in Germany and America, it did not experience the same degree of collaboration with the public health officials who successfully influenced politicians to support environmental reforms.[79]   This is putting it too mildly as they were rivals: doctors felt that eugenists threatened their role and career prospects[80] and eugenists complained that the medical profession was too 'engrossed' with environmental issues to support eugenics.

Early last century, Britain's environmental cause was invigorated by the rise of the Garden City Movement which greatly influenced town planning around the world.[81] In Australia these reforms began in 1900 after an outbreak of bubonic plague struck 303 residents in the Rocks, then a Sydney harbour-side slum, killing 103 of them. The following May, the Rocks Resumption Board was established in an effort to combat the disease; it marked the birth of Australia's town planning (or housing) movement. The Town Planning Association of New South Wales incorporated public health and eugenist aims for building attractive, clean, disease-free suburbs which would reduce infant mortality and produce a virile, white race. These model communities would enjoy moral health and social stability because the new housing would avert degeneration, disintegration of character and other revolutionary 'isms' which were thought to be associated with slums and poverty.[82]

Many groups were involved with town planning; its supporters included eugenists Arthur, Eldridge, Irvine and Barrett; Labor politicians John D Fitzgerald, J R Dacey and John C Watson; planners Sir John Sulman, Marion and Walter Burley Griffin; and public health official Dr James Purdy. Michael Roe described town planning as one of the great progressive causes which developed in parallel with the country life movement.[83] They really emerged in tandem because although most Australians live in suburbs, fantasies about life in the bush are a national preoccupation. Although the reforms produced more garden suburbs than garden cities, they encouraged home ownership and were fostered by an Arcadian mystique in which country life was noble, healthy and quintessentially Australian. It began in the 1850s when the British started to portray Australia as having progressed from its convict days to become 'a veritable Arcady in which the Golden Age of rural prosperity and individual dignity might be recaptured'.[84] This preoccupation with the bush was fostered by *The Bulletin* whose first bush ballad, *Sam Holt* by Ironbark, appeared on 26 March 1881 and Henry Lawson and Banjo Paterson continued the genre. The bush legend was expounded and expanded by artists, writers and poets in the early decades of last century.[85] In reality, Australia is the world's driest continent with the least arable land and it is extremely urbanised. Although Robert Irvine's idea for garden suburbs was no longer considered the answer to society's ills after 1916, its legacy remains dotted in our suburbs and our minds.

Despite the fact that eugenics organisations did not exist in Australia until the last four years of the 1900 to 1914 period which Bacchi studied, the optimism she described was felt widely, not just by the enthusiastic eugenists. For example, Dr James Jamieson found the 'modern tendency' to minimise the part played by heredity in disease, 'a happy one'.[86] There were some dissenters but most, like Professor Henry Laurie, welcomed the twentieth century's promise of 'brighter hopes for the prevention of disease and vice in spite of an adverse heredity'.[87] Eleven years later, the optimism was still evident in Ramsay Smith's views about the population 'working out its destiny in new and strange surroundings':

> Judging from what is already known, environment will modify the physical structure of the race, the bones, the form of the head, the vocal organs, the appearance of the skin, hair and eyes; it will change the times during childhood at which maximum growth occurs; it will modify the time of adolescence and the climacteric; it will influence the mental and moral characters, the appetites, passions and aspirations of the young and the old; it will reduce the birth-rate; it will modify our medical pathology. All these changes, under intelligent and judicious guidance and by rational living, according to wisely directed education, will contribute to the well-being of the people and expand national life to its fullest possible development.[88]

Mary Cawte discussed two important hereditarian influences at work in Australia which developed after the period Bacchi studied: the social Darwinist treatment of Aborigines and the attempts to segregate or sterilise the unfit.[89] The factors are complex and it is incorrect to claim that the nurture advocates were gentler than their opponents, the nature advocates. This has been dismissed as a myth by Mark Adams with the reminder that supporters of the 'soft' Lamarckian and the 'hard' Mendelian theories could both be 'strident advocates of eugenic sterilisation'.[90]

One man who blurred these distinctions was the New Zealander Dr Truby King who in 1914 said he was 'in sympathy' with the remark that 'environment can knock heredity into a cocked hat'. This phrase from the game of ninepins means to trounce someone in a contest of skill. His views were reported by the *Sydney Morning Herald* which found his Medical Congress paper 'one of the most interesting' although not all would agree with his strong pro-environment 'plea'. For King it was mothers' ignorance and improper infant feeding, not heredity, which caused a large proportion of 'imbecility or idiocy'. However, he hedged his bets and wanted to 'segregate defectives' to stop them breeding.[91]

Similarly, in 1907, Mackellar had argued that environment was 'the explanation *par excellence* of the good or evil in child-life: supervise the environment and you supervise the development of the child'.[92] Ten years later he favoured 'compulsory sterilisation of the unfit'[93], a phrase which the eugenist Arnold White coined in 1910. Although Mackellar had for years believed that environment 'was much the more potent influence', by 1917 'greater experience and a close study of the subject' had made him 'materially alter' his views and state that 'the primary factor is usually found in heredity'.[94] As early as 1902, Professor Laurie had commented 'towards the close of the [nineteenth] century it had become the fashion to exalt nature unduly over nurture. Recently the pendulum has been swaying back again'.[95] Many British doctors kept the debate oscillating: Sir James Barr (a medical eugenist) complained at the 1913 British Medical Association Conference that doctors were so engrossed with the environment that they ignored the future.[96] Eugenics Society President, Lord Horder, argued on an Australian visit in 1935 that heredity had been forgotten and blamed nurture-oriented tinkering by social reformers for causing Britain's problems.[97] In his 1936 history of contraception, Dr Norman Himes directed a blast at the 'misleaders of the people' who were 'preaching unalloyed environmentalism'. He justified his 'outburst' on the grounds that he was 'entitled to show emotion after having devoted 500 pages to fact reporting and cautious comment'.[98]

There were similar nature-nurture fluctuations in Australia. In 1914, W A (Bill) Holman said he rejoiced to hear Truby King deprecating the dismal fatalism produced in the last 20 years by some doctors' misguided study of heredity. Holman, like Catherine Spence, blamed Ibsen's *Ghosts* for the public's widespread fatalistic acceptance of heredity.[99] Meredith Atkinson pointed to the success of Australian soldiers in World War I, claiming that this provided an unparalleled 'demonstration of the efficacy of good food, comfortable homes, shorter hours, higher wages, open-air life, universal education and political freedom'. This, he said, proved that 'pseudo-scientific pessimists' who preached 'hereditarian dogmatism' were wrong. 'Australia has demonstrated beyond question the supreme and infinite potentialities of social environment'.[100] A year later, Griffith Taylor identified the environment 'as having most influence because the changes in it caused civilisations to wax and wane, with different races rising and then sinking into oblivion'.[101]

Popular opinion changed when the 1929 Depression showed that economics, not genetics, was responsible for the unemployment and ruin which affected both eugenic and cacogenic (unfit) people. Public opinion was also jolted by news that fit parents could produce unfit offspring, a possibility which was discussed in 1930 in a Melbourne monthly, *Stead's Review*.[102] Sir John Macpherson, professor of psychiatry at the University of Sydney, dispelled the myths about mentally defective children being more likely if parents were poor, unhealthy or drunken, with the comment that such births could happen 'just as frequently' if parents were rich, healthy and sober.[103]

Racial Poisons

Venereal Diseases – The Sins of the Fathers

Figure 25: The Sins of the Fathers[104]

Some eugenists pedantically argued that venereal diseases (VD) lay outside the pale of eugenics in its strictest sense 'because genetics was not involved'.[105]   However, most were concerned because it caused 'sterilization of the fit': infected women were likely to become sterile, to miscarry or to have stillbirths and congenital syphilis caused many infant deaths.[106] From ancient times, when there was no possibility of a cure, this scourge has been feared as a death sentence for sinners; it has been stigmatised as 'the sins of the fathers'. For example, the Athenian dramatist Euripides, who was born around 480 BC, wrote in *Phoenix,* 'The Gods visit the sins of the fathers upon the children'; the Roman poet Horace (65-8 BC) wrote in his *Odes* , 'For the sins of your fathers, you though guiltless, must suffer'; the *Bible* (Exodus 20:5 and Deuteronomy 5:9) reiterated this warning, 'I the Lord thy God am a jealous God, visiting the inequity of the fathers upon the children unto the third and fourth generation of them that hate me'; and

Shakespeare, in *The Merchant of Venice*, Act III, Scene V, took up the theme: 'The sins of the fathers are laid upon the children'.

Despite 'anxious care' to prevent its introduction to the new Australian settlement, convicts were discovered with venereal disease in April 1788.[107]   A century later Dr Charles (later Sir Charles) Mackellar (1844-1926), who in 1882 became the first President of the NSW Board of Health, reported to the State's government that VD remained a serious problem.[108] Warnings were also given by Brettena Smyth (1840-1898), the self-proclaimed 'pioneer Australian lecturess and female instructor in matters pertaining to health and disease, and the improvement of the race'.[109]

In 1901 the French dramatist Eugène Brieux (1858-1932) caused outrage in Paris with his awful-warning play about VD. It was also performed in English as *Damaged Goods* and fifteen years later, came to Sydney and Melbourne. In 1902 Sir Thomas Fitzgerald (1838-1908) told the Australasian Association for the Advancement of Science that 'syphilis is undoubtedly hereditary'.[110] Others feared its damage would have a combined impact on both nature and nurture, warning that 'the environment of to-day will become the heredity of tomorrow.' The 1980s anti-nuclear slogan 'radiation fades your genes' was making a similar point.

When there was no hope of cure, VD sufferers were sometimes isolated in segregated 'lock' hospitals, initially used to treat people with leprosy.[111] In 1899 plans for a women's lock hospital in Sydney had to be abandoned[112] and a lock ward at Sydney Hospital functioned 'under a cloud', as few people would admit to having been treated there. Laws have been equally contentious and despite the 1860s controversy sparked by Britain's coercive Contagious Diseases Acts, Australia copied this legislation.[113] Queensland in 1868, followed by Tasmania in 1879, gave police the power to detain prostitutes who were thought to have VD. NSW was one of the 'laggards',[114] although it had passed the Police Offences Amendment Bill and the Prisoners' Detention Bill in 1908, which could extend the sentences of syphilitic criminals.[115]

Most politically conservative women's groups were silent about these laws but Rose Scott's Women's Political and Educational League objected, particularly to anonymous notification of women as VD suspects. However, in 1908 after Sir Charles Wade, the NSW Liberal Premier showed Scott children in hospital with congenital syphilis she repudiated her position on pragmatic and eugenic grounds.[116] In 1912 Dr Arthur used similar shock tactics. He gave a shilling to an 'innocent' VD-ravaged boy to accompany him from Sydney Hospital to the neighbouring NSW Parliament House where the unfortunate victim was made to parade for an assembled group of politicians who were instructed to 'look at that!'. Arthur boasted 'this was undoubtedly the most eloquent speech ever made in my life'.[117]

Many statistics were useless because 'syphilis' was only recorded in the 'gravest cases'. To avoid hurting relatives' feelings, doctors usually avoided writing the word on a death certificate. Sydney's Hospital for Sick Children estimated in 1902 that the VD death rate was at least 60 per 1,000 babies treated for the disease: 'after they have contracted it, they are born with it and they die as a result of it'.[118] This was stated by several witnesses at the 1904 Royal Commission on the Decline of the Birth-rate and some argued that VD had contributed to the population decline.[119]

At the 1908 Intercolonial Medical Congress Peter B Bennie (1852-1932), an Honorary at the Melbourne Children's Hospital, claimed that 'fully 25% of sick children' and 10% of children in the community were 'syphilised', a rate as bad as New York's. Sydney's medical establishment felt this was an exaggeration but Bennie was later praised by the National Health and Medical Research Council for being the first person in Australia to recommend that the problem should be tackled by educational means.[120]

Few had learned their lessons; in 1917 Professor Anderson Stuart said that ten cots in a Sydney hospital were occupied by children who had caught VD from 'low-down' men who had raped virgins in the belief that this would cure their syphilis.[121] George Black, a morally-flawed NSW Minister for Public Health, proposed an era of 'sexual sanitation', free from attacks by diseased and depraved men because 'pure blood is more valuable to the State than pure gold'.[122] The nightmare prospects of VD prompted some suffragettes to demand 'votes for women and chastity for men'. In Western Australia, Edith Cowan (1861-1932) urged schools to teach sex hygiene and scientific temperance because:

> There are no two racial poisons to be compared with alcohol and the sex diseases in the awfulness of their results, and it has become unthinkable that men and women can continue, like ostriches, to bury their heads in the sands of ignorance and yet hope the nation can remain unscathed.[123]

Cowan (Nationalist Party) was elected to the WA Legislative Assembly in 1921, the first woman in an Australian Parliament and the second in the British Empire. Her influence shows in a book on sex hygiene by Reginald C Everitt Atkinson, the State's Commissioner of Public Health, and Professor William Dakin. Not only were prospective marriage partners with 'a defective gift', selfish brutes guilty of 'almost criminal' deceit, but the authors also blamed the deceived victims; they were 'deplorably selfish' and 'sublimely ignorant' for not discovering their partner's carefully concealed defects![124] In New South Wales the conservative politician and eugenist Dr Richard Arthur had been making similar pro-chastity exhortations since 1903 in pamphlets produced by the Australian White Cross League's Purity Series. He persevered, writing in the *Medical Journal of Australia* on 28 October 1916:

> I have been for many years a firm believer in the necessity for letting air and light into this subject of sex relations, and I am convinced that we are standing to-day at the opening of a new era, the causes of which are the intellectual emancipation of women, the increasing influence of eugenics, the disappearance of the mock modesty that banned all consideration and discussion of one of the greatest natural functions, and the growing public concern at the menace of venereal disease. These causes will bring about .. a revolution in the mental attitude of men towards illicit intercourse.

As VD began causing increasing havoc in World War I, fears that troops might return not wounded but invalided by syphilis, galvanised governments to support legislation to combat sexual diseases. Strong support came from Dr Arthur, who in 1915 chaired a NSW Legislative Assembly Select Committee on the Prevalence of Venereal Diseases and it produced reports in 1916 and 1919. He also persuaded the very sedate University of Sydney to agree with senior medical students' requests in 1916 to establish a Society for Combating Venereal Diseases. The first meeting was attended by 300 students, staff and graduates. Anderson Stuart, the Chairman, agreed with Professor Welsh that the Society should study 'the problems of venereal diseases, prostitution and kindred evils', educate the public and 'secure suitable legislation'. Office bearers included prominent eugenists such as Meredith Atkinson, Secretary, assisted by Ralph Noble and Jessie Street, with Professors H Tasman Lovell and Robert F Irvine on the Council. The Society published papers and in 1916 participated in Australia's first conference about venereal diseases, the Workers' Educational Association's *Teaching of Sex Hygiene*.[125] However, Jessie Street's paper for the Conference – which advocated preventive sex education and selective 'universal free treatment' for 'innocent' sufferers, but not for the 'promiscuous' – was *not* published in the WEA Conference papers[126] although her presentation of it was mentioned in the *Sydney Morning Herald*.

Shortly after the Conference, Maybanke Anderson produced the WEA's first pamphlet, a tract about VD. She asked 'why prate about a White Australia and erect fine buildings for posterity' when society was 'diseased and dying?' If nothing was done to 'kill this secret enemy', attempting to defend Australia would be 'hardly worthwhile' and it would be a 'mockery to talk about prosperous Australia'.[127] Gonorrhoea was a highly secret enemy but few then recognized it as a principal, often symptomless cause of women's sterility and that it was more harmful than syphilis. The campaign was initiated by women and comments about VD appeared in Australian newspapers surprisingly early. For example, Women's Liberal League founder Laura Bogue Luffman wrote: 'Although Dr Arthur is correct in stating that the year 1913 may be regarded as the opening of a new era (as far as frank discussion in the British press is concerned), it must not be forgotten that women – especially medical women – have been calling attention to this terrible scourge ever since their eyes were opened to its existence'.[128] Australian press, although slightly behind Britain, was almost 20 years ahead of America where the words syphilis and venereal disease did not appear in the *New York Times* until 1935.[129]

Many of the campaigners, who would now be described as purity feminists, thought that early marriage, sex education and higher wages for women, would eliminate prostitution. Membership of the University's anti-VD society was over 600 in 1917 and 1918, but the society disbanded after 1920. A similar fate was suffered by the NSW Social Hygiene Association which was established in 1916 by the feminists Street, Golding and Dwyer, and Victoria's Association to Combat the Social Evil.[130] The NSW Venereal Diseases Act was passed in 1918 and from 1920 it became mandatory for sufferers to receive medical treatment until cured and unqualified people were barred from treating VD. Arthur had campaigned for this for fifteen years and had drafted the legislation.

Professor Welsh warned a health congress audience in 1917 about the need to wage two wars 'to defend our homes and our race' from external military aggression and the internal attack from venereal diseases. He spoke of homes 'made desolate, a nation defrauded by gonorrhoea'.[131] War, as well as eliminating the best of the race, was blamed for maximising the impact of TB, VD and alcohol.[132] In a paper presented at the 1920 Australasian Medical Congress, Cumpston commented that 59,274 pensions were paid to war widows, but no help or effective protection was given to the women and children of 55,000 soldiers who had contracted VD on overseas military service, or to the unknown numbers of infected people in Australia.[133]

State intervention, for the future of the race, was central to the Progressive ideology which underpinned debates about VD. In 1920 the *Eugenics Review* reported that Major W A Sawyer, President of the American-based Social Hygiene Association, supported by the Rockefeller Foundation's International Health Board, would spend five years in Australia to give advice about VD and other infectious diseases. VD became the catalyst for the Commonwealth's involvement in health services and the crisis of war-related illnesses (particularly influenza and VD) was so pressing that the Australian

Government agreed to create the Commonwealth Department of Health in 1921 in order to receive American health funding.[134]

In 1925 the NSW Board of Health funded a VD clinic which became one of the finest in the Commonwealth, according to Dr John Cooper Booth (Director of the Division of Venereal Diseases at Sydney's Rachel Forster Hospital) who later stressed that 'coercive legislation' was 'the basis of all control'.[135] The VD clinic was so well known that many people did not realise that it was part of a general hospital.[136]   When the RHA began in 1926, fighting VD was paramount; at its inaugural meeting Co-President Dr Ralph Lyndal Worrall said 'sex is the mainspring of life, but it is treated like a skeleton in a cupboard.   Nothing could be more fatal than the association of immorality with venereal disease'.[137] The RHA was so closely identified with this work that Dr Cooper Booth reminded delegates at the 1929 Australian Racial Hygiene Congress that it worked in other areas as well. In both the 1928 and the 1929 Annual Report of the Director-General of Public Health, Dr Robert Dick emphasised the help given by the RHA, the Fathers and Sons Welfare Movement and other public spirited citizens in promoting the government's anti-VD message.[138]

The NSW Public Health Department purchased one eugenic-sounding film, *Well Born*, from the British Hygiene Council and borrowed others on VD and sex hygiene with such moralisingly euphemistic titles: *Gift of Life, Social Hygiene for Women, Waste, Memories, The Flaw, Whatsoever a Man Soweth*. The Report listed the RHA-sponsored meetings, films, leaflet distribution, as though the Association (which was given a £500 grant in 1928) was an adjunct to the government's anti-VD work.   Finally, it noted, 'posters kept displayed in public lavatories throughout the State', those terrifying warnings which remained on toilet doors for years after.

Although the NSW Government grant was withdrawn in 1930, the RHA continued to promote its anti-VD message.[139] The propaganda included the play *Just One Slip*, showing films in country areas and interstate, and pressuring the Board of Health to open a 'continuous' VD clinic in June 1933. Their 1936 Annual report noted that Dr Lane from the warship *Canberra* had thanked the Association for lending the 'talkie picture' *Damaged Lives* which he showed to sailors. Although it was useless expecting the boys to read, they had to 'sit out the picture'. The RHA arranged a private screening in Sydney and, the flier for a 15 November 1939 screening in Melbourne, advised that it had been seen by the Archbishop of Sydney; Dr Sydney Morris, Director General of Public Health; Dr Grace Cuthbert, Director Maternal Mortality, Department of Health; Professor Harvey Sutton of the Sydney University, and Mrs Goodisson, 'all of whom were most enthusiastic in their praises of the film'. However, it failed to meet other film companies' approval. Others of this genre were *Damaged Lives* and the film *Damaged Goods,* an adaptation of the 1901 play by Brieux which J C Williamson had successfully staged in Sydney and Melbourne in 1916. *The Triad* denounced it as 'cant' which pandered to 'the public taste for nastiness and morbidity'. The 1937 films were described by the Halliwell *Film Guide* as 'naive even at the time' – they had trouble with the American censors but were 'not otherwise notable'. While the RHA showed these anti-VD films in the 1930s, in 1940 they ignored *Dr Ehrlich's Magic Bullet,* a biographical film about the German scientist Paul Ehrlich (1854-1915) who developed the drug Salvarsan which provided the first effective treatment for VD. The RHA promoted purity films but not the detached documentaries.

Prompted by the need for prestige, publicity and public recognition, the RHA established links with counterpart organisations overseas. In 1929, some members became affiliated with the American Social Hygiene Association, which in 1913 had been formed from an amalgamation of America's Vigilance Association and the Federation for Sex Hygiene. From 1928 to 1935 Ruby Rich, while in London, acted as the RHA representative on Britain's Social Hygiene Council. The RHA reprinted some of the Council's booklets (without acknowledging their source)[140] and proudly announced in their 1938 Annual Report that an address by Dame Maria Ogilvie Gordon, a Vice-President of the Council, had been their 'big share of the Sesquicentenary celebrations'. Two groups boycotted these Australian festivities: the Aborigines' Progressive Association held a day of mourning and, 'despite strenuous efforts', the Sydney organisers could not attract anyone from the Royal family to attend the celebrations.[141] The RHA also lost face when their important visitor said she was 'quite unaware of the work' the RHA was doing in Sydney. Surprisingly, the RHA quoted Dame Maria's humiliatingly public remarks in their Annual Report.

Anticipating recent discussions about AIDS, the views of anti-VD campaigners were split on two issues; both differentiated between 'innocent victims' and 'sinful profligates' and both argued about condoms.[142] Debates about VD invariably include moral judgements and the name itself, *venereal* disease, comes from *venery*, an archaic word meaning 'gratification of sexual desire'. In the fight against men who were venereal not venerable, the anti-condom/pro-chastity group included Jessie Street, Marion Piddington and Angela Booth, who thought that condoms were immoral because they invited promiscuity and condoned vice. Many doctors, and the New Zealand campaigner Ettie Rout, were prompted by World War I to promote condoms.[143] It was a hot issue at the 1929 Australian Racial Hygiene Congress; Mabs Fawkner, writing for the rural newspaper *The Land,* noted that 'Mrs Councillor [Angela] Booth, of Melbourne, made a sweeping attack on the morals of many married women, and considered it a crime to make the use of prophylaxis [condoms] available to young people. Sir James Barrett crossed swords with her on the subject'.[144] Piddington had proposed her own idiosyncratic medical solution for VD.

Dr Joseph Goldsmid argued in a 1933 speech to the Brisbane Rationalist Society, that the rates of prostitution, VD and illegitimacy would be reduced by 'companionate' (non-procreative) marriages.[145] This proposal had been advocated by a liberal American judge, Ben B Lindsey, whose work in children's courts was praised by Edith Onians, who had met him in 1912.[146] In the 1930s Piddington and the RHA worried that such unions would encourage sexual licence.[147] Lindsey carefully defined his concept as 'legal marriage, with legalised birth control, and with the right to divorce by mutual consent for childless couples, usually without the payment of alimony'.[148]

In a 1937 paper on the prevention of VD-caused blindness, two doctors proposed to the NHMRC that 'voluntary sterilization should be available for carriers and sufferers of hereditary eye diseases'.[149] While the NHMRC did not agree to this harsh measure, in World War II they urged authorities to limit alcohol sales to women and control young girls' loose conduct in public places.[150] From 1942 to 1947, state laws were replaced by the wartime National Security (Venereal Diseases and Contraceptives) Regulations. In 1943 Dr Cumpston agreed it would be hard to control the irresponsible promiscuous girl and admitted that he had received vigorous protests about the restrictions, especially from women's organisations. Despite this, he said that the government had proceeded along lines which it felt in duty bound to follow.[151]

Dr Edith Anderson noted, in the October 1948 issue of the *RHA Monthly Bulletin,* that VD had increased after the wartime regulations were lifted. This might have been true but most importantly, the death rate from VD was rapidly falling.[152] After penicillin was introduced in 1943, there was less talk of VD as God's 'scourge for sinners', fewer calls for moral solutions, and less anxiety about female morality. Mercifully, it was no longer a case of 'a night with Venus and lifetime with Mercury' and people were freed from the horrors of mercury-based treatment. In 1950 the RHA broadcast one of their last old-style commercials asking listeners to 'Protect your family – Stamp out VD'.

The Taint of Tuberculosis

The high death rate from tuberculosis (TB) in the cities of eighteenth century Europe was replicated in Australia where, from the first days of European settlement, colonists and Aboriginals were plagued by uncontrolled infections. A contributing factor in the high Australian death rate was the influx of British consumptives who came here in search of a sun-assisted return to health. While each colony tried to isolate or care for people with TB, there was no effective attack on this disease until the National Tuberculosis Campaign began operating in 1950.[153] With false optimism it ceased in 1976. The disease was not beaten and sadly, the World Health Organisation issued a symbolic and literal *Mayday* in May 1993, announcing that TB was a 'global emergency' affecting more than a third of the world's population. Unfortunately, in the twenty-first century many antibiotics are ineffective against drug-resistant TB and VD.

Figure 26: Health + Wealth = Happiness[154]

Consumption was an early name for this disease because it consumed the sufferer, with a reputation, as John Bunyan noted in the seventeenth century, as being the 'captain of the men of death'. John Pearn described an ingenious nineteenth century Australian attempt to provide charitable care for consumptives which was augmented by government financing: in 1877 a philanthropist established what was probably Australia's first sanatorium in the NSW town of Picton. TB, like VD, was surrounded with fear and ignorance. In 1881, a medical textbook listed 'causes' of TB, including 'hereditary disposition', 'unfavourable climate', 'sedentary indoor life', 'defective ventilation', 'deficiency of light' and 'depressing emotions'.[155] The following year, German bacteriologist Robert Koch (1843-1910) discovered the real cause – a bacillus – which was transmitted by infection and not heredity and in 1891 Anderson Stuart made an Australasian report on Koch's treatment.[156] Twenty years later the NSW Government issued the world's first charity postage stamps, with a surcharge to help care for the sufferers.[157] In 1917 TB and VD were the 'two most wasteful and devastating diseases'.[158] Figures help to make this real. In 1921, according to the *Medical Journal of Australia*, more than 3,000 Australians died from pulmonary TB.

In 1910 Karl Pearson claimed that TB tended to affect especially first and second born children and this unfortunately, made some eugenists reject the idea of contraception.[159] Leonard Hobhouse, an early critic of eugenics, was more optimistic in 1911. He told a British audience that it was quite possible that scientific advances might eliminate the tubercle instead of eliminating the tubercular stock. If this happened, tuberculosis would no longer be ranked as a defect. But if such people had been forbidden to marry, society would 'have lost all that they might have contributed to the population and its well-being for the sake of no permanent gain'.[160] Delegates at the 1911 Australasian Medical Congress were reminded that 'many philosophers, poets, scientists, economists, historians and warriors have been tubercular, alcoholic, or insane or degenerate'.[161] It was not a logical argument because the people functioned despite, not because of, their affliction. Opposite but equally emotional tactics have been used by anti-abortion campaigners who warn women that they have selfishly robbed the world of countless new Beethovens. A unspecified 'famous West Australian doctor' used this argument to oppose eugenic sterilisation on the grounds that they might eliminate people such as Robert Louis Stevenson, Elizabeth Browning, Keats, Chesterton, Byron and the Brontes, who suffered from 'inherited tuberculosis'.[162] Illogical responses are understandable in the case of a little-known disease which was usually fatal.

In Australia, mortality from TB has always been much higher than the death rate from VD but morality, not logic or mortality, made eugenists focus attention on VD.[163] However, the RHA showed some concern about TB (see **Figure 26**) and Dr John Hughes' talk in September 1935 prompted a 'very animated discussion' about heredity and contagion. Chest X-rays were also part of the RHA's pre-marriage checks. If X-rays showed TB, the couple were advised not to marry or to postpone childbearing until it was cured. Contraceptives were scarce, even if a husband or wife had TB.[164]   This difficulty caused a young Hobart doctor to write to Marie Stopes in 1922 in the hope that she would help him buy British supplies for a consumptive patient.[165] However, if Stopes had sent a contraception consignment it was unlikely to have been allowed off the wharf in Tasmania. These seem to have posed a great threat to national security in the 1920s: an Australian Archives file describes an extraordinary protocol: in January a Custom Officer 'detained' a 'check pessary' addressed to a woman in Launceston, obtained signatures for the destruction of this hapless 'prohibited import' and then, in May the 'article was destroyed by fire'.[166] Dr Eulalia Richards, who the RHA honoured in 1950 as one of their oldest members, gave this more reasoned advice about TB in the 1945 edition of *Ladies' Handbook of Home Treatment*:

> Whether or not a harvest of disease results depends upon the character of the soil upon which the seeds fall. Tubercle bacilli cannot grow and thrive in a healthy body … but when … the body becomes weakened and the blood impure, the seeds of tuberculosis find suitable soil for growth, and thus begin to multiply and manufacture poisons.   These poisons soon cause fever and wasting, or consumption, of the body.[167]

Prostitution, A Threat to the Family

Eugenists, pronatalists and purity feminists all believed that prostitution was an evil which threatened domesticity and the race. Joseph Kirby (1837-1924), a South Australian pastor, opposed 'commercialised vice', alcohol and Asian invasion but supported sterilisation.[168]   He campaigned relentlessly, publishing his first anti-prostitution lectures in 1882.[169]   In 1898, he was lampooned in an Adelaide magazine by a writer who wanted to regulate prostitution as part of a Contagious Diseases Act.[170]   Kirby, who was vehemently opposed, wanted young people to sign a pledge, similar to the temperance declaration which, he thought, would deter them from 'seduction and fornication'.[171]

In a paper on prostitution given to the 1916 WEA Conference, Angela Booth, Honorary Secretary of the Association to Combat the Social Evil, made an unusual objection:

As a man's bones did not 'set' until he was 25 or 30, what injury must result, physically, to a youth who begins the sexual life at 16 and 17 years of age! If a prostitute's child was fathered by a mentally and physically stunted youth, the baby 'would swell the list of the inefficient'.[172]

She considered the 'traffic in sex' was the 'foci' and 'nursery' of VD and that 'where lust is rife, drink is abundant; where alcohol flows, continence is impossible'. In her comments about alcohol's 'blighting effect' on sperm and foetus, she was quoting Professor Auguste-Henri Forel (1848-1931) the Swiss neuroanatomist, psychiatrist and social reformer who, Booth said, insisted on this topic 'almost to weariness'. Nineteenth century science was not always wrong; in fact the link between a woman's drinking in pregnancy and 'foetal alcohol syndrome' is now acknowledged.

Feminists worried about the risks which 'innocent' women and children faced from infectious men; some provided sex education and anti-VD campaigns hoping to teach children, particularly girls, to be chaste before marriage and faithful after; some tried to help destitute women survive without prostitution but many purity feminists were antagonistic or frightened, considering that prostitutes sent 'disease, sterility, deformity and death' to the 'best of homes' and the 'best stocks',[173] and some thought prostitutes were mentally defective.[174] In 1919 Angela Booth attacked society's double standards in the *Medical Journal of Australia* with a claim that prostitution would go on unless attention was given to 'the chief provoking cause, the demand in the male'. In the 1920s and 1930s Germans quaintly believed that nudism provided a healthy alternative to prostitution because 'hidden defects' such as VD would show and mate selection would made be from those with 'positive' genes.[175]

Figure 27: Sex Education Versus Sex Ignorance[176]

In 1926 Piddington praised Angela Booth for her years of 'unswerving courage' in educating about the need for reform.[177] Like Cassandra, Piddington took up Saleeby's cry about an imperilled society 'hastening to the Niagara of Racial Ruin', inundated by prostitution and 'irregular unions'.[178] In the May 1928 issue of the theosophists' magazine *Advance! Australia*, Goodisson acknowledged that it was futile to try and stop prostitution, and said that the RHA now realised that a greater threat came from the young promiscuous girl. Then Goodisson paid tribute to the earlier work of Josephine Butler (1828-1906) a courageous British feminist who helped women in workhouses and prisons and whose efforts to prevent women-only compulsory medical examinations for VD led to the 1886 repeal of the Contagious Diseases Acts of 1864, 1866 and 1869. Butler and Goodisson exemplify the kindly, pragmatic feminists who irritated their purer, more puritanical sisters.

RHA propaganda included a 1934 *Open Letter to Young Men* which warned boys about VD and the moral, social and physical evils of prostitution. They should avoid prostitutes, unless rescuing them from the 'mire' or making them leave the 'cursed trade'. After the Depression, women's groups more readily acknowledged that poverty could force women into prostitution.[179] In August 1936, RHA Vice-president Ruby Rich spoke on 'Prostitution and its Attendant Evils'[180] but despite the title, the RHA were not prudes. For example, three months later Rich visited Dr Raphael Cilento in Queensland trying to influence him to abolish compulsory medical examination of prostitutes.[181] However, memories are selective, as Jessie Street showed in her 1966 autobiography when she claimed that the efforts which she and sisters Annie Golding and Kate Dwyer made in 1916 to create the NSW Social Hygiene Association to combat 'commercialised prostitution', had failed from prudishness and people's reluctance to be identified with prostitution:[182] Street had prudishly forgotten to mention that the Association was formed to combat the threat of VD.

Degenerate Drinkers

Figure 28: Alcoholism Produces Degeneracy[183]

Drinking was not associated with illness until a Swedish doctor, Magnus Huss (1807-1890) coined the term 'alcoholism' in 1852, giving doctors a longer list of diseases they could prevent or cure. Dr George Archdall Reid, in an extremely influential address to London's Sociological Society in 1905, tried explain its cause. Reid argued that each race's resistance to disease or misfortune varied according to the extent of their prior exposure, so that excessive drinkers were 'weeded out to a greater extent' and the survivors were moderate drinkers and those not susceptible to alcohol. Reid concluded that 'if only a race goes downhill long enough, it will ultimately arrive at the top. It is literally inconceivable that evolution can have resulted from continuous degeneration'.[184]

Those endorsing Reid's view were lampooned by Saleeby as the 'better-dead' school of eugenists who argued that if alcohol eliminated the unfit, society would be better off. Years later, Harvey Sutton found Reid's hypothesis 'one of the most interesting applications' of the 'survival of the fittest' theory.[185] Apparently, no one noticed an identical theory which was described in Australia in 1901, four years *before* Reid's paper. The writer, Dr John Flynn (1859-1926), was not the missionary known as 'Flynn of the Inland' who founded the Royal Flying Doctor Service, but an Irish-born surgeon and anatomy demonstrator at the University of Sydney, who wrote a 60-page article, 'Heredity and Disease', which was published in the *Australasian Catholic Record* and, in five parts in the *Australasian Medical Gazette*. This is the significant extract:

> Alcohol is a source of elimination of those who have the greatest capacity for enjoying it. From this it follows that those nations that have known, and used alcohol for the longest, ought to be the most temperate; the heavy drinkers, owing to indulgence of their inborn capacity, are gradually eliminated, and the race is continued by those with a poor capacity for enjoying alcohol, and a nation of moderate drinkers is by the process of natural selection gradually evolved. And there is no doubt that there is considerable weight to this line of reasoning.[186]

While Sir Thomas Fitzgerald was mistaken in his 1902 conference paper to claim that VD was 'undoubtedly hereditary', he sensibly considered social and environmental aspects; 'strong drinkers are frequently strong thinkers' who need help to contribute to society and to protect infants, because if conceived by drunk parents they would be 'unsound in their mental organisation'. He concluded that if philanthropists relieved workers' boredom or gave them bicycles, it would do more good than a week of temperance lectures.[187]

An April 1905 editorial in the *Australasian Medical Gazette* claimed that 'numerous observations from all parts of the world' justified the conclusion that 'ova or spermatozoa are directly poisoned' by alcohol with the result that families of alcoholics contain many idiots, imbeciles, epileptics and neurasthenics. Havelock Ellis considered that chronic drunkards 'largely belong to the same great family, and do not so much become feeble-minded because they drink, but possess the tendency to drink because they have a strain of feeble-mindedness from birth'. Others debated whether alcoholism was a cause or a symptom of degeneracy. Some doctors worried whether natural selection should be allowed to operate in the case of alcohol. According to this logic, racial decay would spread by treating alcoholics or consumptives but the race would be strengthened if nature eliminated them. The only course likely to be approved by biology, morality and humanity was to care for individual degenerates and to prevent them from multiplying.[188] This prompted Sydney's *Telegraph* to publish a convoluted ultimatum to doctors in September 1911, urging them to decide whether to accept eugenic doctrines or to oppose them by saving individuals and thus weakening the race by weakening the force of disease.

In popular nineteenth century opinion, sobriety was equated with virtue, and drunkenness with sin. Roy MacLeod identified two ideas which reformers had about the causes of alcoholism. Some argued that it was acquired as a result of defective social environment; but the predominant view, supported by most eugenists, was that it had been inherited either directly or as a predisposition passed on from father to son.[189] Irrespective of their views about its causation, in 1910 both camps were shocked by findings released by the Francis Galton Laboratory for National Eugenics which, according to a report in the *Argus* on 16 July, were 'completely subversive' of the 'cordial agreement' of science and religion that the sins of alcoholism were 'visited upon the children'.

The statement in the *Argus* seems to be the first editorial on eugenics to be published in an Australian newspaper.[190] This scholarly article began, 'Eugenics is a modern study, and by some enthusiasts regarded as the password to the millennium'. It then outlined the British inquiry, comparing children of alcoholic parents with those from 'sober stock', which was conducted by Ethel M Elderton, the second Galton Research Scholar, and Karl Pearson, the Laboratory's Director (who was notorious for his belligerence and for not joining the Eugenics Education Society).[191] The conclusions, as reported in the *Times*, were that parental alcoholism did not affect the intelligence or physique of the offspring whose health was 'as good, or on the whole slightly better than, that of the children of the sober, and that parental alcoholism is not the source of mental defects in progeny'. The *Argus* made the observation that because of the study's hopeful message:

> the drunkard would no longer be able to sit helplessly before his failing and say it was his by birth, and that his name was written already in the book of doom. With courage born of new conviction he might march once more breast-forward holding that we fall to rise, are baffled to fight better.

The medical details in the article suggests that its author was activist physician Sir James Barrett, who approved of practical eugenics and on 26 July 1913 wrote an *Argus* article on environmental reforms. This Melbourne newspaper appears to provide the only comment on the Elderton and Pearson findings. While these 'subversive' findings were passionately debated in Britain, the Australian silence may relate to newspaper proprietors' unwillingness to offend the temperance movement.

Reasoned debate was anathema to the anti-prostitution, anti-alcohol, pro-sterilisation preacher Rev Joseph Kirby, who in 1911 petitioned hotels to reduce their opening hours and followed this in 1912 with a deputation to Archibald Peake, the newly elected South Australian Liberal Premier. Peake was sympathetic until he was lobbied by a rival deputation from the Licensed Victuallers' Association. He then revealed his pro-industry stance by opposing Labor MHA Thomas Smeaton's Bill to reduce trading to the hours of 8 am until 8 pm.[192] Smeaton was the President of the South Australian Temperance Alliance and became a member of the Eugenics Committee of the State Branch of the British Science Guild. Feelings ran high. In 1915 Professor Anderson Stuart, while acknowledging that he drank wine with meals, convened a patriotic meeting in Sydney's Town Hall urging the audience to 'follow the King' and sign the pledge to give up drinking to support the war effort. Support for temperance peaked in 1916 and laws for hotel closing at 6 pm began as a war-time measure in all states except Queensland and Western Australia. The last vestiges of it remained in South Australia until 1967.

Women and the church were often allies in their fight against alcohol. The NSW temperance movement published *Grit: A Journal of National Efficiency and Prohibition,* and their values were shared by the Salvation Army and the Women's Christian Temperance Union, which established a Sydney branch in 1882 and fought for women's suffrage in the belief that this would end the misery caused by strong drink; during World War I the Women's Reform League resolved to 'support all movements calculated to minimise social evils' by campaigning for 'liquor traffic reform' and social purity.[193]

Theosophists were staunch temperance allies and the July 1928 issue of *Advance! Australia* advocated prohibition, reminding readers that families who avoided coarse food such as meat and alcohol had finer children and that we were losing the most desirable migrants because they avoided alcohol-rich Australia and 'made their home in Dry America'. However, Australians gave a resounding *No* at the NSW referendum on 5 September 1928 with only 358,000 votes in favour of prohibition and almost 897,000 against. Combating alcoholism was not a high priority for the RHA, although two members were ardent combatants – Canon R B S Hammond and Dr Arthur.[194] As early as 1912, Arthur had warned that alcoholism was a great plague of civilisation in which the habitual inebriate, whose offspring were of no value to the State 'but simply a great incubus', should sacrifice themselves by remaining childless for the sake of the race.[195] Journalist

Linda Littlejohn told the Australian Racial Hygiene Congress that reform of the liquor trade was urgently needed, and Arthur, the NSW Minister for Health, praised the RHA's extremely valuable work and urged others to combat the trade in alcohol 'along the lines followed by this Association'.[196] His comments are strange because the RHA showed little interest in temperance. In 1930 the Victorian Prohibition League reprinted Saleeby's 1922 tract, *Eugenics and Prohibition* in an attempt to forge an alliance between these two movements but in NSW Dr Arthur's attempts to do this failed just as Saleeby's had.

A Tendency to Crime, Pauperism and Other Ills

Governor Arthur Phillip made a proposal which would later have been considered eugenic when, within the first five years of settlement, he wrote:

> As I would not wish convicts to lay the foundation of an empire, I think they should ever remain separated from the garrison, and other settlers that may come from Europe and not be allowed to mix with them, even after the seven or fourteen years for which they are transported may be expired.[197]

However, our forebears displeased Orson Squire Fowler (1809-1887), a charismatic eccentric who 'phrenologised America and Americanised phrenology'.[198] In 1848 he commented that as citizens of NSW were parented mainly by criminals, their general degradation and viciousness was in perfect keeping with the doctrines of 'idiocy and propensities hereditary'.[199] This slur would have outraged even those residents who were sure the race was hurtling down the slope to ruin.

Papers on degeneracy and acquired inheritance featured in Sydney's 1914 meeting of the British Association for the Advancement of Science which was marred by the outbreak of World War I. The speakers included two eugenists, Charles Davenport from the US Eugenics Record Office, and Professor Felix Von Luschan from the University of Berlin, described by Raphael Falk as one of the founders of physical anthropology in Germany who promoted the notion of the poly-racial origins of the Jews. While it was widely believed that 'tendencies' or 'traits' could be inherited, Davenport identified a new one for parents to inflict on their children, that of 'nomadism or the impulsion to wander' but only the abstract of his paper survived. [200]

We only know the title of Von Luschan's paper, 'Culture and Degeneration' but the *Sydney Morning Herald* on 22 August 1914 quoted snippets which related to the 'effort to ward off the spectre of degeneration' and 'the way to cure crime was the complete and utter isolation of the criminal'.   The *Herald* also published a maudlin interview with 'the wife of this great German scientist' who was 'fair and sweet looking' but spoke in 'a mournful voice' with 'tears in her blue eyes' because she was 'so far away from their home in war time'. The *Herald's* report of a 'large gathering' to meet the scientists did not mention any of the eugenics-related papers which were presented although the meeting was chaired by Professor Robert Irvine, a Vice-President of the Eugenics Education Society.[201]   However, a few months later, Davenport lectured at an EES meeting with Dr Arthur presiding and this time eugenics *was* mentioned in the newspaper, *The Liberal Woman*.[202]

In his 1954 autobiography Richard Berry added a fascinating postcript to von Luscham's Culture and Degeneration paper which was 'discreetly' not mentioned in 1914 in the scientific meeting's official proceedings.   Berry was the professor of Anatomy at Melbourne University and the lecture was delivered at the university's anatomy theatre. He explained:

> It is certain that no German scientific journal would have dared or been permitted to publish it, for it was a most damning account of the pedigree of the German Kaiser Wilhelm II … He could hardly have drawn a worse picture than he gave in my theatre of the Kaiser-mit Gott combination. A genealogical tree accompanied the account, and those who heard the paper and saw the chart were dumbfounded at the daring of the man who could read it [after the embarrassed feeble applause and Berry's platitudinous vote of thanks] Von Luschan rushed across to me, shook me warmly by the hand and pressed into it, a small bottle, containing … that rarest thing in the world, a fine specimen of Tasmanian aboriginal's hair … you can see it in the Welcome [sic] Historical Museum in

London, for there eventually I deposited it for safe keeping ... it is as rare as its acquisition was dramatic.[203]

Religion

Religious zealots were prone to categorize everybody, except the elite whose views mirrored theirs, as the unfit and the unsaved. Galton had turned away from religion and had deified eugenics instead. However, religious eugenists were mostly Protestant and some lumped atheists and Roman Catholics in the 'unfit' category.   Not only eugenists were polarised along religious lines and many communities were split by sectarian feuds.   An American doctor, John Cowan argued, in a 1860s book on sale in Australia, that Catholicism caused unfitness; if Protestant women had abortions, the balance would be tipped in favour of Catholics, who would 'attain the ascendancy of this continent, and so hold the balance of power in its management – truly not a desirable prospect'.[204] The eccentric Dr Alan Carroll was the first President of the Sydney Theosophical Society in 1891 but seems to have renounced this because his curiously-spelt list of 'degenerates' in 1903 included 'raving atheists and fanatics and propounders of new sects and religions, such as the Mahomedans, the Irvinites, the Mormans, [and] the Spiritualists'.[205]

An American statistician claimed in 1912 that the higher birth-rate of foreign-born women in the 'originally Protestant State' of Rhode Island, was a 'menace to British influence' and that the 'State was in a fair way of becoming Roman Catholic'.[206]   The bigoted Ernest MacBride (an extreme Ulster Protestant) joined Britain's Eugenics Society in 1914 specifically to campaign for compulsory sterilisation of Irish Catholics and was later to embarrass the Society by writing to the *Times* in praise of Hitler.[207]   In 1927, Knibbs the Commonwealth Statistician complained privately to Marie Stopes that Mussolini was using the Catholic Church to keep the Italian birth-rate as high as possible.[208]   An Anglican Bishop complained about this openly in 1932, telling the *Sydney Morning Herald* that the Catholic opposition to birth control was really 'based on a desire for power'.[209] Catholics, although opposed to the idea of 'better people', unwittingly practised positive eugenics by producing large families; Papal encyclicals in the

1930s and 1940s, as well as prohibiting birth control, directed them to reject eugenics and sterilisation.

Despite pronatalist hectoring about the need to provide a 'quiverful', family size shrank from the 1870s. The government's response was to issue Indecent Publications Acts, which from 1876 prevented the advertisement or supply of contraceptives. While Annie Besant's birth control pamphlet *The Law of Population* was not legally challenged in Britain, it was in Australia, although the civil libertarian Justice Windeyer won the case magnificently in 1888. These laws and attempts to censor show that the American reformer, Dr Adolphus Knopf, was wrong to claim in 1917:

> In Australia and New Zealand, the means of artificial restriction are in free circulation and the restriction of families is almost universal. Yet these two English colonies have furnished their mother country in these hours of struggle with the most efficient, and physically and mentally best equipped regiments. [These] soldiers … have shown themselves to be brave and fearless fighters and certainly equal, if not superior as far as their English brethren. In the latter country it is well known that birth control is frowned upon by the legal and nearly all the ecclesiastical authorities.[210]

This could have been propaganda to support American birth control campaigner Margaret Sanger (1879-1966) who was sent to the workhouse for 30 days in 1917 for opening America's first birth control clinic. However, Dr Norman Haire in the 1938 preface to the 3rd edition of *Birth-Control Methods* made it clear that Australia continued to be a birth-controller's nightmare. Little had changed in the 20 years he had been away, medical students received no training in contraceptive techniques and many doctors knew as little about it as did their patients.[211] In 1942 he could find only two birth control clinics in the whole of Australia; the subject was not quite respectable and overpriced contraceptives were sold like drinks at a sly-grog shop.[212] When, in the 1940s and 1950s, Haire wrote a weekly family planning advice column for the Australian magazine *Woman*, the Catholic Church added the magazine to its list of prohibited books.

Some Australian opposition to eugenics was on the grounds that eugenists advocated birth control, a practice which was widely condemned until the Pill became available in the 1960s. Early last century, between a quarter and a third of the population was Catholic and the clergy – particularly the sizeable segment with Irish roots – exerted a powerful influence on its flock, the public service and politics. Subsequently, Catholic opposition to birth control and eugenics had more impact here than it did in Britain or America where a smaller proportion of the population was Catholic. In politics, after the 1916 and 1917 split over the Conscription Referenda, Catholics made up at least 50% of the Labour party, rising to 68% between 1927 and 1930.[213] Another distinctive difference about Australian eugenics is the way in which non-Catholic clergy were mostly silent on this issue, unlike their British colleagues. As Richard Soloway explained, British eugenists sought religious support by reminding the clergy that both groups promoted 'self sacrifice and beneficence to the whole of humanity, including generations to come'.[214] Some eminent British clergymen were supportive but others felt that eugenic plans for selective breeding were improper.

Unemployment and Other 'Evils'

In 1923 Sir George Syme, the President of the Australasian Medical Congress, warned delegates that it was 'harmful' to add to the population 'those who cannot or will not work'. In his opinion, reported in the *Medical Journal of Australia* on 16 February 1924, sterilisation was the best option for such 'drones' because 'incapacity for work is largely due to impaired physical condition, inherited or acquired'. A similar view was expressed in 1927 by Ernest Lidbetter in his contentious paper on heredity and pauperism at the first World Population Conference in Geneva.[215] There is conflicting information about the numbers of Australians who attended. At the time, the *Sydney Morning Herald's* leading article for 3 January 1928 reported that Australia was *not* represented, but years afterwards, the *ADB* entry for the women's rights' campaigner Alice Frances Mabel (May) Moss (1869-1948) claimed that she had been the conference's 'Australian delegate'. Despite the impression this gives, a news item indicates that she did *not attend*: on 4 January the *Sydney Morning Herald* , prompted by Lillie Goodisson, issued a correction to their previous day's leading article to inform readers that the Racial Hygiene Centre 'was invited to send a delegate and appointed [May] Mrs I H Moss, who was in Europe at the time. Unfortunately Mrs Moss could not be present but she wrote to the conference on behalf of the centre.'[216] This was opportunistic self-promotion for the RHA as Moss was not one of their 100 subscribers in 1928-29. However, at least one Australian *did attend*: Wickens who gave a paper and Knibbs (whose rejected paper was mentioned in Chapter 4) was a member of the Conference's General Council.

At Leonard Darwin's suggestion, Lidbetter, with financial support from Henry Twitchin, had spent many years compiling 'pauper pedigrees' in the East End of London and had concluded that 'destitute dependents' did not benefit from welfare assistance.[217] His views had changed little since the *Times* reported his comments in 1910:

> The existence amongst us of a definite race of chronic paupers, a race parasitic upon the community, breeding in and through successive generations. The existence of families of habitual criminals, preying upon the public in a somewhat similar manner, has long been known – but the analogous facts in relation to pauperism have perhaps never before received the full recognition to which they appear to be entitled. The subnormals are unable to appreciate the significance of social relationships and duties. In all respects they are mentally primitive; this is why they are so prolific and thus constitute a most serious menace to our civilization.[218]

Conference delegates were divided in their responses to Lidbetter's paper, but Jean Bourdon, in a plea for liberalism, reminded the audience that although Nietzsche's father had died in an asylum and he had himself gone mad, his 50 years of work while sane, although open to criticism from certain moral points of view, were far superior to an ordinary individual's work.[219] Cora Hodson agreed it was 'a difficult case since Nietzsche was an unfortunate syphilitic who ended his life as a paralytic' but she concluded that it was not the same as cases of real heredity.[220] In Australia, the debaters worried about degenerates who had weak minds and strong sexual appetites. For example, Lidbetter's influence is apparent in a 1930s talk which Marion Piddington wrote for *Smith's Weekly*:

In every part of Australia there are families of feeble-minded persons living and multiplying. Baby after baby is born either to inherit definite feeble-mindedness or become future carriers of the trait which will appear in their descendants. Tubercular parents are passing on to their children the predisposition for future tubercular infection. Alcoholic parents are transmitting such scourges as epilepsy, feeble-mindedness and weakened resisting powers. Criminal parents bring babies into the world with antisocial propensities inimical to society and the race.[221]

Dr Stanley Boyd was one of the few Australian eugenists to consider the impact of both parents' health on their offspring. In a book published in 1944, he wrote that alcohol, syphilis, gonorrhoea, lead and certain radiations were rightly described as racial poisons because of their effects even when only the male parent is exposed to them.[222] More recently, researchers reached similar conclusions after monitoring data on reproductive risks from exposure to toxic substances. In Britain, Sir Thomas Oliver and in America, Professor Alice Hamilton and Dr William Rom, were among the first to document the effects of lead on male and female reproduction.[223] They confirmed findings in the 1860s that males and females exposed to lead in Britain's potteries had higher rates of sterility, miscarriage, stillbirth and infant deaths than other workers. Without the benefit of such knowledge, eugenists struggled to eliminate 'racial poisons' and their efforts did not cease until medical advances made them irrelevant. Acknowledgment that environment and disease, not biology, caused most of the racial poisons, including pauperism, alcoholism and 'a tendency to criminality', removed the rationale for eugenists' concerns.

---

[1]Eugene Talbot, quoted by Steven A Gelb, in 'Degeneracy theory, eugenics, and family studies', *Journal of the History of the Behavioral Sciences*, 26 (July 1990), 243.

[2]Manning, *A Contribution to the Study of Heredity* (Sydney: Govt. Pr., 1886), 7.

[3]Gelb (1990), 243, 245.

[4]S J Holmes, *A Bibliography of Eugenics* (Berkeley: Univ of California Press, 1924), 496.

[5]See Francis Galton, *Essays in Eugenics* (London: EES, 1909), 37-38.

[6]See Jeffrey Weeks' *Coming Out: Homosexual Politics in Britain From the Nineteenth Century to the Present* (London: Quartet Books, 1977), 134, 137, 139-40 and 151-55.

[7]Report of Address on Eugenics by Dr Richard Arthur, MLA, Sydney, 18 Nov 1912, 5.

[8]R F Irvine, 'Eugenics Education Society', *SMH*, 26 February 1914, 5.

[9]'Socialism and eugenics', *SMH*, 22 August 1914, 9 (c), shows that Irvine chaired a joint meeting of the Economics and Commerce Association and the EES on this date.

[10] F A Bland, quoted by Brian H Fletcher in *History and Achievement: A Portrait of the Honours Students of Professor George Arnold Wood* (Sydney: Braxus Press, 1999), 45.

[11]'Care of the Feeble-minded in Australasia', *AMCT* (1914), 701-02.

[12]'Care of the Feeble-minded' (1914), 722-23.

[13]Fishbourne, 'The segregation of the epileptic and feeble-minded', *AMCT*, 2 (1911), 893.

[14]R J A Berry, *Report ... on Mental Deficiency in the State of Victoria*, with Suggestions for the Establishment of a Child Guidance Clinic (Melbourne: Wilson and MacKinnon, 1929).

[15]R J A Berry and Stanley D Porteus, 'A practical method for the early recognition of feeble-mindedness and other forms of social inefficiency', *MJA* (3 August 1918), 87.

[16]Porteus, 'A new definition of feeble-mindedness', Vineland, New Jersey, *Training School Bulletin*, no 14, 1920, 4.

[17]In 1912 Goddard wrote *The Kallikak Family: A Study in Feeblemindedness*, using the composite name 'Kallikak" (from the Greek words 'kallos' (beauty) and 'kakos' (bad).

[18] R J A Berry and R G Gordon, *The Mental Defective: A Problem in Social Inefficiency* (London: Kegan Paul, Trench, Trubner, 1931), 19-20, 19-20.

[19]Sir John Gorst quoted in *State Endowment For Families* (Sydney: Govt. Pr., 1919), 5. 'Undernourished, not defective. Eat more prunes, Dr Arthur says', *Guardian*, 25 Sept 1929.

[20]*Royal Commission on the Decline of the Birth-rate and on the Mortality of Infants in New South Wales* (Sydney: Govt. Pr., 1904), Question 4098.

[21]*ADB* entry and A V K Jones, 'Our own home-grown piano pioneer', *SMH*, 15 Dec 1994, 16.

[22] Hicks, *'This Sin and Scandal': Australia's Population Debate, 1891-1911* (Canberra; ANUP, 1978), 100-102.

[23]Richard Soloway, *Demography and Degeneration: Eugenics and the Declining Birthrate in Twentieth Century Britain* (Chapel Hill: University of North Carolina Press, 1990) 44-45.

[24] Rhodes, quoted by Robert Colls, in Colls and Philip Dodds (eds.), *Englishness: Politics and Culture, 1880-1920* (London: Croom Helm, 1986), 46.

[25]Michael Rosenthal, *The Character Factory: Baden-Powell and the Origins of the Boy Scout Movement* (London: Collins, 1986), 8. See also 150-60, 189.

[26]John Carey, *The Intellectuals and the Masses: Pride and Prejudice Among the Literary Intelligentsia, 1880-1939* (London: Faber and Faber, 1992), 15. See also 12-14, 62-63, 124-25, 202-03.

[27]Leonard Darwin, 24 November 1926 letter to the Heads of State attending the Imperial Conference. Eugenics Society Archives SA/EUG D166.

[28]Charles Bond, *Some Causes of Racial Decay: An Inquiry Into the Distribution of National Capacity in the Population: The Need for a National Stock Taking* (London: ES, 1928).

[29]Archibald Brockway, 'Physical education', *AMG* (21 March 1910), 123-25.

[30]Sydney Morris, 'Physical education in relation to national fitness', *ANZAAS* (January 1939), 194.

[31]*The Nation's Forum of the Air*, vol 1 (no 2), August 1944, 6.

[32]Jill Roe, *Beyond Belief: Theosophy in Australia, 1879-1914* (Kensington: UNSWP, 1986), 80.

[33]Roe (1986), 231-32.

[34]William Cleland, *The Chronic Insane*, the Habitual Offender and the Endemic Unemployed, with a View to Treatment: A Comparative Study of Degenerates (Adelaide: Webb, 1897).

[35]John H Kellogg, *Ladies' Guide in Health and Disease* (Melbourne: Echo, 1904), 386-87.

[36]Quoted by Lawson Crowe, in *Social Biology*, 32, nos 3-4 (1985), 158.

[37]Gould, *Life's Grandeur: The Spread of Excellence from Plato to Darwin*, London: Jonathan Cape, 1996, 222.

[38]Stirling, 'Weismann's theory of heredity', *Royal Society of South Australia. Transactions*, vol 13, Part 2 (December 1890), 257-68.

[39]Ramsay Smith, *The Practical Aspects of Heredity and Environment* (Adelaide: Whilas & Ormiston, 1899), 16-17.

[40]Laurie, 'The theory of use inheritance, psychologically considered', *AAASR*, vol 9 (1902), 778.

[41]William Dakin, *Journal and Proceedings of the Royal Society of Western Australia*, vol 1 (1914-1915), 239.

[42]Charles Bage, 'Race suicide' in *Social Sins*. St Paul's Cathedral, Melbourne, Lent 1912, Melbourne Diocesan Synod (Melbourne: Church of England Messenger, 1912), 21.

[43] *New York Times*, 20 November 1921, Section 7, 13 (a).

[44]'Acquired character transmission' (leading article), *Times*, 12 October 1932, 13 (c) and correspondence, 18 October 1932, 10 (e) and 11 (e).

[45]W E Agar, 'A Lamarckian experiment involving a hundred generations with negative results', *Journal of Experimental Biology*, 8 (1931), 95-107.

[46]Julian Huxley, *Memories* (Harmondsworth, Middlesex: Penguin), 1972, 241, 272.

[47]Saleeby quoted in *Sociological Review*, 7 (1914), 128 and Holmes (1924), 2.

[48]Hamilton, 'Heredity in relation to eugenics', *Australian Highway* (1 December 1922), 176.

[49]*Australian Racial Hygiene Congress,* 15-18 September 1929 (Sydney: RHA, 1929), 11.

[50]Rodwell's paper is in the Proceedings of the *21st Annual Conference of the Australian and New Zealand History of Education Society,* (Adelaide: St Marks College, October 1992), 475-90.

[51]Rodwell (1992), 488, footnote 1 and Abstract: 'Evidence is advanced which contends that female and male circumcision was practised on "precocious masturbators" in Australian kindergartens'.

[52]Frank Moorhouse, *Grand Days* (Sydney: Macmillan Australia, 1993), 543, 566. Cecil Woodham-Smith's definitive 1950 biography of Nightingale outlines her friendship with an army engineer called Captain Sir Douglas Galton who died in 1898.

[53]Rob Watts, 'Beyond nature and nurture: Eugenics in twentieth century Australian history', *Australian Journal of Politics and History*, 4 no 3 (1994), 319.

[54]An exception is environmentalist Thistle Harris (1902-1990) whose eugenics interest is discussed in Chapter 3. This interest was not mentioned in *Thistle Y Harris (A Biography of Thistle Yolette Stead)* (Chipping Norton, NSW: Surrey Beatty & Sons, 1998) and the author, Joan Webb and Harris' nephew, Alan Clark, did not know about it when I contacted them. None of the eugenics articles Harris wrote for the *Journal of Sex Education* from 1948 to 1950 are in her papers – David George Stead and Thistle Yolette Harris, ML MSS 5715, Boxes 2 and 3 (25).

[55]Galton, quoted by Bateson in the *MJA* (29 August 1914), 203. Galton probably derived this alliteration from Shakespeare's *The Tempest* (Act IV, scene I, pp. 188-189: a "devil, a born devil, on whose **nature/Nurture** can never stick"). Shakespeare, in turn borrowed it from Richard Mulcaster, an Elizabethan educator who wrote in 1582 that "**Nature** makes the boy toward, **nurture** sees him forward" (quoted by Judith Rich Harris in *The Nature Assumption* (New York: The Free Press, 1998), p.4.

[56]Peter J Bowler, *The Mendelian Revolution: The Emergence of Hereditarian Concepts in Modern Science and Society* (London: Athlone Press, 1995).

[57]Nicholas Pastore, *The Nature-Nurture Controversy* [1949] (NY: Garland, 1984), 176.

[58]John Horgan, 'Trends in behavioral genetics. Eugenics revisited', *Scientific American* (June 1993), 92-100.

[59]Catherine Helen Spence, *Heredity and Environment.* Delivered before the Criminological Society of South Australia, 23 October 1897 (Adelaide: Webb and Son, 1897).

[60]Spence (1897), 2-4.

61 Richard Dugdale, *The Jukes: A Study in Crime, Pauperism, Disease and Heredity*, 6th edn. (NY: Putnam's, 1900). First published in 1877.

62Dugdale (1900), 66 and 113.

63 Havelock Ellis, *The Task of Social Hygiene* (London: Constable, 1912), 42.

64Ramsay Smith, *On Race-Culture and the Conditions that Influence it in South Australia* (Adelaide: Govt. Pr., 1912), 22.

65Charles E Rosenberg, quoted by Gelb (July 1990), 243.

66 Daniel Kevles, *In the Name of Eugenics: Genetics and the Uses of Human Heredity* (New York: Knopf, 1985), 71.

67Crowe (1985), 159.

68'Dr Cumpston on Rational Dwellings', *Daily News*, 19 August 1909, in Cumpston Papers, NLA, MSS 434, 613.

69Carol Bacchi, 'The nature-nurture debate in Australia, 1900-1914', *Historical Studies*, 19 (October 1980), 212.

70Those accepting Bacchi's views include Graeme Davison, 'The city-bred child and urban reform in Melbourne 1900-1940', in Peter Williams (ed.), *Social Process and the City* (Sydney: Allen and Unwin, 1983), 153; Stephen Garton, 'Insanity in New South Wales: Some Aspects of its Social History, 1878-1958' (PhD thesis, UNSW, 1984), 318; Marilyn Lake, *The Limits of Hope: Soldier Settlement in Victoria, 1915-38* (Melbourne: OUP, 1987), 20; Milton Lewis, *Managing Madness: Psychiatry and Society in Australia 1788-1980* (Canberra: AGPS, 1988), 130 and Grant McBurnie, 'Constructing Sexuality in Victoria 1930-1950: Sex Reformers Associated with the Victorian Eugenics Society' (PhD thesis, Monash University, 1989), 81.

71For example, Garton, 'Sound minds and healthy bodies: re-considering eugenics in Australia, 1914-1940', *Australian Historical Studies*, 26 (October 1994), 163 and Rob Watts (1993).

72Pastore (1949), 176.

73Leonard Darwin, 'Heredity and environment', *ER*, 5 (1913), 153-54.

74Charles V Drysdale, *Neo-Malthusianism and Eugenics* (London: Bell, 1912), 13.

75Sanger, *Dangers of Cradle Competition* (1922), in Carl Jay Bajema (ed.), *Eugenics. Then and Now* (Stroudsburg, Pennsylvania: Dowden, Hutchinson and Ross, 1976), 188.

76Charles Davenport, *Heredity in Relation to Eugenics* (London: Williams & Norgate, 1912), iv.

77Norman D Harper, 'Notebooks', Sociology (Hons) Course, University of Melbourne, (1926), 18. Dr Helen Bourke, who gave me a copy of these notes, said that the 'lectures on eugenics were almost certainly given by Professor W E Agar'.

78These are discussed by Steven Fraser (ed.), *The Bell Curve Wars: Race, Intelligence and the Future of America* (New York: Basic Books, 1995); Stephen Jay Gould, *The Mismeasure of Man* (London: Penguin, 1984), and William H Tucker, *The Science and Politics of Racial Research* (Urbana and Chicago: University of Illinios Press, 1994).

[79]Dorothy Porter, 'Enemies of the race: Biologism, environmentalism, and public health in Edwardian England', *Victorian Studies*, 34 (Winter 1991), 159-78.

[80]Geoffrey R Searle, 'Eugenics and class', in Charles Webster (ed.), *Biology, Medicine and Society 1840-1940* (Cambridge: CUP, 1981), 223-25.

[81]Robert Freestone, 'The new idea: The garden city as an urban environment ideal 1910-1930', *Journal of the Royal Australian Historical Society*, 73 (October 1987), 94-108.

[82] J M (Max) Freeland, in *Architecture in Australia: A History* (Melbourne: Cheshire, 1968), 226. On pages 98-99 Professor Freeland wrote 'In 1913 the Town Planning Association produced a pamphlet with the caption 'degeneracy stamped in every line. Man is the product of his environment: and like begets like – or worse!' The eugenic link is clear.

[83] Michael Roe, *Nine Australian Progressives: Vitalism in Bourgeois Social Thought, 1890-1960* (St Lucia: QUP, 1984), 15.

[84] J M Powell quoted by Ann R M Young in *Environmental Change in Australia since 1788* (Melbourne: OUP, 1996), 3.

[85] Russell Ward, *The Australian Legend* (London: OUP, 1958) and P R Proudfoot, 'Arcadia and the idea of amenity', *Journal of the Royal Australian Historical Society*, 72 (June 1986), 3-18.

[86] Jamieson, 'Heredity in disease', *Intercolonial Medical Journal of Australasia*, vol 5 (no 2), 20 Sept 1900, 428.

[87]Henry Laurie, 'The theory of use-inheritance psychologically considered', *ANZAAS*, 9 (1902), 771.

[88] Ramsay Smith, *On Race-culture and the Conditions That Influence it in South Australia* (Adelaide: Govt Pr., 1912), 10 and 15.

[89]Mary Cawte, 'Craniometry and eugenics in Australia: R J A Berry and the quest for social efficiency', *Historical Studies*, vol 22 (April 1986), 35.

[90]Mark Adams (ed.), *The Wellborn Science: Eugenics in Germany, France, Brazil, and Russia* (New York: OUP, 1990), 218.

[91]Quoted in Bacchi (1980), 204.

[92]Charles Mackellar, *The Child, the Law and the State* (Sydney: Govt. Pr., 1907), 19.

[93]Charles Mackellar and David A Welsh, *Mental Deficiency: A Medico-sociological Study of Feeble-mindedness* (Sydney: Govt. Pr., 1917), 28 and 62.

[94]Mackellar felt that environmental factors were of primary importance 'until at least 1912'. After this, 'enquires abroad caused him to modify his views', *ADB* vol 10, 298.

[95]Laurie (1902), 771.

[96] Sir James Barr, 'Discussion on 'Eugenics'', *BMJ*, (2 August 1913), 230.

[97] Right Hon Lord Horder, 'Eugenics', *MJA,* (5 October 1935), 438.

[98] Norman Himes, *Medical History of Contraception* [1936] (New York: Schocken Books, 1970), 419, footnote 34.

[99] *Australasian Medical Congress Transactions* (1914), 90.

[100] Meredith Atkinson, *Australia: Economic and Political Studies* (Melbourne: Macmillan, 1920), 19.

[101] Griffith Taylor, quoted in Roy MacLeod and Philip Rehbock (eds.), *Darwin's Laboratory: Evolutionary Theory and Natural History in the Pacific* (Honolulu, Univ of Hawaii Press, 1994), 449.

[102] R G MacLachlan, *Stead's Review* (1 January 1930), 38 and (1 August 1930), 52.

[103] Quoted in *SMH*, 17 April 1925, p. 12 (e).

[104] Herman H Rubin, *Eugenics and Sex Harmony: The Sexes, their Relations and Problems*, 2nd edn. (New York: Pioneer Publications, 1942), 31.

[105] Davenport, *Heredity in Relation to Eugenics* (London: Williams and Norgate, 1912), 2.

[106] W Atkinson Wood, 'The feeble-minded', *Australian Medical Journal* (10 Aug 1912), 641.

[107] John Cobley, 'Medicine in the first 20 years of the colony in New South Wales', *MJA* (7-21 December 1987), 567, quoting Judge Advocate David Collins.

[108] Charles K Mackellar, *Management of the Sydney Hospital: Report of the Committee of Inquiry into Certain Complaints* (Sydney: Govt Pr., 1883).

[109] Brettena Smyth, *The Social Evil: Its Causes and Cure* [Melb: Rae Bros, 1894], title page.

[110] Fitzgerald, *AAAS* (1902), 721.

[111] The word 'lock' comes from the French 'logues' and refers to the rags which were used in the Middle Ages to cover leprosy sufferers' sores.

[112] 'A lock hospital for female patients in Sydney', *AMG* (20 December 1899), 555-56.

[113] F B Smith, *The People's Health, 1830-1910* (London: Weidenfeld and Nicholson, 1979), 166.

[114] Welsh, 'The Prevention of venereal disease', in *The Public Health*. From the Addresses at the Health Congress, Sydney, 25-27 July 1917(Sydney: Govt. Pr., 1918), 19.

[115] Judith Allen, in Kay Daniels (ed.), *So Much Hard Work: Women and Prostitution in Australia* (Sydney; Fontana/Collins, 1984), 210.

[116] Scott, 'On the Social Evil', 1908 speech in Rose Scott Papers, quoted by Allen (1984), 212.

[117] Report of an Address by R Arthur, 18 November 1912, 7.

[118] RCDBR, vol 2 (1904), evidence of Drs William Litchfield and Charles MacLaurin, Q 2380-2405. Also discussed by E Sydney Morris, *MJA* (12 September 1925), 301-45.

[119]See for example doctors Stanham MacCulloch, Q 2517; Andrew Watson-Munro, Q 2785-89; George Taylor, Q 3690-97 and Fourness Barrington, Q 3442 in *RCDBR*, vol 2 (1904).

[120]Peter B Bennie, *AMCT*, vol 3 (October 1908), 10.

[121]*Stages in a Woman's Life*, Lecture at the Salvation Army Congress, Sydney (29 May 1917) by Sir Thomas Anderson Stuart, University of Sydney Archives.

[122]Black, *The Red Plague Crusade* (Sydney: Govt. Pr, 1916), 23, 25. For examples of Black's disrepute see Sally McInerney, *The Confessions of William James Chidley* (UQP, 1977, xxii). After the *Truth* attacked Black's morals in 1892 he sued them for £5,000. The judge awarded him damages of a farthing, saying Black and the newspaper were both morally reprehensible.

[123]Cowan, *Light! Light! Let There Be More Light!* (Perth: Colortype Press, [1913?]), 4.

[124]Atkinson and Dakin, *Sex Hygiene and Sex Education* (Sydney: Angus & Robertson, 1918), 133.

[125]Jill Roe (1986), 231.

[126]Street's paper, 'The place of treatment of venereal disease in social reform' (Canberra: NLA, Street Papers, MS2683, Box 1, 10-11). It was mentioned *SMH*, 27 November 1916, 3 .

[127] Mrs Francis [Maybanke] Anderson, *The Root of the Matter: Social and Economic Aspects of the Sex Problem*, WEA Pamphlet no 1 (Sydney: WEA, 1916), 4.

[128]Laura Bogue Luffman's 1914 letter was reprinted in *The Woman's Voice*, 1 August 1916.

[129]Syphilis was mentioned in the index to London's *Times* in 1908 and an explicit series about VD (by Professor D A Welsh) appeared in the *SMH* on 22, 23 and 24 November 1916.

[130]RHA Annual Report (1920), 7. If Goodisson <u>was</u> the RHA, Mrs James [Angela] Booth <u>was</u> the Association to Combat the Social Evil. Booth's *The Prophylaxis of Venereal Disease: A Reply to Sir James Barrett* (Melbourne: Norman Bros, 1919), was distributed by the Association.

[131]Welsh (1918), 8-9, 17.

[132]Victor Roberts, 'Peace and racial improvement', *AHRC* (1929), 54.

[133]Cumpston, 'The new preventive medicine', *MJA* (4 September 1920), 221.

[134] For more about the Department's creation, see J H L Cumpston, *The Health of the People: A Study in Federalism*, [written in 1928 but not published until 1978], 45: 'In January 1921, Dr V G Heiser, a senior Executive of the Rockefeller Foundation, visited Australia, and offered... to provide certain specialists from the United States, and four fellowships for Australian graduates to study in America. To provide some guarantee that the results of this assistance should not be dissipated, the offer was made strictly contingent upon "the creation of a separate Ministry of

Health and the establishment of a Department of Health by the Commonwealth Government".

[135]NHMRC, 9th Session, (November 1940), Appendix III, 25.

[136]John Cooper Booth, in *ARHC* (1929), 40.

[137]Dr Ralph Worrall, quoted in 'Women and hygiene: men absent', *Sun*, 24 June 1926.

[138]Venereal Diseases Act, 1918. Seventh Report by the Commissioner (Dr Robert Dick) for the Year ended 31 December 1928, page 47 in the *Report of the Director-General of Public Health NSW for the Year 1928* (Sydney: Govt Prt., 1930).

[139]The RHA sold pamphlets by the British Social Hygiene Council and *Just One Slip* was sponsored by the RHA six times at the Playbox Theatre, RHA Annual Report (1930), 6 and staged at the Savoy Theatre in 1931.

[140]1933 booklets by the British Social Hygiene Council reprinted by the RHA: *Sex in Life: Young Men*, by Douglas White and Dr Otto May; *Sex in Life: Young Women*, by Violet D Swaisland and Mary B Douie, and *What Parents Should Tell Their Children*, by Mary Scharlieb and Kenneth Wills.

[141]Peter Spearritt, 'Royal Progress: The Queen and her Australian subjects', *Australian Cultural History*, no 5 (1986), 76.

[142]Dennis Shoesmith, 'Nature's Law': The Venereal Disease Debate, Melbourne, 1918-1919', *ANU Historical Journal*, 9 (December 1972), 20-23.

[143]Those favouring condoms included Arthur, in *MJA* (20 May 1916), 411-14 and (28 October 1916), 361-65; Barrett, in *Eighty Eventful Years* (Melbourne: Stephens, 1945), 102-06 and W J Thomas, *Venereal Disease: A Social Problem* (Sydney: Corson, 1922).

[144]Mabs Fawkner, '"Racial Hygiene": Annual Congress "Prophylaxis"', *The Land*, 20 September 1929, p. 17. Also 'Prophylaxis', RHA Annual Report (1928-29).

[145]Joseph Goldsmid, *Companionate Marriage: From the Medical and Social Aspects* (London: Heinemann, 1934), 38.

[146]Edith Onians, *The Men of To-morrow* (Melbourne: Lothian, 1914), 50.

[147]'Companionate marriage', *HPC* (July 1930), 16-17, 57; RHA Annual Report (1938), 8 and 'Trial marriage not approved. Mrs Goodisson in reply', *Sun*, 25 March 1938, 9 (d).

[148]Ben B Lindsey and Wainwright Evans, *Companionate Marriage* (New York; Brentano's Ltd, 1928), Preface, v.

[149]J B Hamilton and W D Counsel, NHMRC, First Session (February 1937), Appendix 2

[150] *NHMRC* (May 1943), 6.

[151]Cumpston, 20 January 1943 to the Queensland Branch of the Australian Workers Union, AA/461, Item R347/1/7.

[152]See Wray Vamplew, (ed.), *Australians: Historical Statistics* (Sydney: Fairfax, Syme and Weldon, 1987), 317, Tables HM-17-34.

[153]Anne Crichton, *Slowly Taking Control? Australian Governments and Health Care Provisions, 1788-1988* (Sydney: Allen & Unwin, 1990), p. 225, noted that a Commonwealth Act giving financial assistance to encourage TB patients to undertake long treatments had 'failed to achieve its purpose' because it was not well thought out. The legislation was revised in 1948 and following this, major anti-TB campaigns were launched.

[154]Racial Hygiene Association of NSW, Leaflet about Tuberculosis [1948].

[155]Quoted by Susan Sontag in *Illness As Metaphor* (Harmondsworth, UK: Penguin, 1983), 58.

[156]Anderson Stuart, *Report to the Governments of New South Wales, South Australia and New Zealand on the Koch Method of Treating Tuberculosis* (Sydney: Govt. Pr., 1891).

[157]John Pearn, 'Phthisis and philately – an account of the Consumptives Home stamps of NSW: the world's first charity stamps', *MJA* (7-21 December 1987), 575-78.

[158]Welsh (1918), 9.

[159]'Pearson, first study of the statistics of pulmonary tuberculosis', *ER*, vol 2 (1910-1911), 3. Pearson's claim was much quoted, for example by William A Lind, in 'Aetiology of congenital mental deficiency', *MJA* (14 Oct 1916), 316.

[160]Leonard Hobhouse, 'The value and limitations of eugenics', *Sociological Review*, vol 4 (October 1911), 284.

[161]*AMTC*, vol 1 (1911), 100.

[162]'Would class great men as mental defectives. Doctor's warning to eugenists', *Guardian*, 31 October 1929, 8 (d).

[163]For statistics see Vamplew (1987), 317, Tables HM 17-34. Kathryn Antioch and others, in *Disease Costs of Tuberculosis and Syphilis in Australia: A Discussion Paper* (Canberra: AGPS, November 1993), 1, estimated that total costs (for treatment, foregone earnings and premature deaths) for TB in 1989-90 were $12 million while syphilis cost $1.5 million.

[164]'Birth control. Dr Arthur's advice: Will instruct wives', *Sun*, 1 August 1928.

[165]Dr Eric Jeffrey to Dr Marie Stopes, 30 November 1922, quoted in Daniels and Murnane (1980), 150.

[166]A A (Tas), P347/1. Item no 1922/290, 'Birth control – prohibited import of pessary'.

[167]Eulalia S Richards, *Ladies' Handbook of Home Treatment*, rev. edn. (Victoria: Signs, 1945). First edn. 1917 [?], 656-57. There is no record of her RHA membership.

[168]'The Chinese invasion of Australia', *Adelaide Observer*, 4 February 1888.

[169]Kirby, *Three Lectures Concerning the Social Evil: Its Causes, Effects and Remedies* (1882), and *Remedies for the Great Evil Which Injures Social Purity* (1883). Both published in Port Adelaide, SA by E H Derrington.

[170]Anon, 'Letters to Public Men. The Reverend J C Kirby, Congregational Minister', in *Quiz and Lantern*, 27 October 1898. South Australia's VD Act was not passed until 1920.

[171]Kirby (1882), 44.

[172]Booth, in *Teaching of Sex Hygiene* (1918), 17-18.

[173]Booth (1918), 32.

[174]For example, M S Wallace, 'Prostitution and venereal disease', *MJA* (19 July 1919), 59 and 'Feeble-mindedness and prostitution', ibid 26 July, 71-72 and (13 March 1920), 240.

[175]Arnd Kruger, '"There goes the art of manliness": Naturism and racial hygiene in Germany', *Journal of Sport History*, vol 18 (no 1) 1991), 156.

[176]Rubin (1942), 387.

[177]Marion Piddington, *Tell Them!* (Sydney: Moore's Book Shop, 1926), 191.

[178]Piddington, *The Unmarried Mother and Her Child* (Sydney: Moore's, 1923), 13.

[179]Linda Littlejohn, in *ARHC* (1929), 8, claimed that 90% of prostitution had poverty as its driving force. This link was also emphasized by Maybanke Anderson (1916), 12-13.

[180]RHA Annual Report (1937), 4.

[181]RHA Annual Report (1937) 2, noted the RHA's Queensland branch was still alive but Mr Peters the Hon Secretary was unlikely to be able to carry on much longer without assistance.

[182]Jessie Street, *Truth or Repose* (Sydney: Australasian Book Society, 1966), 79.

[183]Rubin (1942), 411.

[184]George Archdall Reid, 'The biological foundations of sociology', in *Sociological Papers*, vol 3 (London: Macmillan, 1907), 7-8, 9. Reid's paper was read to the Sociological Society at the University of London's School of Economics and Political Science on 24 October 1905.

[185]Harvey Sutton, *Lectures in Preventive Medicine* (Sydney: Consolidated Press, 1944), 7.

[186] John Flynn, 'Heredity and disease', *AMG* (20 March 1901), 103.

[187]*AAASR* (1902), 720, 727, 729.

[188]Francis A Pockley, President's Address, *AMCT*, vol 1 (1911), 98-100.

[189]Roy MacLeod, 'The edge of hope: Social policy and chronic alcoholism, 1870-1900', *Journal of the History of Medicine* (July 1967), 244.

[190]*Argus*, 16 July 1910, 18 (d). T F MacDonald applied for a Galton Eugenics Fellowship, after reading about it in Australia, but possibly it was a British paper. University College London, Archives, Galton Papers, Item 133/5A, 7 Jan 1905.

[191]Elderton and Pearson: *A First Study of the Influence of Parental Alcoholism on the Physique and Ability of the Offspring*, Eugenics Laboratory Memoirs, no 10 (London: Dulau, 1910).

[192]Milton Lewis, in *A Rum State: Alcohol and State Policy in Australia, 1788-1988* (Canberra: AGPS, 1992), 63.

[193]The Women's Reform League [leaflet] (Sydney: WRL, [1917?]).

[194] Robert Brodribb Stewart Hammond (1870-1946), a reformer and idealist, was a leader of the Prohibitionist Movement in NSW and edited their journal, *Grit*. He addressed the RHA in 1931 about the 'slow poison'. See also *SMH*, 27 February 1934, 10 (h).

[195] 'Report of Address on Eugenics by Dr R Arthur', 18 November 1912, 6, ML.

[196] *AHRC* (1929), 8, 31. *Grit* published an obituary for Dr Arthur on 2 June 1932.

[197]Historical Records of New South Wales, Vol 1, Phillip 1783-1792 (Sydney: Govt. Pt., 1892), 53.

[198]Quoted in the exhibition on phrenology, *Ruling Heads and Ruling Passions*, 2 March to 18 August 1995, Macleay Museum, University of Sydney.

[199]Orson Squire Fowler, *Hereditary Descent* (New York: Fowler and Wells, 1848), 159.

[200]Charles Davenport, 'Heredity of some emotional traits' [Abstract], Report of the 84th meeting of the BAAS, Australia: 28 July – 31 August 1914, Transactions of Section D, (London: John Murray, 1915), 419.

[201] 'Socialism and Eugenics', *SMH*, 22 August 1914, 9 (c) reported a meeting of the Economics and Commerce Association, held in conjunction with the EES NSW.

[202] 'Eugenic Education', *The Liberal Woman*, 1 November 1914, 28-29.

[203] Chance and Circumstance, as told by R J A Berry, 1954, pages 139-140 – On the cover: 'Typed copy of Professor Berry's autobiography was sent by him to his old friend and colleague Mr D Murray Morton, who passed it on to Dr John Horan, who lent it to Leonard Murphy and gave his permission to have copies made, 23 December 1983. Lodged in the Wellcome Medical History Unit, Medical Library, University of Melbourne.'

[204] John Cowan, *The Science of a New Life* (Melbourne: Ferguson and Mitchell, 1882), 303. First published in 1869 in New York by the phrenologists, Fowler and Wells.

[205] Sydney Theosophical Society. President's address by Alan Carroll (Sydney: W S Ford, 1891). His denunciation is in the *Science of Man*, 25 May 1903, 59.

[206] Dr Frederick L Hoffman's paper at the First International Eugenics Congress was reported in the *Times*, 27 July 1912, 4 (a).

[207] Peter J Bowler, *Biology and Social Thought: 1850-1914* (Berkeley, Ca: Office of History of Science and Technology, University of California at Berkeley, 1993), 83, quoting MacBride, *Textbook of Embryology* (London, 1914), vol 1, 662. His plan for sending degenerate people to Australia was discussed in Chapter 4.

[208] Knibbs to Stopes, 11 July 1927, Stopes Papers, Add MS 58,573, ff. 25-26.

[209] 'Birth control. An outspoken preacher' [Canon Dearmer, from London's Sloan Square], *SMH*, 13 May 1932, 10 (f).

[210] Adolphus Knopf, *Aspects of Birth Control* (Little Blue Book, no 209) [1917?], 14.

[211] Haire, *Birth Control Methods...* 3rd edn. (Sydney: Allen & Unwin, 1945), 11.

[212] Haire, *Sex Problems of Today*, 2nd edn. (Sydney: Angus & Robertson, 1942), 29. He probably meant Piddington whose charges were criticised in Sanger Papers, v 22, 30 May 1933.

[213] G N Hawker, *The Parliament of New South Wales, 1856-1965* (NSW Govt Pr., 1971), 213.

[214] Montague Crackanthorpe, quoted by Soloway (1990), 82.

[215] E J Lidbetter, 'Heredity, disease and pauperism', in Margaret Sanger (ed.) *Proceedings of the World Population Conference* (London: Arnold, 1927), 326-47.

[216] See *ADB* entry for Moss in vol 10, 599, which states that in 1927 she was appointed as an alternate Australian delegate to the League of Nations Assembly at Geneva where she was also the delegate to the First World Population Conference. She became the first president of the National Council of Women of Australia in 1931-36. Her grazier husband was Isador Henry Moss.

[217] Lidbetter (1927), 333-36.

[218] Lidbetter, quoted by L J J Nye, in the *International Knowledge for Living Series* (no 5: The May Book – 'Sex, Marriage and Eugenics') 3rd edn. (Brisbane: Smith & Paterson, 1961), 43.

[219] Jean Bourdon [French delegate], in Sanger (1927), 341-42. In 1900 the German philosopher Friedrich Wilhelm Nietzsche had gone mad and died in Weimar at the age of 55.

[220] Cora Hodson [British delegate and ES secretary], in Sanger (1927), 344.

[221] [Talks on Racial Health by Marion Piddington], *Smith's Weekly*, 20 February 1932, 19.

[222] Stanley Boyd, *Doctor's Conscience: Or all Illness is Preventable* (Sydney: Currawong, 1944), 76.

[223] See Thomas Oliver, 'Lead poisoning and the race', *ER*, vol 3 (1911-1912), 83-93; Alice Hamilton, *Industrial Toxicology* (New York: Macmillan 1934); William Rom, 'Effects of lead on the female and reproduction: a review', *Mount Sinai Journal of Medicine*, 43 (1976), 542-52. Hamilton (1869-1970) was a pioneer of industrial medicine and the first woman to be appointed to Harvard University's Medical Faculty.

6. Eliminating the "Unfit"

While ancient tribes fought to eliminate unfit neighbours, last century eugenists tried to do it scientifically. Eugenists wanted laws to deal with mentally defective people but in the Depression support for sterilisation 'went far beyond eugenicists' in the United States and Britain.[1] This was also true in Australia and in the 1930s many politicians, women's groups and churches – often with no known sympathy for eugenics – clamoured for sterilisation.

Fertility of the Unfit

In *The Human Harvest* (1907) Professor David Starr Jordan argued that 'the survival of the unfittest is the primal cause of the downfall of nations'.[2] This idea was being expressed as early as 1872[3] and Dr William Chapple reiterated it at the 1899 *Intercolonial Medical Congress of Australasia*.[4] The theme was that misguided social welfare efforts, by allowing the unfit to survive and outnumber the fit, had caused racial decay which would escalate if the unfit continued to have large families while the fit limited theirs. As well as these social Darwinian and eugenic fears, Australians had the extra fear that the declining birth rate would cause racial suicide, a myth which was finally 'laid to rest' by the post-war baby boom.[5] Ideas about unfitness were revised once the world-wide Depression in 1929 forced people to realise that unemployment was related to economics, not heredity.

The prejudices took a long time dying; in 1945 the University of Sydney student newsletter *Honi Soit* was reprimanded for reporting a 'blasphemous' debate between Jeff Wilkinson, a science student and member of the Catholic Newman Society, who opposed contraception and Paul Foulkes, another science graduate, who defended it. Wilkinson said it was morally wrong and an offence against nature and the church, and rejected Foulkes' suggestion that Catholic antagonism to birth control was prompted by a 'vested interest in souls'.[6] There are unusual features in Foulkes' defence of contraception 'on eugenic grounds', for use by the 'lower classes' who were 'unfitted to support children'. Such elitist views about class were rarely expressed by

Australian eugenists and it was a particularly strange remark for that time because, as Dr Victor Wallace noted, few people thought about eugenics in wartime because fears about immediate survival replaced fears about future harm to the race.[7]

During the five decades when beliefs about racial decay and racial suicide were current in Australia, they evoked extreme responses. Assumptions that the feeble-minded were 'markedly more prolific than those normally constituted' were widely publicised by leading figures such as the Sydney physician, politician and businessman, Sir Charles Mackellar, who from 1903 to 1904 dominated the NSW Royal Commission on the Decline of the Birth-Rate.[8]   At this time Dr Chapple told society to accept 'the startling fact that this army of defectives' was 'increasing in numbers and relative fertility' because they were all prolific and transmitted their 'fatal taints'.[9]

Fears were increased in 1908 by findings of the *Royal Commission on the Care and Control of the Feeble-minded*, a British study which stimulated Australia to produce its own study report in 1914.[10]   The Australian Committee on the Feeble-minded, appointed by the 1911 Medical Congress, concluded that the hereditary character of feeble-mindedness was an 'ascertained fact confirmed by numerous far-reaching inquiries, particularly in America'. No references were given for statements such as 'the exceptional fertility' of the feeble-minded could be 'taken as proved' and 'the sexual instinct in particular is apt to be utterly uncontrolled in feeble-minded persons'.[11]   Committee members worried that few outside the medical profession realised the gravity of this problem.[12] Dr Harvey Sutton was a Committee member who held grave fears long after these ideas were discredited. In 1944 his views about 'differential fertility' were almost identical with his 1911 comments that 'the families of feeble-minded are large, and often mentally defective. Their numbers exceed the average number of the ordinary family, so that our problem increases with each generation'.[13] Much earlier, a heretic had suggested that the high fertility rate of the unfit might be 'handed on to the eventual benefit of the race'.[14]

Phillip Reilly, in his history of sterilisation in America, referred to Dr Walter Fernald's pioneering surveys of the feeble-minded, published in

1919, which showed that, contrary to accepted opinion, feeble-minded people had a low marriage rate and a very low birth rate. Fernald noted that eugenists had not distinguished between the fertility rates of the feeble-minded and those of the poor.[15] Gradually, scientists throughout the world accepted such findings. Edmund Morris Miller, from 1924 the Chairman of the Mental Deficiency Board of Tasmania, was one of the first to explode the myth; in May 1929 he explained in the *Sydney Morning Herald* that most feeble-minded people did not have excessively large families, and that the old 'scarifying figures' had been due to questionable estimates which 'had not been scientifically determined'. In this instance, Australian thinking was more advanced than it was in Britain; three years later Berry, as Chairman of the British Medical Association's Committee on Mental Deficiency, reported that recent critical examination of the data did not support the often-repeated statements about the excessive fertility of the feeble-minded.[16] Paul Dane, a psychiatrist, dismissed the myth in the *Argus* on 20 January 1934, calling claims about the fertility of the unfit 'an idea brazened forth by scaremongers', adding that 'the truly mental defective person does not breed, so that their stocks as a rule tend to die out'.

Detecting Unfitness

The Anglo-Irish Sir Redmond Barry (1813-1880) was the judge who sentenced Ned Kelly to death three weeks before his own death and, although hating novels, was the prime founder of Melbourne's University and father of the city's public library. He helped make it one of the world's greatest, ordering it to purchase every work listed in Gibbon's *Decline and Fall of the Roman Empire* in his mission to transplant the values of civilized Europe to Australia.[17] The dignified, memorable and eccentric Barry in 1875, while he was Chancellor of the University of Melbourne, compared the physique of Victorian and American young men in an attempt to discover whether 'the race in its transplantation to Australian soil retains undiminished the vigour and fire and stamina of the strong old stock of which it is an offshoot'.[18] Twenty years later, Dr Joseph Ahearne concluded, after taking the chest measurements of British and North Queensland school boys, that 'the heat and taxing educational requirements in the tropics had sapped the Queenslanders' physiques'.[19]

By the early 1900s, there were numerous attempts to detect mental and social unfitness and unfit women caused particular concern; while a writer described 'people' who were blind, deaf, epileptic or mentally defective as the 'dregs of the human species', he really meant women and this became clear when he said they would be 'better protected than pregnant'.[20] In 1908 a Victorian doctor recommended institutions for defective children as 'the first practical step' to lessen 'crime and immorality.[21] The NSW Department of Public Instruction provided school medical inspections in 1908 and 1910 'upon the physical condition of children attending public schools in NSW (with special reference to height, weight and vision), based upon statistics obtained as a result of medical inspection, with anthropometric tables and diagrams.[22] However, the Sydney Branch of the British Science Guild said the Department's first survey was 'incomplete' and in 1909 began its own studies.[23] The authors were two prominent doctors: Dr George Abbott and Dr William Quaife and two educationalists: Rev John Marden (1855-1924) who in 1887 became the first headmaster of the Presbyterian Ladies' College, Sydney and the Rev Charles Prescott (1857-1946) who in 1900 became the headmaster of Sydney's Newington College. They compared vital statistics of local boys and girls with the statistics of the American and British children, using the studies of W S Christopher, Smedley and McMillan (Child Study and Education Departments in Chicago, 1893 to 1903); Porter, Bowditch and others (from the American Statistical Association in Boston, 1894); Arthur McDonald (from the US Bureau of Education in Washington, 1899) and 'older studies' by Charles Roberts in London. The Australian authors concluded that the narrow chests of Australia's youth posed a serious evil in national life and suggested that the provision of playing fields would help to overcome this problem.[24]

In 1911, Labor Prime Minister Andrew Fisher, most state governments, the Royal Anthropological Institute, the Australasian Association for the Advancement of Science (AAAS) and the Australasian Medical Congress agreed on the desirability of periodic measurement of all children and adults, 'to detect whether all the races

of the Empire were improving or deteriorating'.[25]   Concern about
child-bearing explains why the National Fitness Council recommended
in 1945 that school medical services should investigate whether
gymnastics and competitive athletics affected the growth of children,
particularly adolescent girls.[26]   A 1946 Conference of School Medical
Officers proposed that Cumpston should take whatever action he
considered necessary. There is no report that he did.

Two items in the Galton Papers relate to Australian interest in
Galton's work. While in London in 1892, Professor T P Anderson
Stuart left a card at Galton's Anthropometrical Laboratory stating that
he planned to establish a similar one in Sydney.[27] Two years later, the
renowned British anthropometrist E F J Love told Galton that an
AAAS Committee had been formed in Melbourne to consider the best
means of promoting psycho-physical and psychometric investigations
of Australian primary school children in every state and compare the
results with those of other countries to discover if there was any
evidence of 'climatic influence' at work. Love reported that these
investigations would be made easier because in Australia the state
provided education for all social classes, unlike the situation in Britain,
and because the Committee had the support of State Education
Departments and Dr Ramsay Smith, the Head of the South Australian
Department of Public Health.[28]

Alison Turtle noted that no reports of the AAAS Committee's
measurements and mental testing are available, although the old racial
betterment objectives were still evident in a 1932 AAAS Report which
stated that considerations of racial improvement or deterioration were
of primary importance and such questions were frequently asked about
tropical Australia.   In her view, these early tests emulated British
methods to a greater extent than in any other field of Australian
science.[29]

The radical Professor Robert Irvine and the conservative Sir James
Barrett were both enthusiastic about advances in Britain, Germany and
America, and decried the backwardness and conservatism of Australian
universities.[30] In 1914 Irvine complained that Australian universities'
pupil relationship with English universities was even more apparent in

our relationship with Scottish ones, absorbing not the current thinking of these universities but that of the 1850s and 1860s. When Patricia Morison examined the records of the 22 professorial appointments at the University of Sydney between 1880 and 1910, she found 'a preponderance of Scots' – eleven of them – (eight from Edinburgh and three from Glasgow), eight from England (six Oxford and two Cambridge graduates), and only three who had graduated from Sydney.[31] In 1914 the medical faculty was still dominated by the Scottish trio known as 'Andy, Jummy and Taffy'.[32] They were T P Anderson Stuart (Andy) who was appointed in 1883, J T Wilson (Jummy – from the pronunciation of his name Jimmie) who became foundation professor of anatomy in 1890 and D A Welsh (Taffy) who became the first professor of pathology in 1902. Irvine was brave but foolhardy in his criticism and in September 1922 the expatriate Scots on the Senate dismissed him for 'living in sin'.[33] By the end of the decade Professor E Morris Miller was despondent about Australian philosophers' need 'to conform to the tasks' set from afar and hoped this period of 'tutelage' would pass.[34] Some relished this relationship; Charles Lloyd Jones, the first ABC Chairman, announced in 1932 that the ABC would 'walk in the footsteps of the BBC and fall in behind Britain'. However, it continued to irritate others and in the 1960s Patrick White protested that 'English throw-outs flock here to teach us'.

The conviction that children were unfit was followed by demands that authorities should seek them out and take action. An entrepreneurial crank who advocated this practice was Alan Carroll, a medical practitioner, anthropologist and philanthropist, who arrived in Sydney in the 1880s and, in the 1890s, founded the Child Study Association of Australia and the Royal Anthropological Society. He planned to use his high-level support to establish a school and a laboratory to measure and test children, making the ridiculous claim that he could reverse the trauma suffered by brain-damaged children.[35] The Victorian Government passed an Act in 1890 to absolve them from any responsibility to educate defective children; for the next 11 years this was left to charities[36] such as Melbourne's Idiot Asylum in Kew which operated from 1887 to 1908 and again from 1929.[37] Dr

John Fishbourne (1843-1911) also provided education from 1897 in the Melbourne suburb of Moonee Ponds, when he and his daughter ran the first residential school in Australia for mentally defective children.[38] After the death of 'dear, kind, old Dr Fishbourne', the school closed, and the *Australasian Medical Gazette* (19 October 1912) noted that his 25-year 'labours did not bear much fruit'. This was not completely true because he persuaded the 1911 Australasian Medical Congress to seize an 'unparalleled opportunity' to make a national census of school children. Dr Mary Booth reported that Fishbourne, who died a few days after giving the paper, had the gratification of knowing that the AMC had resolved to appoint a special committee to gauge feeble-mindedness in all states.

Assistance for children who were 'heavily handicapped in life's race'[39] was advocated by the feminist journalist Alice Henry (1857-1943) and the National Council of Women of Victoria.[40] They were supported by eminent doctors, including the 'great Springy', John Springthorpe (1855-1933), and Sir Richard Stawell (1864-1935), a specialist in children's diseases, who in 1900 discussed the 'physical signs of mentally defective children'. His article stressed the need for reformers to emulate Britain's Departmental Committee on Defective and Epileptic Children, which aimed to provide 'favourable surroundings' and education to help these children 'take their place in the world' rather than 'become inmates of workhouses, asylums, or prisons'.[41] An attack on this work was made recently in the book *Minorities: Cultural Diversity in Sydney* which included these introductory words: 'Nowhere is it more clearly spelt out how misconceptions and prejudices can blight lives'.[42] They refer to a chapter by Paul Ashton who quoted Stawell in a way which implied that doctors who 'drew up lists' of 'signs' might be involved in musters of the feeble-minded 'who could sometimes remain undetected in society'.[43]

Dr Mary Booth stressed the need for a survey of mental defectives in 1912, informing delegates at the Australasian Association for the Advancement of Science that eugenists relied on such data to study 'what the race may become'.[44] The following year Booth, in her role as Honorary Secretary of the AAAS-appointed Central Committee on the Care and Control of the Feeble-minded, stated that, as no special investigation had been made, it was impossible to know the extent of mental deficiency in NSW. As 'eugenics is a difficult word that is beginning to have a fascination for the public', she recommended a census of the feeble-minded as an 'indispensable preliminary to theorising'.[45] In 1913 details of the surveys were published. Booth seemed unaware that some states had examined children from the 1880s, and that the first systematic survey was made in Sydney in 1901; the results showed that although Sydney boys were taller than English boys, their chest expansion was less than that of European boys. Booth wanted to increase anthropometrical studies so that 'the future of the British race in Australia' could be properly studied.[46] Eldridge called these surveys 'one of the most important events' in NSW's history.[47] However, the RHA went too far in June 1928: the *Sydney Morning Herald* reported that the Senate of the University of Sydney had decided to tell the RHA it could not give approval to their proposal to medically examine all university entrants. The account marks the end of the Association's honeymoon with the press and the RHA wrote nothing about this galling episode in its annual report.

In 1918 Dr Richard Berry, with Stanley David Porteus (1883-1972), a researcher seconded from the Victorian Education Department, claimed after examining nearly 10,000 Victorian school children, that at least 15% of them were mentally subnormal. Berry was confident that, as methods of diagnosis improved, 'the percentages of feeble-minded will be found to be higher' and, like Carroll, called for the establishment of a child study clinic and a segregation colony.[48] The term 'segregation' was first used medically in the 1850s to mean 'selective isolation' or 'quarantine' and eugenic segregation directly echoes the ancient practice of using quarantine in an attempt to limit infectious diseases.

Porteus moved to New Jersey in 1919 after being appointed as Director of Research at the Vineland Training School for Feeble-minded Boys and Girls. Despite his lack of academic qualifications, his invention of the Porteus maze intelligence tests earned him world fame and, in 1922 at the age of 39, he became Professor of Clinical Psychology at the University of Hawaii.[49] Meanwhile, Dr Berry, with Wilfred Agar as his new research partner, embarked on another extensive examination of children in 1922, with support from the Melbourne *Herald*. In 1925 Berry showed the part that skull-measurements (craniometry) played in his estimates of children's intelligence. He exhorted paediatricians to make an early diagnosis in cases of children who were mentally deficient, to protect society from trauma, to save siblings from an unfair upbringing and because 'aments' (people with mental deficiency) were 'unsuitable subjects for surgery'. In view of the rivalry between Berry and his former partner, there is little doubt that Berry had Porteus in mind when he complained in the *Medical Journal of Australia* (12 September 1925) about 'extravagant literature' and 'mere ephemeral rubbish' produced by 'lay psychologists'. Porteus struck back at Berry in his first Vineland study: 'Head capacity alone cannot be used as a measure of intelligence'.[50]   In his autobiography published when he was 86, Porteus commented on a 'startling' study which his predecessor at Vineland, Dr Henry Goddard, had released in 1912. After noting the tendency of 'that age' (the early 1900s) to consider that feeble-mindedness was the root cause of all social insufficiency (unfitness), Porteus commented that Goddard's *The Kallikak Family, a Study in the Heredity of Feeble-mindedness*:

> was a most impressive demonstration, and Australians, including Berry, were fully convinced that if legislative action could stop the propagation of such cases, a host of social problems would be solved.[51]

As Berry was an admirer of Goddard but most Australians were not, this provides a tantalising fragment in the history of Australian-American eugenic relations.   Possibly, expatriate Porteus felt that Australia had not appreciated his talents, forcing him to go abroad to win recognition.   Perhaps he was retaliating against Berry or felt inferior about his origins.   He may have thought that truth might offend Americans and considered it more tactful to imply that gullible Australians were the only people deceived by Goddard. This was not so: while many Australian reformers approvingly discussed Dugdale's 1877 study of the Jukes family, in 1912 they scarcely mentioned Goddard's Kallikak study.[52]

There were also Australian criticisms of the Kallikak study. For example, in the March 1931 issue of the *Australian Journal of Psychology and Philosophy*, Pierre Bachelard criticised the 'implicit faith' which many Americans accorded Goddard's work and, in 1934 Harold Wyndham, in study *Ability Grouping*, commented on the intense American publicity for the work produced by Goddard and his colleagues at Vineland, which 'seem to have been penned with the proselytising zeal of the devotees of a new faith'. In many parts of the world this material 'functioned as a primal myth of the eugenics movement for several decades'.[53] Its impact was greatest in America and Britain, where Goddard's 'research impressed the corps of people' who concerned themselves with 'social deviants'.[54] The comments which Porteus made about legislation are particularly ironic as no eugenics-related laws were passed in Australia, but Goddard's work helped to create a favourable climate for the passage of harsh sterilisation and immigration laws in many American states.

In 1925 Morris Miller, on behalf of the Tasmanian Psychological Clinic, built on the 1917 to 1918 studies which Berry and Porteus had conducted. Miller measured the skulls of more than 4,000 schoolboys and university students from Victoria and Tasmania and compared them with the skull sizes of retarded children and prisoners in Hobart's gaol.[55] He agreed with the Italian educationalist Maria Montessori that food and mental stimulation influenced brain development, but rejected Karl Pearson's view that there was only a 'slight correlation between the size of head and intelligence'. Miller argued that his evidence proved a physical basis for providing higher education. He found that his prisoner subjects were 'much smaller-headed than the law-abiding' and concluded that this proved 'a physical basis for mental deficiency, pauperism and delinquency'. Morris Miller's conclusions about the relationship of head size to criminal behaviour reflected the widespread views which predated eugenist ideology and were made popular by the once influential, now generally rejected, theories of Italian criminologist Cesare Lombroso (1836-1909). It had also been argued that as men's heads (and brains) were bigger than women's, men's intelligence was superior. This notion was rejected by Millicent Preston Stanley, the politician who had fought for 'horses' rights for women' and who, in addition to her NSW Parliamentary income, was employed as the Women's Editor of the Daily Telegraph. She made her point in the 28 January 1926 supplement of this Sydney paper by surveying the hat sizes of her Parliamentary colleagues. Her finding that the Prime Minister had the smallest hat demonstrated that head size was not correlated with intelligence.

In 1925 Dr Harvey Sutton and the NSW Department of Public Health's School Medical Division began a three-year survey of mentally defective children in the state's primary schools.[56] Two years later, Sutton stated in a letter to Graham Butler, President of the Queensland Branch of the BMA, that describing attempts to educate 'markedly retarded or mentally deficient children' was difficult. There were seven residential schools for them in Sydney which provided Montessori-style education. Others in NSW included a new school in rural Glenfield for 128 children; Brush Farm, an institution run by the Child Welfare Department in Eastwood; two others at Mittagong and Carlingford; about 300 children under the jurisdiction of the Lunacy Department at Newcastle and 'a large number of male juvenile insane including difficult sex cases' at Rabbit Island (now called Peat Island) on the Hawkesbury River, north of Sydney.[57] Rabbit Island (which was built in 1905 as an Asylum for Inebriates) and the adjacent Milson Island housed mentally defective males once they became too old for Newcastle; Stockton (another mental asylum) did the same for females.[58] In this way, life-long segregation was provided for a few hundred mentally defective people who were detained under a variety of laws and three separate authorities administered their care. Eugenists wanted a co-ordinated approach in which one law would authorise one authority to segregate and care for all mentally deficient people.

In 1927 Harvey Sutton showed his statistical innumeracy by his claim that 'somewhere about 3.4% or 7.4% (sic) per thousand' school children were mentally defective. He estimated there would be between 2.5 and 5 per 1,000 in the general population.[59] In 1931 Dr Ernest Jones estimated that school-age mental defectives in Australia (in schools, mental hospitals and institutions) were about 22,217 or 2.89% of all children.[60] Judge Walter Bevan, at the RHA's One Day

Conference on 14 October 1931, called for 'fully 50%' of NSW children to be examined to ensure that no defective ones would be 'left out'. The possibility of defective children being among the 50% *not* examined did not occur to the judge, who in 1932 called for records to be kept of the 'mentality' of all school children 'as a help towards preventing maladjustments'.[61] Two years later psychiatrist Ralph Noble reported that approximately 5% of Australian children were mentally defective and should receive special instruction.[62]

In 1935 only two institutions in NSW were provided solely for mental defectives, although 603 male and 816 female mentally defective adults were 'scattered throughout our institutions'.[63] In 1936 Glenfield was still NSW's only state school for mentally deficient children under the age of 12. However, there are no statistics for the numbers of feeble-minded in private institutions in the NSW Archives of the Inspector-General of Mental Hospitals. A reason for this was suggested in a 23 February 1929 letter from a solicitor on behalf of Dr Lorna Hodgkinson, which said that she refused to supply information to the Education Department 'on the grounds that it would breach the confidentiality of families with relatives in her privately-run institution'. Presumably other private institutions were similarly unresponsive. There had been a low response to the 1914 survey of school children – the medical profession's response was 'deplorable' – and, as the fortunes of eugenics declined, responses to subsequent surveys were even lower.[64]

In 1928, the federal government was alarmed about mental deficiency, calling it 'a problem of supreme national importance, because of its impact on the physical and mental health of individuals and on the country's economic prosperity and efficiency'.[65] In response to a resolution which the Federal Health Council passed at its second session in 1928, the Government immediately set up a national inquiry to try and establish the causes of mental deficiency so that it could implement 'preventive measures'. The Inquiry was led by Dr William Ernest Jones (1867-1957), the man who later became Victoria's Inspector-General of the Insane, not the Dr Ernest Jones who was the Welsh Freudian. The Victorian Ernest Jones was a psychiatrist with eminent credentials in this field, whose appointment to head the Inquiry was announced in the *Sydney Morning Herald* on 3 August 1928. He was instructed to report at the next session of the Council and concluded after his examination of local and overseas studies, that 'five active steps appear to be indicated'. His response, which must have delighted eugenists, included proposals for the detection and segregation of the unfit, marriage bars, sterilisation, elimination of syphilis and the control or prohibition of alcohol. His main recommendation was to establish Psychological Clinics in each state to examine all mentally defective children and young adults. The findings, released on 23 December 1929, affirmed that feeble-mindedness was a widespread and serious problem.[66]

Psychological clinics operated in Tasmania and in 1929 the State's Mental Defectives Board, the body established to administer the Tasmanian Mental Deficiency Act (passed in 1920 with amendments in 1925 and 1929), listed its main work as 'the ascertainment of which persons in the State were mental defectives'. [67]   Ernest Jones was chairman of the Board and it is unlikely that they would have undertaken such a task if it had already been done, or if officials felt that unfitness was not a problem. The public continued to see mental deficiency as a problem: in 1927 and 1928, delegations from NSW women's organizations advised the State's Minister for Health that 'there was a strong need for a census of all mentally-defective people in the State'.[68]   In June 1930 Mr Drummond, the NSW Minister for Education, gave details to the *Sydney Morning Herald* of his Department's policy on mental defectives, which involved psychologically testing children where headmasters had identified them as 'mentally subnormal, epileptic, nervously unstable or eccentric'. The inquiry was 'in accordance with the request made by Resolution 13 at the 5th Session of the Federal Health Council, 24-25 March 1931'. This shows that feeble-mindedness continued to cause widespread concern in the 1930s.[69]   Angela Booth commented in the *Argus* (26 January 1934) that the British government would not have initiated a Royal Commission into degeneracy 'unless unquestionable evidence had been submitted to it'. Australian governments shared this concern and it was also held by many other governments in the 1930s. However, the Australian authorities hesitated because of the 'practical difficulties' of implementing sterilisation. These hurdles were discussed in one of the papers at the 1930 Australian Directors of Education Conference in Tasmania:

1. There is the necessity of favourable public opinion. [In Tasmania] a large body of public opinion … is in favour of it, and one hears little expressed opinion against it. The need is for enlightenment.

2. There is the fear of religious difficulties. It appears that this fear is unnecessary. Most churches have humanitarian and welfare organizations within them, and when the facts of deficiency become known, in the majority of cases religious objections disappear. I know of no case of a social welfare worker who is not in favour of the practice.

3. It is supposed that sterilization means castration. Information on this point is needed to overcome many scruples.

4. There is extensive ignorance of the meaning and extent of mental deficiency. Where deficiency is associated with crime, there is little prejudice against the practice of sterilization, but the tendency is to look on the operation as a punishment, instead of being, as it is, a means to a happier and more self-dependent life.

After this summary, the author – probably the Tasmanian Director-General of Education – concluded that some combination of segregation and sterilisation was 'probably the most effective', following the Californian model of offering 'release or parole' to a mentally defective person 'provided they submitted to sterilization'.[70] He was vague about the intended 'beneficiaries' and whether the proposals were to be voluntary or compulsory.

The Consequences of Unfitness

There were fears that racial poisons would cause reductions in intelligence and fitness which would result in escalating economic burdens for the fit. Ignorance and utopian dreams also increased eugenics' popularity. The eugenic utopias (or 'eutopias') found in Plato's *The Republic*, Thomas More's *Utopia*, and Galton's unpublished *Kantsaywhere*, were revisited in William McDougall's *Eugenia*, in H G Wells' predictions of the future and in works by Aldous Huxley, J B S

Haldane, Lancelot Hogben and H J Muller. Alberto Manguel quotes from a 1941 study which lists 215 utopian travel books published in Europe between 1700 and 1800[71]. The Greek word for utopia can mean either 'nowhere' or 'good place' and while some Australians left the country in search of utopia, others hoped to create a 'Workers' Paradise' at home. Utopias frequently become dystopias, as happened in the case of the Paraguayan settlement 'New Australia' for which William Lane and his followers optimistically left home in the 1890s. Many Australians hoped to find a 'Millennial Eden' within Australia and others believed it already was 'God's domain' but Robert Irvine claimed in *National Efficiency*, a booklet he wrote for the Victorian Railways Institute in 1915, that utopia would be an 'unutterably stupid place'. Despite the doubters, in the optimistic pre-war years, many called Australia the 'social laboratory of the world'. From the 1920s, others began to agree with Irvine that 'Australia, instead of being a Paradise, was a working man's hell'.

Dr Cumpston expressed his optimism in the *Medical Journal of Australia* on 4 September 1920:

> It is fitting that we, who aspire to use this opportunity, who dream of leading this young nation of ours to a paradise of physical perfection, should critically examine ourselves and our methods in order to assess our fitness to point to the people the paths they must tread to that paradise of perfection.

He was looking forward to a brighter future in those first years after the war which was supposed to end all wars. By the 1930s such dreams had turned to pessimism as the world plunged into new, more destructive wars and unprecedented numbers of economic and natural disasters. In the 1980s newly emerging reproductive technology offered the possibility of genetically-engineered utopias, but Charles Kerr, Professor of Preventive and Social Medicine at Sydney's Commonwealth Institute of Health, warned these 'have a tendency to end in nightmares'.[72] He reminded Australian teenagers that before adopting such advances it was necessary to ask the 'central and age-old' questions about eugenics:

'What qualities are desirable or undesirable?', 'To what ends are eugenic policies to be directed?' and 'Who is going to make the decisions?'. Eugenics is an idea which ebbs and flows with the times. The cranks, bigots, racists and opportunist politicians who perverted the former version are still with us.[73]

There was greater prejudice and it was less camouflaged in the 1920s and 1930s, despite the occasional counter-claim, such as one in the *Australian Worker* on 10 June 1920, in which the writer argued that the behaviour of the rich was an indication of their unfitness, the words 'rich' and 'poor' often being used as synonymous for 'fit' and 'unfit'. This showed the belief that being poor, unemployed or working class was an indication of unfitness. For example, in volume 2 of *Studies in the Psychology of Sex*, which was published in 1897 and revised in 1937, Havelock Ellis wrote that the 'lower classes' procreated 'most copiously, most recklessly, and most disastrously'. And Margaret Sanger, in her 1939 autobiography, said that birth-controllers, rather than encouraging larger rich families, should 'stop the multiplication of the unfit'. Two early eugenic slogans were particularly blatant – questioning whether educationists were 'trying to force a thousand-dollar education into a one-dollar boy' and the claim that 'the fit turn a slum into a palace but the unfit turn a palace into a slum'. Similar class snobbery was shown by this Australian doctor:

> By inferior we are entitled to refer to the labouring classes, not in the sense of social distinction, but in regard to unskilled and inefficient workers. The lower class are the labouring class, the higher strata are there because they merit being there.[74]

In 1924 Gregory Sprott, the President of the Tasmanian branch of the British Medical Association, reiterated a eugenist cliché: 'The reproduction of the unfit only creates further burdens and has a demoralising and degenerating effect on the whole race'.[75] However, few were as blatant as James Stewart, whose Presidential address to the West Australian Branch of the BMA was reported in the *Medical Journal of Australia* on 19 June 1926. He regretfully concluded that 'the intelligent do not escape the expense of a large family by restricting their own output, but have to support the comparatively useless progeny of the proletariat'. Such elitist class eugenics, while frequent in Britain, was rare in Australia.

In Britain, a rare example of *anti-elitism* was printed in London's *Times* in a 30 July 1912 report of the Eugenics Congress in which Russia's 'Anarchist Prince', Peter Kropotkin was cheered for questioning the class *status quo*. Only an aristocrat who had rejected his class roots could have got away with such a comment. Sensitive to the charges of class snobbishness prompted Leonard Darwin to report, 'if the wastrel was replaced by capable men' the working classes would benefit most because 'the rates of insurance would fall or the benefits available would be increased' and, in November 1914, the *Medical Journal of Australia* found it worth repeating this improbable eugenics sweetener. Another unusual claim was made by Professor William Jethro Brown in the May 1927 *Economic Record*. In his view the 'really poor' would breed less if they became richer. Certainly, parents with greater resources for food and medicine are likely to limit their family size if they are certain that their children will survive to maturity and would also be more willing to invest more time and money in each child's future. However, the topic of family size decision-making is almost as circular as the argument about whether the chicken comes before the egg.

The Influence of Genetics

Wilhelm Johannsen coined the term 'gene' in 1909 but for the next three decades, values rather than science provided the basis for studies of human genetics. J B S Haldane said that genetics did not become a recognised part of the British medical syllabus until 1938.[76] While Professor Wilfred Agar pioneered the teaching of genetics at the University of Melbourne from the 1920s, there was no 'departmental representation' for such courses in any Australian university before 1960. In 1960, one out of the ten universities included genetics, rising to seven out of 19 in 1980.[77]

David Barker has very convincingly shaken the 'recent orthodoxy' that British and American geneticists began to distance themselves publicly from eugenics in the 1920s, if not earlier. Raymond Pearl (one of the first geneticists to publicly disown eugenics) called it 'the biology of superiority' in the November 1927 issue of the *American Mercury* and a 'concerted and effective critique did not develop until after 1930'.[78] Before the 1940s, Australia was particularly reliant on overseas news, and this explains why people frequently made and believed assertions which now appear dubious. For example, no one questioned the conclusions reached by a committee of experts who claimed at the 1914 *Australasian Medical Congress* that 'a very large proportion of our habitual criminals, drunkards, prostitutes and wastrels are feeble-minded'.[79]

Mackellar and Welsh repeated these views in a booklet 'intended to show that, in the absence of provision for its legal control, we are directly fostering the increase of Mental Deficiency with all the evils that follow in its train'. This, Mackellar claimed, would 'provide an ever-increasing burden of work for the philanthropists of the next generation'. Welsh claimed that 'the class of the feeble-minded forms a vast recruiting ground for the criminal, the pauper, the vicious, the prostitute, and the habitual drunkard'.[80] Dr Lorna Hodgkinson threw in a few more problems for the philanthropists to deal with: 'VD, bad housing and poor sanitation'.[81] Dr Arthur, Chairman of the *NSW Parliamentary Enquiry Into Lunacy Law and Administration* in 1922 to 1923, warned that the apparently normal 'higher grade of defectives' formed the 'derelict elements in the community'.[82] This group caused high anxiety to eugenists who argued that because they looked normal, they could cause more havoc than the obviously defective.

Even in wartime some people worried about the feeble-minded. For example, in December 1914 Berry delivered an address called 'One of the Problems of Peace: Mental deficiency'. In 1920 he claimed that military records revealed an 'unduly large and increasing proportion' of unfitness in the population, making it 'impossible to make good the ravages of war'.[83] On 2 June 1923 the *Medical Journal of Australia* published an article by Ralph Noble who warned that 'if nothing was done for the retarded children of Australia, Bolshevism would spread'. He may have felt that helping such children would maintain the status quo and avoid conflict. It was not a new idea and similar statements had been made in 1876 by an Australian public servant and polemicist, Henry Keylock Rusden, who argued in the *Melbourne Review* that letting the unfit survive would lower the quality of the race and destroy it 'almost as effectively as if we were openly to resort to Communism'. 'A Netzer' claimed in the March 1930 issue of *Millions* that eugenics offered 'the only solution to the problems that confront us and the only alternative to anarchy and the horrors of Communism'. In Britain the following year, Julian Huxley argued that the alternative to eugenics was 'a Bolshevik revolution'.[84] In the *Sydney Morning Herald*, Professor John Anderson (1893-1962), the controversial Professor of Philosophy at the University of Sydney, said the opposite in March 1933. The *Herald* was quoting Anderson's comments at a Workers' Educational Association Conference, in which he described the 'notion of the superior, better-bred people' as 'capitalist' and urged working-class people to oppose eugenics.

The debate began in the *Australasian Journal of Psychology and Philosophy,* which published a Canadian article in March 1928 with the title, 'Psychology, leadership and democracy', reprinted with the permission of the author, William D Tait, who was Chairman of the Department of Psychology at McGill University, then an important centre of Canadian eugenic thought.[85] It is important as a rare example of Australian-Canadian contact, rather than for its restatement of stale arguments about the harm caused by misguided maternal mollycoddling of misfits and the need to save the race, not the individual. The article stimulated Professor Anderson to respond:

> There is in America a body known as the Ku Klux Klan, whose mission is to suppress all deviations from right thinking and right living by chastising, sterilizing or annihilating the deviator. … To Dr W D Tait … it would no doubt appear that there is all the difference in the world between the operations of the Klan and the system of scientific tests which he proposes. But the claim to be scientific is hardly supported by the character of the argument that he puts forward.[86]

Anderson's 'review' attracted the attention of David McCallum who made a Foucaultian analysis of Australian eugenics at a 1992 education conference.[87]   McCallum argued that Anderson, representing those opposed to the hereditarian position, had 'identified eugenicist thinking with the activities of the Ku Klux Klan, and accused the eugenicists of flabby logic'.[88]   McCallum drew the wrong conclusions himself: Anderson did not explicitly connect theories proposed by Tait or other eugenists with the Klan, and Anderson's comments were about Tait, not about eugenists in general. McCallum made an overstatement to suggest that Anderson's idiosyncratic response was shared by all eugenists who opposed the hereditarian position.

Marriage Restrictions

Most calls for marriage restrictions, for other people, came from those who were smugly sure about their own superior fitness. In 1900 Dr Carroll said it was more important to stop the unfit marrying than to keep undesirable aliens out.[89]   Marriage restrictions became a eugenics prerequisite and other people shared this view.   In 1912 Galton wanted to introduce pre-marital checks but Havelock Ellis warned him about the expense.[90]   He also feared that Galton's proposal might antagonise doctors who were already annoyed by the Eugenics Education Society's zeal.[91]   Eugenists would have alienated an even more powerful group if they tried to restrict aristocratic inter-marriage or had proposed that European royalty should be sterilized because haemophilia ran in the family.

Happily, in Australia medical alienation was not a problem because most of the medical profession either *were* eugenists or believed that it would help foster national fitness. An article in the *Australian Medical Journal* in October 1912 forecast a future in which 'medicine and eugenics advance hand in hand, for their missions, if not identical, will, I venture to think, be in complete sympathy'. It was written by R J A Berry, whose comment that 'letters with pedigrees had reached [his] laboratory' was his way of circumventing his profession's requirement for anonymity.   In 1914 the renowned Melbourne physician and lecturer J W Springthorpe included a section on eugenics in Australia's first textbook on hygiene. He urged doctors 'to do all in their power to learn its laws and advance its claims in every reasonable and tactful manner', while conceding that problems about child-bearing by the unfit were 'difficult, complex and even uncertain'.[92]

In June 1912 the *Australian Medical Gazette* quoted Dr Henderson, Professor of Sociology at the University of Chicago, who said, 'in recent years the futility of such legislation has become apparent. Propagation of the irresponsible, abnormal, and criminal goes on without regard to legal wedlock'. Eugenists were reminded that plans to restrict marriage were as utopian as the naive hope that such directives would prevent illegitimacy or ensure 'celibacy of the diseased'.[93] The *Argus* made the point in April 1913 that 'irregular unions among the rejected might prove to be worse than the marriages' but added realistically that preventing marriage would not prevent procreation. The *AMG* in September mentioned an American law banning marriage 'between people with transmissible diseases, or between people not mentally or physically sound'. While the editorial agreed with the laws, it disagreed with a social reformer who proposed to breed people as though they were animals. In 1949 a backward-looking RHA doctor still regretted that people were interested in 'pure breeding' of animals and did not think about it in their own case.[94]

In 1961 Sir (Frank) Macfarlane Burnet (1899-1985) rejected such thinking. This shy genius later commented that winning the Nobel Prize for Medicine in 1960 had given him the confidence to speak out on a wide range of issues. This inspiring man, now honoured as Australia's greatest scientist, suggested that any such breeding scheme for humans would be 'fantastically wrong', adding it is 'fortunate that no opportunity is ever likely to arise which will allow deliberate breeding of human stock towards a desired pattern. It would be only too easy to make terrible mistakes'.[95] Many prominent Australians did believe that human breeding could and should be controlled. In 1912, Dr Arthur proposed in a speech on eugenics, that 'every man, before he is allowed to marry, should have to produce a certificate of a clean bill of health'.[96] Tensions between Arthur and Professor Anderson Stuart, both prominent members of the Eugenics Education Society of NSW, are suggested by comments made at an EESNSW dinner which was chaired by the President, Dr Arthur. Anderson Stuart's opinion was reported in the *Telegraph* on 24 February 1914:

> The idea of demanding a medical certificate of fitness before either party to a marriage should be permitted to contract a union, would present such complications as to be quite impossible. That,

however, was quite apart from what this Society proposed to advocate.

Anderson Stuart's act of publicly contradicting the Society's President, and a later comment by the RHA's Lillie Goodisson, reveal ambiguity about what legitimately constituted eugenics work: Goodisson told the British Eugenics Society in 1939 'though [the RHA] is not a Eugenic Society, we decidedly do a good deal of eugenic work and our pre-marital health examinations have been very successful'.[97] There has even been confusion about who *really* were eugenists. It was recently argued that strong-willed Billy Hughes was 'a little cauldron of eugenic theories and degenerationist anxieties'.[98] Hughes has been described as a 'politician who had been in all political parties but belonged to none'. In reality, he was a 'cauldron' of political rather than eugenic machinations and, unlike many of his political colleagues, he had never joined a eugenics society.[99] Neither had he belonged to *all* the parties: Prime Minister Curtin, in his 1944 speech honouring Hughes' half century in politics, asked the old man why he had been in every political party except the County Party. Billy replied, 'Good God, man, you have to draw the line somewhere'.[100] Billy also baulked at eugenic societies although his implicit eugenic assumptions were widely shared from the 1890s to the early 1900s. In 1913 Hughes drafted a Federal Bill proposing that only couples who had both produced certificates of good health could marry. He had to abandon the Bill, following strong pressure from church groups and even his own party.[101]

In 1916 the South Australian Branch of the British Science Guild recommended that marriage licences should be denied to people with 'eugenic unfitness' (defined as 'TB, epilepsy, insanity, VD, confirmed criminal tendency, sex perversion and confirmed alcoholism', unless they could produce a certificate of a cure, signed by two doctors.[102] The *Argus* reported in July 1917 that delegates at Sydney's Health Congress passed a similar resolution to safeguard the 'future of the race'. The 1922 Report of the Commonwealth and States Conference on Venereal Disease recommended testing pregnant women for syphilis and wanted compulsory VD testing for people who wished to marry.[103] This activity probably relates to news that several American states had implemented 'practical eugenics' marriage and sterilisation laws.[104] The US declared these laws were constitutional in 1927 and they became the basis of Hitler's eugenics program – Dr Harry Laughlin, the biologist who headed the Eugenics Record Office and had drafted the legislation, was given an honorary doctorate in Germany in 1936 for his contribution to 'race hygiene'. In Australia as in Britain, nothing came of calls for eugenic sterilisation.

In the Wellcome Institute's Eugenics Society Archives there is a very odd letter and memorandum about 'A proposed Bill for the proposed Qualification of Marriage Act' which Lionel Lewis sent to Britain's Eugenics Education Society on 25 August 1925. He was not a member of any Australian eugenics society and apart from his address, at 4, The Avenue, East St Kilda, Victoria, his identity is a mystery. Lewis informed the Society that Victoria had to check an 'alarming' and 'appalling' increase of degenerates ('deformed, consumptive and diseased') who were 'degrading and perverting' the 'sacred institution of marriage'. This he said, was a 'very grievous evil' from the economic perspective and the 'very essence of folly' politically: once enfranchised, those 'most unfitted to exercise such power' were likely to be controlled by 'incompetent, tyrannical and irresponsible [political] juntas'. He said the Bill was very strongly and decisively supported both by eugenists and 'representative men' in Australia and added that Lady Forster, the wife of the former Governor-General of Australia, had the material and would probably contact the Society directly.[105] Lewis claimed that all necessary steps had been taken for the Bill's enactment in the Commonwealth Parliament but asked the EES to support the Bill's discussion at both the International Eugenics Congress and the League of Nations. Sensibly, the EES contacted the Agent-General for Victoria, asking for more information about these fantastic claims. They replied 'there is no Qualification of Marriage Act in operation in Victoria, nor is anything known of any proposal to restrict marriages either by reason of any medical or physical defects on the part of the contracting parties'.[106] Lewis may have been delusional, one of the cranks which eugenics tended to attract.

However, aspects of the idea had reputable support; in 1927 economist Jethro Brown proposed that 'within limits', 'rational selection' should supplement 'natural selection', although he said he was not suggesting that 'a scientist should go around with an axe and a bath, smashing half the men and drowning half the women' because such things were 'not done in polite society'. His idea (a possible precursor to rational economics) was for pre-marriage certificates and segregation or sterilisation for 'obviously defective types' on the grounds that 'any religious or humane objection scarcely deserves consideration'.[107] The following year Dr Cumpston called for 'the production of the medical certificate declaring the absence of certain obvious physical defects such as venereal disease in communicable form, epilepsy, deaf-mutism, and feeble-mindedness should be made a legally essential condition of marriage'. In 1929 Cumpston's evidence about eugenic considerations was quoted by the Royal Commission on Child Endowment or Family Allowance:

> For this purpose it would be necessary that the Commonwealth should exercise its constitutional powers in relation to marriage and divorce, as such legislation could only be effective if it were applicable to the whole Commonwealth. It would also be desirable that revision should be made of the position in respect of feeble-mindedness and the segregation and control of those individuals declared to be feeble-minded.[108]

From the outset in 1926 the RHA stressed the 'necessity of a health examination before marriage'.[109] At the 1929 *Australian Racial Hygiene Congress*, Arthur and Hughes both favoured such tests; Hughes hoped that the Association would get a law passed for a compulsory certificate of health before marriage.[110] Barrett said that his organisation had repeatedly asked couples to make pre-marriage health declarations.[111] However, in 1937 when Hughes was asked whether he would revive his 1929 proposal for certificates, he replied 'once bitten, twice shy'.[112] In fact Hughes had twice been 'bitten', in 1913 and 1929. Goodisson claimed in the *Sydney Morning Herald* in October 1931 that certificates of health before marriage were almost unknown in NSW until 1929 but had increased enormously since the RHA began advocating them in that year. In a November 1935 article in the

Progressive Journal she endorsed these examinations because 'dishonesty is prevailing'. The RHA Marriage Advisory Centre leaflet was itself dishonest in the claim that Hughes continued to be 'strongly in favour' of compulsory pre-marriage health certificates. The leaflet quotes Hughes as stating this in a May 1937 letter to the RHA and repeating it to a deputation which 'waited on him' on 22 July 1937.[113]

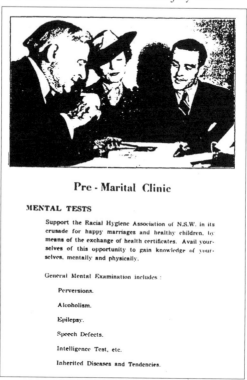

Figure 29: RHA Pre-Marital Health Examinations

The RHA's pre-marital examinations were voluntary but Goodisson seemed ambivalent about this. For example, in October 1936 she maintained in the *Sydney Morning Herald* that only a Hitler could compel such measures. However, in the 1937 Annual Report she said that tests would probably become compulsory once the necessity was appreciated by the government, as it had been by Argentina's President in 1937. Ironically, the RHA's marriage certificates were based on a British motion which in 1934 was withdrawn almost immediately because Lord Kilmaine (1878-1946) who proposed it, agreed it was unworkable. The RHA's lack of access to the Hansard record explains their garbled report. For example, the Annual Report for 1938 said the proposal was 'introduced into the House of Commons by Lord Kilmainham', and the RHA's Marriage Advisory Centre leaflet said that 'Lord Kilmain' had proposed it in the 'House of Lords in November 1935'. In fact, the RHA certificate specifying four levels of fitness was based on Lord Kilmaine's short-lived November 1934 *Motion to Amend the Marriage Act*.[114] The RHA provided premarital checks from 1936 until the 1950s and engaged couples who had undergone these tests were given a certificate. The general medical examinations included 'Blood tests, chest X-Ray, blood pressure, diabetes, bodily defects'. The special mental tests included 'Perversions, alcoholism, epilepsy, speech defects, intelligence test, inherited diseases and tendencies'.[115] Tantalisingly, there are no records of how these tests were done or which 'perversions' they were looking for.

Calls for marriage control continued throughout the 1930s and 1940s. The Presbyterian Church in Queensland made a 1934 proposal which echoed Dr Arthur's 1912 call for 'health certificates for bridegrooms'.[116] Perhaps RHA staff who conducted the tests, like some legislators in North and South America, believed that examining both parties would offend 'pure' women.[117]

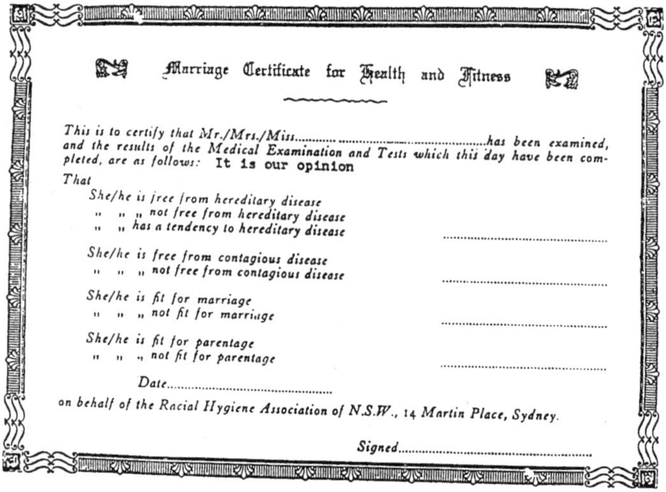

Marriage Certificate for Health and Fitness

This is to certify that Mr./Mrs./Miss...has been examined, and the results of the Medical Examination and Tests which this day have been completed, are as follows: It is our opinion

That

She/he is free from hereditary disease
" " " not free from hereditary disease
" " has a tendency to hereditary disease ....

She/he is free from contagious disease
" " " not free from contagious disease ....

She/he is fit for marriage
" " " not fit for marriage ....

She/he is fit for parentage
" " " not fit for parentage ....

Date..

on behalf of the Racial Hygiene Association of N.S.W., 14 Martin Place, Sydney.

Signed..

Figure 30: RHA Marriage Certificate for Health And Fitness

The NSW Health Week Committee held a conference on *The Need for a Health Certificate Before Marriage* in October 1935. It was chaired by Jessie Street and papers were given by Dr Andrew Davidson, President of the BMA; Dr Cooper Booth, Director of the Venereal Diseases Clinic; and Dr Frances Harding, one of the RHA's honorary medical officers.[118] Women kept up the pressure; in May 1937 the *Sun* newspaper reported that representatives from 15 women's organisations (including the RHA) planned to ask Mr Fitzsimons, the NSW Minister for Health, to impose compulsory pre-marriage health certification. Goodisson wrote to the British Eugenic Society in June 1939 asking Dr Blacker to send the RHA a film on heredity. She included a leaflet about the RHA's Marriage Advisory Centre and concluded her letter, which I have mentioned earlier, with this cleverly ambivalent remark, astutely having 'a bob each way': 'though our Society is not a Eugenic Society, we decidedly do a good deal of Eugenic work and our Pre-Marital Health Examinations have been very successful'.[119]

Concerns about marriage restrictions were raised in the first session of the Commonwealth Government's National Health and Medical Research Council, held in February 1937, which included a report on blindness, 40% of which was said to be preventable. In response, the NHMRC proposed voluntary sterilisation for carriers and sufferers from hereditary eye diseases [including those with VD], the prohibition of consanguineous marriages and the use of voluntary premarital certification.[120]

Dr Norman Haire was tired of such speculations and argued in 1941 that if Australia had not the courage to legislate to make these certificates compulsory, 'at least we might provide facilities for voluntary examination before marriage'.[121]   Not surprisingly, Haire pointedly ignored the RHA's examinations because the RHA had frequently used his help privately but, on the grounds that he was a controversial figure, would not allow him to become a member. There was still no progress by 1943, although the NHMRC wanted the public to be 'steadily educated' so that they would 'voluntarily subject themselves to medical examination before marriage'.[122]

At the 1949 Hobart meeting of the Australasian Association of Psychiatrists, Dr Charles Brothers joked that 'Cupid was never taught genetics' and proposed to remedy this by extending the work of Marriage Guidance Councils to 'control marriages'.[123]   He recognised that 'in the present state of our civilization' this would have to be advisory because 'compulsion' was not yet 'practicable'.[124]   His article was included in the RHA papers.

Simplistically, eugenists hoped that if the unfit did not marry, the would not have children. Their faith was shared by purity feminists who, alarmed about VD and the terrible death toll of mothers and babies, wished to save women and children from infected and infectious men.[125] The campaigners included such high-profile women as Marion Piddington, Jessie Street and Millicent Preston Stanley, and organisations such as the RHA and the United Associations of Women, which was formed in 1929 from an amalgamation of three feminist women's groups: the Women's Service Club, the NSW Women Voters' Association and the Women's League of NSW. Most of the groups made deputations to politicians recommending marriage restrictions. The Eugenics Society of Victoria did not call for restriction or inspections, but gave the RHA a veiled compliment, saying they did approve that it was being done by 'some progressive eugenic centres'.[126]

Legislation for Care, Control or Sterilisation

Politicians and governments are responsive to influential lobby groups and, more recently, opinion polls. For instance, in the 1970s protests from green groups, and their strong public support, prompted governments to save threatened heritage. Surprisingly, historian Michael Roe put the government 'cart' before the Eugenics Education Society of NSW 'horse' in his claim that the Society was 'founded in 1912 as a result of the Government's planning to legislate on mental defectives'.[127] The Society clearly took the initiative when they established a lobby group to pressure the NSW Government to take action. In 1913 Alexander Lewers mentioned 'the somewhat excited demand for drastic action under the heading of Eugenics which rose up suddenly a year or two ago has apparently subsided in the same remarkable manner'.[128] In South Australia it was maintained by the fire-and-brimstone Rev Joseph Coles Kirby (1837-1924) and his ideas were supported by the Women's Liberal League of NSW.[129] He was in favour of prohibition and compulsory sterilisation along lines promoted by a British surgeon, Robert Rentoul, whose books were criticised in March 1904 by the *British Medical Journal* which did not like the 'public executioner' role Rentoul proposed for doctors.[130]

People shocked by previous generations' enthusiasm for harsh penalties need reminding that until 1973 the death penalty was in force in the Australian Capital Territory and the Northern Territory and that the call to sterilise criminals is 'an old perennial blazoned forth every now and then by the lay Press'.[131] In 1872 Henry Keylock Rusden (1826-1910) called for convicted criminals to be used 'as subjects for physiological, medical and surgical experiment'[132] or 'permanently eliminated'. In his view 'the lunatic, the stupid, the weak, the diseased and the incompetent', should be 'pressed out or down'. Rusden even claimed in 1893 that he had convinced 'Mr Darwin' of the importance of extinguishing habitual criminals.[133] Similarly, historian Gyles Turner (1831-1920) suggested a plan in 1899, in which offenders with three convictions were to be given essentials and sent to an island. They should be 'self-supporting, if possible', but kept from 'licentious freedom and its concomitant brood of demoralised and demoralising offspring'.[134] These advocates were office-bearers (Rusden as the President and Turner as Secretary and Treasurer) of the Eclectic Association of Victoria, a group which Melburnian free-thinkers, rationalists and humanists established in 1867. Rusden said he was an 'atheist in theology, a determinist in philosophy, a Malthusian and a radical in sociology and an ultra free-trader'. Ironically, although he helped win the fight to make cremation legal, he was buried with religious rituals. A New Zealand surgeon and politician with a diametrically opposed outlook prescribed the same remedy to deal with 'the Fitman's Burden'. He was William A Chapple (1864-1936) who in 1899 called for 'the painless extinction' of the burdensome, those 'mental and moral and physical defectives who are unable or unwilling to support themselves'.[135]

These proposals predated eugenics but similar proposals *were* made by eugenists in the early years and caused great harm to the movement. In Britain, the Eugenics Education Society probably saw George Bernard Shaw as their biggest burden (although he was never a member) and were mortified by his sporadic use of the title 'eugenist', usually coinciding with his highly publicised and deeply shocking proposals, such as his March 1910 call for the use of a lethal chamber.[136] There were similar Australian demands: in 1911 Dr Edward Steven wanted 'emasculation' or death for 'palpable imbeciles' and the next year Professor Berry wanted to cure 'the evil at its root'.[137] Moderates feared that people regard eugenists as 'a savagely tyrannical clique who regard the lethal chamber as more valuable than the hospital, and castration the greatest good to be got out of a surgeon'.[138] At this time, some doctors and many lay people confused castration with sterilisation.

In 1912 Havelock Ellis stressed that Galton wanted eugenic reforms to come from public education, not legislation. Ellis added 'the compulsory presentation of certificates of health and good breeding forms no part of Eugenics, nor is compulsory sterilisation a demand made by any reasonable eugenist'.[139] Some Australian eugenists and organisations wanted both. Segregation was proposed in 1912 by the *Australian Medical Journal* and similar debates about the 'unfit' were held in Britain at the BMA's 1913 Annual Conference by members of the Medical Sociology Section. It was contentious but some eugenists saw birth control as the way to cull the 'unfit'. For example Dr Arthur, who became a fervent supporter of contraception, said in 1922 that birth control would be 'sheer madness' in Australia, and in 1928 agreed with Mussolini that it 'should not be encouraged among healthy people'.[140] Some wanted segregation *and* sterilisation measures.[141] And there were frankly mad schemes such as Dr Carroll's 1899 proposal that 'degenerates', if segregated and supervised, could lose their 'hereditary abnormality' and be trained 'into a moral character'.[142] From comments by the Women's Reform League President Laura Bogue Luffman in the January 1919 issue of *The Woman's Voice*, the community was clearly resistant to segregation. To make the idea acceptable, she pointed out:

> Dr Saleeby thinks the expression 'permanent care' will satisfy those kind-hearted but mistaken people who imagine a feeble-minded girl is 'freer' on the streets than in an institution.

However Berry, who was obsessive about sterilisation and lethal chambers, resurrected his invidious idea in 1921 in a Workers' Educational Association newsletter, with the disclaimer that such extreme measures would not be needed if an Act allowing segregation were passed.[143] During the 1920s the subject was discussed extensively in Australia's medical periodicals and the lay press.[144] In Britain a plea for moderation was made in 1921 by the geneticist William Bateson who, alarmed by American proposals to sterilize habitual criminals, emphasized the lack of any scientific justification for taking such action. He added this prudent reminder, 'proscription is a weapon with a very nasty recoil'.[145]

The querulous Xavier Herbert (1901-1984), whose 850,00 word novel *Poor Fellow My Country* won the Miles Franklin award in 1975, knew of Berry in the 1920s and was amused by his 'irascible ways'. He offered *Smith's Weekly* a piece about Berry, including a caricature of Berry's skull, horn-rim glasses and cigarette in a long holder. Herbert claimed in his autobiography that this material was plagiarised by

Smith's editor and his caricature was redrawn.[146]   Berry, on his return to England in April 1930, again called for a state-controlled lethal chamber to painlessly exterminate 'the grosser types' of mentally defective people. When shocked and angry eugenists complained in the *Eugenics Review*, Berry replied that he had not 'seriously suggested this'. However, he admitted writing in the *Times* that 'such an act of extinction would be the kindest, wisest, and best thing we could do for all concerned', and wondered why people should be 'so anxious to preserve the life of the almost brainless, senseless, speechless idiots and imbeciles when it seems almost pathetic to condemn them to live their lives as helpless automata.'

Extreme proposals were also made by Australians such as Angela Booth, who in 1916 noted approvingly that the advice from some unspecified 'biologists' was not to be concerned about the unfit but to prevent their 'continuance', and complained that London's *Spectator* would not publish a letter by a 'Melbourne physician' who advocated the 'reform' of sterilizing the unfit.[147]   In 1929 she suggested that humanitarianism had 'gone mad' by sustaining people 'who should never have been born or who should have been allowed to die'.[148] Booth urged Australians to act swiftly before the unfit multiplied the way they had in America which was forced to adopt a policy of sterilisation because segregation cost too much; 'though sterilization of the insane might rob the world of some future genius, sterilization of the feeble-minded would not, [as] feeble-minded parents only produce feeble-minded progeny'.[149]

Dr Waddy, another speaker, argued that as 90% of the feeble-minded had inherited their condition, 'measures' to eliminate them from the community 'would be very desirable'. He said 'If people are unhealthy, you can't tell them they must not marry! You can't tell them they must be continent! But you can sterilize them, or, by teaching them methods of birth control, restrict the size of their offspring'. Sterilisation of people with mental deficiency, epilepsy and 'nervous debility' would 'be good for the community'.[150]

There is no record of the audience's reaction to an astoundingly heartless speech which Victor Roberts gave at the end of his 1932 term as President of the RHA; he was utterly opposed to 'thousands of mental defectives' receiving food from the state. Roberts, who ironically belonged to the Peace Society, was quoted in the *Sydney Morning Herald* on 19 July 1932 as urging the RHA to try to change the thinking of those 'mentally wanting' persons who favoured such government support.[151] Disappointingly, the paper did not print any outraged letters and the RHA did not attempt to distance themselves from his views.

By July 1938 Angela Booth had modified her sterilisation message. In the first publication issued by the ESV, she stressed that it should be voluntary 'as recommended by the famous Brock Report in England, and not compulsory sterilization as practised in Germany'.[152] In September 1938 the Eugenics Society's Dr Blacker answered Booth's query about delays in introducing the Sterilization Bill into the House of Commons. It was, he said, because the government was 'acutely aware' of Roman Catholic and Labor Party opposition, on the grounds that the Bill would be 'a potential threat to the working class.' Citing the example of the Germay's compulsory methods, they called it the 'thin edge of the wedge'.[153] Fears that 'unemployed workers' or the 'poor but normal' might be sterilized had been expressed in Australia many years earlier than this.

The other option of segregation was frequently emphasized. Australian proposals for special schools and colonies for the unfit had begun in the 1890s and continued for the next three decades, with South Australia (in 1898) and NSW (in 1908) being the first states to provide them.[154] Oliver Latham, in the 8 October 1927 issue of the *Medical Journal of Australia*, warned doctors of the 'ludicrous situation' if attempts were made to segregate the thousands of mentally defective children. However, reality did not deter delegates at the National Council of Women Conference who, according to the *Sydney Morning Herald* on 19 July 1928, urged the government to establish 'residential centres' for mentally defective children and colonies for adults. Many women's groups favoured such segregation, fearing that the alternative of the feeble-minded being sterilized and living in the community might have the result that feebleminded men would commit sexual crimes and the women would be a promiscuous 'focus for contagion' and spread venereal disease.[155]

The RHA modified its position in 1931 by accepting that keeping all mentally defective people in institutions was neither possible or desirable 'as we formerly thought'. However, they did want this to apply to the 'worst' cases and an RHA Advisory Board Member proposed establishing 'mental clinics' to 'deal with all school age mental defectives in NSW'.[156] In 1933 Mrs Goodisson wrote to Dr C A Hogg, the NSW Inspector-General of Mental Hospitals, expressing pleasure that he and Reginald Weaver (the State's Minister for Health) were 'in favour of a farm colony for the mentally defective members of the community'.[157] The 10 September 1935 issue of the *Argus* reported that the Mothers' Club of Victoria voted in favour of voluntary sterilisation of the mentally and physically unfit to ensure that in Australia there 'should not only be a white race, but a race of the best whites'. Also that year the United Australia Party's Annual General Convention, with support from John A L Wallace, Inspector-General of Mental Hospitals, called for the segregation of the unfit.[158]

In 1913 one doctor described rejection of undesirable migrants as a 'second form of segregation'.[159] Another, Ernest Jones, said in the *Sydney Morning Herald* in 1928 that 18 years earlier, he had been the 'unfortunate' person with the task of informing the Victorian Parliament that many immigrants were mentally defective. However, plans for segregation had widespread support; for example, Dr Andrew Davidson told the Health Society of NSW in August 1911 that 'a complete system for the control of mentally-defective children from childhood upwards' would soon be established, which, although causing the State 'some initial expense' would be more than repaid by the reduction in money needed to maintain 'weak-minded criminals, inebriates, and the illegitimate children of the feeble-minded'. He was sure the initial opposition would 'die down, and the excellent results would lead those who in ignorance objected to heartily support'.

Eugenics was frequently described as a branch of preventive medicine because one of its aims was to prevent the unfit from breeding.[160] In 1935 Lord Horder told a Melbourne audience that 'eugenics was the soundest and most profitable form of preventive medicine'.[161] In the same year Mrs Muscio, President of the NSW Branch of the National Council of Women viewed it in the same way in her endorsement which appeared in the RHA pamphlet *What Racial Hygiene Means!!;* 'The work that the Racial Hygiene Association is doing is undoubtedly a valuable contribution to sex education, and so, to preventive medicine'. Before 1920 this goal resembled a religious crusade for some: 'each defective strain, as it makes its appearance, must come to an end. There need be no inhumanity. There must be no compromise'.[162]

From the 1890s until the late 1930s there was high-level support by Australian psychiatrists and eugenists for sterilisation and debates were extensively covered in journals such as the *Medical Journal of Australia*.[163] For example, the prestigious surgeon Sir George Syme (1859-1929) recommended in his presidential address to the 1923 Australasian Medical Congress that voluntary sterilisation 'could and should be tried'. The *Eugenics Review* reported Syme's comments under the heading, 'Sterilization: Views in Australia'. In 1929 unanimous support for sterilisation at the *Australian Racial Hygiene Congress* astounded the organiser who said 'Dr Addison's paper on sterilization was the surprise of the Congress. We all expected much hot discussion on this debatable subject, but not so, his seven resolutions were carried without any objection at all'. The decision was more extreme than that of the RHA's Advisory Board, which noted on 8 August 1929, 'It was felt that [sterilization] was a dangerous matter and that some of the American States have rescinded their laws on the subject'. Even so, the audience could not be called 'a small minority of zealots' as it included such prominent citizens as Sir Thomas Henley, Dr Richard Arthur, Dr Sydney Morris, Sir James Barrett, Sir Benjamin and Lady Fuller, Mrs Angela Booth, Mr Cresswell O'Reilly and Dr Lorna Hodgkinson. The author of the surprise paper was Phillip Addison, surgeon, reserve army captain and member of the RHA's Advisory Board. These are the internally contradictory resolutions, half of which related to compulsory sterilisation:

> 1. That the general public should be educated to the facts that it is
>   in the interests of the common weal and posterity that those

individuals who come from hereditary [sic] defective families should be sterilized

2. That the sterilization should be voluntary

3. That individuals convicted of criminal offences and found to be mentally defective, should be compulsorily sterilized

4. That the group of submental defective adults and children committed to the care of the state, if there is any likelihood of their returning to everyday society, should be compulsorily sterilized

5. Strict enforcement of immigration laws, not only in relation to British born subjects, but also aliens; if found deficient within a certain period, they should be either deported or sterilized

6. The vigorous enforcement of the VD Act as a contributory factor to sterilization

7. That any person found to be a menace to society should be compulsorily sterilized.[164]

The RHA reaffirmed these resolutions at their One Day Conference on 14 October 1931. Later that same day the Rev H N Baker attempted to overturn this decision but his motion was narrowly defeated, by nine votes to eight, a marked shift from the unanimous support expressed in 1929. The fact that only 17 people voted on such a contentious issue shows the small size of the RHA membership at the ARHC meeting. This needs emphasis – in their best early years the RHA had 100 subscribers listed in their 1928-29 Annual Report and by 1931, page 5 of the Annual Report listed only 25 members.

The debate continued in RHA annual reports: in the 1931 report Dr H G Wallace criticised the resolutions at a meeting of the Newcastle Branch of the Association but most of the audience opposed him and in the 1932 report the Rev Baker again warned about the dangers of sterilisation. In 1929 Ralph Noble had reminded Racial Hygiene Congress delegates of the need for a Mental Defectives Bill, which 'for years past had been promised by successive Ministers for Health'.[165] Millicent Preston Stanley, President of the Feminist Club said this was something the Club had been urging for 12 years.[166] In expressing this support Noble had changed from his 1924 stance when he urged doctors to 'encourage the intelligent use of segregation' to prevent 'lay extremists' from succeeding in their 'clamour for sterilization'.[167] Miss Preston Stanley, in 1925, made history as the Nationalist Party's Member for Sydney's Eastern Suburbs, the first woman to be elected to the New South Wales Parliament. However, this eminent woman deserved Noble's rebuke if we believe the remark which the *Labor Daily* attributed to her, 'What are we doing to dam the endless stream of degenerate and moron human stocks?'.[168]

A special meeting of the RHA Executive tried to agree in June 1934 whether to segregate or sterilize the 'mentally unfit' and to determine who had 'the right to be sterilized'. In 1936 the RHA discussed this 'several times' and found the lack of any legal ruling 'very unsatisfactory'. However, by 1950 this no longer roused passions and Dr Brothers, Chairman of the Tasmanian Mental Deficiency Board, praised Britain for 'her usual wise conservatism' in refraining from passing any laws about sterilization'.[169] No Bill for the sterilisation of defectives was ever passed in NSW despite several mistaken reports that Dr Arthur's Bill became law, although he certainly tried.[170]

In 1913 Arthur spoke about the 'provision of his Bill' but still nothing happened. [171] The history of the delay was given by Greg McGirr, the NSW Minister for Motherhood; in 1920, responding to a women's delegation who 'urged the segregation of these unfortunates for the welfare of society', McGirr said the Bill had been 'prepared some years ago' but had 'lain in the Department of Education'. After it came to the Health Department McGirr promised to bring the Bill 'forward this session' and asked for 'the assistance of the deputation [from the Women's Reform League] in making the measure as complete and perfect as possible'.[172] Nothing came of this and in 1929 Dr Arthur said 'sterilization is an inevitable necessity, but the time is not ripe for its introduction'.[173] *Hansard* shows that Arthur 'was inclined to accept an amendment in connection with sterilization if such was moved'.[174] There was no amendment and the Bill would have lapsed because institutional care was so expensive that the scheme was opposed even by Arthur's own party.[175] The publicity for this Bill led Cora Hodson, the Secretary of the Eugenics Society in London, to mistakenly include NSW in her list of 'countries' which had sterilisation laws. She apologised after learning from the NSW

Government offices 'that no such Act appears in their legislation lists'.[176]

In March 1931, the Federal Health Council, a body of Commonwealth and State Ministers for Health, adopted a resolution requesting the Commonwealth Department of Health to gather information from countries with laws relating to sterilisation of mental defectives and 'to obtain any related information from the various States'.[177] There were also public concerns about sterilisation; in the 1932 Health Week address given by William Dawson, the Professor of Psychiatry at the University of Sydney, Dawson noted that although some American states had passed sterilisation legislation 'very few medical men would venture to suggest it' because they knew too little about heredity to suggest this 'dangerous course'. Earlier that year Dr Cumpston had contacted Australia House in London for clarification about the legal status in Britain of eugenic sterilisation.

In response to his letter, Frank McCallum, the Chief Medical Officer for the Commonwealth, wrote that 'it would appear that a "mark time" policy has been adopted' in Britain. This was 'understandable', he wrote, 'because enthusiasm for sterilization was largely confined to people whose zeal was greater than their scientific knowledge'.[178] Dr Frank Kerr, a Medical Officer with the Commonwealth Department of Health, presented the findings of this investigation to the Federal Health Council in 1933. His *Federal Inquiry into the Sterilization of Mental Defectives* recommended laws to allow selective voluntary sterilisation of people with, or likely to transmit, a mental defect or disorder. The report proposed that sterilisation should first be approved by state boards, with provision for appeal.[179]

Neither the Commonwealth nor individual states acted on this report. Cumpston had changed his opinion since advising the *Royal Commission on Child Endowment* in 1929 that the Commonwealth should exercise its constitutional powers on the matter. In 1934, the Inspector-General of Mental Hospitals in NSW obtained an opinion from the State Crown Solicitor's Office about the legality of sterilizing a man who had requested this procedure. The Office advised that such an operation would not be lawful, either for 'healthy' individuals who could give informed consent or for mentally defective people who lacked the capacity to do this. The Crown Solicitor stated that any such operation would amount to a 'maiming' and that before this procedure could be lawful 'there would have to be an advancement of the frontiers of what is lawful'.[180]

Australia, like other Commonwealth countries, followed established British practices. Consequently, Cumpston's decision to now take an anti-sterilisation stance, was made as a result of Britain's decision in 1933-1934 that doctors performing eugenic sterilisation operations risked prosecution on the grounds of mutilation.[181] In 1935 Cumpston advised the RHA

> There is no Commonwealth law in the matter [of sterilization] and, except in the Territories, I would consider that the constitutionality of any Commonwealth legislation would be questioned.[182]

In 1944 Harvey Sutton complained that 'no court decision has been given on an actual case, and till the legal aspect is cleared up, no hospital will permit doubtful operations, though in private practice no such prohibition exists'.[183] Although in 1967 the procedure as a eugenic measure was still in legal limbo, by 1980 sterilisation had become the most widely used contraceptive measure worldwide.[184]

Paradoxically, although the clamour was for mentally defective women to be sterilized, eugenists' clinics could only perform the simpler male sterilisation (vasectomy). Piddington, with her Institute of Family Relations, was the only person brave, or foolish, enough to talk about it in the 1930s. Doctors did not want to be involved in a legal test case and the fear of the associated costs and publicity suggests why the RHA avoided such work, or kept quiet about it. In fact, while others had also performed these operations, they did not acknowledge this until the 1970s. The RHA (under a new name) opened its first Vasectomy Clinic in Sydney in 1972 and the following year, Dr Victor Wallace gave details about the vasectomies his Victorian clinic had performed from 1936.[185]

Dr William Ernest Jones noted in his 1929 *Report on Mental Deficiency in the Commonwealth of Australia* that while they had passed sterilisation laws in many American states, 'principally in California', most states had ceased the practice. Recently, researchers have suggested why California (with forced sterilisations of 20,100 mental patients in government institutions) surpassed other states' tally: from the pioneering gold rush days it had been a xenophobic 'State of strangers'.[186]   Ernest Jones found 'Segregation and guardianship infinitely preferable to sterilization [and stated that] sterilization will never be resorted to in any of the countries of the British Empire until the economic pressure, arising from the increasing burden of lunacy and mental deficiency, has become very much more acute than it is at the present time'.[187]

Ernest Jones must not have known that in March 1928 the Province of Alberta in Canada became the only jurisdiction in the British Empire to pass a eugenic sterilisation law (for compulsory sterilisation of psychiatric and mentally defective people as a condition of their discharge from institutions).[188]   In 1997 the reality was publicly revealed and D Wahlsten has analysed the way in which the Alberta Eugenics Board operated 'away from public and legislative scrutiny' from 1928 until 1972 when the Sexual Sterilization Act was repealed and in 1996 the Board was tried and prosecuted.[189]

The truth was not known in 1929 when the provisions in Alberta's Sexual Sterilization Act were quoted approvingly in the Western Australian Parliament.[190]   Others forgot, or never knew about it. For example, in the *Sydney Morning Herald* on 20 January 1934, Dr Richard Dick, the Director-General of Public Health in NSW, repeated Ernest Jones' mistake by commenting that 'no British community' had permitted sterilisation. In 1935 Angela Booth supported her argument with the claim that 'two countries' in the British Empire had advocated sterilisation: 'Alberta passed a law legalizing voluntary sterilization in 1928, and British Columbia in 1933'.[191]   Using the word 'voluntary' is wrong for these Canadian Acts because the Alberta Act was coercive in 1928 and became more so in 1937 when it was amended to allow compulsory sterilisation.[192]   Both continued to function until their repeal in 1972. Although militants in the 1930s could have cited precedents in the United States, they did not. Possibly, this was because Australia was so strongly pro-British and pro-Commonwealth that an appeal to follow an American example would have been counter-productive.

Attempts to pass legislation controlling marriage had failed and no eugenics-related organisations succeeded in their clamour for laws to regulate the education, care, control or sterilisation of mental defectives. Several Bills were prepared but only one, relating specifically to mental deficiency, was passed. In addition, Lunacy Acts or Prisons Acts more appropriately described some 'mental defectives' laws which were passed, not for eugenic reasons, but to maintain law and order. In 1920 Tasmania became (and remained) 'the first and only State in Australia to legislate especially for the feeble-minded class as well as for the lower grades'. In 1923 the passage of this law was cited as indicating that Tasmania was 'more advanced than other states of the Commonwealth', unlike the 'woefully unenlightened and woefully behind' state of NSW.[193]

Ironically, the only law with eugenic intent was passed in a state which did not have a eugenics organisation. In 1925 Professor Morris Miller drafted an amended Tasmanian Mental Deficiency Bill with the help of the humane Emanuel Sydney Morris, Director of Public Health.[194] The Bill, like the British legislation of 1913, distinguished between mental deficiency and insanity.[195] Such a distinction was important to eugenists, who pointed out that although South Australia had passed a Mental Deficiency Act in 1913 (with 1914 and 1922 amendments), it was really a Lunacy Act, because it dealt in part with low-grade defectives and made no distinction between mental disorders and mental deficiency.[196]

Western Australia's Legislative Council in 1929 did not pass the non-party Mental Deficiency Bill, despite 'exhaustive' consideration by a Select Committee and lengthy discussion in both Houses of Parliament.[197] The Bill had a provision for sterilisation of mental defectives in it, but after its defeat the State's only legislation for 'this class' was the *Lunacy Act* for their admission to hospitals for the insane.[198] Attempts that year by the Victorian Parliament to pass a *Mental Deficiency Bill* also failed. Victoria's National Council of Women (whose unintentionally ironic motto was 'Do unto others as ye would they should do unto you') sent this resolution to their State Minister for Health in October 1933:

> We urge our governmental authorities to take further effective measures to prevent mental defectives from reproducing their own kind, and so creating expenditure by the community on welfare work, gaols and mental hospitals.[199]

Dr Ernest Jones, Victoria's Director of Mental Hygiene, maintained his interest in the subject, sending a request in 1936 to his Sydney equivalent, Dr John A Wallace, for a copy of the draft Bill which the NSW Cabinet was considering 'for the control of mental defectives who were criminally inclined'.[200]   Jones thanked Wallace for the confidential material and mentioned the polarisation of Victoria's judiciary, who wanted an institution for sexual offenders, and the psychiatrists who planned to 'cure these perverts by talking them to death'.[201]   Edward Paris Nesbitt, a lawyer with the unique distinction of having been an inmate of gaols and lunatic asylums, showed that such arguments were not new when he stated in 1892 that 'for years doctors and lawyers had disputed this, with doctors expressing most of the acrimony'.[202]   The NSW Bill, which Ernest Jones asked to see in 1936, became the *Mental Defectives (Convicted Persons) Act* of 1939, which amended the 1899 *Prisons Act*.[203]

When the Queensland Parliament considered mental deficiency legislation in 1930, Sydney's *Telegraph* reported that it would soon introduce a non-party Bill for the sterilisation of mental defectives, which in the words of the State's Home Secretary, James C Petersen, 'would arrest the propagation of thousands of children who would be of no use to the community or to themselves'.[204]   This Bill related to day and residential schools for 'idiots, imbeciles, feeble-minded persons and moral defectives' but it lapsed 'owing to financial stringency'.[205]   In 1934 the Queensland Branch of the BMA prepared a report on the sterilisation of the unfit as a 'preventive measure'.[206] These attempts failed.[207]

On 8 July 1936 Walter Hamilton moved a 'sterilization of unfit persons' motion in the South Australian Parliament.   The State's Premier wrote to Joseph Lyons, the Prime Minister, to inform him of the resolution and to ask what opinion the Commonwealth and other state governments had on the matter.[208] Dr Cumpston's memorandum to the Prime Minister's secretary was that the Commonwealth Minister for Health advised:

> That the government has not at any time considered this question, and as the government has no constitutional powers which would enable it to take any action … it is difficult to foresee an occasion upon which a policy could be formulated.

The Premier was referred to the 1934 United Kingdom Departmental Report for advice on precedent and authority.[209] Cumpston *had* considered the question and in 1929 advised the Royal Commission on Child Endowment or Family Allowance that the Commonwealth did possess such constitutional powers.[210] The South Australian Parliament agreed on 23 September 1936 'that the question of (voluntary and compulsory sterilisation) of persons suffering from unsound mind or other dangerous malady or maladies known to be transmissible to their offspring should receive the earnest and immediate consideration of this House' but they did not discuss it again.[211] This was long after most support had waned; by 1933 support for sterilisation on eugenic grounds was diminishing and no law sanctioning eugenic sterilisation was ever passed in Australia. Reasons for this include:

- At least a third of the Australian population was Catholic and the Pope's 1931 *Casti Connubii* specifically forbade sterilization on the grounds that self-mutilation was unlawful and that the rights of the individual should prevail over the welfare of the community.[212]

- By 1931 it was recognised that most mentally defective people had normal parents, so that plans to sterilize the unfit would only minimally reduce their numbers.[213]

- In 1931, a Bill for voluntary sterilization of people with mental deficiency had been rejected by 167 votes to 89 in the British House of Commons.[214]

- In 1932, a BMA Committee on Sterilization had agreed that sterilization would not lead to a marked reduction in the incidence of mental deficiency and that there were no grounds for the previous alarmist views about racial deterioration.[215]

- In June 1933, the Secretary of the Eugenics Society in London had expressed repugnance about the Nazi sterilization program,[216] and news about this program was starting to be reported in Australian newspapers.[217]

- In 1933, the British psychologist Cyril Burt had 'flung a bombshell amongst the upholders of wholesale sterilization, by pointing out that, in order to wipe out the evil [of mental deficiency], it would be necessary to sterilize one-fifth of the population'.[218]

- In 1934 rejection of the recommendations in the Brock Committee's report for voluntary sterilization in Britain was a result of lack of government interest and the growing disrepute which Nazi 'eugenics' was bringing to the field.[219]

- Britain's pro-sterilization eugenists failed to mobilise support from the scientific community and faced opposition from the labour movement and the Catholic Church.[220]

In 1933 the Commonwealth's conservative Government, after hearing of a British legal decision on the matter, decided against sterilisation on legal and medical grounds. Although initially favouring it, and supported by the pro-sterilisation recommendation of its 1933 Kerr Report, they abandoned the idea. Legal and medical factors, rather than party politics or eugenists' advocacy, had most influence in the decision-making.

However, many attempts to pass eugenic legislation were made by the Labor Party or had bipartisan support.[221] For example, Mark Adams stated that

The fact that eugenics could flourish in both Weimar and Nazi Germany, in Coolidge's America and Lenin's Russia, and that it could count among its adherents renowned communists, socialists, liberals, conservatives and fascists, suggests that any simplistic political classification of the movement cannot sustain analysis'.[222]

Daniel Kevles emphasized the political diversity among British and American eugenists who were united only in being largely 'middle to upper middle class, white, Anglo Saxon, predominantly Protestant and educated'.[223] Australian eugenists, including those in the medical professions, had similarly diverse political views.

Sterilisation had fewer Australian supporters after 1935, but it is not accurate to say that they were all cranks or people seeking notoriety. There was no doubting the sincerity of supporters such as Marion Piddington, Canon R B S Hammond and Professor William Dakin. In Sydney, the Catholic *Church Standard* stated that Hammond's views in support of sterilisation were 'utterly immoral'[224] and Dakin's 1935 comments: 'Sterilize unfit.   Would end evil in generation says Professor' were probably published for their shock value.[225]   There is no record of Australian responses to the 1936 book by John Bostock and Leslie John Javis Nye which praised Hitler and Mussolini's 'triumphs of autocracy' and advocated the sterilisation of 'those individuals who possess such serious transmissible diseases as would make their progeny a burden to themselves and to the state'.[226]   The same year, the extremist Australian Legion in Perth wanted a referendum question about the sterilisation of the unfit posed at the next federal election.[227]

The fact that moderation was the norm was shown even earlier when Mr J H Disney failed to have his 1934 Bill introduced in the Victorian Legislative Council because the Attorney-General refused to allow the Parliamentary Draughtsman 'to prepare any private Bill containing contentious matter' and sterilisation of the unfit was 'very contentious'.[228]   In 1935 a member of the ESV expressed his opposition to eugenic sterilisation in a paper given to the Victorian Council of Mental Hygiene.   The author, psychiatrist Paul Dane, described the 'cry for sterilization' as a 'spurious remedy' which would divert people's minds from 'real reforms'.[229]   It was a divisive issue for the ESV but the Society's President ignored dissent and urged the Chief Secretary of Victoria to include voluntary sterilisation in a *Mental Deficiency Bill*.[230]

Even as late as 1954, a Feminist Club deputation demanded segregation and/or sterilisation for 'incurable sex perverts'.[231] However, public opinion and world events ensured that in Australia such strident demands for eugenic sterilisation never resulted in action.

In 1929, six months before his premature death, the eminent Australian biochemist, Professor Thorburn Brailsford Robertson (1884-1930) made a prescient plea for moderation. Fearful about breeding for fitness, he warned that unless sterilisation of the unfit was limited to the 'conspicuously feeble-minded', it could become

> an appallingly dangerous weapon in the hands of a profession which is possessed of notoriously little social or historical perspective, and still less spirit of toleration for whatever they do not understand.[232]

In 1936 Norman Haire could verify Robertson's prediction from his experience of world events. He opposed compulsory sterilisation: 'for if once the State is given legislative power, there is always the likelihood, as we have seen in Germany, that such powers may be used for political ends. It seems therefore wiser not to put such powers into the hands of the State if the desired result can be obtained voluntarily by educating public opinion'.[233] In 1939, shortly before his death, Havelock Ellis showed no interest when Haire repeatedly attempted to warn him of the fate of the Jews in Germany.[234]

Similarly, embarrassment, ignorance or approval are three possible reasons why many Australians, including eugenists, were not critical in those early years. Mark Hayne has examined Australian responses to Hitler's rise to power, noting that the Australian Government failed to denounce Germany's anti-Semitic policies or condemn the fascist regime, that the Australian press was more favourable to Germany than the British press, and that the Catholic Church praised Germany's actions as opposing communism.[235] It was, to quote W H Auden, 'a low, dishonest decade', although there were exceptions, such as the Sydney historian Stephen (later Sir Stephen) Roberts (1901-1971) who spoke fluent German and had experienced the stark truth of the 'German experiment' during a visit to Germany from November 1935 to March 1937: when he forecast war with Hitler in *The House that Hitler Built*,[236] the *Bulletin* jeered and Germany banned his book.[237]

In 1936 the Australian government agreed to admit a restricted number of Jewish refugees from Germany but many officials took a pro-German stance; in July 1936 Sydney police tried to prevent a performance at the Savoy Theatre of Clifford Odets' anti-Nazi play *Till the Day I Die* and Robert Pullam, in *Guilty Secrets: Free Speech in Australia*, noted that at the start of World War II this play was banned by the Australian Censor after the German Consul protested that it was 'an insult and a caricature of the German nation and its government'. In January 1939, seven months before Australia was at war with Germany, Prime Minister Joseph Lyons publicly rebuked H G Wells for his 'needless affront to other nations'. Wells, the literary giant who Roy MacLeod described aptly as 'the world's best-known historian of the future', was in Australia to address the 1939 ANZAAS Congress. He had denounced Hitler as a 'certifiable lunatic' and derided Mussolini as a 'fantastic renegade' from the Socialist movement, describing both as 'freaks' and 'criminal Caesars'.

Few Australian eugenists openly supported fascist regimes but those who did included prominent people such as Sir Raphael Cilento, Professor Harvey Sutton, and two members of the Eugenics Society of Victoria; on 7 July 1938, Dr Fritz Duras spoke in the ESV lecture series on 'Eugenics in Germany today' and the *Age* reported his contentious views the following day. Duras, the Director of Physical Education at Melbourne University, applauded Nazi measures for racial improvement as 'one of the most interesting biological experiments in the world'.[238] His views were not a solitary aberration and similarly extremist views appeared in 1939 in the second of the Society's publications. They were written by the Society's President, Professor Agar, who praised German pronatalist taxation incentives for the fit, which were introduced in 1933 'to improve the eugenic quality of the nation and to stem the fall in its birth-rate'. Agar commented that if the increase in the German birth rate continued, it would be 'largely due to psychological factors, such as a more optimistic outlook on the future of their nation'.[239] While the ESV had indulged in melodramatic rhetoric, they posed no threat as they were a powerless and moribund organisation whose calls for action were ignored.

By the 1930s both Australia and Britain had rejected the idea of legislation to control the unfit. Events of the 1930s weakened support for sterilisation and, after the news of German practices in World War II, contemplation of eugenics or sterilisation became utterly repugnant. In 1932 it was rejected by Dr Grey Ewan (1896-1992), fondly known at Newcastle's Stockton Mental Hospital as 'the Grey Ruin', who was one of the first psychiatrists trained in NSW and who later became the Deputy Inspector-General of Mental Hospitals in NSW. In his view, using the procedure on the unfit would have a practically negligible impact on preventive medicine and that it was atrocious to suggest that the sterilisation of patients with a mental disease should be a condition of their discharge from hospital.[240]   In addition, suggestions about eugenically 'good' births were unpopular once peace came and with it a resurgence of the pronatalist patriotic imperative to have as many births as possible, whatever the physical or mental status of the parents.   Finally, effective medical treatment for venereal disease, a greater understanding of genetics and the realisation that the unfit were not swamping the fit, undermined the credibility of eugenics. As John Maynard Smith mused in his classic text, *The Theory of Evolution*, while it seems likely that in future the progress we have made in directing the evolution of plants and animals may extend to humans, at present the most that can be said is that

> the indiscriminate scattering of radioactive substances into the atmosphere will increase slightly but significantly the number of the genetically handicapped, and that the discouragement of marriages between close relatives will decrease that number.[241]

After World War II, many people who had previously supported eugenics preferred to forget or deny it. For example, in 1932 the RHA had openly advocated sterilisation of the unfit, but their references in the 1950s to the events of the 1930s modified this position to 'there was some effort made to permit sterilization of the eugenically unfit'.[242]

Eugenists were partly right about factors which could be inherited but while genetic defects continue to cause pain, there are new ways to

316　EUGENICS IN AUSTRALIA

tackle such problems. People no longer fear that they might transmit diseases such as TB, or 'tendencies' such as criminality, which are not hereditary. Advances in genetics offer treatment and even cure; at-risk couples, by using genetic counselling and prenatal testing, can make informed choices if tests show that a foetus is severely disabled or has inherited a fatal disorder and most Australians see it as a basic human right for a couple to decide whether to abort or bear a foetus with serious genetic defects. Many would now be shocked by the suggestion that child-bearing decisions should be made by others, for religious reasons or on the grounds of the parents' likely eugenic contribution to the race or state. The notion that their biological inheritance makes some people worthier than others is abhorrent in democratic countries with egalitarian beliefs.

These factors both cause and reflect major changes in attitudes around the world about 'unfitness' and what can or should be done about it. The commitment to the collective good ('For King and Country') has been replaced by distaste for government or religious intrusion into private affairs and support for self-determination and the protection of human rights; now the aims of eugenists have been replaced with the medical concerns of geneticists. While this has largely reassured the public, some developments in human genetics are contentious and history is a reminder of the potential for misuse which such advances can offer. Easy-going, anti-authoritarian people who tend to vote 'No' in referenda also rejected eugenics and calls for sterilisation. In Australia common sense and scepticism prevailed; 'survival of the fittest is a very good doctrine when we are the fittest; it is a very bad one when we are not', as Billy Hughes put it.[243] Catholic opposition to sterilisation was also influential and, as many Catholics were Irish and poor, they often shared the Communist and Labor Party opposition to elitist definitions of unfitness.[244]

---

[1] Daniel J Kevles, *In the Name of Eugenics: Genetics and the Uses of Human Heredity* (New York: Alfred A Knopf, 1985), 115.

[2] Quoted by John Laurent, in Roy MacLeod and Philip F Rehbock, *Darwin's Laboratory: Evolutionary Theory and Natural History in the Pacific* (Honolulu: University of Hawaii Press, 1994), 492.

[3] Rev Charles Kingsley, quoted by Laurent, ibid.

[4] William A Chapple, 'The fertility of the unfit', *ICMCAT* (1899), 474-82. Also, *The Fertility of the Unfit* (Melbourne; Whitcombe and Tombs, 1903).

[5] Richard A Soloway, *Demography and Degeneration: Eugenics and the Declining Birth-rate in Twentieth Century Britain* (Chapel Hill: University of North Carolina Press, 1990), xv.

[6] 'Murder or not', *Honi Soit*, 12 July 1945, 1. It was followed by 'Wilson [the female editor] must go, Catholics demand – "Blasphemous, obscene"', ibid, 19 July 1945, 1.

[7] V H Wallace, 'The Eugenics Society of Victoria (1936-1961)', *ER*, vol 53 (January 1962), 217.

[8] Charles Mackellar and David Welsh, *Mental Deficiency: A Medico-sociological Study of Feeble-mindedness* (Sydney: Govt. Pr., 1917), 8 and 64.

[9] Chapple (1903), xii, xiii.

[10] David Barker, in 'The biology of stupidity: Genetics, eugenics and mental deficiency in the inter-war years', *British Journal for the History of Science*, vol 22 (September 1989), 348-49, noted that Dr Alfred Tredgold claimed that normal couples had four children, while defectives had seven. Tredgold's claim was extensively cited.

[11] 'Care of the Feeble-minded in Australasia', *AMCT* (1914), 719.

[12] 'Doctors in Congress. Care of the mentally unfit. Facing a grave problem', *Argus*, 12 February 1914, 8.

[13] Harvey Sutton, *Lectures in Preventive Medicine* (Sydney: Consolidated Press, 1944), 26, and 'The feeble-minded – Their classification and importance', *AMCT*, 1 (1911), 905.

[14] Anon but probably Alexander Lewers, *AMJ* (13 December 1913), 1342.

[15] Quoted in Philip Reilly, *The Surgical Solution: A History of Involuntary Sterilization in the United States* (Baltimore: Johns Hopkins University Press, 1991), 122.

[16] *Report of the Mental Deficiency Committee* , *BMA* (London: BMA, July 1932), 34.

[17] Geoffrey Serle, *From Deserts the Prophets Come: The Creative Spirit in Australia 1788-1972* (Melbourne: Heinemann, 1973), 27-28.

[18] *Australasian*, 1 Jan 1876, quoted by W F Mandle, in *Journal of the Royal Australian Historical Society* (December 1973), 235. Mandle, 244, footnote 36, was unable to find results for Barry's questionnaire on boys' age, height, weight and their chest and limb measurements.

[19] *AAASR* (1895), 787-97.

[20] Anon, quoted by William Ramsay Smith, in *Peace: An Address delivered at the University of Adelaide on Peace Day, 9 November 1910* (International Peace Society, Adelaide Branch), 5.

[21] Dr James McCreery, 'The psychology of crime', *AMTC*, 8th session, III (1908), 266.

[22]Reports by J A Hogue, NSW Department of Public Instruction, 1908 and 1910.

[23]British Science Guild (Sydney Branch). *Report of Sub-Committee Upon the Provision of Open Spaces for the Use of School Children in Sydney and Suburbs* (Sydney: British Science Guild, 1 October 1909).

[24]BSG, (1909), 18. There were other supporters: Jan Roberts, in *Maybanke Anderson: Sex, Suffrage & Social Reform* (Sydney: Hale & Iremonger, 1993) p. 120, noted that in 1909 the first President of the Parks and Playgrounds Association was Professor Alexander Mackie, the first principal of the Sydney Teachers' College and the first professor of education of at the University of Sydney. However, the 'driving force' was Maybanke Anderson, supported by Margaret Windeyer.

[25]Ramsay Smith, *On Race-Culture and the Conditions that Influence it in South Australia* (Adelaide: Govt. Pr., 1912), 3.

[26]NHMRC, Session 20, November 1945, 10. See also Session 21, May 1946, 6.

[27]Stuart to F Galton, 1892, Galton Papers (London: University College London), 196/8.

[28]Love to Galton, 14 April 1894, ibid.

[29]Turtle (1988), 228-30.

[30]R F Irvine, *The Place of the Social Sciences in a Modern University* (Sydney: Angus & Robertson, 1914), 7.

[31] Patricia Morison, *J T Wilson and the Fraternity of Duckmaloi* (Amsterdam and Atlanta, Ga: Rodopi, Clio Medica 42, The Wellcome Institute Series in the History of Medicine, 1997), 404.

[32]Andy for Thomas Peter Anderson Stuart (1856-1920); Jummy (the Scottish pronunciation of Jimmy) for James Thomas Wilson (1861-1945) and Taffy (a play on his surname, as in Taffy is a Welshman, from Davy, short for David, Wales' patron saint) for David Arthur Welsh (1865-1948).

[33]In 1925 the scholar and poet Christopher John Brennan (1870-1932) became the second and last professor to be dismissed by the University for adultery.

[34]*AJPP* (December 1929), 245.

[35]Alan Carroll (?1823-1911, né Samuel Mathias Curl), edited *The Science of Man*. A hagiography was written by the journal's sub-editor, Mrs D Izett – *Health and Longevity According the Theories of the Late Dr Alan Carroll* (Sydney: Epworth, 1918). Mulvaney, in MacLeod (1988), 202-03, wrote that Carroll's 'useful facts and idiotic theories … were not supported by leaders in the field'

[36]See examples quoted by Brian Williams in *Education With Its Eyes Open: A Biography of Dr K S Cunningham* (Camberwell, Victoria: ACER, 1994), 66.

[37]J W Y Fishbourne, 'The segregation of the epileptic and the feeble-minded', *AMCT*, vol 2 (1911), 890.

[38]Alice Henry, 'Brightening the dull', *Argus*, 27 May 1899.

[39]Richard A Stawell, 'Physical signs of mentally defective children', *Intercolonial Medical Journal of Australasia*, 5 (no 10) 20 October 1900, 476.

[40]Alice Henry file, ML, QA 823/H-CY, Reel 145.

[41]Stawell (1900), 473.

[42]Shirley Fitzgerald and Garry Wotherspoon (eds.), *Minorities: Cultural Diversity in Sydney* (Sydney: State Library of NSW Press in assoc with the Sydney History Group, 1995), Intro, 13.

[43]Paul Ashton, 'Changing approaches to the developmentally-disabled', in Fitzgerald and Wotherspoon (1995), 145.

[44]Mary Booth, 'School Anthropometrics: the importance of Australasian measurements conforming to the schedule of the British Anthropometric Committee, 1908', vol 13, *AAASR* (1911), 690.

[45]Mary Booth, 'The need for educating public opinion on the problem of the feeble-minded', *AMG* (12 October 1912), 378-79.

[46]*Commonwealth Yearbook*, no 6 (1913), 1103-05.

[47]*Navy*, 14 March 1916, 7.

[48]R J A Berry and Stanley D Porteus, 'A practical method for the early recognition of feeble-mindedness and other forms of social inefficiency', *MJA* (3 August 1918), 88.

[49]Stanley D Porteus, *A Psychologist of Sorts: The Autobiography and Publications of the Inventor of the Porteus Maze Tests* (Palo Alto, California: Pacific Books, 1969).

[50]Porteus (1969), 262. Berry's head was larger than Porteus'.

[51]Porteus (1969), 60.

[52]Initially, the only Goddard advocate appeared to be W A Wood, in *Australian Medical Journal*, 20 July 1912, 601-05. Piddington was impressed and called Goddard the world's 'highest authority' on feeble-mindedness, in *HPC* (January 1930), 12.

[53]Stephen Jay Gould, *The Mismeasure of Man* (London: Penguin, 1981), 168 and 158-74.

[54]Kevles (1985), 79. See also Barker (1989), 347-75.

[55]Morris Miller, *Brain Capacity and Intelligence: Including a Comparison of Brain Measurements of Tasmanian School Boys ...* (1926), quoted in *ER*, 18 (1926-27), 151-52.

[56]Reported by Arthur Edward Machin, 'The problem of mentally-defective children in NSW from the educational and vocational points of view', *MJA* (17 March 1934), 371.

[57]Harvey Sutton to Butler, 12 May 1927, State Archives of NSW, Inspector General of the Insane, 2/8566.5. Subsequently cited as State Archives (I-G).

[58]Letter from I-G of Mental Hospitals [NSW] 21 January 1935 to Dr Byam Ellerton, Inspector of Asylums, Mental Hospitals, Qld, ibid, 5/5908.

[59]Public Health, School Medical and Dental Services, 1928-1929. Harvey Sutton, ibid, 2/8566.5.

[60]Quoted by Frank R Kerr, in *The Sterilization of Mental Defectives*, Federal Health Council, Report of the 6th Session 21-23 February 1933 (Canberra: Govt. Pr., 1933), Appendix II, 22.

[61]*MJA* (28 May 1932), 780. Judge Bevan was speaking on behalf of the RHA at the first meeting of the Council for Mental Hygiene for NSW.

[62]'Mental defectives. Among children. Doctor's survey', *SMH*, 16 May 1934, 13.

[63]I-G to Ellerton, 21 January 1935, State Archives (I-G), 5/5908.

[64]'The Feeble-minded in Australasia', *ER*, 6 (July 1914), 156.

[65]William Ernest Jones, *Report on Mental Deficiency in the Commonwealth of Australia* (Canberra: Australian Department of Health, 1929), 3.

[66] William Ernest Jones, (1929).

[67]'Mental defectives. Proposed legislation', *SMH*, 22 November 1927, 10 and 'Mental defectives. Proposed legislation', 17 March 1928, 12 (d).

[68]Kerr (1933), 16-32.

[69]'The Problems of the Mental Deficient', [a 10-page paper] presented at the Australian Directors of Education Conference, Hobart, 1930 (Tasmania: Archives Office, Ed. 73).

[70] Sir J Arthur Thompson, 'The sociological appeal to biology, *Sociological Papers*, vol 3, (1906), 185.

[71] Quoted by Alberto Manguel, in Reading Pictures (London: Bloomsbury, 2000) p. 237.

[72]Charles Kerr, 'Negative and positive eugenics', in Harry Messel (ed.), *The Biological Manipulation of Life* (Pergamon Press, 1981), 281.

[73]Kerr (1981), 282, 308.

[74]Richard Granville Waddy, in *ARHC* (1929), 63.

[75]Geoffrey Sprott, 'Mental deficiencies', *MJA* (22 March 1924), 281.

[76]Haldane quoted by G R Searle, in *Eugenics and Politics in Britain 1900-1914* (Leyden: Nordhoff, 1976), 100.

[77]Ken F Dyer, in *Australian Science Teachers Journal*, 27, no 2 (1981), 13.

[78]Barker (1989), 348 and 375.

[79]'Care of the Feeble-minded' (1914), 719.

[80]Mackellar and Welsh (1917), foreword, 8 and 47-48.

[81]Hodgkinson, 'Mental deficiency as a problem of racial hygiene', *AHRC* (1929), 35-36.

[82]Arthur, 'Idiocy. Its alarming inroads in NSW. Suicidal policies', *Sunday Times*, 26 October 1924.

[83]Berry (1918); *MJA* (14 December 1914), 485-90 and *MJA* (7 February 1920), 140.

[84] Huxley quoted by Elazar Barkan in *The Retreat of Scientific Racism* (Cambridge: CUP, 1992), 188.

[85]Angus McLaren, *Our Own Master Race: Eugenics in Canada 1885-1945* (Toronto: McClelland and Stewart, 1990), 24-25, 109.

[86]John Anderson, 'Another outbreak of virtue', *AJPP*, 6 (June 1928), 151-52.

[87]David McCallum, 'Knowledges, schooling, power: Questions about the eugenics movement in Australia', in *Australian and New Zealand History of Education Society Conference* (Adelaide: October 1992), 75-97.

[88]McCallum, *The Social Production of Merit: Education*, Psychology and Politics in Australia, 1900-1950 (London: Falmer Press, 1990), 67.

[89]*Science of Man* (22 January 1900), 223-24.

[90]Havelock Ellis, *The Task of Social Hygiene* (London: Constable, 1912), 203.

[91]Searle (1976), 100 and *BMJ* (2 August 1913), 230.

[92]John William Springthorpe, *Therapeutics, Dietetics and Hygiene: An Australian Text-Book, vol 1 – Hygiene and Dietetics* (Melbourne: James Little, 1914), 38. Comments by Powles, in MacLeod (1988), 294, 296-97, 300.

[93]Quoted in *ER*, 13 (1921-1922), 476.

[94]Dr Phyllis Burton, in 'Planned parenthood', by Staff Correspondent, *SMH*, 14 January 1949, 2 (d).

[95]Frank Macfarlane Burnet, in 'Migration and race mixture from the genetic angle', *ER*, 53 (April 1961), 97.

[96]Arthur (1912), 7. He was addressing the Women's Liberal League.

[97]Goodisson to Dr Blacker, 21 June 1939, London, Eugenic Society SA/EUG, D69.

[98]David Walker, 'White peril', *Australian Book Review*, September 1995, 33.

[99] Politicians who joined eugenics societies included Alfred Deakin (in his declining years), Richard Arthur, Jack Eldridge, T H Smeaton and F W Young. Eugenist views were also expressed by Henry Parkes, Edmund Barton, the Commissioners of the RCDBR and the *Bulletin*.

[100] Fed Daly, *From Curtin to Kerr* (Melbourne: Sun Books, 1977), 32.

[101]W F Whyte, *William Morris Hughes: His Life and Times* (Sydney: Angus & Robertson, 1957), 163-64.

[102]'Negative eugenics, national aspect of parentage', in *Race Building*, Adelaide's *Mail* (1916), 19-21.

[103]John Cooper Booth, 'Address on the Control of Venereal Disease', quoted in *NHMRC*, 9th Session November 1940, Appendix III, 26.

[104]Described by W E Agar, 'Practical eugenics in the United States', *New Outlook*, 12 May 1923, 164-65.

[105]Lewis to Sec EES, 16 June 1926, SA/EUG, E3B.

[106]Office of the Agent-General for Victoria to Sec EES, 21 October 1925, SA/EUG E3B. In his 1913 Presidential speech, Leonard Darwin had noted this problem: 'Eugenics is always in some danger of being used as a dumping-ground for cranks', quoted in Searle in (1976), 14.

[107]Brown (1927), 28-29, 30-31.

[108]Report of the Royal Commission on Child Endowment or Family Allowances, *CPP*, vol 2 (1929), 1359. H. Eugenic Control, Section 630, Question 12,022.

[109]Goodisson, 'Health examination before marriage', *Progressive Journal* (5 November 1935), 3 and 48.

[110]*AHRC* (1929), 27 and 32.

[111]Ibid, 11.

[112]'Health pass to marriage. Hughes has doubts' [*SMH*, 1937?], United Associations of Women news cuttings, ML.

[113]SA/EUG. D 69. Correspondence. Foreign Countries. The RHA's Marriage Advisory Centre leaflet is attached with Lillie Goodisson's 21 June 1939 letter to Dr C P Blacker.

[114]Lord Kilmaine (John Edward Deane Brown), 'Marriage Laws', House of Lords, 14 November 1934, Session 1933-34, vol 5, 423-31.

[115]The RHA Annual Report (1938), 6, 7 stated that 65 people had had pre-marriage tests in the first 8 months and they had been asked by the ES in London to send a copy of their questionnaire. Dr Lotte A Fink, in *Fifth International Conference on Planned Parenthood*, Proceedings (London: IPPF, 1955), 287-90, said that the RHA's examinations were suspended during the war and listed the numbers of certificates issued as 44 in 1952-1953, 37 in 1953-1954 and 47 in 1954-1955.

[116]Reported in *Sun*, 24 May 1934 and the *Australian Women's Weekly*, 9 June 1934.

[117]Allan M Brandt, *No Magic Bullet: A Social History of Venereal Disease in the United States Since 1880* (New York: OUP, 1985), 148-49.

[118]Reported in *Progressive Journal* (10 March 1936), 12, 16.

[119]Goodisson to Blacker, 21 June 1939. SA/Eugenics Soc. D69. Correspondence Foreign Countries.

[120]J B Hamilton and W D Counsel, NHMRC, First Session, February 1937, Appendix.

[121]Haire, 'Australia's population problem', *General Practitioner* (May 1941), 4.

[122]'Resolutions. No 1, Venereal Diseases', NHMRC, 15th Session, May 1943, 7.

[123]The first of the Marriage Guidance Councils was established in Sydney in 1948.

[124]Charles Brothers, 'Psychiatry and eugenics', *MJA* (5 August 1950), 213.

[125]See *Smith's Weekly*, 23 January 1932, 23; *Guardian*, 21 September 1929, 6; State Archives (I-G), 12/3476, 28 September 1933 and 2 March 1936, W Ernest Jones,

Victoria to Dr John A Wallace, Sydney re NSW Cabinet's proposed Bill on 'the control of mental defectives who are criminally inclined', ibid, 5/5916.

[126]Victor Hugo Wallace, *Women and Children First!* (Melbourne: OUP, 1946), 45.

[127]Roe (1984), 165.

[128][Alexander Lewers], 'Eugenics' *AMG* (13 December 1913), 1342.

[129]The six measures which Kirby advocated, including a proposal to segregate or sterilize the feeble-minded, are listed in *The Woman's Voice,* 1 August 1916.

[130]Joseph Kirby, *The State and the Sterilization of Defectives* (Semaphore, South Australia: Kirby, [1912?]). Archival papers in State Archives (I-G), 12/1212.1, include urgent requests in 1912 to obtain Rentoul's *Race Culture or Race Suicide: (A Plea for the Unborn).*

[131]Brothers (1950), 211-15. Queensland was the first state to abolish capital punishment in 1922 but hangings continued in other Australian states until 1967.

[132]Rusden, *The Treatment of Criminals in Relation to Science: Or Suggestions for the Prevention of Cruelty to Honest Men and Women* (Melbourne: George Robertson, 1872).

[133]Rusden, 'The Survival of the Unfittest', *AAASR* (1893), 524. Bill Bynum at the Wellcome Institute could not find any correspondence between Rusden and Charles Darwin, Pers. comm., 18 and 22 June 1992. Barry Smith wrote 'Rusden would have been bold enough to write to Charles Darwin and possibly bold enough to misrepresent Darwin's reply', Pers. comm., 13 July 1992.

[134]Henry Turner, 'The treatment of paupers and criminals', *Bankers' Magazine of Australasia* (25 April 1899), 617-18. See also Carroll in *Science of Man* (30 January 1904), 186-87.

[135]Chapple, 'The fertility of the unfit', *IMCA* (1899), 474-85 and his 1903 book of this title.

[136]This controversy is discussed in Searle (1976), 14, 121.

[137]Steven, *AMCT*, vol 2 (1911), 893 and Berry *AMG* (14 September 1912), 283.

[138]Edgar Schuster, *BMJ* (2 August 1913), 223.

[139]Havelock Ellis (1912), 30.

[140]'Control of birth. Church opposition. Strong Sydney views', *Daily Mail* [17 July 1922] and *Guardian*, 1 July 1928.

[141]For example, see W Verco *AMG* (20 July 1910), 342 and G A Syme *MJA* (16 Feb 1924), 10. Goddard, quoted by Edward J Larson, in *Sex, Race, and Science: Eugenics in the Deep South* (Baltimore: Johns Hopkins Univ Press, 1995), 29, indicated that 'it is not a question of segregation *or* sterilization, but segregation *and* sterilization'.

[142]*Science of Man* (21 July 1899), 101.

[143]ASW [Berry], 'What of the feeble-minded?', *Australian Highway* (1 August 1921), 6-7. It was anonymous but the words and the idea make it likely that RJA Berry was the author.

[144]Minogue, 'Mental deficiency among the criminal insane', *MJA* (27 October 1923), 438.

[145]Bateson, *ER*, 13 (1921-1922), 327.

[146]Xavier Herbert, in the autobiography of his first 24 years, *Disturbing Element* (1963), 262.

[147]Quoted by Angela Booth in *Teaching of Sex Hygiene*. Report of a Conference by the Workers' Educational Association of NSW, 23-25 November 1916, 2nd edn. (Sydney: Burrows, 1918), 31. Dr W A Wood, in the *Australian Medical Journal*, 20 July 1912, 604, also complained of this refusal to publish his letter by the *Spectator* which had published 'mild' articles on the topic.

[148]Booth, 'Medical prophylaxis and venereal diseases', in *AHRC* (1929), 25.

[149]Booth, 'The Subnormal class', in *AHRC* (1929), 55.

[150]Waddy (1929) 62-63. He was a Rhodes Scholar and lectured in Ophthalmology at the University of Sydney from 1922 to 1939.

[151] Rose Scott formed the Peace Society in Sydney in 1908 as a branch of the London Society.

[152]Angela Booth, *Voluntary Sterilization for Human Betterment* (Melbourne: Brown, Prior, Anderson, 1938), 5.

[153]Letter from C P Blacker to Mrs A Booth, 23 September 1938, SA/EUG, E 3.

[154]A report about a home for 24 feeble-minded children, built near Parramatta by the State Children's Relief Board, appeared in the *AMJ* (20 February 1909), 87. See also *SMH*, 28 June 1911, 5 (b), and 11 May 1928, 15 (a). Articles in the *MJA* include (27 February 1915), 196-97; (5 March 1927), 341-42 and (16 April 1927), 581-82.

[155]At their 1931 Annual General Conference, three branches of the Country Women's Association of NSW passed segregation resolutions, State Archives (I-G), 12/3464. Also see the National Council of Women of NSW, 28 June 1923, 1 April 1937, 1 December 1938 and 1 June 1939.

[156]Dr Fanny Reading, RHA One Day Conference (14 October 1931), 13.

[157]State Archives (I-G), 12/1399.2.

[158]State Archives (I-G), 5/5911.

[159]Albert Wallace Weihen, 'The medical inspection of immigrants to Australia', *AMCT* (1911), 635.

[160]See Schuster (1913), 223 and Baylebridge, *National Notes*, 3rd edn., (Sydney: Tallabila Press, 1936), 30.

[161]Horder, *MJA* (5 October 1935), 438

[162]Mackellar and Welsh (1917), 64.

[163]Material in the *Medical Journal of Australia* includes eugenics editorials: (21 November 1931), 655-56 and (5 October 1935), 438; letters: (26 December 1931),

825-6; (23 January 1932), 143; (6 February 1932), 211 and (27 February 1932), 311-12; articles: (9 March 1935), 295-305 and 318-21. In 1930 pro-sterilization articles appeared in: *Guardian*, 7 May, 1; *SMH*, 23 May, 15; 4 June, 15 and 25 June, 15. Opposition was expressed in *Labor Daily*, 14 June, 10 and 21 June, 17.

164 AHRC (1929): Addison's resolutions, 65-66 and Goodisson's response, 68. RHA Annual Report (1934) 4, indicates that Addison also addressed the RHA on this topic in November 1933.

165 Noble was quoted in *SMH*, 18 September 1929, 19 (c). In 1926, a NSW Mental Deficiency Bill was prepared – see *Commonwealth Yearbook* (1926), 477.

166 'Mental Hygiene', *Telegraph*, 25 July 1933. Other women's deputations on this topic are listed in *SMH*, 22 November 1927, 10; 17 March 1928, 12; 18 May 1928, 8.

167 Noble, *MJA* (12 July 1924), 31-35. Professor William Osborne in *SMH*, 12 August 1929, 15, also warned of the dangers of sterilization. See also *MJA* (21 November 1931), 655-56.

168 Quoted in *Labor Daily*, 28 September 1925, 5 (d).

169 Brothers (1950), 215.

170 Jeff Goldhar, 'The sterilization of women with an intellectual disability', *University of Tasmania Law Review*, 10 no 2 (1991), 171. Bacchi (1980) 205, wrote 'In 1930 Arthur presented a Bill calling for the sterilization of defectives'. Her mistake was repeated by Cawte, in *Historical Studies* (April 1986), 38 and Lewis, in *Managing Madness: Psychiatry and Society in Australia 1788-1980* (Canberra: AGPS, 1988), 130.

171 Dr Arthur on Eugenics, *The Liberal Woman*, 1 September 1913, 193-94.

172 *The Woman's Voice*, 1 July 1920, 10.

173 Danger of the half-wit. Sterilization must come, says Minister', *Telegraph*, 15 July 1929, 4 (d).

174 NSWPD, 27 March 1930, 4182 and *SMH*, 1 February 1930, 18.

175 Minister is opposed by own party', *Labor Daily*, 23 May 1930, 5 (f).

176 Cora Hodson, 'Sterilization laws', *ER*, 21 (January 1930), 324.

177 Resolution 13, 5th Session of the Federal Health Council of Australia, 24 and 25 March 1931, 4.

178 Letter by McCallum to Cumpston, 23 March 1932, AA. ACT, A 1928/1. Item 362/20.

179 See *Federal Inquiry into the Sterilization of Mental Defectives*, 1933, prepared by Kerr as Appendix II of the 6th session of the FHC, 21-23 February 1933, 16-28. See also ibid, H Downes, CMO to the D-G, Summary, 28 March 1934, 2-3 and 24, AA/ACT, A1928/1 – Item 362/20.

180 State Crown Solicitor's Office, Sydney in response to a letter on 20 September 1934 from the I-G of Mental Hospitals, Sydney, State Archives (I-G), 5908.

181 Searle (1976), 100.

[182]Goodisson to Cumpston, 3 December 1935 and 13 December, AA/ACT, A461/1 Item D347/1/1, 'Sterilization of the unfit'.

[183]Sutton (1944), 48.

[184]See for example, O V Briscoe et al, 'Legality of eugenic sterilization in Australia', 185-89 and the editorial, 'The case for eugenic sterilization', 219-220, in *MJA*, 29 July 1967.   The 1980 statistic is quoted by George F Brown and Ellen H Moskowitz in 'Moral and policy issues in long-acting contraception', *Annual Review of Public Health*, vol 18, 1997, 381.

[185] V H Wallace, 'Vasectomy', *MJA* (27 January 1973), 212.

[186]Larson (1995), 38-39 and Ian Robert Dowbiggin, *Keeping America Sane: Psychiatry and Eugenics in the United States and Canada, 1880-1940* (Ithaca, Cornell University Press, 1997), 120.

[187]Ernest Jones (1929), 17.

[188] In 1928 this Canadian Act was reported in the *SMH*, 9 March, 11 (b), and 10 March, 17 (c).

[189]D Wahlsten, 'Leilani Muir versus the philosopher king: Eugenics on trial in Alberta', *Genetica*, vol 99 (2-3), 1997, 185-98

[190] Hon A J H Saw, Mental Deficiency Bill, 12 November 1929, WAPD, 82 (1929), 1459.

[191]Booth (1938), 12, referred to these Canadian provinces as 'countries'.

[192]Angus McLaren, *Eugenics in Canada, 1885-1945* (Toronto: McClelland and Stewart, 1990), 100.

[193]H Tasman Lovell, 'The Tasmanian Mental Deficiency Act', *AJPP*, vol 1 (December 1923), 285.

[194]Emanuel Sydney (Syd) Morris (1888-1957) became Tasmania's Director of Public Health in 1920.   He outlined his plans for a scheme of 'mutual benefit to themselves [people with mental deficiency] and the community of which they form a part' in 'the Administrative control of mental deficiency in Tasmania', *Health*, 2 no 3 (May 1924), 80.

[195]Faith Schenk and Alan S Parkes, quoted by Edward J Larson in 'The rhetoric of eugenics: Expert authority and the Mental Deficiency Bill', *The British Journal for the History of Science*, 24 (March 1991), 48, 57-60. Some British eugenists claimed this as their 'principal legislative achievement', even though it was only passed after all references to eugenics had been removed in response to public hostility.

[196]Miller, *MJA* (7 February 1925), 134 and the *Commonwealth Yearbook* (1926), 477.

[197]WAPD, 82 (1929), Mental Deficiency Bill debates: 14 August, 343; 17 Sept, 739-47; 19 Sept, 823-26; 22 Oct, 1080-82; 30 Oct, 1231; 12 Nov, 1450-62; 20 Nov, 1684-91 and 10 Dec, 2009-20.

[198]J Bentley, I-G of the Insane, WA Lunacy Dept, to Chief Quarantine Officer General, Commonwealth Dept of Health, 10 August 1931, Federal Health Council of Australia.

[199]C Downing, Hon Sec National Council Women of Vic to Mr W C Marr, Minister for Health, 20 October 1933, AA/ACT, A461/1, Item D347/1/1, 'Sterilization of the Unfit'.

[200]Ernest Jones to John A Wallace, I-G of Mental Hospitals Sydney, 2 March 1936, State Archives (I-G), 5/5916.

[201]Ernest Jones to Wallace, 25 March 1936, ibid. On 12 August 1938 Professor Agar, Eugenics Society of Victoria wrote to the Chief Secretary of Victoria asking him to add a sterilization clause to the Mental Deficiency Bill, V H Wallace Papers, University of Melbourne Archives.

[202]Edward Paris Nesbitt, 'Insanity and crime', *AAASR* (1892), 575.

[203]This NSW Act made provision for the special care and treatment of mentally defective prisoners. It was replaced by *Miscellaneous Acts (Mental Health) Repeal and Amendment Act* no 181, 1983.

[204]'Mental defectives. Sterilization Bill for Queensland', *Telegraph*, 7 November 1930, 2.

[205]Home Secretary's Office to Raphael Cilento, Division of Tropical Hygiene, 10 August 1931 forwarded to D-G of Health on 12 August 1931. AA/ACT, A1928/1, Item 362/20.

[206]'Sterilization. Weaver [Qld Minister for Health] will study BMA report', *Sun*, 10 January 1934, 10 (f) and 'Sterilization. Inquiry for Queensland Government', *SMH*, 11 January 1934, 6 (f).

[207] Wayne Jarred from the Queensland Parliamentary Library could not locate any Bill dealing with this between 1930-1935, Pers. Comm, 22 June 1993. Dr Humphrey Crammond, Chairman of the Historical Committee of the Old Branch of the AMA could not provide information about the BMA sub-committee appointed to report to Queensland's Home Department, Pers. Comm, 14 July 1993.

[208]Richard Butler, Premier of SA to Prime Minister, 16 Nov 1936, AA/ACT D347/1/1.

[209]Ibid, J H L Cumpston to Sec, Prime Minister's Department, Canberra, 27 November 1936.

[210]Report of the Royal Commission (1929), 1359, paragraph 630.

[211]SAPD (1936), 696-704, 940-45, 1169-76, 1400-05 and 1557.

[212]John T Noonan, *Contraception: A History of its Treatment by the Catholic Theologians and Canonists*, (Cambridge, Mass: Belknap Press of Harvard Univ Press, 1986), 430-31.

[213]In 'The wider implications of the policy of sterilization' (a paper presented at the RHA One Day Conference, 14 October 1931, 15) the Reverend H N Baker

pointed out that even if no childbearing occurred among the unfit, this would 'prevent only 17%, at the most, of defectives being born'.

214Reported in the *SMH*, 23 July 1931, 10 (d).

215'Sterilization will not reduce idiocy. BMA Committee's conclusions', *Telegraph*, 24 June 1932. In a 1934 lecture to the Catholic Newman Society, Sydney cancer specialist Dr Herbert M Moran said it was wrong to assume that mental deficiency was a single or 'largely a hereditary disease' or that the national stock was degenerating, *SMH*, 25 April 1934, 15.

216C P Blacker, 'Eugenic sterilization in Germany', *Lancet* (10 June 1933), 1265-66. Sheila Block noted that from 1934 until the beginning of the war 'approximately 360,000 people were sterilized – more than 35 times the number reported to have occurred in the US between 1907 and 1930, most against the will of the individual concerned', quoted by Sheila Faith Weiss in *Race Hygiene and National Efficiency: The Eugenics of Wilhelm Schallmayer* (Berkeley, California: University of California Press, 1987), 155.

217AA files on *Sterilization of Mental Defectives* (1933) contained: 'Sterilise millions!, *Telegraph* (Sydney), 30 October 1933; 'Sterilization law. Eugenic reform in Germany', *West Australian,* 18 November 1933; 'Sterilization. 400 thousand marked in Germany', *Canberra Times*, 22 December 1933; and 'Sterilization. German law may defeat end' and December 30, 1933. See also *SMH*, 2 December 1933, 15 and 22 December 1933, 9 (b).

218'Socially unfit. Sterilization idea. Intense controversy in England', *Canberra Times*, 27 October 1933, also reported in *SMH*, 27 October 1933, 12 (b).

219Michael Freeden, 'Eugenics and progressive thought: A study of ideological affinity', *Historical Journal*, 22 (1979), 667-68.

220John Macnicol, 'Eugenics and the campaign for voluntary sterilization in Britain between the wars', *Social History of Medicine*, 2 (August 1989), 147-69.

221Federal Labor politician Billy Hughes introduced a Marriage Certificates Bill in 1913. In 1930 the NSW Mental Defectives Bill was introduced as non-party legislation.

222Adams (1990), 220-21 and 224.

223Kevles (1985), 64.

224'Sterilization called "utterly immoral"', *Telegraph*, 9 December 1933, 3 (e).

225Dakin was quoted as saying this in the *Sun and Guardian*, 18 August 1935, 7 (a).

226*Whither Away? A Study of Race Psychology and the Factors Leading to Australia's National Decline*, by A Psychologist and A Physician [Leslie John Javis Nye and John Bostock] (Sydney: Angus and Robertson, 1936), 40, 79.

227Reported in 'Referenda sought' [on sterilization], *SMH*, 18 May 1936, 7 (h). The April 1936 letter from the Australian Legion, signed by John H Gaffney, Honorary Organiser, is in Perth's Battye Library at PR2485.

[228]'Sterilization of the unfit', *Argus*, 11 July, 9 (c) and 'Proposed legislation. Action by Mr Disney, MLC', *Argus*, 8 August 1934, 8 (e) and VPD, LC (12 September 1934, 1753.

[229]Paul Dane, 'Sterilization of the unfit', *MJA* (23 May 1936), 711.

[230]W E Agar to Hon H S Bailey, Chief Secretary of Victoria, 12 August 1938.

[231]Quoted by Gail Griffith, 'The Feminist Club of New South Wales, 1914-1970: A history of feminist politics in decline', *Hecate*, 14 no 1 (1988), 64.

[232]T Brailsford Robertson, *The Spirit of Research* (Adelaide: F W Preece, 1931), 199-200, reprinting his earlier article from *The Hibbert Journal* (July 1929).

[233]Haire, typescript *Hymen*, 29 January 1936, 22, Sydney: Fisher Library, ibid.

[234]Phyllis Grosskurth, *Havelock Ellis : A Biography* (New York: New York University Press, 1985), 415.

[235]Mark B Hayne, 'Australian reactions to Hitler's accession to power, February-June 1933', *Journal of the Royal Australian Historical Society*, 71 (June 1985), 59-74.

[236]The book was published in London by Methuen in 1937. For comments see, 'War or oblivion. Hitler's alternatives. Professor Roberts's views', *SMH*, 26 October 1937, 17.

[237]'Book banned by Nazis', *Argus*, 13 December 1937, 1 (f) and 'Book of the Week, Why did the Nazis ban Professor Roberts's book?', ibid, 14 December 1937, 10(d).

[238]Grant McBurnie, 'Constructing Sexuality in Victoria 1930-1950: Sex Reformers Associated with the Victorian Eugenics Society' (PhD thesis, Clayton, Victoria: Monash University, 1989), 301, stated that Duras was born in 1896 in Bonn, Germany and trained there as an MD.

[239]W E Agar, *Eugenics and the Future of the Australian Population* (Melbourne: ESV, 1939), 14-15.

[240]Grey Ewan, 'Sterilization of the unfit', *MJA*, (27 February 1932), 311-12.

[241]John Maynard Smith, *The Theory of Evolution* (Cambridge: CUP, 1993), 328, 345.

[242]Fink (1956), 287. In contrast, in 1949 fears that women at refugee hostels had been sterilized in German concentration camps prompted the Commonwealth Department of Health to investigate. The number of their pregnancies provided reassurance, AA/A434/1, Item 49.3/13646.

[243]Billy Hughes, quoted by Douglas Sladen, in *From Boundary-rider to Prime Minister: Hughes of Australia. The Man of the Hour* (London: Hutchinson and Co, 1916), 72.

[244]'The "unfit"', *Australian Worker*, 10 June 1920, 13 and 'A threatened evil. Dangerous sterilization fad', *Labor Daily*, 14 June 1930, 10 (b), and 21 June 1930, 7 (d).

Conclusion

This book has reconsidered the contribution which eugenics made to Australian history by examining three propositions: that eugenics in Australia in the early 20th century was readily accepted because of fears about the declining birth rate; that Australian eugenic ideas, while mainly derivative, had certain distinctly Australian qualities; and that eugenics influenced the developments of Australian health services, particularly family planning and public health.

I used primary sources to fill gaps in the history of eugenics in Australia. In addition, I have suggested ways of redefining and correcting the interpretations of several scholars who have claimed that Australian eugenics was weak before 1914; dismissed the importance of the nature-nurture debate, and neglected the role of environmental eugenics. It is also necessary to qualify the view that concerns about the feeble-minded had waned by 1928 and that only zealots advocated eugenic sterilisation. Eugenists, individuals in sympathy with eugenic goals, and eugenics-related organisations played major roles from the 1920s to 1950s, particularly in the fields of public health and family planning. In the 1920s and 1930s many politicians, academics and the public accepted eugenics and it was a frequent topic in books and in literary, current affairs and women's magazines. Such writing about eugenics, and the language which eugenists used, revealed information about its impact and the extent to which eugenics developed distinctively in this country.

Australia's political and social developments reflected eugenic beliefs and progressivism, which aimed to increase national efficiency and vitality through enlightened state intervention in programs such as sanitation, town planning and quarantine. Progressivism is also visible in the 1904 Royal Commission on the Decline of the Birth-Rate and on the Mortality of Infants in New South Wales, in attempts to eradicate venereal diseases, and in efforts to prove medically that white settlement of the tropics was safe. Other such initiatives were the introduction of baby health centres in 1904, the implementation of child endowment schemes from 1912, the establishment of the Commonwealth Department of Health in 1921, and the decision to establish a Commonwealth Royal Commission on Health in 1925 to again examine the problems of VD, the falling birth rate and the high maternal and infant death rate. In some government reports, including the Report of the Royal Commission on Child Endowment or Family Allowances and the Report on Mental Deficiency in the Commonwealth of Australia, both published in 1929, eugenic ideas were expressed explicitly. The same is true of the Commonwealth report on Sterilisation of Mental Defectives published in 1933, and eugenic ideas were frequently quoted in parliamentary attempts to pass mental deficiency laws. Eugenics was implicit in work of the NSW Director-General of Public Health, Dr Emanuel Sydney Morris who, in the Medical Science and National Health Section of the 1939 Australian and New Zealand Association for the Advancement of Science Congress, reported that the state was continuing to increase its responsibility for managing the whole of an individual's physical life. Eugenics was also evident in the work of the National Fitness Councils, and in reports in 1943 and 1944 by Kathleen Gordon, the Commonwealth Department of Health's National Fitness Officer.

Precursors to Eugenics

In the years between 1904 and 1930, eugenics organizations operated in many countries. Australia responded enthusiastically to these new theories which, emerging after the industrial revolution, occurring first in Britain in the 1780s, and had 'tilled the ground' in which the eugenics 'seed' germinated.[1] The ready acceptance of eugenics was understandable in a new, sparsely populated country which was attempting to establish itself on the fringes of the British Empire. Before 1914, Australia had gained a reputation as the world's social laboratory. In 1909 the first Commonwealth Statistician, Sir George Knibbs, also claimed that Australia was the anthropological laboratory of the world. As Barry Butcher has demonstrated, Australia was used as the world's anthropological quarry, with studies of Australian Aboriginals by Sir Walter Baldwin Spencer and others providing 'evidence' that informed Charles Darwin's theories. These evolutionary theories received world acceptance and gave a scientific legitimacy to the belief that Aboriginals were inferior and destined for extinction, a view which Australian pastoralists and politicians had long held. Social Darwinian beliefs were also a part of the restrictive immigration policy which from 1901 aimed to ensure the continuation of a British-Australian nationality. A eugenist later commented that 'unconsciously, the White Australia Policy was one of greatest eugenics laws ever passed in Australia'.[2] This policy was linked with the themes of Australian nationalism, British imperialism and Caucasian racism which contributed to the early 20th century debates about the dangers facing Australia's 'national stock'. The preoccupations of this young nation provided both stimuli and nurture for eugenics.

Eugenics was attractive early last century because it offered a scientifically respectable option when the idea of white superiority was challenged by declining birth rates in the western world while Asian populations were expanding. As well, in 1905 the Japanese had fought and defeated the Russians, and in 1908 a black boxer had beaten a white one in a world title fight which was held in Sydney. As a result Australians were intensely worried about the dangers of 'yellow peril', fearing an Asian invasion and believing that a declining white birth-rate indicated that a process of 'racial suicide' was already taking place. When NSW Government Statistician Timothy Coghlan produced evidence of this decline it caused such alarm that in 1904 a Royal Commission was set up to determine the causes and find solutions to this problem, defining it as 'a respectable, even pressing public issue' which 'cleared the way for state involvement'.[3] Without this fearfulness about a small and diminishing population and the acceptance of the legitimacy of the government having a role to rectify this problem, it is unlikely that there would have been such a favourable response to eugenists' proposals for improving the 'national stock'.

Added to anxieties about population size, however, was the further fear that national fitness was being eroded by an escalating process of mental, moral and physical decay. In Britain, such fears stemmed from 19th century degeneracy theories which were used to argue that, if counter-measures were not taken, deficiencies would intensify in successive generations. The reduction in family size prompted anxieties about class-linked fertility differences, with the rich having few children and the poor having many. It was also feared that misguided social welfare efforts had allowed the 'unfit' to survive and outnumber the 'fit', and that this differential fertility was the principal cause of national decay. Debate about racial decay was intensified in Britain by the high rejection rates of army recruits and by the reverses which the British suffered in the Boer War. The public and parliamentary demands for national efficiency prompted the establishment in 1903 of an Inter-Departmental Committee on Physical Deterioration. Although the subsequent report stressed environmental causes of ill health, it was widely believed that the urban poor were 'degenerating', even 'degenerate'. It was in this climate, where Britain feared both the loss of its Empire and internal collapse, that Francis Galton successfully launched his plans in 1904 to improve the race. The Eugenics Education Society was established in London three years after the enthusiastic reception of Galton's eugenics proposals.

Defining Eugenics

Caution is needed when considering the enigmatic subject of eugenics because, for many people, like Lewis Carroll's Humpty Dumpty character, 'it means just what I choose it to mean – neither more nor less'. There have been endless disputes about what constituted eugenic fitness and unfitness with the result that people had many different responses to eugenics. At the 1929 Australian Racial Hygiene Congress, Linda Littlejohn mused that even if science knew how to improve the race, it would be difficult to choose whether the model should be 'a Mussolini or a Gandhi, a Darwin or a Ford - a tall man or a short one, a giant in brawn or a giant in intellect - a prohibitionist or an anti-prohibitionist'.[4]

The causes which Australian eugenists endorsed ranged from censorship, sex education, temperance and prevention or eradication of venereal disease, to pure food regulations and the health and happiness of babies. To avoid what Geoffrey Searle has described as an 'absurd situation', I followed his plan for discriminating between the different kinds and levels of commitment to eugenics by dividing eugenists into four main categories. The first are 'strong' eugenists, those for whom eugenics provided the only means of escape from national collapse and decay. The second were 'weak' eugenists who grafted aspects of eugenics onto their underlying political creeds. The third group, which figured importantly in Australia, were the 'medical' eugenists, mainly doctors and health workers who considered eugenics not as a political belief but as a branch of public health which needed government support to improve health or reduce disease and suffering. Also important was the fourth group of 'career' eugenists, consisting mostly of academics and practitioners in such fields as genetics, statistics, education or psychology, who sympathised with the objectives only where they stimulated interest in their own field of study. Finally, there was a marginal group of eugenists who used eugenic ideas to promote unrelated causes.

Few Australians contributed significantly to the eugenics movement and they were largely isolated from overseas eugenists and from each other. However, these eugenists were influential. Most of these would fit Searle's 'medical' or 'career' eugenist categories, factors which helped to determine the direction and impact of the movement. I used Searle's classification in biographical sketches of four people who played major roles: Marion Piddington, John Eldridge, Lillie Goodisson and Henry Twitchin. They were born approximately within the same decade, made their contributions later in life, lacked significant scientific training, and revered overseas eugenic thinking. Two became involved in eugenics because of personal experiences: Twitchin, because he believed he had 'inherited bad health', and Goodisson because she had a syphilitic husband. Australian-born Eldridge and Piddington, and Welsh-born Goodisson, promoted eugenics in this country. English-born Twitchin, a 'career' eugenist who amassed a fortune as a pastoralist in Australia, assisted the cause of the British movement. Piddington, Australia's only 'strong' eugenist, and Goodisson, a 'medical' eugenist, remained unwavering in their commitment to the cause. Piddington believed that human history could be explained in terms of eugenics and crusaded desperately for a eugenic utopia, and Goodisson used both eugenics and politics to further her anti-VD and pro-contraception goals.

Eldridge was a 'weak' eugenist who endorsed eugenics while it aided his political career. The complexity of eugenics is underlined by the fact that the projects of these four eugenists appear to be unrelated to political theory. Eldridge and Piddington were affiliated with the Labor Party, and while he favoured an environmental approach, she espoused hereditarian eugenics. Goodisson and Twitchin were politically conservative but, while she focused on women's health, he dreamed of eradicating the unfit.

Something Old, Something New in Australian Eugenics

Australia frequently sought overseas advice and expertise and this was true of eugenics which was largely derived from the British and, to a lesser extent, American movements. For example, Australia followed the British preference for voluntary rather than regulatory measures to control the 'unfit'. This is not surprising as many Australian doctors, scientists and academics who advocated eugenics were either British-born or had 'appropriated a British culture of science and directed it to colonial and national purposes'.[5] There were also differences: for example, environmental concerns were of great importance in the early years of the Australian eugenics movement, at a time when hereditary determinism dominated the movements in countries such as Britain and America. Australia's colonial circumstances provide obvious reasons for this, as the country's isolation and harsh climate might be inimical to white survival. Eugenics was welcomed by this new nation which needed to boost its population and fitness in order to fill the continent as protection from Asian invasion. While these factors were not unique to Australia, they featured much more prominently than in either Britain or America. In addition, the most committed Australian eugenists before 1914 were ardent supporters of environmental reforms.

In 1916 Marion Piddington launched an unsuccessful crusade for 'eugenic' motherhood. By this she meant artificial insemination, also called celibate or scientific motherhood, and eutelegenesis. While Marie Stopes had reluctantly mentioned this in one of her books,

Piddington's suggestion found little support and she suffered years of censure because of it.

Australia's population was small, so that it is not surprising that although there were some influential eugenists, there was no cohesive 'movement' comparable in any sense to those of Britain or America. Between 1911 and 1936, five Australian states made seven attempts to launch eugenics organizations. Four attempts were made before 1914 but only two groups – the Racial Hygiene Association of NSW (RHA) and the Eugenics Society of Victoria (ESV) - survived more than a decade and they were bitter rivals. Alison Turtle has described the RHA as 'the main outlet of the [eugenics] movement'.[6]   The reality however, was shown in a 1939 letter from the RHA to the British Eugenics Society's Dr Blacker, informing him that the organization was 'not a Eugenic Society.' Eugenics became a 'flag of convenience' for the RHA after the split with Piddington.   When the RHA established a birth control clinic in 1933 (two years after Piddington established hers), the RHA's primary interest was birth control, a controversial cause that faced powerful pronatalist, medical and religious opposition. While many members of the Australian medical profession sympathized with eugenic goals, most doctors (prior to 1960) and the Catholic Church opposed birth control.[7] The RHA allied itself with supportive politicians and sympathetic doctors.

In two important ways the Australian eugenics movement as a whole differed from those of other countries: class was less relevant in Australia than in Britain, and racial tensions played a lesser role in Australia than they did in America or South Africa. In 1887 Timothy Coghlan noted that no Australians were 'born to poverty' and, as it was assumed that the Aborigines were a dying race, from 1901 the restrictive immigration policy ensured the continuation of a predominantly Anglo-Saxon heritage. Consequently, neither class nor race featured prominently in the Australian eugenics experience. In Australia, the 'unfit' who featured in negative eugenics schemes were principally the mentally defective and people affected by 'racial poisons' but not the poor (as in Britain) nor those of non-white races (as in America and South Africa). The class difference is well illustrated by Australian child endowment schemes which provided universal, not class-based benefits. On three occasions, in 1912 and twice in 1922, Britain's Eugenics Education Society complained that the Australian schemes would increase 'pauper stock' and swell 'the less valuable classes'. Economic difficulties in 1928 prompted the Commonwealth Government to consider providing benefits to children of the 'right kind of stock' [determined by health not wealth] and to withhold them from only the 'unmistakeably feeble-minded' and those with genetically transmissible defects.[8]

Another significant difference lies in the antagonism displayed by the medical profession towards eugenics in Britain which was largely absent in Australia, probably because many members of the medical profession were also eugenists. Many Australian doctors became eugenists as young men and their beliefs have left a legacy in the health system which they later helped to build. This was particularly so in the case of Dr John (Howard) Cumpston. At the outset of his career in the first two decades of this century, eugenics was accepted as a science and these beliefs were manifest in the workings of the Commonwealth Department of Health, after he became its first Director-General of Health in 1921. The same was true of Sir Thomas Anderson Stuart, who played an important role in the development of the Faculty of Medicine at the University of Sydney and in the establishment of the Institute of Tropical Medicine in Townsville in 1909 to help develop the tropics. The political significance of the Institute is indicated by the fact that it was one of Australia's first medical research institutes. 'Medical' eugenists such as Dr Richard Arthur, the NSW Minister for Health, were influential as politicians. In addition, this group of eugenists also wielded power as administrators, for example, doctors E Sydney Morris, W Ramsay Smith, Professor Harvey Sutton, Sir Raphael Cilento and Sir James Barrett. The influence of individuals with eugenic sympathies was also evident in many other fields and these too have been considered in this book.

Australian Responses to Eugenics

Australia reacted quickly to eugenics, with enthusiastic responses coming from state and federal governments, professions, the churches and individuals.   In 1912 eugenics enjoyed such prestige and respectability that an invitation to attend the first International Eugenics Congress in London was dispatched from Downing Street to the Australian Prime Minister, and that Australia was represented by four official delegates, headed by Sir John Cockburn, a former Premier of South Australia. Despite this official imprimatur, in two decades the fortunes of eugenics had plummeted so that in 1932 the Australian government declined the invitation to the third international congress.

In the 'golden' years of eugenics before 1914, the Australian government's response to reports of a degenerating population was to undertake anthropological surveys, first to check children's physical fitness, and later to determine the numbers of the 'feeble-minded'. Dr Mary Booth told the Australasian Association for The Advancement of Science delegates in 1908 that eugenists relied on such data to study 'what the race may become'.   The NSW Department of Public Instruction instituted medical examinations of school children: these studies were augmented in 1909 by the Sydney branch of the British Science Guild, which aimed to improve the school children's physical fitness.   In 1916 Jack Eldridge, Secretary of the NSW Eugenics Education Society, described these surveys as 'one of the most important events' in the State's history.   Unlike overseas eugenists' anxieties about differential fertility rates according to class, or about questionable physical prowess, in Australia these were overshadowed by fears that the feeble-minded were increasing and would soon outnumber the 'fit'.

In 1911 the Australasian Medical Congress delegated a committee to find out the extent of feeble-mindedness in each state. The national committee presented its report in 1914 and proposed to respond to the problem with support from the medical profession, educational and charitable bodies, eugenics societies, women's organizations, churches and the press. Assumptions that the feeble-minded were 'markedly more prolific than those normally constituted' were widely publicised by notables such as Sir Charles Mackellar, the dominant figure in the 1904 Royal Commission into the birth rate decline. Studies of school children, undertaken in Victoria by Professor Richard Berry and Stanley Porteus in 1918, and in NSW by Dr Harvey Sutton in 1925, did much to convince Australians that the proportion of mentally deficient people in the community posed a large and growing problem. Before genetics was included in university medical courses in 1938, knowledge about inherited characteristics was rudimentary. This explains why there was such fear of mental deficiency, and why people believed that it could be eliminated in a few generations if affected individuals did not reproduce.

From 1942 Leslie Bailey provided an unusual style of positive eugenics at Hopewood House in Bowral, in which 86 babies born 'under unfortunate circumstances' developed into fine, healthy children with superior teeth. He concentrated on nurtural (environmental) eugenics, paying particular attention to the provision of a wholesome diet, exercise and fresh air. In the 1950s, the *Australian Women's Weekly* sponsored a competition with a hidden positive eugenics agenda which was to encourage childbearing among the 'fit'. Eugenists soon discarded any plans for positive eugenics and instead concentrated on negative eugenics, which aimed to minimise or prevent 'unfit' births by implementing strategies of prevention and control. The first aimed to combat 'racial poisons' which were thought to threaten healthy parenthood. The second attempted to regulate marriage and advocated legislation for the care, control or sterilisation of 'unfit' people.

There is no evidence to support Stephen Garton's claim that a 1927 to 1928 Commonwealth survey had concluded that feeble-mindedness was 'not as rampant in NSW as many eugenicists had argued'.[9] No survey was done at this time. The national survey, which was not announced until August 1928, was headed by Dr Ernest Jones, who was instructed to inquire into the prevalence of mental deficiency and to recommend methods of treatment. Jones' report, published in December 1929, contained nothing at all about levels of feeble-mindedness, but proposed that each state should establish psychological clinics to examine mentally deficient children and young adults. Jones had examined issues of concern to eugenists: detection, segregation, sterilisation and marriage prevention of the unfit, eliminating syphilis, and control or prohibition of alcohol. Contrary to Garton's assertion that by 1927-28 mental deficiency was no longer seen as a problem, many eugenists, significant numbers of the public, and federal and state governments considered that it was an extremely grave problem.

Numerous delegations from eugenics groups and women's organizations to politicians in the 1920s and 1930s urging that mental defectives should be sterilized or placed in custodial care, and the extensive outpourings on the subject in medical journals and newspapers over this period are evidence of a wide concern. As a result of this pressure, and in response to a request made by the Federal Health Council in 1931, the Commonwealth Government conducted an extensive inquiry into the sterilisation of mental defectives.[10]   It recommended laws to allow selective voluntary sterilisation of people with, or likely to transmit, a mental defect or disorder. State boards were to give approval for sterilisation and there was to be provision for appeal.[11]   However, neither the Commonwealth nor individual states took any action. After receiving legal advice that Britain had decided against eugenic sterilisation, Dr Cumpston declared that the Commonwealth had no powers on the subject: in 1929 he had advised the *Royal Commission on Child Endowment* that the Commonwealth should exercise its constitutional powers on the matter.

The evidence of parliamentary debates does not support Garton's claim that Labor governments 'on the whole' were 'more wary' of passing legislation which proposed segregation.[12]   Indeed, many attempts to pass eugenic legislation in Australia were made by the Labor Party or had bipartisan support.[13]   Propositions that eugenists were mostly right-wing politically have been dismissed as a 'myth' by Mark Adams who noted that eugenists included communists, socialists, liberals, conservatives and fascists, all of which 'suggests that any simplistic political classification of the movement cannot sustain analysis'.[14]

Daniel Kevles also emphasized the political diversity of British and American eugenists whose only common bond was in being largely 'middle to upper middle class, white, Anglo Saxon, predominantly Protestant and educated'.[15]   Australian eugenists also had homogeneous backgrounds with similarly diverse political views which both mirrored and shaped those of the wider community. Anthea Hyslop noted that, early this century, Australian liberals, radicals and conservatives had surprisingly similar views, all of which agreed on the 'need for a larger, healthier, racially pure population, and for the preventive and scientific treatment of social problems'.[16]   My findings strongly support those of Adams, Kevles and Hyslop.

While eugenics sought to improve national fitness through better health, it was also frequently described as a branch of preventive medicine because one of its aims was to prevent the unfit from breeding. Before 1920 this goal resembled a religious crusade for some but the literature does not support Claudia Thame's claim that 'the extreme position of sterilisation of the unfit was held by only a small minority of zealots', nor is there evidence that 'the *Medical Journal of Australia* published only two articles advocating the "scientific improvement of the race" during the 1920s and 1930s and made no editorial comment on the subject at all'.[17]   Similarly, there is little evidence to support David McCallum's claim that 'ideas about sterilisation did not gain much acceptance in Australia'.[18]   An examination of contemporary literature disproves both claims. During the 1920s and the early 1930s, there was intense debate and extensive writing about this issue, with many articles appearing in the *Medical Journal of Australia.*[19]   In June 1934 a special meeting of the RHA Executive tried to agree whether it was preferable to segregate or sterilize the 'mentally unfit', and to decide which persons had 'the right to be sterilized'.[20]   In 1936 the RHA discussed the issue 'several times' and found the lack of any legal ruling 'very unsatisfactory'.[21]   In 1950 Dr Charles Brothers, Chairman of the Tasmanian Mental Deficiency Board, praised Britain for 'her usual wise conservatism' in refraining from passing any laws about sterilisation although the subject had been 'discussed for many years'.[22]

Despite widespread debates, no Bill for the sterilisation of mental defectives was ever presented in the NSW Parliament. Several scholars have mistakenly reported that Dr Arthur had done so.[23]   The nearest Arthur came to this was his comment in 1929 that 'sterilisation is an inevitable necessity, but the time is not ripe for its introduction'.[24] Although Arthur said he 'was inclined to accept an amendment in connection with sterilisation if such was moved',[25] no such amendment was proposed and Arthur's own party opposed the Bill.[26] There has been a similar misconception about state legislation on feeble-mindedness. Garton has suggested that 'mental defectives' legislation was passed 'in Tasmania (1920), Victoria (1922), Queensland (1938) and New South Wales (1939)'.[27] Tasmania passed legislation especially for the feeble-minded but it was the only Australian state which did. Although some states passed what might appear to be 'mental defectives' laws, these were Lunacy Acts or Prisons Acts, and related to law and order, rather than eugenics.

Motherhood and migration have always been important for Australia. Pronatalist governments promoted migration in the belief that a large, steadily increasing population was vital for the country's wealth and progress. British migration was encouraged, including the (now notorious) child migrant schemes. The imperial motive was to send the colonies these little 'bricks for Empire building' under the philanthropic guise of 'child rescue'. The eugenic motive was to transplant children, rather than adults, from urban slums in the belief that they would escape slum-induced degeneration. If the British Government could not discourage the poor from having children, they could encourage them to migrate. Some Australian eugenists worried about such migrants, arguing that Australia should only receive 'thoroughbreds', not those affected by 'racial poisons'.

Women as mothers played a central role in the plans for boosting the nation's fitness. Hereditary determinists such as William Baylebridge saw them as 'the sacred vessels of maternity'; pronatalists such as Octavius Beale commented that feminism was 'a formidable adversary of fecundity', and eugenist doctors, including Truby King, Mary Booth and Sir James Barrett, felt that higher education would divert women from the primary role of motherhood. Feminists and eugenists agreed that the mothers of the race needed education. I have considered the links between the women's movement and eugenics in the light of recent criticisms by historians who have examined the work of birth control pioneers in Britain, America and Australia. A more accurate view of the pioneers' aims was obtained by examining the humanitarian work of their clinics than by considering their eugenic rhetoric.

Organised Eugenics

Six months after participating in the discussion on eugenics at the 1913 meeting of the BMA in Brighton (England), Dr William Ernest Jones urged Australians to establish affiliated branches of the London-based Eugenics Education Society. New Zealand already had four such branches and an unaffiliated group was operating in South Australia. Jones differentiated between eugenics groups which wished to improve the quality of the race, and pronatalists who aimed to increase its quantity.

The analysis of much of the historical writing on eugenics in Australia has not been informed by an examination of the archival material on Australian eugenics, particularly that relating to activity before 1914, or to the significant Australian presence at the 1912 International Eugenics Congress. For example, Alison Turtle has argued that 'the organized eugenics movement gained little ground in Australia and almost none at all until after the [1914-1918] war'.[28] Similarly, Stephen Garton reiterated the statement that the eugenics movement was weak prior to 1914.[29] My analysis of these eugenics groups' activities has demonstrated that there was eugenics-related activity in four states before 1914. Indeed, this was the time when many individuals, who later became leaders in their professions, acquired their eugenics beliefs. As a consequence, their pre-1914 learning had an impact on careers which spanned the next three decades, crucial years in the establishment of the state's role in the provision of public health and social medicine.[30] There were also influential decision-makers in the fields of education, science, law and politics but, while these professions wielded power in various spheres, doctors' influence was almost ubiquitous in the first half of this century. Paradoxically, the medical profession largely accepted eugenics because they had limited scientific understanding. Despite this, doctors' public standing was much greater 50 years ago than it is now and doctors' orders were generally followed on social, moral and medical matters. As a result 'medical' eugenists influenced both the developing health services and their patients.

The Style of Australian Eugenics: Nature or Nurture?

The crucially important nature-nurture debate, as explored by Carol Bacchi[31], plays a central role in Australian eugenics. I have engaged with Stephen Garton and Rob Watts over their criticism of Bacchi's emphasis on environment in Australian eugenics and over their dismissal of the importance of the nature-nurture debate. In Garton's view, this debate 'contaminated' enquiries[32] while, according to Watts, it led 'numerous historians' into the 'bog' of 'this oppressive dichotomy'.[33] My examination of archival material supports Bacchi's position on the importance of the debate and her conclusion that between 1900 and 1914 'hereditary determinism found fewer adherents [in Australia] than in England or America'.[34]   While the British eugenics movement was not launched until 1907, the early years of the movement were important ones for eugenics in Australia. Between 1912 and 1914 the Eugenics Education Society of NSW changed its focus: although initially sharing the hereditarian objectives of the parent British body, in 1914 the NSW society changed to the 'nurtural' (environmental) perspective which Caleb Saleeby promoted. These aspects of eugenics suited the social reform orientation of members such as Eldridge, Irvine and Arthur. Eldridge's involvement in economics, eugenics, social sciences and low cost housing was probably stimulated by Irvine who stated that 'the problem of how to produce a superior civilisation is both biological and sociological', a comment which Eldridge found 'entirely in accord with the principles of eugenics', indeed 'the whole basis of the new science'.[35]   Bacchi underestimated the extent of eugenics activity prior to 1914 and was also unaware that the NSW Eugenics Education Society was using Saleeby's objectives rather than creating an environmental position which was uniquely theirs. I argued that Watts and Garton were mistaken in their attack on Bacchi, particularly so in their dismissal of the importance of the nature-nurture debate. This was centrally important to eugenists, both in Australia and overseas, and has resurfaced periodically, the most recent being the fierce arguments surrounding the contentious 1994 American book on class, race and intelligence by the late Richard J Herrnstein and Charles Murray.[36]

The Impact of Eugenics

The impact of eugenics is both complex and paradoxical. There were eugenists in Tasmania and Queensland, but neither state had eugenics organizations.[37] Despite this, Tasmania was the only state to legislate on the feeble-minded, not the states which had such organizations. While all states tried to pass eugenics-related laws, no one who advocated such laws belonged to a eugenics organization. Eugenists were often rivals. The groups were small, vied with each other, and had frequent internal and external disagreements. Attempts to establish eugenics research institutes failed. With the exception of Knibbs, no Australian eugenists participated in or reported on the 1921 and 1932 International Eugenics Congresses – evidence which suggests that the Australian movement was fragmented, isolated and ineffectual.

Certainly, the eugenics movement in Australia was not strong: the Racial Hygiene Association focused mostly on birth control and the Eugenics Society of Victoria was not established until 1936, by which time eugenics' credibility had waned. ESV members argued whether to focus on 'pure' eugenics, or expand to include such issues as welfare, VD, housing, alcoholism and contraception. The ESV remained 'pure' but achieved few results, and it closed in 1961. There were major differences between the ESV and the RHA which determined their respective fates: whereas the ESV strove for an unattainable abstract goal and had little popular, political, or medical support, the RHA had all three, as birth control was a tangible health service which many people wanted.

Despite the weakness of the eugenics movement, there were several eugenics-related achievements which were real and long-lasting. Eugenics attracted many prominent people whose eugenics-influenced thinking is reflected in many of the health and education services which these experts helped to establish. Perhaps the greatest influence was in the medical profession which, both collectively and individually, exerted an influence on Australia's national life, and eugenics helped to shape this influence. The health services which were pioneered before

World War II also bear the stamp of these beliefs. Eugenists' efforts to improve national fitness encompassed maternal and child health, fighting VD and TB, and the provision of sex education and birth control. As well, questions raised by eugenics stimulated the study of genetics. While much of the rationale for eugenics now appears misguided or offensive, such thinking was incorporated into the development of public health; eugenists' crusades helped the public to accept services which had been opposed or ignored. I agree with Dr Victor Wallace that 'the [eugenics] pioneers played a definite part in winning this freedom and in bringing about this enlightenment'.

Many of the preoccupations which fuelled Australian anxieties in the first half of last century were ephemeral: fears of invasion no longer cause concern, pressure to 'populate or perish' has eased, and questions are rarely asked about national fitness. Interest in 'populating' the tropical north had waned by 1930 when the Commonwealth Government closed the Australian Institute of Tropical Medicine in Townsville and relegated this field to a secondary role for the School of Public Health and Tropical Medicine in Sydney. However, the 'survival of the fittest' ideology and debates about national fitness were the foundations from which eugenics developed. It also provided Australia with a welcome and scientifically respectable means for dealing with social problems and sustaining national fitness and pride.

Eugenists were partly right about factors which could be inherited but, while the transmission of genetic defects is still a problem in the 1990s, there has been a vast change in the ethical approach and in the choice of available options. There are a number of reasons for this: people no longer fear the genetic transmission of diseases such as TB, or 'tendencies' such as criminality which are not hereditary. Advances in genetics offer treatment and possibly even cure; at-risk couples, by the use of genetic counselling and prenatal testing, can make informed choices if tests show that a foetus is severely disabled or has inherited a fatal disorder. Most Australians would see it as a basic human right for a couple to decide whether to abort or bear a foetus with serious genetic defects. Most people in our society would be shocked by the suggestion that child-bearing decisions should be taken from individuals and made by others, for religious reasons, or on the grounds of the parents' likely eugenic contribution to the race or state. Finally, eugenic assumptions that some people are biologically 'better' than others are abhorrent in democratic countries with egalitarian beliefs.

These factors both cause and reflect major changes in world attitudes about 'unfitness' and what can or should be done about it. In English-speaking countries early this century, when eugenics flourished, there was considerable commitment to the collective good ('for king and country'). Such unquestioning and altruistic commitment has largely been replaced by distaste for government or religious intrusion into private affairs and by support for self-determination and the protection of human rights. Distinctively Australian reasons for largely rejecting negative eugenics are: the legendary Australian easy-going, anti-authoritarian attitudes; the failure of eugenists and eugenics-related organisations to mobilize support; Catholic opposition to sterilisation; and Communist and Labor Party opposition to class-based definitions of unfitness. For reasons which apply universally, and for such specifically Australian ones, there has been little support for proposals to minimise the 'unfit'. In this we followed the British preference for voluntary measures, rejecting the regulatory procedures of some American states.

Overall, this book has argued that, before and between the two world wars, an ill-defined concept of eugenics was propounded by many leading Australians; that, while largely derived from Britain and America, a variety of specifically Australian circumstances contributed to this acceptance; that many influential Australian politicians enlisted elements of eugenic thinking into their political speeches; and that eugenic ideas played a significant role in the development of Australian policies in the fields of public health and family planning.

Many 'medical' eugenists, striving for national fitness, saw eugenics as a tool for improving public health in the broadest sense, involving all aspects of community and individual well-being, freedom from disease and giving children the best start in life. Their utopian dreams of making Australia 'a paradise of physical perfection' were seen as a possibility in an age of unsophisticated medicine when few questioned doctors' standing in the community.

Careers of some eugenists spanned the rise and fall of eugenics but their amnesia-prone biographers and obituary writers rarely mention this involvement. In Australia and overseas, by the 1950s most eugenists had distanced themselves by adopting new titles such as 'human geneticists', 'sociologists' or 'demographers', just as many eugenics movements and their publications still operate but, from the 1930s, began adopting new names. The discredited 'old' eugenics may have become invisible. While the human rights movement and the horrors of the holocaust make state-imposed eugenics unlikely, new threats loom at home and in the market place – consumers may opt for 'designer' babies or employers and insurance companies might exclude the genetically 'unfit'. Advances in genetic screening, prenatal testing, gene therapy and allied treatment – possibly even human cloning and growing new body parts – present new choices and consequences. In 2002 Professor Gregory Stock, who directs the Program on Medicine, Technology and Society at the University of California at Los Angeles, took an optimistic view of such possibilities in *Redesigning Humans: Choosing our Children's Genes*. He believes the first wave of germinal choice technology may be only a decade away and argued that 'In-depth genetic testing, sophisticated preimplantation genetic diagnosis, egg banking, improved in vitro fertilization, and cloning are poised to transform reproductive choices.'[38] Thirty years earlier Philip Larkin complained that parents 'fill you with the faults they had and add some extra, just for you.[39] In the twenty-first century, children who discover that their parents had chosen their genes might be even more unhappy.

---

[1] J M Thoday and A S Parkes, (eds.), *Genetic and Environmental Influences on Behaviour.* A Symposium held by the Eugenics Society in September 1967 (Edinburgh: Oliver and Boyd), 1968, v. Such metaphors were popular with social Darwinians and eugenists.

[2] Richard Granville Waddy, 'Eugenics', in *Australian Racial Hygiene Congress Report*, 15-18 September 1929 (Sydney: RHA, 1929), 63.

[3] Milton Lewis, '"Populate or Perish": Aspects of Infant and Maternal Health in Sydney, 1870-1939' (PhD thesis, ANU, 1976), 125.

[4] Linda Littlejohn, 'Marriage and Divorce', in *AHRC* (1929), 7.

[5] Roy MacLeod, 'Preface', in *The Commonwealth of Science: ANZAAS and the Scientific Enterprise in Australasia, 1888-1988* (Melbourne: Oxford University Press, 1988), xi.

[6] Alison Turtle, 'Anthropometry in Britain and Australia: technology, ideology and imperial connection', *Storia della Psicologia*, 2 (no 2) (1990), 134.

[7] John Peel and Malcolm Potts wrote 'Within a generation the physician has undergone a remarkable reversal of attitude from being an opponent, or apathetic supporter, of birth control to attempting to create a closed shop of contraceptive techniques', in Don Brothwell (ed.), *Biosocial Man: Studies related to the Interaction of Biological and Cultural Factors in Human Populations* (London: Published for the Eugenics Society by the Institute of Biology, 1977), 78. The 'reversal' was prompted by doctors' role as prescribers of oral contraceptives in the early 1960s.

[8] *Report of the Royal Commission on Child Endowment or Family Allowances*, CPP, 2 (1920), 'H. Eugenic Control', paragraphs 627-633, 888-91, 1046, 1359-60.

[9] Stephen Garton, *Medicine and Madness: A Social History of Insanity in NSW, 1880-1940* (Kensington: UNSWP, 1988), 95.

[10] Frank Robinson Kerr, *The Sterilisation of Mental Defectives*, in Federal Health Council, Report of the 6th Session (Canberra; Govt. Pr., 1933), 16-32.

[11] See *Federal Inquiry into the Sterilisation of Mental Defectives*, 1933. It was prepared by F R Kerr and appeared as Appendix II of the Sixth session of the FHC, 21-23 February 1933, 16-28. See also Ibid., H Downes, CMO to the D-G, Summary, 28 March 1934, 2-3 and 24, AA. ACT, A1928/1 - Item 362/20.

[12] Stephen Garton, 'Insanity in New South Wales: Some Aspects of its Social History, 1878-1958' (PhD thesis, UNSW, 1984), 337.

[13] Federal Labor politician Billy Hughes introduced a Marriage Certificates Bill in 1913 and still favoured such legislation in 1929. In 1930 the NSW Mental Defectives Bill was introduced as non-party legislation.

[14] Adams (1990), 220-21 and 224. See also Diane Paul, 'Eugenics and the Left', *Journal of the History of Ideas*, 45 (January-March 1984), 567-90 and Christopher Shaw, 'Eliminating the Yahoo: Eugenics, social Darwinism and five Fabians', *History of Political Thought*, 8 (Winter 1987), 521-44.

[15] Daniel J Kevles, *In the Name of Eugenics: Genetics and the Uses of Human Heredity* (New York: Knopf, 1985), 64.

[16] Anthea Hyslop, 'The Social Reform Movement in Melbourne, 1890 to 1914' (PhD thesis, La Trobe University, 1980), 12.

[17] Claudia Thame, 'Health and the State: The Development of Collective Responsibility for Health Care in Australia in the First Half of the Twentieth Century' (PhD thesis ANU, 1975), 156.

[18] David McCallum, *The Social Production of Merit: Education, Psychology and Politics in Australia, 1900-1950* (Deakin Studies in Education Series: 7) (London: The Falmer Press, 1990), 17.

[19] *MJA* articles include eugenics editorials on (21 November 1931), 655-56 and (5 October 1935), 438; letters (26 December 1931), 825-6; (23 January 1932), 143; (6 February 1932), 211 and (27 February 1932), 311-12; articles on (9 March 1935), 295-305 and 318-21.

[20] RHA Annual Report (1935), 3.

[21] Ibid (1936), 3.

[22] Brothers (1950), 215.

[23] Bacchi (1980), 205 wrote, 'In 1930, as Minister for Health in the Bavin administration, Arthur presented a Bill calling for the sterilisation of defectives'. This mistake was repeated by Mary Cawte in *Historical Studies* (April 1986), 38 and by Milton Lewis in *Managing Madness: Psychiatry and Society in Australia 1788-1980* (Canberra: AGPS, 1988), 130.

[24] 'Danger of the half-wit. Sterilisation must come, says Minister', *Telegraph*, 15 July 1929, 4 (d).

[25] NSWPD, 27 March 1930, 4182 and *SMH*, 1 February 1930, 18.

[26] 'Minister is opposed by own party', *Labor Daily*, 23 May 1930, 5 (f).

[27] Garton (1994), 164.

[28] Turtle (1990), 134.

[29] Stephen Garton, 'Sound minds in healthy bodies: Reconsidering eugenics in Australia, 1914-1940', *Australian Historical Studies*, 26 (October 1994), 164.

[30] These included Dr J H L Cumpston, Dr W Ramsay Smith, Dr E Sydney Morris, Dr E Morris Miller, Dr W Ernest Jones, Sir T Anderson Stuart, Sir James Barrett, Dr Victor Wallace, Dr Kenneth Cunningham, Dr Mary Booth, Professor R J A Berry, Sir Frank Macfarlane Burnet and Sir George Knibbs.

[31] Carol Bacchi, 'The nature-nurture debate in Australia, 1900-1914', *Historical Studies*, 19 (October 1980), 199-212.

[32] Garton (1994), 163.

[33] Rob Watts, 'Beyond nature and nurture: Eugenics in twentieth century Australian history', *Australian Journal of Politics and History*, 4 no.3 (1994), 320.

[34] Bacchi (1980), 199.

[35] Eldridge (5 March 1914).

[36] Richard J Herrnstein and Charles Murray, *The Bell Curve: Intelligence and Class Structure in American Life* (New York: Free press/Simon and Schuster, 1994).

[37] For example, Sir Raphael Cilento in Queensland and E Morris Miller and E Sydney Morris in Tasmania.

[38] Gregory Stock, *Redesigning Humans: Choosing Our Children's Genes* (London: Profile Books, 2002), 177.

[39] Philip Larkin, *This Be The Verse*, 1974, in Collected Poems, Anthony Thwaite, ed (London: Faber & Faber, 1988), 180.

Appendix

Terminology

I have used terms which were acceptable during the period studied, such as 'unfit', 'feeble-minded' and 'mental deficiency', rather than today's terminology. This Appendix also includes words which have significant meanings in the context of eugenics, are ambiguous or can be interpreted in different ways, or whose meaning has changed.

Degeneracy (Degeneration) Theory was first articulated in 1857 by a French psychiatrist, Benedict Augustin Morel (1809-1873). From 1860 to 1910 this model was widely accepted by psychiatrists and neurologists who proposed that patients who were unresponsive to their treatment had inbuilt deficiencies (also called 'traits' or 'tendencies) which became progressively worse in each generation until the affected individual, family or groups became extinct.

Eugenics is the science of improving the qualities of offspring and those of the human race. The word comes from the Greek *eugenes* meaning well-born and was coined by Sir Francis Galton in his 1883 book, *Inquiries into Human Faculty and its Development*. He decided to use the word *eugenics* because it expressed the idea better, was a neater, 'more generalised one' than 'viriculture' which he had previously used. Drawing on ancient ideas, Galton had expressed eugenic beliefs as early as 1865 but did not feel that the time was right to announce his plan until 1901. He elaborated on it in 1904, describing it as a new 'science which deals with all influences that improve the inborn qualities of a race; also with those that develop them to the utmost advantage'. The prestigious journal *Nature* reported in its 20 August 1998 issue that a workshop on the science and ethics of eugenics at the 18th International Congress of Genetics in Beijing had 'argued that the term "eugenics" is currently used in so many ways "as to make it no longer suitable for use in scientific literature". It was so controversial that one delegate argued that the word 'eugenics' should be banned! Saul Dubow described eugenics 'as one of the most important expressions of social Darwinism, but not synonymous with it' and notes that there is no 'general agreement' about the meanings of 'eugenics' and 'social Darwinism', with some writers offering restrictive and technical definitions and others using it in a more inclusive sense and stressing its pervasive influence.[1] The antonyms are dysgenic and kakogenic.   Allied   terms   are   **racial hygiene**, **social Darwinism** and **stirpiculture**.

Eugenist is defined in the *Oxford English Dictionary* as 'a student or advocate of eugenics', with a note that it is also used as an attribute or an adjective.   I have chosen this British term which Caleb Saleeby coined in 1908, rather than 'eugenicist', because eugenics originated in Britain, the British used the term 'eugenist' prior to World War II and it is shorter and more euphonious than 'eugenicist'.   An argument in favour of 'eugenicist' was made on 3 September 1935 by Professor Charles Davenport, Director of the Eugenics Record Office, in a letter to Dr Ellsworth Huntington, President   of   the   American   Eugenics   Society.   Davenport reprimanded him for using the term 'eugenist', 'like our English cousins', when in his opinion, 'as long as students of genetics call themselves not genists, but geneticists, students of eugenics should be called eugenicists not eugenists'.   The *New York Times* published an article on 28 August 1932 with the title 'The week in science: Eugenists and geneticists are at odds', showing that even then, Davenport's preference for 'eugenicist' was not universally adopted. Recently, Nancy Leys Stepan (in *'The Hour of Eugenics': Race, Gender and Nation in Latin America*) although conceding that the term 'eugenicist' was currently fashionable, explained why she had decided to use the word 'eugenist' in her book.

Feeble-minded is one of the many terms used in the 19th and early 20th century to describe people who lack normal mental powers. Synonyms include 'mentally deficient', 'retarded', 'idiot', 'moron' and 'socially inefficient'.

Nature versus nurture is a hotly disputed debate between those who believe that improving the environment (nurture) will have a genetic benefit, because acquired characteristics would be passed on, and those who believe that heredity (nature) is predominantly or solely responsible.   Central to eugenic debates is that 'convenient jingle of words', 'nature and nurture', which was made popular by Francis Galton's 1874 book, *English Men of Science: Their Nature and*

Nurture. He probably assumed his readers would recognise Shakespeare as the source of the expression and was quoting from the scene in *The Tempest*, in which Prospero described Caliban as 'A devil, a born devil, on whose nature, nurture can never stick'.

Neo-Malthusianism is discussed by Rosanna Ledbetter in the preface of *A History of the Malthusian League: 1877-1927* (Columbus: Ohio State University Press, 1976). She writes, 'the term neo-Malthusian was apparently coined in the late 1870s by Dr Samuel Van Houten, at one time Prime Minister of Holland and a vice-president of the English Malthusian League for many years'. The word 'contraception' was not used until the early 20th century and Lidbetter credits Edward Bliss Foote (1829-1906), an American pioneer in birth control, with being the first to use this term. Neo-Malthusianism was the term used by the birth control movement in Britain, which began in 1877, after the much-publicised Knowlton trial of 1876 in which Annie Besant and Charles Bradlaugh were prosecuted for publishing Dr Charles Knowlton's birth control pamphlet *Fruits of Philosophy*. In 1878 the first Australian edition of the pamphlet appeared and in 1888 the controversial and courageous Justice Windeyer (1834-1897) delivered his famous Judgement that the pamphlet was not obscene. Unfortunately, its contraceptive advice was incorrect.

Charles V Drysdale's 1912 book *Neo-Malthusianism and Eugenics* outlined the tenets of birth control that 'no parents should have more children than they can adequately feed, clothe, and educate. No one having definite hereditary defects should have children, but if they are sufficiently responsible they may marry so long as they do not reproduce'. This extended the proposition made by Thomas Robert Malthus (1766-1834) that as population increased faster than the means of sustenance, it should be checked by social and moral restraints. In 1838, while working on his inquiry into evolution, Charles Darwin acknowledged that he 'had happened' to read Malthus' *Essay on the Principle of Population* 'for amusement'. From it Darwin had 'at last got a theory by which to work', although his *Origin of Species* did not appear until 1859.

Papal Encyclicals were frequently issued about eugenics-related issues. In 1930 Pope Pius XI published *On Christian Marriage* which extended the Catholic Church's ban on contraception and abortion to all those who 'put eugenics before aims of a higher order, and by public authority wish to prevent from marrying all those whom, even though naturally fit for marriage, they consider, according to the norms and conjectures of their investigations would, through hereditary transmission, bring forth defective offspring'. On 8 January 1931 Pope Pius XI called on all Catholics to stem the tide of sexual libertarianism. In a 16,000-word world Encyclical he reinforced the prohibition of divorce, trial marriages and birth control. Decrees, on 18 and 21 March 1931, condemned positive and negative eugenics and two more, on 21 and 24 February 1940, condemned sterilisation.[2]

Positive (or Constructive) Eugenics is the theory that eugenically fit women and men should be encouraged to have large families and, in this way, increase the size of the fit population. There were few serious attempts to implement it.

Progressivism is the vague term used to describe the range of political reforms for 'human betterment' which were proposed from late last century until its 'noonday' in 1915. Drawing from 19th century philosophical ideas, this liberal reform began in America and its influence was felt in Britain, Australia and in eugenics movements throughout the world. These reforms had an impact in the formative years of Australia's health services. Progressives believed that, just as science and industry had developed economic efficiency, the same principles should be applied to perfecting humans and that the state should provide a centralised national health service to promote this.

Pronatalism describes attempts to encourage all women (not just the 'fit') to have large families and to increase the population. Its aims are shown in Billy Hughes' slogan that Australia must 'populate or perish'. Pronatalism was prompted in Australia by fears of **racial suicide** and **yellow peril**.

Purity (or Maternal) Feminism is the term used to describe the style of feminism which was common early this century. It was espoused by feminists who advocated women's rights while endorsing motherhood as women's primary role. The science of eugenics strengthened demands for sexual reforms which the women's movement had previously been making for moral or social purity reasons. However, purity feminists were not necessarily wowsers and at the 1929 Australian Racial Hygiene Congress, Angela Booth quoted Lord Chesterfield's advice to his son to 'spend his days with books and his nights with women, but to have the good editions of each'.

Race is a troublesome term. Its inglorious history dates from Joseph de Gobineau's *Essay on the Inequality of Races* (1853-1855) and racial research was encouraged by politicians and social commentators. Scientists became interested after Swedish botanist Carolus Linnaeus (1707-1778), in *Systema Naturae*, extended animal classification to humans in 1758, dividing them into four groups; Europeans who were 'fair ... gentle, acute, inventive ... governed by laws'; Americans who were 'obstinate ... regulated by customs'; Asiatics who were 'severe, haughty, covetous ... governed by opinions'; and Africans who were 'black ... crafty, indolent, ... governed by caprice'. The term 'race' was first used by the German physiologist Johann Blumenbach (1752-1840), who in the 1860s classified *homo sapiens* into five groups: Caucasian, Mongolian, Malayan, Ethiopian and American. Nineteenth century scientists ranked races by their perceived biological and social worth, always ranking northern Europeans top. Recently the taboo surrounding racial research stimulated the creation of a new term – ethnicity – which has become a euphemism for race and many scientists argue that research into ethnicity and health is similarly racist, unsound and flawed as a social construct.

Race Culture, (a synonym for eugenics) was used by Dr William Ramsay Smith who, in his 1912 book, *On Race-Culture and the Conditions that Influence it in South Australia*, stated that its aim was 'to show how to discover the fit and the conditions that foster fitness, and how to encourage the multiplication of the fit; to show how to find the unfit and the conditions that cause or perpetuate unfitness, and how we may either remove such conditions or discourage the propagation of such persons'. Galton originally used the term **viriculture** from the Latin word for man. Other terms used were **man culture**, **stirpiculture** and **puericulture** (infant nurture, for the Latin for boy).

Racial Decay was the term applied to the belief, widely held early this century, that the human race was progressively degenerating as a result of an increase in racial poisons and in the size of the unfit segment of the population. The words race and racial were often used interchangeably. See also **degeneracy theory** and **racial poisons**.

Racial Hygiene can be defined in several ways. The term 'Rassenhygiene' was proposed by Alfred Ploetz in 1895 but its exact meaning was disputed in the 1920s. In Germany at that time, the use of the terms 'Rassenhygiene' (race/racial hygiene) or 'Eugenik' (eugenics) became 'a kind of political flag, often with the more right-wing members of the movement favouring the first term, the more left-wing members the latter'.[3] The German term for racial hygiene was broader in scope than the English word 'eugenics' and encompassed attempts to improve the quality and the quantity of the population. **Racial hygiene** lacked these connotations in Australia. For example, after investigating the NSW Racial Hygiene Association, the Commonwealth Security Service concluded 1943 that 'It cannot in any manner be regarded as anti-Semitic, since many of its members and supporters are of the Jewish persuasion. The use of the word "racial" in the Association's title, refers to the whole of the human race'.

Racial Poisons was a term coined by Caleb Saleeby in 1907 and used by degeneracy theorists and eugenists to apply to any substance which, regardless of its impact on an individual, was 'liable to injure the race of which he (or she) is trustee'. Venereal disease, tuberculosis, alcoholism and feeble-mindedness were the poisons of most concern.

Racial Suicide was first used in 1901 by American sociologist Edward Alsworth Ross. Prompted by fears of white population decline, it was a major concern for Australians early this century. Fears about racial decay were linked with fears about race suicide, Theodore Roosevelt warned that both could jeopardise the future of the white races.

Social Darwinism, which now has largely pejorative connotations, was first used early this century. *The Penguin Dictionary of Sociology* states that theories of evolution rely on two central assumptions: 'There are underlying, and largely irresistible, forces acting in societies which are like the natural forces which operate in animal and plant communities. One can therefore formulate social laws similar to natural ones; these social forces are of such a kind as to produce evolutionary progress through the natural conflicts between social groups. The best adapted and most successful social groups survive these conflicts, raising the evolutionary level of society generally'.

Social Hygiene is the term used by Havelock Ellis (in his 1912 book, *The Task of Social Hygiene*) to describe an extension of the social reform movement. It was adopted by various groups who expanded the term to apply to attempts to combat VD, prostitution and various other social evils. In the 1910s there was a Social Hygiene Association in America, a Social Hygiene Council in Britain and a Social Hygiene Association in NSW.

Stirpiculture is the name coined by John Humphrey Noyes (1811-1886) from the Latin for stem, root or stock which was used from 1869-1879 in the Oneida Community, New York, to describe the process of 'scientific propagation' this community used in attempts to produce people who were morally and physically perfect. As Noyes coined the word years before Galton proposed the term eugenics in 1883, Noyes not Galton is more entitled to be called the founder of the eugenics movement.[4]

Thoroughbred has many definitions including: 'of pure or unmixed breed, stock or race, as a horse or other animal, bred from the purest and best blood'; 'of or pertaining to the Thoroughbred breed of horses - an English breed of racehorses, developed by crossing domestic and Middle Eastern strains'; (of human beings) 'having qualities characteristic of pure breeding; high-spirited; mettlesome; elegant or graceful; a well-bred or thoroughly trained person'.

The phrase 'human thoroughbreds' was a favourite with eugenists. It was used in 1908 by the pioneer sociologist William Isaac Thomas (1863-1947), a professor at the University of Chicago who, in the *American Magazine* (volume 67, page 552), defined eugenics as 'a science for the production of human thoroughbreds.' In 1914 the cereal magnate John H Kellogg enthused about establishing 'a race of human thoroughbreds,' in his Presidential Address to the first Race Betterment Conference, held at Battle Creek, Michigan. The phrase is often attributed to Margaret Sanger who concluded chapter 6 of her 1920 book *The Pivot of Civilization* with Dr Edward A Kempf's words: 'The noblest and most difficult art of all is the raising of human thoroughbreds.' The Planned Parenthood organisation include this quote on their Internet website as an example of Sanger's ideas which have been taken out of context by anti-choice activists in an attempt to discredit Sanger and the movement she founded. They point out that Dr Kempf was a progressive physician who, in a plea for state endowment of maternal and infant care, was showing how environment may improve human excellence. It was in this spirit that Margaret Sanger used the phrase 'Birth Control: To Create a Race of Thoroughbreds' as a banner heading of the November 1921 issue of her magazine *The Birth Control Review*.

Yellow peril is the term used to describe the alleged danger of a predominance of the yellow (Asian) race over the white race and western civilisation generally. The phrase *die Gelbe Gefahr* (which translates as 'Yellow Peril') was coined by a Germany's startled Kaiser Wilhelm II, who recognised that Japan was a rising power in the East after the Japanese victory over China in their war of 1895. Fears intensified after Japan won the Russo-Japanese war of 1904-1905. In Australia, this scare prompted the strenuous attempts to boost the population. See also **pronatalism** and **racial suicide**.

Select Bibliography

Additional sources are provided in the footnotes

A. Primary Sources

1. Official publications

Commonwealth of Australia, *Official Yearbooks*, 1909 +

Parliamentary Debates and Parliamentary Papers for all states, 1903 to 1939

2. Theses

Bettes, Martha Ellen, 'A Marriage of Motives: Relationship Between Eugenics and the Woman's Movement' (BA thesis, University of Pennsylvania, 1975).

Cowan, Ruth Schwartz, *Sir Francis Galton and the Study of Fertility in the Nineteenth Century* [PhD thesis, Johns Hopkins University, 1969] (New York: Garland, 1985).

Farrall, Lyndsay A, *The Origins and Growth of the English Eugenics Movement, 1865-1925* [PhD thesis Indiana University, 1969] (New York: Garland, 1985).

Foley, Meredith Anne, 'The Women's Movement in New South Wales and Victoria, 1918-1938' (PhD thesis, University of Sydney, 1985).

Garton, Stephen, 'Insanity in NSW: Some Aspects of Its Social History 1878-1958' (PhD thesis, University of NSW, 1984).

Hicks, Neville, 'Evidence and Contemporary Opinion about the Peopling of Australia, 1890-1911' (PhD thesis, Australian National University, 1971).

Hyslop, Anthea, 'The Social Reform Movement in Melbourne, 1890-1914' (PhD thesis, La Trobe University, 1980).

Lewis, Milton J, '"Populate or Perish": Aspects of Infant and Maternal Health in Sydney, 1870-1939' (PhD thesis, Australian National University, 1976).

McBurnie, Grant, 'Constructing Sexuality in Victoria 1930-1950: Sex Reformers Associated with the Victorian Eugenics Society' (PhD thesis, Monash University, 1989).

Thame, Claudia, 'Health and the State. The Development of Collective Responsibility for Health Care in Australia in the First Half of the Twentieth Century' (PhD thesis, Australian National University, 1974).

Wyndham, Diana, 'Striving for National Fitness: Eugenics in Australia 1910s to 1930s (PhD thesis, University of Sydney, 1996) - available at http://setis.library.usyd.edu.au/~thesis/adt-NU/public/adt-NU2000.0015/

3. Archives and Papers of Individuals and Organisations

American Philosophical Society Archives, Philadelphia
    Charles B Davenport Papers, BD/27
        Peyton Rous Papers B/R77

Richard Arthur Papers, ML, MSS 473

Australian Archives. ACT
    A1/1/ Item 1933/3589, 'Sterilization of mental defectives: Northern Territory'
    A425   Prohibited Publications: Blasphemous, indecent or obscene publications:

Item 35/8897, *Eugenics and Sex Harmony*, Herman H Rubin, 1935

A434/I item 49.3/12646, 'Sterilization of DP [displaced person] women'

A461/ Item D347/1/1, 'Sterilization of the unfit 1932-1936'

A461/ Item Q347/1/1, 'Birth control, 1940-41'

A461/ Item R347/1/7, 'VD and contraceptives regulations, 1943-46'

A461/ Item T347/1/1, 'The Eugenics Society of Victoria, 1940'

A981/ Item Conferences 103, 'Third International Congress on Eugenics, 1932'

A/1658/ Item 200/2/48, 'Conferences and Congresses. RHA, 1950'

A1928/ Item 362/20, 'Federal Health Council Inquiry Into Sterilization of Mental Defectives 1933'

A/1928/ Item 369/3, 'Films. Propaganda for combating venereal disease'

A/1928/ Item 680/32, Section 1,3,4, 'Motherhood endowment and child birth rate – decline in birth rate. Suggested Royal Commission, 1944'

A1928/ Item 848/9, 'Public Health. Birth control, 1942-47'

CP 78/22/ Item 1912/209, 'International Eugenics Conference, 1912'

Australian Archives. New South Wales

C443/ Item J19, 'John C Eldridge to Japanese Consul, 1941'.

SP314/ Item I2/12/3, 'Regulation re contraceptives broadcast in news 1942'

SP1063/ Item 635, 'RHA of NSW, 14 Martin Place Sydney, 1930-36'

SP 1063/ Item 6535, School of Public Health and Tropical Medicine'

Inspector General of the Insane, Special Bundles (1888-1949)

Correspondence files (1888-1949), 3/1772.1, 6/5319, 7/6233-2, 12/1396-1411.2 (1893-1933), 3/1771.1, 12/3433-3479.1 (1934-36), 5/5905-12, 4/5914-19, 5/7663, 12/3460-79 7/9997, 'Circulars to Baby Health Centres'

Mental defectives (1927-28), 12/13992.2

Amendment to Lunacy Act (1902-37), 12/1412.1

Australian Archives. South Australia

D1915. 22063 Racial Hygiene Association 1943-44

Australian Archives. Victoria

MP742/1/ Item 211/6/145, 'National Security (Venereal Diseases and Contraceptives) Regulations, 1942-43'.

Mary Booth Papers, ML MSS 1329 1-6

British Library, Department of Manuscripts, London

Additional Papers 58 572, Marie Carmichael Stopes Papers.
'Piddington-Stopes correspondence 1919-40'.
Additional Papers 58 573. 'Knibbs to Stopes', ff 10-11, 17.

Sir Joseph Hector Carruthers Papers, ML CY431

John Howard Lidgett Cumpston Papers, NLA, MS 434 and MS 614

John Chambers Eldridge Papers, ML MSS 933

Mary Fullerton Papers, ML MSS 2342

Norman Haire Papers, Fisher Library, Rare Books

Alice Henry articles and cuttings, ML QA824/H-CY, Reel 1453

International Eugenics Congresses

Problems in Eugenics. Papers communicated to the first International Eugenics Congress, held at the University of London, 24-30 July 1912. The EES, London (facsimile, New York: Garland, 1984) 2 vols.

Eugenics, Genetics and the Family, vol 1 and *Eugenics in Race and State*, vol 2 (1923), Scientific Papers of the second International Congress of Eugenics, American Museum of National History, New York, 22-28 September 1921 (New York: Garland, 1985). Laughlin, Harry Hamilton, *The Second International Exhibition of Eugenics* held 22 September to 22 October 1921 in connection with the [Congress] (Baltimore: Williams and Wilkins, 1923).

A Decade of Progress in Eugenics , Scientific Papers of the third International Congress of Eugenics, 1932 (New York: Garland, 1984).

Library of Congress, Manuscript Division, Margaret Sanger Papers

George H Knibbs to Sanger, 13 December 1927, Sanger Papers, vol 21

Edith How-Martyn, Birth Control International Information Centre, London to Miss F Rose, National Committee on Federal Legislation for Birth Control, New York, 30 May 1933, Sanger Papers, vol 22

Note on Mrs Piddington, Sanger Papers, vol 23, 2935

National Council of Women of New South Wales. Biennial Reports, 1912-1914, 1926-1928, 1933-1934, 1937-1940, ML 396.06/26

Dowell O'Reilly Papers, ML MSS 231

Racial Hygiene Association of New South Wales

Australian Racial Hygiene Congress, 15-18 September 1929 Report Conference Papers, 1931, 1932; 'Memorandum and Articles of Association', 18 August 1932.

Annual Reports, 1928-1929, 1938-1939, 1939-1940

General Secretary's Report, 1930-1938; Annual Meeting 1932
Birth Control Clinic Report 1937, 1938, RHA Monthly Bulletin, no 1 (May 1940) to no 36 (November-December 1951).

Racial Hygiene Centre

Papers of Racial Hygiene Association and Family Planning Assocn, ML MSS 3838

Includes: RHC minute book, 1926-1927; RHC Appeal Committee minute book, 1927-1928; RHC, Subcommittees' minute book, 1927-1932; RHA minute book, 1931-1933; 1932, Memorandum and Articles of Association; Newspapers cuttings 1927-35 re Aborigines, public health, birth control, mental defectives etc., Folder labelled 'Papers of Dr Lotte A Fink (1898-1960)', 1945-1958; Certificate of Incorporation of Change of Name, 18 October 1960; FPA Minute books etc.

Ruby Rich, Interview by Hazel de Berg, Canberra: NLA
Oral History tapes 954-55 and 994-95, 1976

Bessie Rischbieth Papers, NLA, Series 12 MS 2004

Jessie May Grey Street Papers.

'The place of treatment of venereal disease in social reform', for a conference on 'The Teaching of Sex Hygiene', 22-25 November 1916, NLA, MS 2683. [This did not appear in the WEA conference's published Report].

Tasmania. Archives Office

Australian Directors of Education Conferences, 1926 and 1930. Position statements on Mental Deficiency. Ed 73 file

University College London, Francis Galton Archives – correspondence
Professor Thomas Anderson Stuart, 1892 (324-5)
Sir John Alexander Cockburn, 22 March 1905 (133/5A)
Dr Thomas Fauset MacDonald, 7 January 1905 (133/5A)

University of Melbourne Archives
Victor Hugo Wallace Papers (includes Eugenics Society of Victoria)

University of Sydney Archives
Robert Francis Irvine, M283, no 1101
Thomas Peter Anderson Stuart, M312, no 1196

Victoria. Public Record Office. Education Department
Special Case Files, SP 1106 – Sex education in schools. Leonard Darwin's 4 May 1918 letter to Frank Tate, Director of Education

Wellcome Institute for the History of Medicine, London. Eugenics Society Archives. SA/EUG

C. People

C 86 Sec, ES to Major Leonard Darwin, 27 January 1927

C 87 Major Leonard Darwin: Eugenics Society correspondence with Major Darwin. Found amongst Mr Twitchin's Papers. L Darwin, May 1930 (1922-1930). Uncatalogued and not included in ML material.

C176 Mrs Edith How-Martin (1930-1954)

C343 Henry Twitchin (1922-1930)

D. General Correspondence

D 69 Correspondence – Foreign countries

D 103 Immigration and Emigration (1925-1958)

D 105 Imperial Conference 1926

D 122 Migration Council

D 166 Premiers, India and Colonies (1922-1927)

E. Branches and Other Societies (1909-1962)

2-5 Australian Eugenics Societies

E2 Eugenics Education Society of NSW (1912-1930)

E3 Eugenics Society of Victoria (1914-1939)

E4 Eugenics Society of Victoria (1940-1961)

E5 Western Australia (1933)

E19 New Zealand (1933-1936)

H. Henry Twitchin Bequest

Miscellaneous Collections (PP/MCS)

Marie Carmichael Stopes Papers

A307 *Married Love*, Australia. Mrs Marion Piddington

A308 Australia. General. A copy of these files is in ML, Reel 2573

Women's League of NSW, NLA, MS 2004/5/957

Women's Reform League (formerly Women's Liberal League), ML, 329.21/2

Workers' Educational Association (NSW), Minutes Books, Annual Reports, etc.

4. Newspapers and Periodicals

Advance! Australia (Australian Section of the Theosophical Society, Sydney) 1926-1929

Age (Melbourne) 1888 to 1923

Argus (Melbourne) 1901 to 1938

Australasian Journal of Psychology and Philosophy (Sydney) 1924 to 1927

Australasian Association for the Advancement of Science Reports, 1892 to 1924

Australasian Medical Congress Transactions, 1911 to 1929

Australasian Medical Gazette, 1898 to 1914

Australian Highway (Newsletter of the Workers' Educational Assocn) 1921-1944

Australian Medical Journal, 1912 to 1924

Australian Worker, 1920 to 1929

Boomerang (founded by William Lane and Alfred Brown, Brisbane) 1887-1992

Daily Guardian (Sydney) 1923 to 1931

Eugenics Review (London) 1909 to 1968

Figaro, incorporating the Bohemian (Brisbane) 1919

Grit (A Journal of National Efficiency and Prohibition, Sydney) 1932-1935

Health and Physical Culture (Sydney: Health and Physical Culture Publishing) 1929-1943.

Herself (Nell B B Dungey, ed., Sydney) 1928-1931

Home (Sydney) 1920-1942

Intercolonial Medical Journal of Australasia (Melbourne: Stillwell) 1896-1907

Labor Daily (Sydney) 1925 to 1940

The Liberal Woman (Women's' Liberal League of NSW), August 1910 to February 1915.

Medical Journal of Australia (Sydney) 1914-1973

Millions (the official magazine of the Sydney Millions Club) 1921-1930

Navvy (Journal of the Railway Workers' and General Labourers' Association, Sydney) 1915 to 1916

New Outlook (supported by the Public Questions Society of the University of Sydney) 1922-1923

Progressive Journal (Anne Marsh, ed., Sydney) 1935-1936.

Science of Man (Dr Alan Carroll, ed., Sydney) 1898-1911

Smith's Weekly (Sydney) 1931-1941

Stead's Review (Melbourne) 1921-1931

Sydney Morning Herald, 1903-1996

Telegraph (Sydney) 1905-1950

Triad (Sydney) 1915-1927

Woman Voter (Women's Political Association, Vida Goldstein, ed.) 1914-1918

Woman's Voice (newsletter of the Woman's Reform League, Sydney) 1916-1923

5. Books and Articles

Ackermann, Jessie A, *Australia: From a Woman's Point of View* (Sydney: Cassell, 1981) [London: Cassell, 1913].

Agar, Wilfred Eade

'The Australian in the tropics', *Bulletin*, 29 September 1900.

'The Biographical view of human diversity', *New Outlook*, 12 July 1922, 151-52.

'Practical eugenics in the United States', *New Outlook*, 12 May 1923, 154-65.

'Individual differences from an evolutionary stand-point', *AJPP*, 2 (1924), 320.

'Some problems of evolution and genetics', *AAASR*, 17 (1924), 347-58.

'A Lamarckian experiment involving a hundred generations with negative results', *Journal of Experimental Biology*, 8 (1931), 75-107.

'The eugenic outlook for the future', ESV lecture, 7 October 1937.

'The relative influence of heredity and environment', ESV lecture, 9 June 1938.

Eugenics and the Future of the Australian Population, Publication no 2 (Melbourne: Brown, Prior, Anderson for the ESV, 1939).

Science and Human Welfare (Melbourne: MUP in assocn with OUP, 1943).

Ahearne, Joseph, 'Effect of the Queensland educational regulations on the physique of the present and future North Queenslander',

AAASR, vol 6 (1895), 787-97 and 'The Australian in the Tropics', *The Bulletin*, 29 September 1900.

Arthur, Richard

The Choice Between Purity and Impurity: An Appeal to Young Men (Purity Series [Australian White Cross League] no 3) (Sydney: William Brooks and Co, 1903).

Select Committee on the Prevalence of Venereal Disease. Progress Report to the NSW Legislative Assembly (Sydney: Govt. Pr., 1916).

State Endowment for Families and the Fallacy of the Existing Basic Wage System. Statement to NSW Board of Trade, 4 September 1919 (Sydney: Govt. Pr.).

Report on the Existing Facilities for the Treatment of Venereal Diseases in NSW, with Recommendations for their Extension and Improvement (Sydney: Govt. Pr, 1919).

'The decreased birth-rate in NSW', *AMG* (21 November 1898), 502-03.

'The success of the White Australia Policy', *Westminster Gazette*, 20 Oct 1908.

'The birth rate', *Telegraph*, 25 December 1915, 15 (g).

'Problem of venereal disease', *Telegraph*, 3 May 1916, 10 (f).

'Some aspects of the venereal problem', *MJA* (28 October 1916), 361-65.

'Settlement of tropical Australia', *MJA* (23 April 1921), 345.

'Idiocy. Alarming inroads in NSW', *Sunday Times*, 26 October 1924, 6.

'Problem of child endowment', *Advance! Australia* (February 1927), 55-59.

'Dr Arthur and birth control', *Labor Daily*, 30 November 1927, 4 (h).

'Health before marriage. Should the bridegroom give clergyman a certificate? Dr Arthur says "yes"', *Telegraph*, 3 July 1928, 2 (d).

'Morons to be segregated. Dr Arthur's colony scheme. Law of humanity', *Daily Guardian*, 4 April 1929, 9 (c).

'Birth control desirable. Dr Arthur says so', *Daily Guardian*, 1 July 1930, 6.

Atkinson, Reginald Cyril Everitt

'Notification of venereal diseases in Western Australia', *Journal of Social Hygiene*, 10 (1924), 187

and William J Dakin, *Sex Hygiene and Sex Education* (Sydney: Angus & Robertson, 1918).

Bateson, William, 'Presidential address at the Melbourne meeting of the British Association for the Advancement of Science', *MJA* (22 August 1914), 173-81; (29 August), 187-204.

Barrett, James William

    'Presidential address', *Intercolonial Medical Journal*, 1 (20 January 1901), 1-28.

    The Twin Ideals: An Educated Commonwealth (London: Lewis, 1918), 2 vols.

    Eighty Eventful Years (Melbourne: Stephens, 1945).

Baylebridge [né Blocksidge], William, *National Notes*, 3rd edn. (Sydney: Tallabila Press, 1936).

Beale, Octavius Charles

    Racial Decay: A Compilation of Evidence from World Sources (Sydney: Angus & Robertson, 1910).

    'The birth-rate', *SMH*, 5 June 1923, 11 (e).

Berry, Richard James Arthur

    Synopsis of Four Lectures On the Past History and Future Development of Man (Melbourne: Ford, 1912).

    'One of the problems of peace: Mental deficiency', *MJA* (14 Dec 1914), 485-90.

    'Brain weight in congenital mental deficiency', *MJA* (10 January 1920) and (7 February 1920), 139-40.

    'The physical basis of social inefficiency', *BMJ*, 2 (1921), 72-75.

    'The causes and effects of feeble-mindedness', *New Outlook* (1 Nov 1922), 43-44.

    'The problem of the unfit', *Herald*, 3 May 1924, 11.

    'Lethal chamber proposal', *ER*, 22 (July 1930), 155-56.

    'Brain and mind', *ER*, 23 (1932-1933), 70, 163.

    'Mental deficiency. Part 1. Some family histories of an unselected group' *ER*, 24 (1932-1933), 285

    Report of the Mental Deficiency Committee (London: Macmillan, 1933).

    'Some modern views of human mind and its disorders', *ER*, 26(1934-35), 127.

Birtles, Francis, in RHC Papers.

    'Starving natives. Why the Aborigines are dying out', *Sun*, 16 September 1923.

    'Blacks inhumanly treated. Startling allegations', *Daily Standard*, 13 March 1932.

Black, George

The Red Plague Crusade: Ignorance a Racial Enemy – Cures and Preventives – Sexual Education Advocated (Sydney: Govt. Pr., 1916).

Blacker, Carlos Paton.

'Eugenic sterilization in Germany', *Lancet* (10 June 1933), 1265-66.

Voluntary Sterilization (London: OUP, 1934).

'Eugenic problems needing research', *ER*, 29 (1937), 181-87.

Eugenics in Prospect and Retrospect (London: Hamilton, 1945).

Eugenics: Galton and After (London: Duckworth, 1952).

'Family planning and eugenic movements in the mid-twentieth century', in Pincus, ed. (1956), 126-34.

Booth, Angela

The Prophylaxis of Venereal Disease: A Reply to Sir James Barrett by Mrs James Booth (Melbourne: Norman Brothers, 1919).

'Feeble-mindedness and prostitution', *MJA* (9 August 1919), 123.

The Prophylaxis of Venereal Diseases (under the auspices of the Association to Combat the Social Evil), 2nd edn. (Melbourne: Norman Bros, [1920s?].

'Mentally deficient children', *MJA* (4 July 1923), 18.

'Negative eugenics. How shall we deal with feeble-mindedness?', *Argus*, 12 January 1934, 6 (e).

'Sterilising mental defectives', *Argus*, 26 January 1934, 8 (e).

Voluntary Sterilization for Human Betterment (Publication [Eugenics Society of Victoria] no 1) (Melbourne: Brown, Prior, Anderson, 1938).

'The Sterilization of the unfit', ESV lecture, 21 July 1938.

Booth, James

'Moron breeds moron', *Steads Review* (1 November 1929), 17-18.

'The cost of the moron', *Steads Review* (1 July 1930), 22-23, 42.

Booth, Mary

'The scope of hygiene in modern education', *AMG* (21 March 1910), 126-28.

'School anthropometrics', *AAASR* (1911), 689-96.

'On the need for educating public opinion on the problem of the feeble-minded', *AMG* (12 October 1912), 377-79.

'Report of Central Committee of the Australian Medical Congress on the Care and Control of the Feeble-minded', *AMJ* (1 March 1913), 929.

William Beattie Smith and Mary Booth, 'Report on the care and control of the feeble-minded', *AMG* (April 1913), 40.

'Mental deficient children', *SMH*, 4 July 1923, 18.

Bostock, John

'Mental deficiency. Its mental and physical characteristics', *MJA* (19 February 1927), 255-60 (5 March 1927), 325-28.

'Mental hygiene', *AMTC* (1929), 302-05.

'Mental hygiene and the art of living. Psychology needed in all social relations. Psychiatrist [Bostock] states laws', *Daily Standard*, 6 April 1933.

and Leslie John Jarvis Nye, *Whither Away? A Study of Race Psychology and the Factors Leading to Australia's National Decline*, 2nd edn (Sydney: Angus and Robertson, 1936).

Bottomley, William

'The Church and Eugenics', ESV Lecture, 18 August 1938.

Boyd, Stanley

'A plan for racial health', *MJA* (8 March 1941), 285-89.

Doctor's Conscience: Or all Illness is Preventable (Sydney: Currajong, 1944).

Boylan, Eustace

Factors in National Decay (Melb: Australian Catholic Truth Society, 1917).

Breinl, Anton and W J Young

'Tropical Australia and its settlement', *MJA* (3 May 1919), 353-59 (10 May 1919), 373-83 and (17 May 1919), 395-404.

British Association for the Advancement of Science, Report of the 84th meeting [held in] Australia, 28 July – 31 August 1914 (London: Murray, 1915).

British Science Guild. South Australian Branch

Eugenics: Report of a Sub-Committee [Adelaide, 1911].

Race Building: Work of the Local Branch. Reports of Sub-Committees on Infant Care, Nutrition, Physical Culture, Ethical Education, Science in Schools, Eugenics, Venereal Disease, and the Establishment of a Research Institute, *The Mail* (Adelaide, 1916).

Brothers, Charles R D, 'Psychiatry and eugenics', *MJA* (5 August 1950), 211-15.

Brown, William Jethro

The Underlying Principles of Modern Legislation (London, 1912).

'Economic welfare and racial vitality, *Economic Record*, 3 (1927), 15-34.

Bryden, William, 'The Principles of Heredity', ESV Lecture, 12 August 1937.

Burnet, Sir (Frank) Macfarlane

Migration and Race Mixture from the Genetic Angle, prepared at the request of the Department of Immigration, 1959. Also in *ER*, 51 (July 1959), 93-97.

Endurance of Life: The Implications of Genetics for Human Life (Melbourne: MUP, 1978).

Chapple, William A

'The fertility of the unfit', *Intercolonial Medical Congress of Australasia. Transactions* (1899), 474-82 and *The Fertility of the Unfit* (Melbourne: Whitcombe & Tombs, 1903).

Cilento, Raphael West

The White Man in the Tropics: With Especial Reference to Australia and its Dependencies (Melbourne: Govt. Pr., 1925).

'Health and vitality in Northern Australia', *United Empire*, 5 (1925), 670-76.

'White settlement of tropical Australia', *Economic Record*, 3 (1927), 117-26.

Clapperton, Jane Hume

Scientific Meliorism and the Evolution of Happiness (London: Kegan Paul, Tench, 1885).

Clark, Colin, 'The menace of depopulation', ESV lecture, 29 July 1937.

Cleland, William Lennox

The Chronic Insane, the Habitual Offender and the Endemic Unemployed, With a View to Treatment: A Comparative Study of Degenerates. The Criminological Society of South Australia, 30 September 1897 (Adelaide: Webb and Son, 1897).

Coghlan, Timothy Augustine

The Wealth and Progress of New South Wales 1886-1887 (Sydney: Robertson, 1887.

Childbirth in New South Wales: A Study in Statistics (Sydney: Govt. Pr., 1900).

The Decline of the Birth Rate in New South Wales and Other Phenomena of Childbirth: An Essay in Statistics (Sydney: Govt. Pr., 1903).

Cowan, Edith Dircksey *Light! Light! Let There be More Light! For Parents* (Perth: Colortype, [1910-1920?]).

Cumpston, John Howard Lidgett

'Tropical Australia', *AMTC*, 27 August 1920 (Melbourne: Govt. Pr., 1921).

The History of Plague in Australia 1900-1925, Service publication no 32, Australian Department of Health (Melbourne: Govt. Pr., 1926).

'The Development of the Australian people', *MJA* (13 October 1934), 469-76,
The Health of the People: A Study in Federation [1927-28] (Canberra: Union Offset, 1978).

Curle, James Herbert, *To-day and To-morrow: The Testing Period of the White Race* 7th edn. (London: Methuen, 1928)

Dane, Paul G

'Eugenics or economics? Problem of the mental defective. Sterilization and sophistry', *Age*, 20 January 1934, 20 (f).
'Sterilization of the unfit', *MJA* (23 May 1936), 707-12.
'The sterilization of the unfit', ESV lecture, 21 July 1938.

Darwin, Charles Robert *The Illustrated 'Origin of Species'* [1859], Abridged by Richard E Leakey (London: Faber and Faber, 1986).

Darwin, Leonard

'The need for eugenic reform', *Lancet* (8 November 1913), 1324-25.
The Need For Eugenic Reform (London: Murray, 1926).
What is Eugenics? [London: Watts, 1928] (Melbourne: Lothian Publishing Co, 1930).
'An Account of the Society's most generous benefactor', *ER*, 22 (July 1930), 91-97.

Davidson, Andrew

'Mental diseases from a sociological point of view', *AMG* (21 Sept 1908), 449-57
'Feeble-minded children', *AMG* (21 August 1911), 436-441.

Devanny, Jean

'Eugenic reform and the unfit', *Stead's Review* (1 May 1930), 21-22.
'What do I know of eugenics?', *HPC* (May 1930), 6, 54.
'More light on eugenic reform', *HPC* (August 1930), 18, 47.

Dugdale, Richard, *'The Jukes': A study in Crime, Pauperism, Disease and Heredity. Also Further Studies of Criminals* [1877] 6th edn. (New York: Putnam's, 1900).

Duras, Fritz, 'Eugenics in Germany today', Eugenics Society of Victoria, 7 July 1938.

Eldridge, John Chambers

'The science of eugenics', *Telegraph*, 30 July 1912, 11(e).
'Eugenics', *Telegraph*, 5 March 1914, 4 (e).
The Housing Problem: What it Means and How to Approach it (Sydney: The Worker Trade Union Print, 1915).

'Eugenics', *Navy* (Sydney), [in 35 parts], Part 1 (17 May 1915), 3 to Part 35 (26 September, 1916), 5.

'Motherhood endowment in Australia. Surveys of events and legislation', *ER*, 14 (April 1923), 54-58.

'John C Eldridge, Martin (NSW)', *Australian Worker*, 11 December 1929, 7.

'J C Eldridge, Labor MHR for Martin (NSW)', *Bulletin*, 10 June 1931, 13.

Motherhood Endowment Bibliography [typescript], 31 June (sic) 1921, in Pamphlets. Capital and Labour, ML.

Elkington, John Simeon Colebrook, *Tropical Australia: Is it Suitable for a Working White Race?* (Melbourne: Govt. Pr., 1905).

Ellery, Reginald Spencer

'Sterilization of the unfit', *MJA* (26 December 1931), 825-26.

'Mental deficiency and insanity', ESV lecture, 9 September 1937.

'The social problem group', Eugenics Society of Vic lecture, 23 June 1938.

Ellis, Henry Havelock

The Problem of Race-regeneration (London: Cassell, 1911).

The Task of Social Hygiene (London: Constable, 1912).

'Birth control in relation to morality and eugenics', *Birth Control Review*, 3 (1919), 7-9.

Eugenic Sterilization, 2nd edn. (London: Eugenics Society, Committee For Legalising Sterilization [1935?]).

Ewan, Grey, 'Sterilization of the unfit', *MJA* (27 February 1932), 311-12.

Fishbourne, John William Yorke

'The Lunacy Statute', *AMJ*, 9 (1887), 272-76.

'Segregation of the epileptic and the feeble-minded', *Australasian Medical Congress Transactions*, vol 2 (1911), 885-91.

Flynn, John, 'Heredity and disease', *AMG* (20 March 1901), 94-109; (20 June 1901), 225-38; (20 Sept 1901), 376-81; (21 Oct 1901), 430-40; (20 Jan 1902), 18-23

Galton, Sir Francis

Inquiries Into Human Faculty and Its Development (London: Macmillan, 1883).

Essays in Eugenics (London: EES, 1909).

Giblin, Lyndhurst F, 'Endowment of motherhood', *ER*, 3 (1911-1912), 265.

Goldsmid, Joseph Albert, Companionate Marriage From the Medical and Social Aspects (London: Heinemann, 1934).

Goldsmith, Frank, *The Necessity for the Study of Tropical Medicine in Australia*, as read before the Australasian Medical Congress of 1902 (Adelaide: Govt Pr., 1903).

Goodisson, Lillie Elizabeth
    'Contagious diseases', *SMH*, 10 August 1927, 12.
    'Racial Hygiene', *Advance! Australia* (May 1928), 221-22.
    'Birth control', *Advance! Australia* (September 1928), 41.
    'RHA at Newcastle', *Australian Highway* (10 April 1929), 127-28.
    'Birth control', *SMH*, 17 October 1931, 17.
    'Maternal mortality', *SMH*, 7 January 1935, 4 and 11 July 1935, 8.
    'Sterilisation', *Progressive Journal* (5 January 1936), 3, 48.
    'The RHA', *Progressive Journal* (10 March 1936), 32.
    'RHA. Australia's population want', *Progressive Journal* (10 April 1936), 7
    'Address to women voters', *SMH*, 13 June 1936, 20.
    'Mentally unfit', *SMH*, 15 July 1936,10.
    'The mentally deficient', *SMH*, 27 March 1937, 7.
    'Marriage Advisory Bureau. Health tests', *SMH*, 25 November 1937, 8.
    'The mentally unfit', *SMH*, 22 June 1938, 8.
    'Declining birthrate', *SMH*, 16 July 1938, 11
    'Abnormal offenders', *SMH*, 23 June 1939, 3.

Gordon, Kathleen M
    Youth Centres. Department of Health (Canberra: Govt. Pr., 1944).
    Community Centres. Paper presented at the 7th session of the Commonwealth National Fitness Council, Canberra, 29 September 1943.

Haire, Norman, *Sex Problems of To-Day* (Sydney: Angus and Robertson, 1942).

Hamilton, Ellice E P, 'Heredity in relation to eugenics', *Australian Highway* (December 1922), 174-75; (January 1923), 195-97; (February), 195-97.

Henderson, John, *Observations on the Colonies of New South Wales and Van Diemen's Land* [1832] (Adelaide: Libraries Board of South Australia, 1965).

Henry, Alice

Collection of articles in ML (QA824/H-CY, Reel 1453) which include:

'Home for epileptics. Examples from other countries', [*Argus*, 1898?].

Wynua, 'The latest in education', *Australian Herald*, March 1898, 125-26.

'Brightening the dull', *Argus*, 27 May 1899.

'The education of weak-minded children', *SMH*, 18 February 1903 [?].

'Caring for epileptics. A colony projected', *Argus*, 18 June 1904.

Himes, Norman E, *Medical History of Contraception* [1936] (NY: Schocken, 1970).

Hodgkinson, Lorna Myrtle

'Mental defectives. Education of children. New appointment', *SMH*, 18 January 1923, 8.

'The feeble-minded. Care of children. America's example', *SMH*, 19 October 1922, 9.

'Care of the feeble-minded'. *SMH*, 28 November 1922, 9.

'Workers or wasters? The feeble-minded in America', *SMH*, 30 November 1922, 13 and 1 December, 7.

'Mental patients. Care of children. New system recommended', *SMH*, 8 May 1923, 7

Holman, William A, quoted in 'More people. A Labor view. "Baby the best immigrant"', *Telegraph*, 18 September 1905, 7.

Holmes, Samuel J

'Some misconceptions of eugenics', *Atlantic Monthly*, 115 (1915), 222-27.

A Bibliography of Eugenics, University of California Publications in Zoology, no 25 (Berkeley, California: University of California Press, 1924).

'The opposition to eugenics', *Science* (21 April 1939), 351-57.

Horder, Right Hon Lord, 'Eugenics', *MJA* (5 October 1935), 438.

Huntington, Ellsworth

West of the Pacific (New York: Charles Scribner's Sons, 1925).

'Natural selection and climate in Northern Australia', *Economic Record*, 5 (1929), 185-201.

Mainsprings of Civilization (New York: John Wiley and Sons, 1945).

Irvine, Robert Francis

Report of the Commission of Inquiry into the Question of Housing of Workmen in Europe and America (Sydney: Govt. Pr., 1913).

'Eugenics Education Society', *SMH*, 26 February 1914, 5.

The Place of the Social Sciences in a Modern University (Sydney: Angus and Robertson, 1914).

Izett, D, *Health and Longevity According to the Theories of the Late Dr Alan Carroll. With an Account of the Work of the Child Study Association* (Sydney: Epsworth, 1915).

Johns' Notable Australians, 1906, 1908 (Adelaide), *Fred Johns' Annual* (with varying subtitles), 1912, 1913, 1914 (Adelaide, 1912) (London, 1913, 1914).

Jones, William Ernest
  'Eugenics in relation to the feeble-minded question, *AMJ*, 8 March 1913, 935-37
  'Eugenics', *AMJ*, 3 January 1914, 1370-73.
  'Law of eugenics. Who should marry?', *Argus*, 6 March 1914, 10.
  Report on Mental Deficiency in the Commonwealth of Australia (Canberra: Australian Department of Health, 1929).

Kerr, Frank Robinson, *The Sterilization of Mental Defectives*, Federal Health Council Reports, 6th Session (Canberra: Govt. Pr., 1933), 16-32.

King, Frederick Truby, 'Education and eugenics', *AMTC* (Feb 1914), 42-45, 80-96.

Kirby, Joseph Coles
  Three Lectures Concerning the Social Evil: Its Causes, Effects and Remedies (Port Adelaide: E H Derrington, 1882).
  The State and the Sterilization of Defectives (Semaphore, South Australia: Kirby [1912?]).

Knibbs, Sir George Handley
  '"Healthiest country". Striking improvements. Australian statistics', *SMH*, 11 June 1912, 7.
  'The fundamental elements of the problems of population and migration', *ER*, 19 (1927-1928), 267-89.
  The Shadow of the World's Future or the Earth's Population Possibilities and the Consequences of the Present Rate of Increase of the Earth's Inhabitants (London: Benn, 1928).

Lang, John Thomas
  I Remember (Sydney: Invincible Press, [1956]).

'Three words that blasted a politician's career', *Truth*, 6 April 1958, 37 (a).

The Turbulent Years (Sydney: Alpha Books, 1975).

Leslie, Robert Murray

    'Woman's progress in relation to eugenics' *ER*, 2 (1910-1911), 282-98.

    'Birth rate in Australia', *ER*, 3 (1911-1912), 353.

L'Estrange, Guy, 'Eugenics in light of higher civilisation', *AMG* (20 Jan 1910), 1-6.

Lewers, Alexander, *Medicine and Mediation: Occasional Writings* (Melbourne: Ford, 1915).

Lind, William Alexander Teao

    'Aetiology of congenital mental deficiency', *MJA* (14 October 1916), 313-16.

    'Preventive medicine in mental disease', *MJA* (15 April 1922), 403-08.

    'On insanity', *MJA* (3 April 1926), 373-74.

Lindsey, Benjamin B and Wainwright Evans, *The Companionate Marriage* (New York: Brentano's Ltd, 1928).

Lovell, Henry Tasman, 'The Tasmanian Mental Deficiency Act', *AJPP*, vol 1 (December 1923), 285-89.

Macfie, Matthew, 'How can tropical and sub-tropical Australia be effectively developed?' *AAASR*, with discussion (Adelaide: Govt. Pr., 1907).

Mackellar, Charles Kinnaird

    Child-life in Sydney (Sydney: Govt. Pr., 1903).

    The Treatment of Neglected and Delinquent Children in Great Britain, Europe and America: With Recommendations as to Amendment of Administration and Law in NSW (Sydney: Govt. Pr., 1913).

    'Mental deficiency', *SMH*, 21 August 1915, 9 (g).

    and David Arthur Welsh, *Mental Deficiency: A Medico-sociological Study of Feeble-mindedness* (Sydney: Govt. Pr., 1917).

    "'Faddists and Ministers". Problem of the feeble-minded' *Telegraph*, 25 May 1920, 6.

Macpherson, John, 'Legislative machinery for the care of the feeble-minded in Britain', *MJA* (7 June 1924), 403-08.

Mee, Arthur (ed.), *Harmsworth Popular Science*, 7 vols (London: Educational Book Co, [1912]). The work's 45 chapters on eugenics were written by Caleb C Saleeby.

Mental Defectives Bill
NSWPD (13 March 1930), 3753-70; (26 March), 4137-42; (27 March), 4174-90.
Report of Select Committee, with minutes of proceedings and evidence. Journal and papers of the Tasmania Parliament (1920-21), Report no 43, 12.
VicPD (1929), 698, 799-823, 1654-1712, 2087-2111, 2150, 2489-98.
WAPD (1929), 343, 739-47, 823-26, 1080-82, 1450-62, 1684-91, 2009-20.

Miller, Edmund Morris
The Mental Hygiene Movement and Organisation in Australia (Sydney: Australasian Medical, 1923).
'Observations (mainly psychological) on the concept of mental deficiency', *MJA* (7 February 1925), 133-40.
Criminality and Levels of Intelligence: Being a Report of a Mental Survey of the Hobart Gaol (Hobart: Govt. Pr., 1925).
Brain Capacity and Intelligence Including a Comparison of Brain Measurements of Tasmanian and Victorian School Boys … (Sydney: Australasian Association for Psychology and Philosophy, 1926).

Money, Leo Chiozza, *The Peril of the White* (London: Collins, 1925).

Morris, Emanuel Sydney
'The administrative control of mental deficiency in Tasmania', *Health*, 2 (May 1924), 78-80.
'An essay on the causes and prevention of maternal morbidity and mortality', *MJA* (12 September 1925), 301-45.
'Physical Education – An outline of its aims, scope, methods and organization' in NHMRC Reports, 5th session (November 1938), Appendix 1, 12-20.
'Physical education in relation to national fitness', *ANZAASR* (January 1939), 194-98.
'Hygiene and social progress' in *The Health Inspectors' Association of Australia, NSW Branch, 22nd Annual Conference* (25-30 September 1933), 9-17.

Noble, Ralph Athelstone
'Detection and prevention of mental deficiency', *MJA* (7 June 1924), 400-03.
'Some observations on the treatment of the feeble-minded in Great Britain and America', *MJA* (12 July 1924), 31-35.
'The mental hygiene movement and its possibilities in Australia' *AMCT* (1929), 300-02.

Nye, Leslie John Jarvis, *Sex, Marriage and Eugenics* [Booklet 5 in the International Knowledge of Living series] (Brisbane: Smith and Paterson (rev edn) 1961).

Onians, Edith C, *The Men of To-morrow* (Melbourne: Lothian, 1914).

Pastore, Nicholas, *The Nature-Nurture Controversy* (New York: King's Crown Press, Columbia University, 1949) [New York: Garland, 1984].

Pearson, Charles Henry, *National Life and Character: A Forecast* (London: Macmillan, 1893).

Pearson, Karl, The Scope and Importance to the State of the Science of National Eugenics (London: Dulau, 1911).

Piddington, Albert Bathurst

'Child endowment. System in Europe. Piddington's lecture', *SMH*, 22 July 1924,10.

'Piddington takes a gloomy view. "A dying nation"', *Labor Daily*, 2 March 1925, 4 (d).

'Child endowment', *Labor Daily*, 17 June 1927, 5 (f).

'Families have no security. Case for increase in endowment rates', *Labor Daily*, 21 December 1936, 6 (c).

'Larger families are a national asset. Child endowment', *SMH*, 13 August 1941, 6.

Piddington, Marion Louisa

'Lois' (pseud), *Via Nuova or Science and Maternity* (Sydney: Dymock's Book Arcade, 1916).

Scientific Motherhood: For the Lonely Woman and Childless Widows After the War: Proposal to set up a Federal Eugenic Fund and Institute to Foster Artificial Insemination of War Widows (Sydney [1918?]).

'Eugenics', *Daily Mail*, Brisbane, 10 July 1920, 9.

'Breffny', 'Eugenics', *Australian Highway* (1 December 1921), 11-12.

'A Mother', 'Marie Stopes', *Telegraph*, 19 May 1923, 14 (c).

Tell them! Or the Second Stage of Mothercraft (Sydney: Moore's Bookshop, [1926]).

'Sterilisation of the unfit' *HPC* (January 1930), 12, 43.

'Breeding out the unfit. Eugenics and sterilisation.', *HPC* (February 1930), 19, 42.

'The race. Ban, censor, suppress, but why not educate?', *HPC* (March 1930), 15, 43.

'Mothers in jeopardy. Race destruction and its alternative', *HPC* (April 1930), 18-20.

'The moron mother', *HPC* (May 1930), 12, 50.

'Early and companionate marriage. Panic suggestion', *HPC* (July 1930), 16-17. 57.

'Eradication of venereal disease and promiscuity', *HPC* (August 1930), 10, 44.

'Parental metaphylaxis', *HPC* (September 1930), 10, 44, 46-47

'Venereal disease and promiscuity. The new method of sex training', *HPC* (1 November 1930), 41 and (1 December 1930), 41.

'Talks on racial health, sex education', *Smith's Weekly* (16 January), 16; (23 January) and (20 February 1932), 19.

'The frustration of the maternal instinct and the new psychology', *AJPP*, 15 (September 1937), 205-220.

Phillips, Philip David and Gordon Leslie Wood, eds., *The Peopling of Australia*, by W E Agar et al (Melbourne: Macmillan in assocn with MUP, 1928).

Popenoe, Paul and Rosewell Hill Johnson, *Applied Eugenics* (New York: Macmillan, 1933).

Porteus, Stanley D, *A Psychologist of Sorts: The Autobiography and Publications of the Inventor of the Porteus Maze Tests* (Palo Alto, California: Pacific Books, 1969).

Price, Archibald Grenfell
   A White Man in the Tropics and the Problem of North Australia [Text of radio broadcasts 11 and 18 July 1934]. Reprinted in *MJA* (26 January 1935), 106-110.
   White Settlers in the Tropics (New York: American Geographical Society, 1939).

Purdy, John, 'Health week. Multiplication of the fit', *SMH*, 11 October 1930, 9.

Reid, George   Archdall, 'The biological foundation of sociology', *Sociological Papers*, vol 3 (1906), 3-52.

Rentoul, Robert Reid, *Race Culture: Or Race Suicide?* (London: Scott, 1906).

Roberts, Stephen, *The House That Hitler Built* (London: Methuen, 1937).

Robertson, Clutha, 'A threatened evil. Dangerous sterilisation fad', *Labor Daily*, (14 June 1930), 10 (b) and (21 June 1930), 7 (d).

Robertson, Thorburn Brailsford, *The Spirit of Research* (Adelaide: Preece, 1931).

Roper, G Allen, *Ancient Eugenics* (Oxford: Blackwell, 1913).

Rout, Ettie A

The Morality of Birth Control (London: Bodley Head, 1925).

Safe Marriage: A Return to Sanity (London: Heinemann, 1923).

Royal Commission

Royal Commission on the Decline of the Birth-Rate and on the Mortality of Infants in New South Wales (Sydney: Govt Prt, 1904).

Royal Commission on Child Endowment or Family Allowances, Report, CPP, 2 vols (1929).

Royal Commission on Health: Minutes of Evidence (Melbourne: Govt. Pr., 1925).

Rubin, Herman Harold, *Eugenics and Sex Harmony: The Sexes, Their Relations and Problems, Including Recent Fascinating Medical Discoveries, Prevention of Disease and Special Advice on Common Disorders*, 2nd edn. (New York: Pioneer, 1942).

Rusden, Henry Keylock

The Treatment of Criminals in Relation to Science: Or Suggestions for the Prevention of Cruelty to Honest Men and Women (Melbourne: George Robertson, 1872).

Selection. Natural and Artificial (Beechworth, Victoria: Warren, 1874).

'Labour and capital', *Melbourne Review*, vol 1 (1876), 67-83.

'The survival of the unfittest', (abstract) *AAASC* (Adelaide: 1893), 523-24.

Saleeby, Caleb Williams

Parenthood and Race culture: An Outline of Eugenics (New York: Cassell, 1909).

Author of the 45 Chapters on eugenics, in Arthur Mee (ed.), *Harmsworth Popular Science*, 7 vols (London: Educational Book Co [1912]).

The Progress of Eugenics (London: Cassell, 1914).

The Eugenic Prospect: National and Racial (London: T Fisher Unwin, 1921).

Guard Your Race (Melbourne: Australia Publishing, 1930).

Sanger, Margaret (ed.),

Proceedings of the World Population Conference, Geneva (London: Arnold, 1927).

and Hannah M Stone (eds.), *The Practice of Contraception: An International Symposium and Survey*. From the Proceedings of the Seventh International Birth Control Conference, Zurich, September 1930 (London: Bailliere, Tindall and Cox, 1931).

Smith, William Beattie and Mary Booth, 'Report of the Central Committee on the Care and Control of the Feeble-minded', *AMG* (26 April 1913), 400-01.

Smith, William Ramsay
  Practical Aspects of Heredity and Environment (Adelaide: Whillas and Ormiston, 1899).
  Peace: An Address Delivered at the University of Adelaide on Peace Day, 9 November 1910 (International Peace Society, Adelaide Branch, 1910).
  On Race-culture and the Conditions that Influence it in South Australia (Adelaide: Govt Pr., 1912).
  'Australian Conditions and Problems From the Stand Point of Present Anthropological Knowledge', Presidential Address, Anthropology Section AAAS (Sydney: Angus and Robertson, 1913).

Smyth, Brettena
  The Limitation of Offspring: Being the Substance of a Lecture Delivered in the North Melbourne Town Hall, and Elsewhere, to Large Audiences of Women Only, 8th edn. (Melbourne: Rae Brothers, 1893).
  The Social Evil: Its Cause and Cure (Melbourne: [Rae Brothers?], 1894).
  Diseases Incidental to Women: Their Cause, Prevention and Cure. 19th edn (Melbourne: Prender, 1895).

Society for Combating Venereal Diseases (Sydney: Univ of Sydney, June 1917).

Southern, George William R, *Making Morality Modern: A Plea for Sexual Reform on a Scientific Basis : Addressed to Working People* (Mosman: [Southern], 1934).

Spence, Catherine Helen, *Heredity and Environment*, delivered before the Criminological Society of South Australia, 23 October 1897 (Adelaide: The Society, 1897).

Spence, William Guthrie, *The Child*, *The Home and the State* (Sydney: Worker Print, 1908).

Springthorpe, John William
  'Sanitary science and hygiene' *AAASR*, 6 (1895), 173-82.

Stirling, Edward Charles, 'Presidential address. Weismann's theory of heredity', *Royal Society of South Australia*, *Transactions*, 13 (December 1890), 257-68.

Stopes, Marie, *Radiant Motherhood: A Book for Those Who Are Creating the Future*, 6th edn. (London: Putnam, 1934).

Storer, Robert Vivian

Sex and Disease (Sydney: Butterworths, 1929).

Sex in Modern Life: A Survey of Sexual Life in Adolescence and Marriage (Melbourne: James Little, 1933).

Street, Jessie May Grey, *Truth or Repose* (Sydney: Australasian Book Soc, 1966).

Sutton, Harvey Vincent

'The cure of feeble-mindedness', *AMG* (7 June 1913), 556.

'The Importance of nationality' and 'The feeble-minded – their classification and importance' in *AAASR* (1911), 508-10 and *AMCT* (Sept 1911), 894-907. 'Mental hygiene', *Australian Highway* – four articles: in 1930 (10 June, 150-51 and 10 July, 165-67) and in 1931 (10 Oct, 194-96 and 10 November, 208-10). 'The Australian child and progress of child welfare', *MJA* (14 Nov 1931), 603-16.

Lectures on Preventive Medicine (Sydney: Consolidated Press, 1944).

Swan, Henry Waterman [pseud.], *Facultative Motherhood Without Offence to Moral Law: Every Woman's Right to Motherhood – A Suggestion* (Melbourne: Australasian Authors' Agency, 1918).

Syme, George Aldington,

Presidential Address, *MJA* (16 February 1924), 5-12.

Tait, William D, 'Psychology, leadership and democracy', *AJPP*, 6 (1928), 28-34.

Taylor, Thomas Griffith

'Future settlement in Australia', *New Outlook* (19 April 1922), 9-11.

'Racial misconceptions', *Home* (1 October 1927).

Environment and Race: A study of the Evolution, Migration, Settlement and Status of the Races of Man (London: OUP, 1927).

Environment, Race and Migration. Fundamentals of Human Distribution: With Special Sections of Racial Classification, and Settlement in Canada and Australia (Toronto: University of Toronto Press, 1937).

Australia: A Study of Warm Environments and Their Effect on British Settlement, 4th edn. (London: Methuen, 1947).

Teaching of Sex Hygiene

Report of a Conference organised by the Workers' Educational Association of NSW [at] Sydney University 23-25 November 1916 (Sydney: Burrows, 1918).

Turner, Henry Gyles, 'The treatment of paupers and criminals', *Bankers Magazine of Australia*, 12 (25 April 1899), 611-19.

Twitchin, Henry

'Funds for eugenics. Pastoralist's large bequest', *SMH*, 2 May 1930, 12.

'Legacy for eugenics', *SMH*, 3 May 1930, 16.

'An account of the Society's most generous benefactor' [Obituary], *ER*, 22 (July 1930), 87-88, 91-97.

Verco, William Alfred, 'The influence of the medical profession upon the national life in Australia', *AMG* (20 July 1910), 339-44.

Wallace, M S, 'Feeble-mindedness and prostitution', *MJA* (9 August 1919), 123.

Wallace, Victor Hugo

'Birth control and eugenics', lecture given to the Eugenics Society of Victoria, 23 September 1937

'Birth control for the poor?', *New Times*, 10 June 1938.

Women and Children First: An Outline of a Population Policy for Australia (Melbourne: OUP, 1946).

'The Eugenics Society of Victoria (1936-1961)', *ER*, 53 (January 1962), 215-18.

'Family planning in Melbourne', *MJA* (29 March 1969), 706-07.

'Vasectomy', *MJA* (27 January 1973), 212.

Walters, George Thomas

Eugenics; or Scientific Race Culture, A lecture delivered at the Hyde Park Unitarian Church, Sydney (15 December 1912).

Eugenics Problems and the War, Address auspiced by the EES of NSW (Sydney: Bell, 1916).

Welsh, David Arthur

'The enemy in our midst. Venereal disease', *SMH*, 22 November 1916, 10 (f); 23 and (24 November), 6 (h).

'The wrecker of life. Venereal disease', *SMH*, 14 and 15 June 1917, 6 (h).

Wickens, Charles Henry

Census of the Commonwealth of Australia, 4th, April 1921 (Census Bulletin no 26) Summary for Tropical Australia (Melbourne: Govt. Pr., 1923).

'Vitality of the white races in low latitudes', *Economic Record*, 3 (1927), 117-26.

Windeyer, John C, 'Pre-maternity work', *MJA* (16 September 1922), 325-27.

Wood, W Atkinson, 'The feeble-minded', *AMJ* (10 August 1912), 641.

Yule, John Sandison

'The feeble-minded Census', *AMJ* (27 July 1912), 616.

'The feeble-minded', *AMJ* (10 August 1912), 6421.
'Report by the Victorian Committee, *AMJ* (1 March 1913), 929-30.
'Census of feeble-minded in Victoria, 1912', *AMCT* (February 1914), 722-30.

B. Secondary Sources

Abrams, Philip, The Origins of British Sociology: 1834-1914: An Essay With Selected Papers (Chicago: University of Chicago Press, 1968).

Adams, Mark B
'The politics of human heredity in the USSR, 1920-1940', *Genome*, 31 (1989), 879-84.
'The Soviet nature-nurture debate' in Graham (1990), 94-138.
(ed.), *The Wellborn Science: Eugenics in Germany, France, Brazil and Russia* (New York: OUP, 1990).

Allen, Garland E, 'Eugenics and American social history, 1880-1950', *Genome*, 31 (1989), 885-89.

Allen, Judith A, "'Our deeply degraded sex" and "The Animal in man": Rose Scott, feminism and sexuality, 1890-1925', *Australian Feminist Studies*, nos 7 and 8 (Summer 1988), 64-91.

Aly, Gotz et al., *Cleansing the Fatherland. Nazi Medicine and Racial Hygiene*, Belinda Cooper (trans.) (Baltimore: Johns Hopkins University Press, 1994).

Ashton, Paul, 'Changing approaches to the developmentally-disabled', in Fitzgerald and Wotherspoon (1995), 140-56.

Australian Dictionary of Biography (*ADB*), vols 1 and 2 (1788-1890), vols 1-12 (1891-1939 and vols 13-14 (1940-1980), John Ritchie (ed.) (Melbourne: MUP).

Bacchi, Carol Lee
'The nature-nurture debate in Australia, 1900-1914', *Historical Studies*, 19 (October 1980), 199-212.
'Evolution, eugenics and women: The impact of scientific theories on attitudes towards women, 1870-1920', in Windschuttle (1980), 132-56.
'First wave feminism: History's judgement', in Grieve and Grimshaw (1981), 156-67.

Barker, David, 'The biology of stupidity: genetics, eugenics and mental deficiency in the inter-war years', *British Journal for the History of Science*, 22 (September 1989), 347-75.

Bean, Philip and Joy Melville, *Lost Children of the Empire: The Untold Story of Britain's Child Migrants* (London: Unwin Hyman, 1989).

Barkan, Elazar, *The Retreat of Scientific Racism: Changing Concepts of Race in Britain and the United States between the World Wars* (Cambridge: CUP, 1992).

Bourke, Helen, 'Sociology and social sciences in Australia, 1912-28', *Australian and New Zealand Journal of Sociology*, 17 (March 1981), 26-35.

Bowler, Peter J
'The role of the history of science in the understanding of social Darwinism and eugenics', *Impact of Science on Society*, 40 (1990), 273-78.
Biology and Social Thought: 1850-1914. ... (Berkeley: Office for History of Science and Technology, University of California, 1993).
The Mendelian Revolution. The Emergence of Hereditarian Concepts in Modern Science and Society (London: Athlone Press, 1995).

Brandt, Allan M, *No Magic Bullet: A Social History of Venereal Disease in the United States Since 1880* (New York: OUP, 1985).

Burleigh, Michael, *Death and Deliverance: "Euthanasia" in Germany 1900-1945* (Cambridge: CUP, 1994).

Cawte, Mary, 'Craniometry and eugenics in Australia. R J A Berry and the quest for social efficiency', *Historical Studies*, 22 (April 1986), 35-53.

Clay, Catrine and Michael Leapman, *Master Race: The Lebensborn Experiment in Nazi Germany* (London: Hodder and Stoughton, 1995).

Cohen, Deborah A, 'Private lives in public spaces: Marie Stopes, the Mothers' Clinics and the practice of contraception', *History Workshop Journal*, Issue 35 (Spring 1993), 95-116.

Cole, Douglas, 'The crimson thread of kinship: Ethnic ideas in Australia, 1870-1914', *Historical Studies*, 14 (April 1971), 511-25.

Conley, Margaret, '"Citizens: Protect your birthright". The Racial Hygiene Association of NSW', *Bowyang*, 6 (1981), 8-12.

Cravens, Hamilton, *The Triumph of Evolution: American Scientists and the Heredity-environment Controversy 1900-1944* (Philadelphia: University of Pennsylvania Press, 1978).

Crook, D Paul
'Darwinism, the political implications', *History of European Ideas*, 2 (1981), 19-34.

'Nature's pruning hook? War and evolution, 1890-1918: A response to Nancy Stepan', *Australian Journal of Politics and History*, 33 (1986), 237-52.

'War as genetic disaster? The First World War debate over the eugenics of warfare', *War and Society*, 8 (May 1990), 47-70.

Curthoys, Ann, 'Eugenics, feminism, and birth control: The case of Marion Piddington', *Hecate*, 15 (1989), 73-87.

Daniels, Kay

'Political pathfinders and a strange sexual radical. Forgotten women in Australian History', *National Times*, 9-15 January 1983, 25-26.

and Mary Murnane (comps.), *Uphill all the Way: A Documentary History of Women in Australia* (St Lucia: QUP, 1980).

and Anne Picot (eds.), *Women in Australia: An Annotated Guide to Records* (Canberra: AGPS, 1977) 2 vols.

Davin, Anna, 'Imperialism and motherhood', *History Workshop*, no 5 (Spring 1978), 9-65.

Farrall, Lyndsay A, 'The history of eugenics. A bibliographical review', *Annals of Science*, 36 (1979), 111-23.

Fitzgerald, Shirley and Garry Wotherspoon, (eds.), *Minorities: Cultural Diversity in Sydney* (State Library of NSW Press in assocn with Sydney History Group, 1995).

Fraser, Steven (ed.), *The Bell Curve Wars: Race, Intelligence and the Future of America* (New York: Basic Books, 1995).

Freeden, Michael, 'Eugenics and progressive thought: A study of ideological affinity', *Historical Journal*, 22 (1979), 645-71.

Garton, Stephen,

'Sir Charles Mackellar: Psychiatry, eugenics and child welfare in NSW, 1900-1914', *Historical Studies*, 22 (April 1986), 21-34.

'The rise of the therapeutic state: Psychiatry and the system of criminal jurisdiction in NSW, 1890-1940', *Australian Journal of Politics and History*, 33 (1986), 378-88.

Medicine and Madness. A Social History of Insanity in New South Wales, 1880-1940 (Kensington: UNSWP, 1988).

'Sound minds and healthy bodies: reconsidering eugenics in Australia, 1914-1940', *Australian Historical Studies*, 26 (October 1994), 163-81.

Gelb, Steven A, 'Degeneracy theory, eugenics and family studies', *Journal of the history of the Behavioral Sciences*, 26 (July 1990), 242-45.

Gill, Alan, *Orphans of the Empire: The Shocking Story of Child Migration to Australia* (Sydney: Millennium Books, 1997).

Gillespie, James A, *The Price of Health: Australian Governments and Medical Politics 1910-1960* (Cambridge: CUP, 1991).

Goldhar, Jeff, 'The sterilization of women with an intellectual disability. A lawyer looks at the medical aspects' *University of Tasmania Law Review*, 10 (1991), 157-96.

Goodwin, Craufurd D, 'Evolutionary theory in Australian social thought', *Journal of the History of Ideas*, 25 (1964), 393-416.

Gould, Stephen Jay, *The Mismeasure of Man* (London: Penguin, 1984).

Graham, R Loren
'Science and values: The eugenics movement in Germany and Russia in the 1920s', *American Historical Review*, 83 (1978), 1133-64.
(ed.), *Science and the Soviet Social Order* (Cambridge, Mass: Harvard University Press, 1990).

Hall, Lesley A, 'Illustrations from the Wellcome Institute Library: The Eugenics Society Archives in the Contemporary Medical Archives Centre', *Medical History*, 34 (1990), 327-33.

Haller, Mark, *Eugenics: Hereditarian Attitudes in American Thought* (New Brunswick, New Jersey: Rutgers University Press, 1963).

Halliday, R J, 'The sociological movement, the Sociological Society and the genesis of academic sociology in Britain', *Sociological Review*, 16 (November 1968), 377-98.

Hayne, Mark B, 'Australian reaction to Hitler's accession to power', *Journal of the Royal Australian Historical Society*, 71 (June 1985), 59-74.

Heller, Robert, 'Chance or choice? Eugenics from Frank to Galton', *Society of Social History and Medicine Bulletin*, 15 (1974), 9-10.

Hicks, Neville
'Theories of differential fertility and the Australian experience', *Historical Studies*, 16 (October 1975), 567-84.
'This Sin and Scandal': Australia's Population Debate, 1891-1911 (Canberra: ANUP, 1978).

Hodson, Kathleen, 'The Eugenics Review 1909-1968' *ER*, 60 (1968), 162-75.

Hofstadter, Richard, *Social Darwinism in American Thought*, rev. edn. (Boston: Beacon, 1955).

Horgan, John, 'Eugenics revisited', *Scientific American* (June 1993), 92-100.

Jones, Greta, *Social Hygiene in Twentieth Century Britain* (London: Croom Helm, 1986).

Kevles, Daniel J

In the Name of Eugenics: Genetics and the Uses of Human Heredity (New York: Knopf, 1985). Also Harvard University Press paperback edition, 1995.

Keynes, Milo (ed.), *Sir Francis Galton, FRS: The Legacy of His Ideas* (Studies in Biology, Economy and Society, Galton Institute) (London: Macmillan, 1993).

Kingsland, Sharon

Modelling Nature: Episodes in the History of Population Ecology (Chicago: University of Chicago Press, 1985).

'Evolution and debates over human progress from Darwin to sociobiology', in Teitelbaum and Winter (1989), 167-98.

Koonz, Claudia, 'Ethical dilemmas and Nazi eugenics: single-issue dissent in religious contexts', *The Journal of Modern History*, 64, Supplement (December 1992), S8-S31.

Kuhl, Stefan, *The Nazi Connection: Eugenics, American Racism, and German National Socialism* (New York: OUP, 1994).

Larson, Edward J

'The rhetoric of eugenics: Expert authority and the Mental Deficiency Bill', *British Journal for the History of Science* (24 March 1991), 45-60.

Sex, Race, and Science: Eugenics in the Deep South (Baltimore: The Johns Hopkins University Press, 1995).

Lerner, Richard M, *Final Solutions: Biology, Prejudice and Genocide* (Pa: Pennsylvania State University Press, 1992).

Lewis, Milton J

and Roy MacLeod, 'A workingman's paradise? Reflections on urban mortality in colonial Australia 1860-1900', *Medical History*, 31 (1987), 387-402.

'Medical politics and the professionalisation of medicine in NSW, 1850-1901', *Journal of Australian Studies*, no 22 (May 1988), 69-82.

(ed.), *Health and Disease in Australia: A History by J H L Cumpston* (Canberra: AGPS, 1989).

MacLeod, Roy Malcolm

'The edge of hope: Social policy and chronic alcoholism 1870-1900', *Journal of the History of Medicine* (July 1976), 215-45.

(ed.), *The Commonwealth of Science: ANZAAS and the Scientific Enterprise in Australasia, 1888-1988* (Melbourne: OUP, 1988).

and Milton Lewis (eds.), *Disease, Medicine and Empire: Perspectives on Western Medicine and the Experience of European Expansion* (London: Routledge, 1988).

and Donald Denoon (eds.), *Health and Healing in Tropical Australia and Papua New Guinea* (Townsville: James Cook University, 1991).

and Philip F Rehbock, *Darwin's Laboratory: Evolutionary Theory and Natural History in the Pacific* (Honolulu: University of Hawaii Press, 1994).

Macainsh, Noel, *Nietzsche in Australia: A Literary Inquiry into a Nationalistic Ideology* (Munich: Verlag fur Dokumentation und Werbung, 1975).

Macnicol, John, 'Eugenics and the campaign for voluntary sterilization in Britain between the wars', *Social History of Medicine*, 2, no 2 (August 1989), 147-69.

Mandle, William Frederick, 'Cricket and Australian nationalism in the nineteenth century', *Journal of the Royal Australian Historical Society*, 59 (December 1973), 225-246.

McLaren, Angus, *Our Own Master Race. Eugenics in Canada, 1885-1945* (Toronto: McClelland and Stewart, 1990).

McQueen, Humphrey, 'Freud: Letter to our subcontinent', *Bowyang*, no 4 (September-October 1980), 140-43.

Paul, Diane B
'Eugenics and the Left', *Journal of the History of Ideas*, 45 (January-March 1984), 567-90.
and Hamish Spencer, 'The hidden science of eugenics', *Nature* (23 March 1995), 302-04.

Pickens, Donald K, *Eugenics and the Progressives* (Nashville, Tennessee: Vanderbilt University Press, 1968).

Porter, Dorothy, '"Enemies of the race": Biologism, environmentalism, and public health in Edwardian England', *Victorian Studies*, 34 (Winter 1991), 159-78.

Pringle, Rosemary, 'Octavius Beale and the ideology of the birth rate: The Royal Commissions of 1904 and 1905', *Refractory Girl*, no 3 (Winter 1973), 19-27.

Rafter, Nicole Hahn (ed.), *White Trash: The Eugenic Family Studies, 1877-1919* (Boston: Northeastern UP, 1988).

Reilly, Philip

'The surgical solution: The writings of activist physicians in the early years of eugenical sterilization', *Perspectives in Biology and Medicine*, 26 (September 1983), 637-56.

The Surgical Solution: A History of Involuntary Sterilization in the United States (Baltimore: Johns Hopkins University Press, 1991)

Roe, Jill

Beyond Belief: Theosophy in Australia, 1879-1939 (Kensington: UNSWP, 1986).

(ed.), *Social Policy in Australia: Some Perspectives 1901-1975* (Sydney: Cassell, 1976).

Roe, Michael

'Efficiency: The fascist dynamic in American Progressivism', *Teaching History*, 8, Part 2 (August 1974), 38-55.

'The establishment of the Australian Department of Health. Its background and significance', *Historical Studies*, 17, no 69 (1976), 176-92.

Nine Australian Progressives: Vitalism in Bourgeois Social Thought, 1890-1960 (St Lucia: UQP, 1984).

Roll-Hansen, Nils

'The progress of eugenics: Growth of knowledge and change in ideology', *History of Science*, 26 (1988), 295-331.

'Eugenic sterilization: A preliminary comparison of the Scandinavian experience to that of Germany', *Genome*, 31 (1989), 890-95.

Rose, June, *Marie Stopes and the Sexual Revolution* (London: Faber and Faber, 1992).

Schenk, Faith and Sir Alan S Parkes, 'The activities of the Eugenics Society', *ER*, 60 (1968), 142-61.

Searle, Geoffrey Russell

Eugenics and Politics in Britain 1900-1914 (Leyden: Noordhoff, 1976).

'Eugenics and politics in Britain in the 1930s', *Annals of Science*, 36 (1979), 159-69.

'Eugenics and class', in Charles Webster (ed.), *Biology, Medicine and Society 1840-1940* (Cambridge: CUP, 1981), 217-42.

Siedlecky, Stefania and Diana Wyndham, *Populate and Perish: Australian Women's Fight For Birth Control* (Sydney: Allen and Unwin, 1990).

Smith, F B (Barry), *The People's Health 1830-1910* (London: Weidenfeld and Nicholson, 1990).

Smith, John Maynard, 'Eugenics and utopia', *Daedalus* (Summer 1988), 73-92. Originally published, ibid, (Spring 1965), 487-505.

Soloway, Richard A, *Demography and Degeneration: Eugenics and the Declining Birthrate in Twentieth-century Britain* (Chapel Hill: University of North Carolina Press, 1990).

Spallone, Patricia (ed.), *Beyond Conception: The New Politics of Reproduction* (London: Macmillan, 1989).

Stepan, Nancy Leys
The Idea of Race in Science: Great Britain 1800-1960 (London: Macmillan, 1982).
The Hour of Eugenics': Race, Gender and Nation in Latin America (Ithaca, New York: Cornell University Press, 1991).

Teitelbaum, Michael S and Jay M Winter
The Fear of Population Decline (Orlando, Florida: Academic, 1985).
(eds.), *Population and Resources in Western Intellectual Traditions* (Cambridge: CUP, 1989).

Tolerton, Jane, *Ettie: A Life of Ettie Rout* (Auckland: Penguin, 1992).

Tregenza, John, *Professor of Democracy: The Life of Charles Henry Pearson, 1830-1894 – Oxford Don and Australian Radical* (Melbourne: MUP, 1968).

Thearle, M John
'The saga of the Australian leech worm', in Pearn (1988), 79-92.
'The rise and fall of phrenology in Australia', *Australian and New Zealand Journal of Psychiatry*, 27 (September 1993), 518-25.

Turney, Clifford et al., *Australia's First: A History of the University of Sydney, Vol 1, 1850-1939* (Sydney: University of Sydney, 1991).

Turtle, Alison M
'Education, social science and the "Common Weal"', MacLeod (1988), 222-46.
'Anthropometry in Britain and Australia: Technology, ideology and Imperial connection", *Storia della Psicologia*, 2, no 2 (1990), 118-43.
'The first women psychologists in Australia', *Australian Psychologist*, 25, no 3 (November 1990), 239-55.
'Person, Porteus, and the Pacific Islands Regiment: The beginnings of cross-cultural psychology in Australia', *Journal of the History of the Behavioral Sciences*, 27 (January 1991), 7-20.

Watts, Rob, 'Beyond nature and nurture: Eugenics in twentieth century Australian history', *Australian Journal of Politics and History*, 4, no 3 (1994), 318-34.

Weiss, Sheila Faith
   Race Hygiene and National Efficiency: The Eugenics of Wilhelm Schallmayer (Berkeley, California: University of California Press, 1987).
   'Race and class in Fritz Lenz's eugenics', *Medizinhistoriches Journal*, 27, nos 1-2 (1992), 5-25.

Willard, Myra, *History of the White Australia Policy to 1920* (Melbourne: MUP, 1923)

Wilde, William H, Joy Hooton and Barry Andrews, *The Oxford Companion to Australian Literature*, rev edn. (Melbourne: OUP, 1991).

---

[1] Saul Dubow, *Scientific Racism in Modern South Africa* (Cambridge: CUP, 1995), 121.

[2] The Encyclical, *On Christian Marriage* (Washington, DC: National Catholic Welfare Conference, 1931), 23-24, quoted in R Loren Graham, *American Historical Review*, 83 (1978), 1139-40.

[3] Loren R Graham, 'Science and values: The eugenics movement in Germany and Russia in the 1920s', *American Historical Review*, 83 (1978), 1138-39.

[4] Wilson Yates, 'Birth control literature and the medical profession in nineteenth century America', *Journal of the History of Medicine and Allied Sciences*, 31 (1976), 56, 65.

Index

ALSO AVAILABLE

MARIE STOPES, EUGENICS AND THE ENGLISH BIRTH CONTROL MOVEMENT

EDITED BY ROBERT PEEL

Proceedings of the 1996 Conference of the Galton Institute

CONTENTS

ISBN 0950406627

Available post paid from the Institute's General Secretary Price £5.00

ALSO AVAILABLE

ESSAYS IN THE HISTORY OF EUGENICS

EDITED BY ROBERT PEEL

Proceedings of the 1997 Conference of the Galton Institute

CONTENTS

ISBN 0950406635

Available post paid from the Institute's General Secretary Price £5.00

ALSO AVAILABLE

HUMAN PEDIGREE STUDIES

EDITED BY ROBERT PEEL

Proceedings of the 1998 Conference of the Galton Institute

CONTENTS

ISBN 0950406643

Available post paid from the Institute's General Secretary Price £5.00

ALSO AVAILABLE

POPULATION CRISES AND POPULATION CYCLES

BY

CLAIRE RUSSELL AND W M S RUSSELL

Series Editor: ROBERT A PEEL

CONTENTS

ISBN 0950406651

Available post paid from the Institute's General Secretary Price £5.00

ALSO AVAILABLE

A CENTURY OF MENDELISM

EDITED BY ROBERT PEEL and JOHN TIMSON

Proceedings of the 2000 Conference of the Galton Institute

CONTENTS

ISBN 095040666X

Available post paid from the Institute's General Secretary Price £5.00